Contents

Figures, Tables and Boxes

Acknowledgements

I should like to thank the many people who have helped with this book. Background research extended from the Cro-Magnon cave paintings at Lascaux to the dot.com boom of 1999–2000, from Auckland to Zanzibar. I am grateful for the help of Magnus Feldmann, Tim Harford, Adrian Lewis, Robert Metz, Scott Reeves, Jorim Schraven and Alex von Tunzelmann. Julian Bene, David Bodanis, Andrew Dilnot, Leslie Hannah, Richard Layard, George Richardson and Bridget Rosewell provided comments on earlier drafts which helped structure the argument more effectively. My agent Michael Sissons and editor Stuart Proffitt helped turn an idea in the autumn of 1999 into a reality in the summer of 2002. And Jo Charrington organized both me and the process of production throughout that period with great calm, efficiency and unvarying good humour. I am grateful to them all.

John Kay

PENGUIN BOOKS

THE TRUTH ABOUT MARKETS

'Provides another foundation stone for trying different, less arrogant ways of running our companies. The truth about markets is that there are alternatives, after all' *Observer*

'Insightful and laconic . . . a delight . . . quite possibly the only book on economics you will ever need to read' *Accounting & Business*

'Kay is one of the leading British economists of his generation . . . He gives answers to those puzzling questions that nag the non-specialist. Why are some countries rich and others poor? Why do people doing the same job in Mexico and the US, a few miles apart, get completely different wages?' Hamish McRae, *Independent*

'Both a lucid guide and a salutary warning' *Scotsman*

'He compares greedy boardroom fat cats to corrupt African dictators. He think anti-globalization protestors are naïve and wrong. He takes sideswipes at his old Oxford colleagues and believes Tony Blair could be the best thing for the centre-left since Roosevelt. John Kay sounds like the archetypal polemicist, an economist with attitude, the dismal science's answer to David Starkey. Wrong on all counts. Kay argues that Keynes was right when he wanted economists to be treated like dentists. They should use their skills to remedy specific problems rather than launch ideological crusades. Grand narratives are out. Gentle probing is in' Larry Elliott, *Guardian*

'His explanation of how markets really work is a salutary reminder that the scope for screwing up is greater than the DIY economists imagine and that large scale attempts to interfere with market mechanisms are doomed' *Time*

ABOUT THE AUTHOR

John Kay is a Fellow of St John's College, Oxford, and a Visiting Professor of Economics at the London School of Economics. He has been Professor of Economics at the London Business School and Professor of Management at the University of Oxford. He has been director of an independent think tank, set up and sold a highly successful economic consultancy business and has been a director of several public companies. He now writes a fortnightly column for the *Financial Times*.

JOHN KAY

The Truth About Markets

Why Some Nations are Rich
but Most Remain Poor

PENGUIN BOOKS

PENGUIN BOOKS

Published by the Penguin Group
Penguin Books Ltd, 80 Strand, London WC2R ORL, England
Penguin Group (USA) Inc., 375 Hudson Street, New York, New York 10014, USA
Penguin Books Australia Ltd, 250 Camberwell Road, Camberwell, Victoria 3124, Australia
Penguin Books Canada Ltd, 10 Alcorn Avenue, Toronto, Ontario, Canada M4V 3B2
Penguin Books India (P) Ltd, 11 Community Centre, Panchsheel Park, New Delhi – 110 017, India
Penguin Group (NZ), Cnr Airborne and Rosedale Roads, Albany, Auckland 1310, New Zealand
Penguin Books (South Africa) (Pty) Ltd, 24 Sturdee Avenue, Rosebank 2196, South Africa

Penguin Books Ltd, Registered Offices: 80 Strand, London WC2R ORL, England

www.penguin.com

First published by Allen Lane 2003
Published in Penguin Books with new material 2004
11

Copyright © John Kay, 2003, 2004

Typeset by Rowland Phototypesetting Ltd, Bury St Edmunds, Suffolk
Printed in England by Clays Ltd, St Ives plc

ISBN-13: 978–0–140–29672–3

www.greenpenguin.co.uk

Mixed Sources
Product group from well-managed
forests and other controlled sources
www.fsc.org Cert no. SA-COC-1592
© 1996 Forest Stewardship Council

Penguin Books is committed to a sustainable future
for our business, our readers and our planet.
The book in your hands is made from paper
certified by the Forest Stewardship Council.

Note to Readers

The superscript [N], as in Mirrlees[N], means the individual referred to has been awarded the Nobel Prize for Economics. The superscript [W], as in JOKES[W], means that relevant weblinks can be found by visiting http://www.TheTruthAboutMarkets.com and typing JOKES. Other updated material related to this book is also available at this website.

Part One

THE ISSUES

I

Welcome to the World of Bloomberg Television

If you have ever spent a night in one of the international hotels that cater to the travelling businessman or businesswoman, you will have zapped the channels on the hotel television network and reached Bloomberg television, or its almost indistinguishable competitor, CNBC. There is something rivetingly awful about Bloomberg television. It is like a movie so bad you cannot bring yourself to stop watching.

In the right-hand corner of the screen, flashing lights tell you the Dow-Jones index is going up, or down. Across the bottom, there is a constantly moving border of share prices – Cisco is up 0.75 on the day. The left-hand section is occupied by talking heads. The producers of Bloomberg television have the unenviable task of filling this space with interviews and pronouncements for twenty-four hours of every day. Bloomberg television never sleeps. Often the talking head is a Bloomberg employee. A man in red braces describes the action on the Bloomberg Big Board with irrepressible excitement.

But frequently the talking head is an economist. I have done it myself. But mostly he – or often she – works for one of the major securities houses, like Merrill Lynch or Goldman Sachs. The talking head stands before a picture of the firm's trading room: Bloomberg gets free programming in return for free advertising. The economist will be answering a question, such as 'How should we interpret the latest month's figures from the National Association of Purchasing Managers?'[1] I am not making this up: if you do not believe me, turn on, tune in to Bloomberg television.

Bloomberg television is a visible manifestation of the rise of popular capitalism in the last two decades of the twentieth century. In 1979

Margaret Thatcher became the British Prime Minister and a year later Ronald Reagan was elected President of the United States. With these changes of government came a reversal of the trend towards greater government economic intervention and higher state spending:[2] a trend which had been characteristic of most of the twentieth century and had continued uninterrupted since the Second World War. This change of direction was reinforced by the collapse of the Russian Empire in Eastern Europe and the disintegration of the Soviet Union. The fall of the Berlin Wall in 1989 symbolized Western victory in the cold war. One of the most extraordinary episodes in the economic history of the world followed.

It was, above all, an American decade. As the Berlin Wall came down, the American political scientist Francis Fukuyama proclaimed 'the end of history'. Fukuyama's article in *National Interest* extended into a best-selling book.[3] The collapse of Communism was the prelude to convergence on a common model of economic, social and political organization, based on liberal democracy and lightly regulated capitalism. The model bore, of course, a strong relationship to late-twentieth-century America.

The triumphalism expressed in Fukuyama's careful prose was overtaken by more assertive accounts from business people and popular commentators. Walter Wriston, former chief executive of Citicorp, wrote of *The Twilight of Sovereignty*. In his book, he claimed that markets should and would undermine the traditional role of governments. By the end of the decade, this diagnosis of the subordination of government to market was shared by those – like Naomi Klein – who deplored it as well as those – like Wriston – who applauded it.[4]

Wriston provides an articulate account of one view of how market economies work. Self-regarding materialism is the principal determinant of economic behaviour, and government should not restrict it. Financial markets are the main regulator of economic activity. The economic role of the state is the protection of property rights and the enforcement of contracts; I call this the American business model.

The spread of these ideas around the world was brilliantly captured in Daniel Yergin and Joseph Stanislaw's *The Commanding Heights*. They took their title from Lenin, via the British Labour Party: the goal of socialism was to seize the 'commanding heights' of the economy for the people. Now, they argued, 'the decamping of the state from the commanding heights marks a great divide between the twentieth and twenty-first centuries'.[5]

For Reagan and Thatcher, reducing the economic role of the state had involved a deliberate political choice. In the world Wriston described a decade later, there was no longer any choice. International trade and capital flows made the decline of national government inescapable. Throughout the 1990s the term 'globalization' took over from 'privatization' as the label for market-oriented reforms. Wriston anticipated the emerging consensus of the 1990s: the global dimension of markets and the importance of new technologies. His themes of internationalization and technology were taken up more stridently by later commentators. The leading chronicler of globalization was Thomas Friedman. In his introduction to *The Lexus and the Olive Tree* (1999), based on his *New York Times* columns, Friedman asserted that 'the world is ten years old'. The theme was globalization but there could be no doubt where the centre of this new world was found. 'If 100 years ago you had come to a visionary geo-architect and told him that in the year 2000 the world would be defined by a system called "globalization", what sort of country would he have designed to compete and win in that world? The answer is that he would have designed something that looks an awful lot like the United States of America.'[6]

The US economy performed well in the 1990s. *Business Week* proclaimed the 'new economy' – technology had transformed America's long-term growth potential.[7] With the aid of Bloomberg television, this strong economic performance was translated into an extraordinary stock market boom. In 1996 the Chairman of the Federal Reserve Board, Alan Greenspan, warned of 'irrational exuberance'.[8] As he spoke the valuation of stocks was at the highest level ever recorded in American history – surpassing the records of 1929 – but far more was to come. The Chairman, having once put his head above the parapet, retreated.

Greenspan famously speaks in riddles. His partner, Anthea Mitchell, failed to understand what was being said when he first proposed marriage.[9] But as the paper wealth of Americans continued to grow, Greenspan acquired heroic stature. History will judge whether

Greenspan was the man who made millions of Americans rich – or the man who could not bear to tell them that they had only imagined it.

The triumphalism expressed by Friedman developed into hubris and finally into collective madness. The boom became the bubble. The trigger was belief in the limitless potential of new technologies, most of all the Internet. In the mid-1990s knowledge of the Internet began to extend beyond computer nerds and academics. It was repeatedly asserted that the Internet would revolutionize economic activity, that it would be even more significant than previous technological innovations such as railways, telecommunications, electricity or automobiles – although it was always hard to find specifics about the nature of the prospective change.[10]

New companies were set up to exploit the Internet's commercial potential. Businesses that had earned only cents in revenues were floated on the stock market for billions of dollars. The research analysts of securities houses – the talking heads of Bloomberg television – such as Mary Meeker, the 'Internet goddess', and Henry Blodget of Merrill Lynch, were paid multi-million-dollar bonuses for rationalizing absurd valuations.[11] The NASDAQ index of high technology stocks doubled and doubled again.[12]

Intellectuals were wheeled out in support of the values of the 'new economy'. Lester Thurow, economist and former dean of the Sloan School of Management at the Massachusetts Institute of Technology, lauded its heroes. 'Wealth has always been important in the personal pecking order, but it has become increasingly the only dimension by which personal worth is measured. It is the only game to play if you want to prove your mettle. It is the big leagues. If you do not play there, by definition you are second rate.'[13] Only by the pursuit of wealth was it possible to 'leave footprints in the sands of time'.

More measured support came from President Clinton's Assistant Treasury Secretary, Larry Summers. Nephew of both Paul Samuelson[N] and Kenneth Arrow[N] – possibly the two greatest economists of the second half of the twentieth century – Summers was himself an economist of considerable distinction, a winner of the John Bates Clark medal for the best US economist under 40. Greenspan had no strong technical credentials as an economist – he had dabbled with the far right cult figure, Ayn Rand[14] – but he displayed legendary political skills and antennae. With the Treasury Secretary, Robert Rubin – former chief of Goldman Sachs, the most respected securities business – they made an impressive trio. Summers succeeded Rubin in 1999, before returning to Harvard in 2001 as its President.

The greatest admiration for the American business model was to be found in the American business community. Arbitrariness and disparities in the distribution of income are justified – even morally justified – simply because they are market outcomes. What could be more congenial to executives and successful entrepreneurs than the discovery that their good fortune not only benefits them but is essential to the welfare of society as a whole? Thus fortified, they greatly enlarged that good fortune. As the 1990s rolled on, an increasing proportion of the profits of US corporations was diverted into the pockets of its senior managers.[15]

Still, Europeans always displayed some scepticism about the universality of the American business model. The G7 group of the world's largest industrialized nations[16] met in Denver in 1997 and was subjected to a diet of what the *Financial Times* called 'effusive self-praise' from Clinton. The *Financial Times* went on to quote one European official as saying: 'They keep telling us how successful their system is. Then they remind us not to stray too far from our hotel at night.'[17]

But the inexorable rise of the American business model provoked a loss of European self-confidence. In Britain and Germany, speculation in technology stocks paralleled the bubble on Wall Street.[18] A paean of praise for America by journalist Jonathan Freedland, *Bring Home the Revolution*, was said to be the favourite reading of Britain's New Labour politicians.[19] At Lisbon in February 2000, European leaders signed up to a 'new economy' agenda: the market liberalization required by globalization and new technology.

These ideas were also transmitted to poor countries. The phrase 'Washington consensus'[20] came to describe the general nostrums put forward by the principal international economic agencies, the International Monetary Fund and the World Bank, whose head offices are located beside each other in downtown Washington DC.[21]

But globalization and the American business model provoked reaction. The World Trade Organization met in Seattle in November 1999. Rioters filled the streets and the conference ended in disarray. Every similar subsequent meeting attracted crowds of demonstrators. The next was the annual World Economic Forum, which is held in the pretty ski resort of Davos in Switzerland.[22] The January 2000 meeting was intended to be the culmination of a decade of American triumphalism. Clinton flew in above the demonstrators to wave farewell to the business people who had gained so much during his tenure.

Yet it didn't quite work. The e-business sessions were overflowing, but the reception given to Clinton and Summers was muted. The ball was over. A few weeks later, the NASDAQ index reached its peak. Two years later, it had lost three-quarters of its value. Most of the Internet businesses established in the bubble failed.

However, the American business model is only bruised. It remains the working hypothesis of most business people and consultants. Self-regarding materialism is the dominant human motivation. Greed in politics is disastrous, because politicians can use the coercive power of the state to get other people's money. Greed in business is virtuous because producing the goods and services people want is the only way to extract money from them. The political sphere should be as small as possible and the business sphere as large as possible.

So the premises of the American business model lead directly to market fundamentalism – the belief that interference with the functioning of free markets is almost never justified – and to the doctrine of the minimal state, whose economic role should extend little beyond the definition of property rights and the enforcement of contracts. With greed the mainspring of the market economy, redistributive taxation inhibits its progress.

There is an obvious problem: if society is dominated by very greedy people and the role of the state is minimal, won't the result be anarchy? The most intellectually interesting part of the American business model is its explanation of why this need not be so, and a significant part of this book will be devoted to that question.

This technical, though vitally important, issue does not greatly concern most friends of the American business model. For them, the model meets a deep-seated need for simple, universal explanations of complex phenomena. Its appeal directly parallels that of the Marxist doctrines it has supplanted. Its prescriptions are not just right, but inevitable. Its proponents show the same ingenuity in attributing all social and economic problems to government that Marxists displayed in attributing all social and economic problems to capital. The American business model offers to its adherents the same confident certainties as Marxism.

With Marxism dead, the public interest in economic questions which was traditionally directed to political activity is channelled through Bloomberg television. And the talking heads define the public image of the economist. If I introduce myself to a dinner guest as an economist I encounter expectations that I shall be boring, opinionated, obsessed by money, and usually wrong. People ask what I think is going to happen to exchange rates, without much interest in the answer. If I respond that I am not that kind of economist, they express surprise that there is any other kind of economist, and turn to talk to the person on the other side.

Most economists do not forecast exchange rates. But the belief that they do is largely responsible for the subject's poor public reputation. It is easy for a chairman introducing an economist to raise a laugh by saying that whenever you meet two economists you encounter three opinions.[23] I myself have contributed to the popular readiness to poke fun at the poor forecasting record of the talking heads.[24] The economists who fill these roles earn large salaries but less respect, and the work they do appears trivial. No doubt it is necessary that someone should be studying statistics from the National Association of Purchasing Managers, but as an intellectual pursuit it hardly ranks with the understanding of great art and literature or the hunt for subatomic particles.

Bloomberg television fosters another misunderstanding. It describes what is happening 'in the markets'. Friends warned me against putting the term 'markets' in the title of this book. They suggested that libraries would shelve it with books about stocks and shares. Perhaps Amazon would report that 'people who bought this book also bought books like *How to Become Rich by Sitting All Day Looking at Bloomberg Television*. In 1999 people really did believe that, and for some of them it was true. But selling bits of paper to one another at ever-higher prices creates only the illusion of wealth, and that only for a time.

Most markets are not securities markets. There are markets for food and clothing, for flowers and for electricity, and these latter markets are the principal concern of this book. The activities described on Bloomberg television are only peripherally related to the operations of the real market economy – not wholly irrelevant, but largely irrelevant. To call it 'business television' is a serious misnomer.

The issues raised on Bloomberg television – 'How should we interpret the latest figures from the National Association of Purchasing Managers?' and even 'Will the Federal Reserve raise interest rates at its next meeting?' – are indeed boring and unimportant. The real issues of economics are vital and fascinating, and raise some of the most important social and political questions of our time.

Why are some people and some countries rich, and others poor? Why did centrally planned regimes fail in economic competition with market economies? How do decentralized market economies co-ordinate complex products and global distribution? How do economic systems handle risks? How do they deal with inequalities of information in markets for technologically sophisticated products? How do they distribute the rewards between different members of the teams which manage complex production processes? How do markets co-ordinate networks? How do they stimulate knowledge and innovation? What really determines our economic behaviour – how we work and what we consume? What should be the role of government in a modern economy?

These are the questions with which this book is concerned. In answering them, I shall show that the American business model is not, and could not be, a correct description of how the American economy works. The countries that most closely resemble its prescriptions of unrestrained individualism with minimal government are among the poorest on the planet. Effective market economies are embedded in an elaborate social, political and cultural context, and could not function outside that context.

The search for the truth about markets will take us not just to Wall Street and Washington, but to Switzerland and New Zealand, South Africa and Russia. We shall visit the flower market at San Remo, the used-car showroom and the corner shop, and the control room of the National Grid. The economists whose work is described in this book rarely appear on Bloomberg television. They do, however, win Nobel Prizes (see Appendix).

Like other economists, I use models. Most people imagine that economic models are complex lists of equations which predict the future through computer simulations. There are economic models of these kinds, such as the forecasting models used by finance ministries and central banks and even by some of the talking heads on Bloomberg television. But most economic models are different in structure and intention. They reduce a complex problem to a few essentials and illustrate the relationships between them. A good model is one which is wide in scope and unexpected in implications. To appreciate models of this kind, turn on, tune in to George Akerlof's[N] market for lemons (Chapter 18) and Albert Tucker's Prisoner's Dilemma (Chapter 20). A good model is like a biblical parable and, like parables, is neither true nor false: only illuminating or unilluminating. These economic models are what I shall call, in Chapter 16, little stories.

Positively the last word on Bloomberg television: the channel symbolizes, but does not exemplify, the American business model. Bloomberg television is not really a commercial venture. Bloomberg's primary business is the provision of financial information through closed networks to traders in large securities houses. Bloomberg television has never been particularly profitable but has made the company's eponymous founder known to a much wider audience.[25] In November 2001, after spending more money per voter than any other politician in history, Michael Bloomberg was elected Mayor of New York City.[26]

2

People

Economic Lives

Heidi is playing with her children in the garden of their four-bedroom villa in Küssnacht, an elegant suburb of Zurich. She has just driven home in her Nissan Micra from the primary school where she teaches. Heidi earns $2,500 per month. Heidi is married to Hermann, who studied economics and business at the University of St Gallen and is an executive in a Zurich bank. The Micra is their runabout but Hermann drives to work in their Mercedes. Heidi and Hermann enjoy eating out in Zurich, where there are many good international restaurants as well as cheerful Swiss taverns. They like opera, and play tennis at a club in Küssnacht. In winter they ski most weekends. In summer they visit their small holiday house in Umbria.

Ravi is cycling to his job at the State Bank of India in Mumbai, where he earns $320 per month. Ravi is a recently qualified accountant, and also recently married. Ravi and his wife Nandini live with Ravi's parents in a two-bedroomed apartment in the favoured district of Worli. The rent of the apartment is $280 per month, paid by Ravi's father. Nandini does not work. It is relatively uncommon in India for the wives of men of Ravi's income and social status to seek employment. A housekeeper visits each morning to clean and cook: she is paid around $25 per month.

Sven is running in the forest near Kivik in Sweden. He is a farm-worker and earns the union rate corresponding to his age and experience, which is $1,700 per month. Sven lives with his girlfriend, Ingrid, in a three-bedroomed house in the village and the couple have a four-month-old daughter. Ingrid is employed on the same farm, but is on maternity leave. Swedish parents are entitled to share a year's leave. In a few months Ingrid will return to work and Sven will spend the balance of leave at home with his daughter. Sven and Ingrid have a mobile phone each and a Volvo 740; they love sport and go skiing in the north of the country. Summer holidays may be spent in Mallorca or in Sven's parents' summer house on an island in the Baltic Sea.

Ivan is taking the metro to work. He is a maintenance engineer for AT&T, the American telephone company. Ivan has a doctorate from MTUSI (Moscow Technical University of Communications and Information) and earns $900 per month. He lives with his mother, Lyudmila, his wife Olga and two children in Yugo-Zapadnaya, a Moscow suburb. Ivan's father was killed in Afghanistan and his mother receives a pension of $40 per month. Olga teaches English linguistics at MTUSI, where she earns $100 per month but, in a good month, she receives an additional $300 or more from English translations for businesses. Ivan and Olga have a ten-year-old Ford Sierra which was imported second-hand from Holland.

Heidi and Hermann in Switzerland and Sven and Ingrid in Sweden have very different economic lives from Ravi and Nandini in India, and Ivan and Olga in Russia. Heidi and Hermann, Sven and Ingrid have more material goods. They have more choices in work and leisure. This wider range of experiences leaves them better placed to develop their interests and talents. But their economic lives are only part of their lives. With choices come mistakes and material goods do not meet all our needs or theirs. Ravi and Ivan do not think of themselves as poor. Like most people, they derive their frame of reference from their local environment. They are well aware that they are much better off than the many destitute people in the streets of Moscow and Mumbai.

Which of these four couples is happiest? The answer depends far more on their personal relationships than the size of their house or the reliability of their car. But Ravi and Ivan would like to have the resources and opportunities available to Heidi and Sven. And the issue of why their economic lives differ so much is interesting whatever its consequences for their happiness. The economic question is important even if it is not the only question, or the whole story.

The answer to the economic question – why their economic lives are so different – is not at all obvious. Heidi and Ravi, Sven and Ivan are different people. But they are sufficiently similar for us to be able to see that the differences in their economic lives are mainly the product of differences in the environments within which they operate, not differences in the innate capabilities of the individuals themselves. Heidi and Sven have higher material living standards, not because they are more talented, or more hard-working, but because they were born and live in Switzerland and Sweden. Ravi and Ivan have lower material living standards, not because they are less talented or hard-working, but because they were born and live in India and Russia. We often talk of globalization as if the world were becoming homogeneous. But globalization has emphasized, not eliminated, these facts of geography.

Facts of geography have an overriding importance for Raoul and Pedro, too. The Rio Grande is a wide, sluggish river, of no great natural beauty or interest, but because it forms the border between the United States and Mexico for 1,000 miles it has great political, social and economic significance. Raoul is a skilled and experienced machinist in a factory in northern Mexico. He earns $700 per month, a good wage in Mexico. His brother Pedro works illegally as a kitchen porter in a Los Angeles restaurant. Pedro takes home twice as much as Raoul. Raoul has sometimes thought of joining Pedro but he prefers to stay with his friends and family in Mexico; he thinks that money is only part of life.

Why Do Economic Lives Differ?

What features of the environment into which people are born or migrate make such a difference to their economic lives?[1] For most of economic history, it was believed that the explanation was found in the availability of physical resources. What mattered was access to fertile land, or valuable minerals – gold and silver, coal and oil – or the availability of scarce, specialist goods like sugar cane or saffron. The attempt to gain access to these resources has been a principal cause of wars for thousands of years.

Yet differences in standards of living between countries today are not the product of differences in endowments of natural resources. Many of the richest countries in the world – like Switzerland and

Table 2.1 Resource availability in various countries

Resources per head, US $000 (includes mineral resources, oil and gas, agricultural land, forests)

Top ten countries:		Other rich states:*	
Saudi Arabia	71.9	Austria	7.6
New Zealand	51.1	Belgium	1.8
Canada	36.6	Denmark	11.1
Australia	35.3	France	8.1
Norway	30.2	Germany	4.2
Venezuela	20.8	Italy	3.4
Ireland	17.8	Japan	2.3
USA	16.5	Netherlands	4.1
Finland	15.9	Sweden	14.6
Uruguay	14.8	Switzerland	3.1
		UK	4.9

*These are the other countries listed in Table 3.5. Hong Kong and Singapore were not included in the study; the figures for both would be extremely small.

Source: World Bank (1997), appendix table 1.

Sweden – have few natural resources. Britain once had large reserves of coal, and is now exploiting significant reserves of oil. But it has far less of either than Russia. It is a modern cliché that Silicon Valley is not built on reserves of silicon. Heidi in Switzerland and Sven in Sweden have greater access to the world's natural resources than Ravi in Mumbai or Ivan in Moscow because they have the financial resources to buy them, not because of their geographic proximity. That prior fact requires explanation.

If not resources, perhaps technology. While Sven is an employee on a Swedish farm, Sicelo owns his own farm. But Sicelo's farm is in a small village in KwaZulu Natal. He lives in a hut with his own wife, the two wives of his brother Patrick, and five of the six children of the marriages. The hut has no electricity or sanitation. Sicelo earns around $150 per month from the sale of milk and vegetables. The women help on the farm and contribute to household earnings by making baskets. Patrick works in a gold mine in Carletonville, 500 miles away. He earns $250 per month and sends most of this back to support the family. He usually returns to the village twice a year. Sicelo's eldest son is a domestic worker in Durban and sends $75 per month to his parents.

There is a world of difference between the sophisticated modern agricultural machinery which Sven uses every day and the simple tools available to Sicelo. In principle, the global marketplace makes the same technology available everywhere in the world. For Ivan, this is a reality. AT&T deploys the same equipment in Russia as in the United States. But for Sicelo access to modern technology is a dream. Like most South Africans, Sicelo has neither the education nor the capital to use the equipment to be found on every farm in Sweden.

Is it education that makes the difference? Ravi and Ivan are more skilled than most workers in rich countries. It is hard to imagine that Sven could do either of their jobs, but they could probably do his. But if Sicelo had a better education that would probably not, of itself, raise his productivity much. Is it capital that is key? Since common sense tells us that rural South Africa needs capital far more than Sweden, why does Sven have so much and Sicelo so little? In a global capital market, owners of capital can readily shift funds from country to country and from business to business. They do so, not on sentimental or patriotic grounds, but in hope of higher returns. In the 1990s foreign investors formed exaggerated views of the prospects in South-East Asian economies such as Thailand and Indonesia, which, though still poor, were developing rapidly. Far more capital flowed into these economies than they could absorb.[2]

Globalization of capital markets has brought little benefit to South African agriculture because the infrastructure readily available in Sweden is missing. A better social infrastructure would give Sicelo the education to operate competently capital equipment that others might pay for. A better physical infrastructure – proper roads, for example – would give him access to markets in which he could sell his output easily and cheaply. A better institutional infrastructure would enable capital to be passed to Sicelo in an intelligent and discriminating way, and give investors confidence that they will earn profits from their investment if it succeeds. None of these infrastructures exists for Sicelo.

Raoul and Pedro were born in the same Mexican town, and received the same education. Pedro in Los Angeles makes *less* use of his education and capabilities than Raoul. The average American worker has far more capital at his disposal than the average Mexican.[3] Yet Raoul, whose employer manufactures for an American corporation, utilizes more capital equipment than Pedro. Mexico has ready access to American technology and firms have established plants, like Raoul's, to use American technology in lower-cost locations such as Mexico. We cannot explain all the differences in outcomes by differences in skills, education, capital or technology: none of these factors, nor all of them together, are sufficient to account for the differences between the economic lives of Pedro and Raoul, between the prosperity of the United States and the poverty of Mexico.

Economic Systems Matter

Productivity is not simply the result of the availability of capital and technology, of differences in the skills of individual workers. In the modern world, skills can be developed everywhere, and capital and technology flow freely between countries. Economic differences persist because output and living standards are the complex product of the intersection of the economic environment with associated social, political and cultural institutions. The economic lives of individuals are the product of the systems within which they operate.

No modern experience illustrates this as starkly as the difference between the economic lives of the brothers Friedrich and Heinz. They were born between Hitler's accession to power in 1933 and the outbreak of war in 1939 and brought up in a suburb on the outskirts of Berlin. At school during the war, they experienced acute privations after much of Berlin was razed, and the physical infrastructure of Germany destroyed, by the Allied advances in 1944–5. After the war they began engineering apprenticeships. Both trained in plants which had been established by Siemens, Germany's largest engineering business. Friedrich moved to Nuremberg, while Heinz started work in a plant formerly owned by Siemens but then controlled by the East German state. Both married in their early twenties and rented apartments in the cities where they had settled. In the early 1950s the differences in the economic lives of the two brothers were still small.

Their families saw each other regularly although, as the boundaries between the German occupation zones became more marked, visits became less frequent. After the building of the Berlin Wall in 1961 they talked to each other only by telephone, and less and less often.

When the Wall came down in 1989, Heinz, like millions of other Easterners, drove his Trabant into the Western zone to see for himself. He had heard that the range and quality of goods in the shops was far superior: now he knew it as a reality. His clothes, his furniture looked shabby compared with Friedrich's: his cramped apartment in a barracks-style block hardly matched Friedrich's semi-detached house with garden. When Heinz described the equipment he used at work, Friedrich laughed.

Heinz and his colleagues enthusiastically supported reunification, believing that Western living standards would soon be theirs. It didn't happen. Today Heinz lives on a pension from the German government. Friedrich, with a Siemens pension added to his state entitlement, receives twice as much. The Siemens company reacquired the plant in which Heinz worked, scrapped virtually everything inside it, and runs it today with a workforce of less than half the number Heinz remembers. Many of his former colleagues, like Heinz himself, have never worked again.

In 1945 the roads, railways and factories of Germany had been destroyed. The country had been victim of a bombing campaign designed to reduce its productive capabilities. But, within a few years, West Germany was again among the richest and most productive economies in the world.[4] While the Eastern zone struggled, the division of Germany into two economic zones was the nearest approach ever made in social science to a controlled experiment. The results were decisive. From 1961 the Berlin Wall divided the two zones. Otherwise, the experiment would have ended prematurely with the flight of population from the East. Twenty-eight years later the citizens of the two zones literally tore down the wall which separated them.

The destruction of physical capital does not lead to enduring differences in economic performance; the implementation of different mechanisms of economic management does. The stark differences in economic lives around the world are not the result of differences in the availability of resources, or education, or capital, or skills. They are the product of differences in the structure of economic institutions. These latter differences in turn determine the availability of resources, education, capital and skills.

This book is about the institutions that define our economic lives. It will become apparent that it is not just economic institutions which matter. Economic institutions function only as part of a social, political and cultural context. This is what I describe as the embedded market.

3

Figures

There are no average people, only real individuals, like Heidi and Ravi. But only by using aggregates and averages can we move from the particular to the general. Economic statistics are simply the averages of the daily economic lives of households and firms.

The World Bank provides a range of indicators for comparison of the economic lives enjoyed in different countries. These include estimates for 2001 for Gross National Income (GNI) per head for 208 countries.[1] Switzerland is at the top, with GNI of $37,000 per head, and the Congo, where the average income is around $100, at the bottom.

Table 3.1 lists the countries with highest GNI per head, down to Italy, whose income level is just over half the Swiss average. Thirteen of these nineteen rich states are in Western Europe, including eleven of the fifteen members of the European Union.[2] But Norway and Switzerland, which head the list, have chosen to stay out of the EU.

There are six other rich countries: Australia, Canada and the United States, and three Asian economies – Japan, Singapore and Hong Kong. The total population of the nineteen is around 800 million, of which 300 million live in North America and slightly more in Europe.

Below that level, GNI per head is more than half that of Italy in eight states ranging from Israel to Slovenia. 'Poor intermediate' countries such as Hungary, Mexico and Saudi Arabia rank behind but have per capita GNI more than half the Slovenian level.

Many of these intermediate countries – Spain, South Korea, Slovenia – are clearly on the way up, and will one day join the rich states of Table 3.1. One is on the way down: New Zealand would until the 1980s have been grouped with the prosperous economies of Western Europe.

Countries whose economic performance lags Hungary have GNI

Table 3.1 The world's richest countries

GNI per head, 2001, current US$ at market exchange rate:

Switzerland	38,330	Finland	23,780
Norway	35,620	Belgium	23,850
Japan	35,610	Germany	23,560
United States	34,400	Ireland	22,850
Denmark	30,600	France	22,730
Hong Kong	25,780	Canada	21,930
Sweden	25,400	Singapore	21,100
United Kingdom	25,120	Australia	19,930
Netherlands	24,330	Italy	19,390
Austria	23,940		

Source: World Bank.

Table 3.2 Intermediate economies

Rich intermediate: GNI per head between one quarter and one half of Swiss levels, 2001:		Poor intermediate: GNI per head between one quarter and on eighth of Swiss levels, 2001:	
	Population (m)		Population (m)
Israel	6.4	Saudi Arabia	21.4
Spain	41.1	Mexico	99.4
New Zealand	3.8	Czech Republic	10.2
Greece	10.6	Hungary	10.2
Portugal	10.0		
Taiwan	22.3		
South Korea	47.6		
Slovenia	2.0		

Sources: World Bank; Centre for Economic Planning and Development, Taiwan.

per head less than one eighth of the Swiss level. Economic life there is altogether different. This environment defines the economic lives of most people in the world – Ravi and Nandini, Ivan and Olga, Sicelo and his family: five-sixths of the world's population. But the list of intermediate economies is short – thirteen countries. Their total population is 300 million, one-third of whom live in Mexico and a further third in Korea and Spain.

The distribution of GNI is 'twin-peaked', whether we measure it by the number of states or by their population.[3] At first sight, this gulf between rich and poor may not seem surprising. There is indeed a wide gulf between rich and poor in the world economy: Heidi's economic life is different from Ravi's, and Bill Gates's economic life is different from mine. But the gulf is not empty. However you define rich and poor households, there are many households in between.

Distributions of most variables – height, weight, examination performance – are clustered round the average.[4] The further away from the centre of the distribution, the fewer observations you find. The distribution of income *within* a country is like that.[5] Most incomes are close to the local average, and as you move away from that average there are fewer households.

These distributions of income within countries have the shape of a conventional statistical distribution known as the log normal or Pareto. There is no sharp distinction between rich and poor households, simply a gradation.[6] The distribution of income among states is different. There is a large number of poor states, a small number neither rich nor poor, and a persistent group of about twenty rich countries.

Table 3.1 raises two immediate questions. What do these figures mean – what exactly is GNI? And what is the explanation of the extraordinarily wide range of economic performance which they record? This book is directed towards the second of these questions, but it is necessary to begin by answering the first.

Accounting for our Economic Lives

Economic lives have three different aspects – work, income, consumption. We mostly work in organizations. Heidi teaches in a Swiss school, Ivan works for a Russian subsidiary of AT&T. Sicelo works for himself, but in a co-operative South African community. Organizations are teams. A meal in Pedro's Los Angeles restaurant requires the services of a chef, a waiter and a washer-up. The owner of the restaurant and the bank which finances it also receive a share of what the diner pays. The revenues of the organization become the incomes of individuals – employees, investors, shareholders.[7]

Figure 3.1 The distribution of world income

(a) Number of states

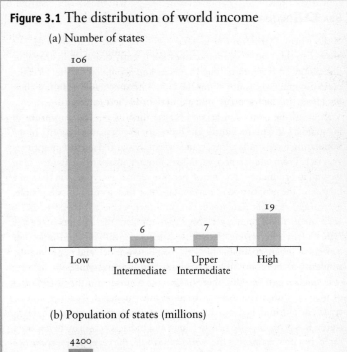

(b) Population of states (millions)

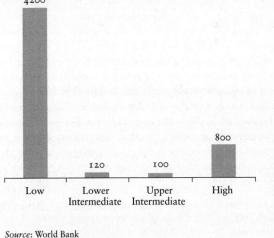

Source: World Bank

Box 3.1 Inequality in world income distribution

Is the world distribution of income becoming more or less equal? The answer to this central economic question is hotly disputed, in academic discussion, among international agencies and in popular debate.* Yet the main disagreement is not about the facts – most protagonists draw their data from the same sources – but about the way these facts are described.

Some of the confusion arises because there is no single measure of inequality.† In a poor country like India, for example, the majority of the population have similar, low, standards of living, and a small minority is very rich. From one perspective, this is a more egalitarian distribution than we find in productive economies, because almost everyone is in the same boat, and the proportion of national income that accrues to rich people, even in aggregate, is quite small. From another perspective this structure is very unequal. We cannot sensibly say that one of these points of view is right and the other wrong. Each draws attention to different and important aspects of Indian economic life – the gap between rich and poor, and the similarity of the economic lives of most of the Indian population.

In the last two decades, there has been a tendency for the distribution of income within countries to become more unequal. This is certainly true in Britain and the United States, and probably true in some other rich states. It is probably also true in China and India, where growth has been rapid, but uneven. Across the world as a whole, the very poorest countries – mostly in Africa – have become poorer and the rich have become richer. But the population of these countries is relatively small. Two populous poor countries – China and India – have enjoyed much more rapid economic growth than the rich countries of the world. Since these two countries alone account for about a third of world population, the overall effect of this growth on the world distribution of income is huge.‡

If I was forced to vote on one side or another, I would conclude that world income inequality – as measured by the distribution of income on a per household basis – had probably gone down. But it is far more important to understand the complex changes which have occurred, and why they have occurred, than to engage in rhetorical debate about rising or falling inequality.

*See for example Wade and Wolf in *Prospect*, March 2001, Firebaugh (1999), Melchior, Telle and Wiig (2000), D. Henderson (2000), Castles (1998).
†See Atkinson (1970, 1983), Kakwani (1980) for discussion of the problems of statistical measurement of inequality.
‡Pritchett (1997), Sala-i-Martin (2002).

We work in organizations, earn as individuals and consume as households. Sven and Ingrid work in the same business unit, receive separate pay cheques and make joint consumption decisions. The way households pool resources differs across cultures. Sven and Ingrid, unmarried, live together with their child. Ravi, though married, lives with his parents. Sicelo's tribal village is supported by family members working elsewhere; Pedro sends money back to his family in Mexico. The units in which individuals work and consume are determined by economic necessities and social norms.

These perspectives on our economic lives – work, income, consumption – are interrelated. What we earn depends on what we produce, what we spend depends on what we earn, what we consume depends on what we make. The links between earnings, production and expenditure apply to individuals, households, business organizations, and for the economy as a whole.

National income accounting systematizes these aggregate relationships, just as financial accounting provides the framework for our business activities. Modern national accounts are still based essentially on the framework derived by Simon Kuznets[N], in the Unites States and James Meade[N] and Richard Stone[N] in Britain during the Second World War, which records and integrates the three elements of economic life – incomes, output and expenditure. All converge on the central concept

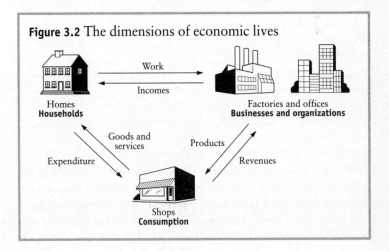

Figure 3.2 The dimensions of economic lives

Table 3.3 What the United Kingdom spends, 2001

	(£billion)
24.5m households spend on average £25,900	634
Government spends (equates to £3,211 per head of population)	192
Business investment	189
Trade deficit (net purchases from abroad)	−22
Gross domestic product	993

Sources: Annual National Accounts; OECD; UK National Statistics.

Table 3.4 What the United Kingdom earns, 2001

	(£billion)
29m workers earn on average £19,200	559
Profits of businesses	302
Taxes (less subsidies) on businesses	132
Gross domestic product	993

Sources: Annual National Accounts; OECD.

Table 3.5 Redistribution of United Kingdom income among households, 2001

	(£billion)
Earnings of workers	573
Investment income (net)	80
Total household income from current production	653
Benefits and pensions	246
Total resources	899
Taxes	−131
Other Social contributions	−101
Left for households to spend	668

Source: UK National Statistics.

of national income accounting, gross domestic product (GDP). When politicians talk about economic growth, or pundits discuss booms and recessions, they are talking about growth in GDP. International agencies have encouraged countries to produce national accounts in a common framework, and this data is the basis for the rankings in

Table 3.6 What the United Kingdom produces: 2001 (£billion)

	Total output	Sold to other businesses	Sold directly
Agriculture	18	7	11
Mining	32	22	9
Manufacturing	376	117	259
Electricity, gas & water supply	46	13	33
Construction	127	52	75
Trade	294	157	137
Transport & communication	153	71	82
Finance intermediation	485	290	196
Public administration	85	45	40
Education, health & social work	219	108	111
Other	80	40	40
Gross domestic product			993

Source: UK National Statistics.

Table 3.1. GNI is derived by adjusting GDP, a measure of a country's output, for the income its residents derive from assets they own overseas.

Ravi's income is in rupees. Ivan is paid in roubles, although his wife may earn dollars. Comparisons across countries are easiest if figures are translated into a common currency. The simplest way of doing this is to look up the quoted exchange rate, but such exchange rates fluctuate from day to day. Since the euro was established in 1999 its value has ranged from 82 cents to $1.25. Table 3.1 is based on a three-year average in order to reduce this volatility.

Kivik and Palanpur

Switzerland's GDP is not much smaller than India's. Yet the population of India is over a hundred times larger. About 5 million people work in Switzerland and 600 million in India. Can these staggering differences in productivity really be true?

Box 3.2 What GDP is and isn't

GDP is often criticized because it is not necessarily a measure of sustainable output, or of economic welfare. Two frequent criticisms are that it fails to take account of degradation (or improvement) in the environment and that it does not measure unpaid work undertaken within the home.*

There is some validity in these claims. But the measurement of GDP and the framework of national income accounts should be seen primarily as a way of organizing information about the national economy, rather than as an attempt to measure welfare. It is difficult to maintain this position because economic data is widely used in political debate.

In the 1990s the Bureau of Economic Analysis, which compiles the US national accounts, was under obvious pressure, particularly from Chairman Greenspan, to support the assertions then made about the 'new economy'. On the other side of the political fence, those who argue that GDP should account for environmental costs or unpaid work are more concerned to make environmental or feminist arguments than to enhance the integrity of national accounting frameworks.

GDP and other economic measurements are likely to be of greatest use to a wide range of users if as far as is possible the measurement relates to issues of objective fact. Users can then modify these measures to reflect their own particular requirements. The pursuit of objectivity and comparability is preferable to repeated modification in pursuit of a concept of accuracy which is both subjective and elusive. (The same is true of commercial accounting.)

*For substantive academic discussion of these issues, see Kenrick (1979), and Nordhaus and Kokkelenberg (1999).

Sven's farm at Kivik produces wheat. Since wheat is grown in many countries, we can make approximate comparisons between the productivity of Sven's farm and the productivity of Indian farming. For several decades now, a group of economists has regularly visited the village of Palanpur in Rajasthan, living with the people and studying its economy as anthropologists study culture.[8]

Sven's farm produces about twenty times as much wheat per person employed as does Palanpur. Yields vary from year to year: rather more in Palanpur than in Kivik. But the trend is upward. Since 1960 the green revolution (the adoption of new crop varieties adapted to tropical climates) has almost doubled the Palanpur crop. There have been productivity gains in Sweden, too.

The average yield at Kivik is around four times that at Palanpur. If you were to choose a climate in which to grow wheat, you would probably not select either Kivik or Palanpur. Kivik is too cold and Palanpur is too dry (except in the monsoon, when it is too wet). The Canadian prairies, and the American Great Plains, have the best blend of temperature and moisture for wheat. Land at Kivik is more fertile than at Palanpur, but it is hard to say how much of that is intrinsic and how much the result of poor farming in the Indian village.

Sven has much more machinery and uses more fertilizer and modern pesticides. The village employs about five times as many people per acre. The difference in labour input both causes and is caused by the difference in income levels. Because Swedish labour is expensive, Swedish farmers use costly equipment, and Swedish agriculture is consolidated into large plots. Palanpur villagers use bullocks, ploughs and scythes, as they have done for centuries, and many work their own smallholdings.

Every aspect of economic life is different, so there is no single explanation of productivity differences. Wheat cultivation is one of the few activities for which Indian and Swedish output are comparable: wheat is more or less wheat wherever it is grown.[9] Many Swedish goods simply could not be manufactured in India. There are no Indian cars of Volvo quality. Goods like Volvos command high prices in world markets and that is why the average difference in GDP per worker is well above a ratio of twenty to one.

Material Living Standards

Sven and Ingrid ski in Northern Sweden and have access to modern ski-lifts, built to exacting standards; Ivan and Olga ski in Northern Russia where the few lifts available are old and poorly maintained. The Swedish environment is immacutely preserved, but Ivan and Olga ski in the forests of the Komi Republic, which has suffered sustained damage from atmospheric pollution and inappropriate logging.[10]

But a week's skiing in Sweden costs ten times what Ivan and Olga pay. Sven and Ingrid have a better experience – both couples would prefer Swedish facilities and equipment. But is that experience ten times better? Most of the pleasure comes from snow and sun, freedom and companionship, and these are as exhilarating for Ivan and Olga as for Sven and Ingrid.

Heidi and Hermann share an income whose dollar value is more than thirty times that of Ravi and Nandini. They are much better off, in material terms, with all the material goods that Ravi and Nandini have, and many more: The Indian couple would readily exchange their economic lives for those of Heidi and Hermann, but Heidi and Hermann would not want the economic lives of Ravi and Nandini. Though not necessarily happier, Heidi and Hermann are better off.

But is Heidi thirty times as well off as Ravi? An objective approach to the measurement of material living standards might ask what it would cost Heidi and Hermann to live the economic life of Ravi and Nandini, or Ravi and Nandini to live the economic life of Heidi and Hermann. But the question is tough. The Swiss authorities would not allow an apartment like that of Ravi and Nandini to be built there. You can find a house like that of Heidi and Hermann in India, but in an enclosed compound with private security guards. Yet the food which Nandini buys cheaply every day in the market is available in Zurich only from an expensive delicatessen. And Heidi does much of the housework herself, while Nandini does have a housekeeper, and does very little domestic work. An automatic dishwasher costs three years of a housekeeper's earnings in India: But Heidi's salary pays for her machine in less than a week.

The more distant comparisons are in space and time, the more strained they become. Nathan Rothschild, probably the richest man in the world in 1836, died despite the best medical attention money could buy. The infection which killed him could today be cured by antibiotics available even to Sicelo for a few coins.[11] Isn't Sicelo, alive, better off than Nathan Rothschild, dead?

Despite these difficulties, international agencies make estimates of purchasing power parity (PPP): the cost of maintaining a given material standard of living in different countries.[12] International disparities in material living standards are less wide than international disparities in productivity because services and property are generally cheaper in poor countries than in rich countries: they are also cheaper in Australia and North America than in Europe or Japan.

Productivity and Material Living Standards

These national accounts concepts are the building blocks for the measurement of all aspects of representative economic lives. Table 3.7 provides estimates of material living standards – private consumption per head – and of productivity – output per working hour – for the nineteen rich countries of Table 3.1

These countries are both the nineteen most productive countries in the world and also the nineteen countries with the highest material standard of living. This equivalence is not inevitable, but is likely, given the fundamental connections between the different aspects of our economic lives – output, incomes and consumption. And it has an important implication which will be developed fully in the course of this book. The main reasons why some countries are better off than others is to be found in the internal economic organization of these countries themselves, rather than the product of international economics. Heidi is not rich because Sicelo is poor.

It is probably best to measure productivity at market exchange rates, because market exchange rates measure what, on average, global markets are willing to pay for a country's output. But market exchange rates are subject to large short term fluctuations and, in 2001, the value of the euro was extremely low: so rankings by purchasing power parity in Table 3.7 may be a better overall guide to the underlying levels of productivity in the various countries.

However measured, Norway, which combines large and profitable oil extraction with an efficient industrial sector, has the highest productivity of any country in the world. Elsewhere, output per hour worked converted at market exchange rates ranks Japan at the top ($43) and Australia at the bottom ($23), although the less misleading purchasing power parity basis discloses a narrower range, from Belgium's $46 to around $30 in the still emerging Hong Kong and Singapore. Average output of about $40 per hour is what a productive modern economy with current technology can expect to achieve.

Table 3.7 Living standards and productivity, 2001, US$

	Consumption per head, PPP exchange rates	Output per hour, PPP exchange rates	Output per hour, market exchange rates
Australia	16300	32.3	22.6
Austria	15600	40.0	33.2
Belgium	14700	46.3	37.0
Canada	16000	33.6	25.9
Denmark	13500	39.0	39.8
Finland	13500	36.4	32.0
France	14300	45.2	37.1
Germany	15000	40.1	34.5
Hong Kong	15600	30.9	30.0
Ireland	13400	40.2	36.6
Italy	15600	40.1	28.9
Japan	14700	35.3	43.4
Netherlands	14300	42.0	34.5
Norway	15200	54.0	55.1
Singapore	11500	29.6	26.9
Sweden	12200	33.5	31.8
Switzerland	17400	34.6	39.5
United Kingdom	16900	34.2	31.5
United States	24500	39.5	39.5

Sources: OECD, Hong Kong Census and Statistics Department; Statistics Singapore.

Among the rich states themselves, variations in productivity are poorly correlated with variations in material living standards. Table 3.8 explores why. There are large differences in private consumption as a share of national income – almost 70 per cent in the United States as against just over 40 per cent in Norway. Norway enjoys a trade surplus, the United States a deficit. Norway has higher personal savings, higher business investment and higher public spending.

Variations in the proportion of the population working are less dramatic, but still considerable: 55 per cent of the Swiss population is in employment but in Belgium, where early retirement is common, unemployment is high and it is still unusual for married women with children to work, the figure is only 39 per cent. But annual working

Table 3.8 Why material living standards differ, 2001

	Household consumption as a share of GDP (%)	Number working per 100 of population	Hours worked (annual average)	PPP local cost of $ of consumption of $1
Australia	60.1	47.3	1779	0.70
Austria	55.6	46.2	1519	0.83
Belgium	53.2	38.8	1547	0.80
Canada	55.1	48.0	1789	0.77
Denmark	46.4	50.4	1482	1.02
Finland	47.8	45.5	1612	0.88
France	54.0	40.5	1474	0.82
Germany	57.5	44.5	1467	0.86
Hong Kong	57.8	49.7	1760	0.97
Ireland	44.7	44.6	1674	0.89
Italy	59.6	40.6	1606	0.72
Japan	55.2	50.4	1780	1.23
Netherlands	48.9	50.6	1376	0.82
Norway	41.2	50.2	1364	1.02
Singapore	42.3	51.1	1798	0.91
Sweden	47.0	48.6	1603	0.95
Switzerland	58.4	55.3	1566	1.14
United Kingdom	63.8	45.7	1656	0.92
United States	69.7	48.4	1878	1.00

Figures in italics indicate median figure.

Sources: OECD, Hong Kong Census and Statistics Department; Statistics Singapore.

hours vary considerably. Norwegians take a large part of the benefit of oil revenues in leisure. The United States is a complete outlier, with much longer typical working hours than other countries, and is also the only country in which average hours of work have been rising. The normal trend around the world is for working hours to fall as incomes rise and, if the United States is excluded, there is a strong tendency for longer holidays and shorter working weeks in richer countries.

The final column of Table 3.8 shows the cost of living in different countries: in 2001 it would have cost $1.23 in Japan, and $1.14 in Switzerland, but only 70 cents in Australia, to buy the goods that would have cost $1 in the United States. This table makes the United States look expensive but this is another consequence of the low value of the euro in 2001. If the same calculation were repeated in 2003 the cost of living in Belgium, France, Germany and the Netherlands would be similar to that of the United States.

The group of factors described in Table 3.8, taken together, lead to a striking conclusion. The United States, with average productivity levels, achieves much higher private consumption levels than any other country in the world. The principal reasons are the high level of consumption, relative to GNP, and longer working hours. Government spending in the United States – primarily on health, education and infrastructure – is much lower than average, business investment is lower than average, and high consumption is financed by extensive borrowing from the rest of the world, particularly Asia. And Americans work more than residents of other rich countries, with later retirement, shorter holidays and longer hours. Through this relentless focus on private consumption, American levels are 40 per cent above those of the next highest countries, Switzerland and the United Kingdom.

Other Dimensions

The nineteen countries of Table 3.1 are the rich states and productive economies of the world. They are distinguished from other countries in many other respects. Here are some correlations.

climate Productive economies are cooler. With the exceptions of Hong Kong and Singapore, and a large area of Australia in which very few people live, there are no rich states in the tropics.[13]

democracy Rich states are normally democracies.[14]

environmental standards Productive economies mostly have higher environmental standards (less atmospheric pollution, better water quality) and more environmental activism.[15]

freedom of expression Free speech is less restricted in productive economies.[16]

gender equality Rights and freedoms of women are more extensive in rich states than in poor ones.[17]

happiness, self-reported The population of productive economies mostly gives positive answers to the question 'Are you generally happy with your life?' The same is true in some poor countries (Cuba, India). In other unproductive economies, surveys show that very few people are happy. This is particularly true of Eastern Europe.[18]

health Life expectancy is higher in rich states.[19]

height The population of productive economies is taller.[20]

honesty Rich states are less corrupt. Citizens give positive answers to questions like 'Do you find you can trust other people?'[21]

inequality Inequality can be measured in many ways. The ratio of total income of the richest 20 per cent of the population to total income of the poorest 20 per cent is lower in rich countries: they are more egalitarian. Most ways of measuring inequality would lead to a similar conclusion.[22]

inflation Prices rise less rapidly in rich states.[23]

literacy The population of productive economies is almost entirely literate. This is also true in Eastern Europe, but only occasionally elsewhere.[24]

materialism People in poor countries more often give positive answers to questions of the kind 'Is money the most important thing?'[25]

openness Productive countries have fewer restrictions on trade with other countries.[26]

population growth Population growth is lower in rich states.[27]

property rights Property rights are more secure in rich states.[28]

religion From the standpoint of earthly productivity, it is better to live in a society whose traditions are Christian and, among Christians, it is better to live in a predominantly Protestant tradition than in a mainly Catholic one.[29]

tolerance More people in rich states answer 'yes' to such questions as 'Should people be allowed to live as they choose?'[30]

Correlation does not imply causation. Average height is greater in rich states. Are tall people more productive than short people? Or does higher productivity make people taller? I doubt if either of these things is true. Higher standards of living, which result from higher productivity, lead to better nutrition. In turn, better nutrition leads to greater adult height and still higher productivity. The relationship works in both directions, and only in association with other factors which are themselves associated with height and productivity.

Most of the relationships above are similarly complex. Few of these correlations are simply causal: they are the product of a mixture of factors associated with higher productivity. Our economic lives are embedded in our social and political lives.

That embeddedness is the continuing theme of this book. Different cultures have made different choices about the ways in which the capacities of their economies are reflected in the economic lives of their citizens. These choices are partly the result of individual decisions – how long to spend over lunch – and of collective decisions – what resources to devote to public schools or transport systems. There are no economic criteria that enable us to conclude that some choices are right, and others wrong. Nor is there an inevitable convergence. Diversity is an important feature of economic life.

In the decade since the cold war ended, admiring eyes have switched from Japan – whose boom ended with its bubble in the late 1980s – to Germany – whose successful social market economy struggled with the burden of reunification in the 1990s. Attention was diverted to the Asian tigers – Singapore, Korea, Hong Kong – but ended with the financial crisis of 1997. Since then America's New Economy has occupied centre stage.

Trends of a few years or even months are often projected into an indefinite future. But differences in economic performance and experience among rich states are small and temporary, differences between rich and poor states large and enduring. Any theory of the relative success and failure of economic systems must explain this central fact. A good starting-point is to ask how today's rich states became rich.

4

How Rich States Became Rich

Beginnings[1]

A modern economic system is a complex, interacting set of institutions which has evolved over thousands of years. Objects made from materials which were only available hundreds of miles away are found at the campsites of our Cro-Magnon ancestors, who arrived in Europe 40,000 years ago. The Neanderthals, whom they displaced, used only local materials. The Cro-Magnons moved from barter to trade, and bought objects, not for their own immediate use, but for resale. Cro-Magnons also innovated. Neanderthal tools do not change much. Cro-Magnon tools became steadily more effective and more specialized. The key difference between Neanderthals and Cro-Magnons was probably language.[2] Communication is essential to specialization and exchange.

Agriculture began in the fertile crescent of Mesopotamia between 8,000 and 10,000 years ago.[3] People had always 'owned' clothes and tools. But agriculture requires property rights over land and animals, and these rights had to be codified and recognized. The new institutions created opportunities for further technological innovation. Selective breeding and domestication of crops and species came with ownership of seeds and animals. New technologies and new institutions gradually spread out from their places of origin.[4]

Technologies and institutions sped rapidly across plains and along rivers, slowly over hills. Agricultural practice can be transferred more easily along an east–west axis than a north–south one, because climate changes less. Today's rich states are in temperate climates not too different from those of Mesopotamia 10,000 years ago. The seeds of European economic hegemony were planted then.

In ancient Greece there were people who organized production and trade. Business and management had been invented, but were not well regarded by the philosophers and writers of the time.[5] Intellectual disdain for the market is not new. Tourists in Athens can still visit ancient marketplaces – physical locations where competitive buyers met sellers. These marketplaces were public facilities, provided by the state to assist commerce. The Greeks invented the notion of politics. With a political realm comes the possibility of a government whose economic activities are distinct from the economic interests of those who control it. Market economies require disinterested government.

Ancient Greece was a pluralist society. Its citizens began to question the functioning of the natural world and the structure of social organization. This restless spirit lay quiescent through the Dark Ages, to revive in medieval times.[6] The Renaissance is associated with the growth of pluralism and experiment in art, architecture and literature – a pluralism and experiment which extended to economic organization, economic institutions and new ventures and to markets for risk and capital. Paper rights to commodities as well as commodities themselves could be traded. These were the beginnings of modern securities markets. Businesses developed that were distinguishable from the individuals who ran them, such as trading companies and banks. Their records were maintained through double-entry bookkeeping.[7]

From the Reformation to the Industrial Revolution

The religious reformation in Northern Europe followed; economic growth accelerated in Northern Europe. In rich states with religiously mixed populations (such as Switzerland, Germany and the Netherlands) the economic role of Protestants was disproportionate to their numbers. Catholic Italy and Ireland became rich states only in the later part of the twentieth century and Spain will become one only in the twenty-first. The architectural legacies of Italy and Spain demonstrate the difference between their relative economic position at the time of the Reformation, and today.

The correlation between religion and economic development is inescapable, but the nature of the connection is controversial. Max Weber explained how belief in predestination led to the austere, hard-working morality we still call 'the Protestant ethic'. R. H. Tawney and Robert Merton gave greater weight to the intellectual ferment that followed the breakdown of clerical authoritarianism: the opportunity to challenge established ideas and practices which is essential to the coevolution of technology and institutions.[8] The combination of moral rigour and free enquiry is the basis of disciplined pluralism – the defining characteristic of the successful market economy.

The shape of that market economy began to emerge. Britain and the Netherlands became major trading nations in the seventeenth and eighteenth centuries. While Spanish colonists were soldiers in search of gold, British and Dutch colonization was managed by businesses such as the East India Company and the VOC (Vereenigde Oostindische Compagnie), and its purpose was commercial exploitation. The beginning of the eighteenth century was a period of rapid financial innovation, which culminated in the boom and bust of the South Sea Bubble.

The first blast-furnace iron was made at Coalbrookdale in 1709 by Abraham Darby. The invention of the flying shuttle (by my namesake John Kay) was one of many advances in technology in the textile industry. These discoveries, together with the invention of steam power, made it efficient to organize businesses on a larger scale. The mill Richard Arkwright built to exploit the spinning frame – the invention of another namesake of mine – was the largest in the world. Technical institutions were established to disseminate and extend the new technologies.

The establishment of agriculture; the creation of public marketplaces; the development of banking and insurance; the invention of corporate organization. Each was a step in the coevolution of economic institutions, social developments and technological innovation. It is a coevolution because there is no linear cause: each strand of development both supports and requires the other.

Productive Economies, Rich States

In the second half of the eighteenth century there was little difference between living standards in Western Europe and those in the rest of the world.[9] The nineteen rich states which today account for about three-quarters of world output then produced only a quarter of it. But the modern pattern had been set by 1820. Economic historians have reconstructed historic series of GDP (even attempting to assess what national income statisticians would have calculated a million years ago).[10] We have roughly comparable estimates for twenty-six countries in 1820.[11] The most productive state then was the UK, but in sixteen of the twenty-six productivity was more than half the British level. All but one of these (Spain) are now rich countries. Of the ten others, only two (Finland and Japan) are now rich. History evidently matters.

Still, the range of productivity in 1820 was small by modern standards. Output per head in the richest countries (the UK, the Netherlands) was then three times the level of the poorest (India, China). The gap today is a factor of thirty to fifty. This widening has been almost continuous for two centuries. In the first half of the nineteenth century, a small group began to pull away, and in each subsequent period a few other states caught up, mostly those which were more productive to begin with. And the newly productive countries have almost always been on the geographic borders of those that are already productive.

If history is important, so is geography. There were ten productive economies in 1870: Belgium, Denmark, Germany, the Netherlands, Switzerland, the UK and the four European settlements of Australia, Canada, New Zealand and the United States. The European group form a contiguous geographical block.[12]

Before the First World War, three further European countries – Austria, France and Sweden – became productive. Each is on the periphery of the established group. Norway emerged, first as an independent state and then an economic force, in the first half of the twentieth century. The geographical cluster of productive economies continued to expand after the Second World War with the accession of Finland, Ireland and Italy.

Table 4.1 Rich and poor states, 1820 (income per head, 1990 $)*

Rich countries today:†		Others in Maddison's sample:	
UK	1,756	Spain	1,063
Netherlands	1,561	Czechoslovakia	849
Australia	1,528	Mexico	760
Austria	1,295	USSR	751
Belgium	1,291	Brazil	670
USA	1,287	Indonesia	614
Denmark	1,225	India‡	531
France	1,218	China	523
Sweden	1,198		
Germany	1,112		
Italy	1,092		
Norway	1,004		
Ireland	954		
Canada	893		
Finland	759		
Japan	704		

*Estimates relate to 1990 boundaries as far as possible.
†Figures for Switzerland in 1820 are not available: the other two rich countries (of 19) are Hong Kong and Singapore.
‡Includes Pakistan and Bangladesh.
Source: Maddison (1993).

If we look at potentially productive economies – those likely to qualify before 2050 – the geographic theme continues. The Czech Republic, Greece, Hungary, Poland, Portugal, Slovenia and Spain[13] all border existing rich states. There could hardly be a more striking refutation of the claim that globalization, and improvements in transport and communication, have made economic geography irrelevant. Geography, or something closely related to geography, matters a great deal, and continues to matter.

Settlements

There are three productive economies outside Europe and Asia: Australia, Canada and the United States. At first sight, their success refutes the thesis that geography has been important to history. Australia is 10,000 miles away from Western Europe and 3,000 miles from its nearest rich neighbour, Singapore.

But there is no real inconsistency. Australia, Canada and the United States are all European settlements. They were established by North-West European immigrants. These settlers annihilated the culture of the native population and largely annihilated the native population itself. The inhabitants of Australia, Canada and the United States speak North-Western European languages, and their legal systems and political and social institutions are European in origin. Outside French-speaking Quebec, the principal language is English. Colonies such as India or Indonesia in which immigrants were a minority are not rich states: not even those colonies where settlements were large, as in South Africa, Kenya or the West Indies.[14]

Australia, Canada and the United States – the 'Western offshoots' – imported technology and institutions from Western Europe: they also imported people familiar with that technology and those institutions. In European colonies the native population was not encouraged – and often, until late stages of colonialism, not permitted – to assimilate to and be assimilated by the imported culture. The transfer of technology and institutions was superficial and transitory.

The Western offshoots played a major role in the development of the institutions of the market economy. The revolution was brought home, in an economic sense, before the end of the nineteenth century, as the United States became a centre for new technology and financial innovation. In the twentieth century, the United States became dominant in management theory and product innovation; by its end Americans sincerely believed that the market economy was an American invention, and a comparatively recent one: 'The world is ten years old.'

But even if the building-blocks of the market economy were imported, there was one problem which these new countries had to solve for themselves. By the nature of settlement, there is no established system of property in land when settlers arrive in an empty territory. (The territories were not empty and land claims existed, if not property on a European model. But the settlers ignored these claims or extinguished them.) There are two principal ways of creating new property rights. They can be allocated, or sold, by the state; or government can recognize and enforce the rights of those settlers who actually occupy the land.[15]

The ability to award, or sell, tracts of empty land is a congenial source of patronage and revenue for government. But decisions made in Washington or London did not necessarily relate to what was happening on the ground thousands of miles away.[16] Settlers developed local norms to define and protect each other's rights. In the gold rushes – the largest were in California and in Victoria, Australia – government was ineffective. A degree of spontaneous order, in which the mining communities regulated and enforced each other's claims, emerged rapidly.[17] These models influenced the general development of land rights. In the end, settlers' claims – squatters' rights – were the principal determinant of property rights in English-speaking settlements (but not in English-speaking colonies).

Argentina and New Zealand

These two once rich states have many things in common. Both are low-cost agricultural producers. Both play international rugby. There are many differences, however. The most famous Argentines are Eva Perón ('Evita'), movie-star wife of a populist dictator, and the sceptical writer Jorge Luis Borges. The most famous New Zealanders are Ernest Rutherford, who first split the atom (in England), and Edmund Hillary, who climbed Mt. Everest (in Nepal). The symbol of Argentina is the gaucho, of New Zealand the kiwi. Both are geographically peripheral countries. Geographic contiguity had a large influence on the development of rich states in Western Europe. The two countries that have ceased to be rich states are the two that are most detached geographically.

Transport costs hardly explain why countries that were rich a century ago are less rich today. In Chapter 23, I shall examine the unconvincing dependency theory of the Argentine economist Raoul Prebisch, which claims that all peripheral countries are disadvantaged. But one consequence of peripheral location is that it gives countries greater freedom to pursue economic policies that are different from those of other rich states. The geographical contiguity which worked so well in Europe is ineffective. This freedom has been exploited in both Argentina and New Zealand, to dismal effect. The fame of Evita and her husband is not based on skill in economic management, and New Zealand has inflicted unsuccessful economic experiments on itself.

Argentina was never as well off as Australia or New Zealand. But a visitor to Buenos Aires is still impressed by century-old buildings which match the opulence of late-nineteenth-century European capitals. The shabby surroundings measure the decline in Argentina's relative position. Argentine development was strikingly pluralist (a pluralism which is maintained today in the vitality of Argentine cultural life). Immigration from Italy was almost as important as immigration from Spain. Despite the famous Welsh enclave in Patagonia, few settlers were attracted from Northern Europe. But British economic influence was pervasive: Britons not only built tramways and railways but organized markets for Argentine meat.[18]

But economic institutions are only part of the structures relevant to economic development. While the economic growth of English-speaking settlements has matched or outperformed England, Spanish-speaking settlements have struggled to match the performance of Spain, itself unexceptional. And there is a key economic difference between English and Spanish settlements. In English-speaking countries, tension over property distribution was resolved largely in favour of settlers. In Latin America, central control over land allocation was more effective. Even today the structure of land ownership in Latin America is dominated by the descendants of a small number of founding families. This had direct consequences for the management of the land: absentee proprietors are generally poor proprietors. But the indirect economic consequences were more important still. The unequal distribution of income and wealth lacked legitimacy. These economic and political inequalities have shaped the destructive and confrontational nature of Argentina's politics from the overthrow of Rivadavia by landowners in 1827 to the street demonstrations of 2002.[19]

The problems of New Zealand are more recent in origin. Twelve thousand miles distant, New Zealand became a major agricultural producer focused on the British market. Even in 1960 more than half of New Zealand exports were to the mother country. This relationship fractured as Britain moved closer to continental Europe and, more hesitantly, New Zealand moved towards Australia and Asia.

New Zealand could find alternative markets only at lower prices and its economic performance deteriorated. In 1975 Robert Muldoon became Prime Minister. His slogan was 'think big', and he sponsored the construction of aluminium smelters and petrochemical plants and favoured detailed economic intervention. Most of the 'think big' projects were eventually written off with large losses. Muldoon was defeated in the 1984 election.[20] The new Labour government appointed Roger Douglas as Finance Minister. Douglas pursued enthusiastic free market policies, supported by an able and ideologically committed group of Treasury officials led by Graham Scott. If ever a country has been run by economists, it was New Zealand. From 1984 to 1999 New Zealand followed policies of privatization and deregulation, and pursued labour market flexibility and reductions in social benefits. During this period, the country experienced the worst economic performance of any rich state. Its decline was bleakly symbolized in January 1998 when the supply cables of the unregulated Mercury Energy failed, blacking out the Central Business District of Auckland. Seven weeks elapsed before regular power supplies were restored with the aid of the New Zealand army.[21]

No country has modelled its policies more deliberately on the American business model – applause for self-interest, market fundamentalism, and the rolling back of the economic and redistributive functions of the state – than New Zealand after 1984, not even the United States.[22] When one branch of the US government has maintained a strong ideological position – as under the Reagan presidency or the Republican congress of 1994–6 – checks and balances operated within the US system of government. The parliamentary structure which Britain gave New Zealand has few restraints on executive authority

(New Zealand even has a unicameral legislature). In 1999 the New Zealand electorate tired of economic experiments and returned a Labour government with conventional policies. After three phases of adverse economic experience, one externally created, two self-inflicted, New Zealand GDP per head had fallen from 125 per cent of the average of rich states in 1960 to 60 per cent of the average in 2000.[23]

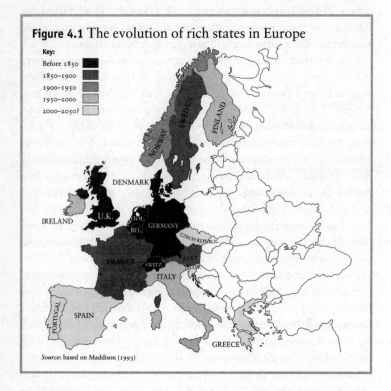

Figure 4.1 The evolution of rich states in Europe

Key:
Before 1850
1850–1900
1900–1950
1950–2000
2000–2050?

Source: based on Maddison (1993)

The Asian Contrast

Fig. 4.1 shows the geography of the rich states of Western Europe. The group expanded steadily from a central core, gradually encompassing peripheral areas. In Asia, geographic contiguity seems to be equally significant, but in precisely the opposite direction. Richer states

(Fig. 4.2) are peripheral and, even within China itself, coastal regions have higher incomes. It is as though an economic blight had centred on Beijing – and perhaps this is the right way to see it.

Why did the Industrial Revolution happen in Britain and in North-West Europe and not in South-East China?[24] This is one of the great puzzles of economic history. Earlier in the millennium, Chinese technology had fully matched that of the West. In the second half of the eighteenth century there are many similarities between the two regions – in industrial structure, agricultural techniques, in capital per head, and the mild but increasing pressure of population on available land.

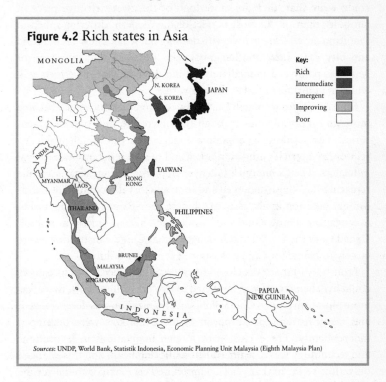

Figure 4.2 Rich states in Asia

Sources: UNDP, World Bank, Statistik Indonesia, Economic Planning Unit Malaysia (Eighth Malaysia Plan)

But the Industrial Revolution in Europe was not a purely technological phenomenon. China's institutions lagged behind its productive capability. And the pluralism which was so important to the evolution of Western European science and Western European institutions was largely absent. China was – is – a more or less unitary state while Europe has always been fragmented. This contrast can be overstated: the imperial writ ran uncertainly over large areas of China, and European fragmentation produced the disadvantages of military conflict as well as the advantages of economic competition. More important is the degree of pluralism within states, and within societies.

The China of that period has given the English language the term 'mandarin'. Mandarins were the civil servants of the Chinese court, and the values they prized were the values of tradition and ritual. At the start of the eighteenth century a French missionary visiting China could write that 'they are more fond of the most defective piece of antiquity than of the most perfect of the modern, differing much in that from us, who are in love with nothing but what is new'. A hundred and fifty years later another missionary observed that 'any man of genius is paralyzed immediately by the thought that his efforts will win him punishment rather than reward'.[25]

China's failure to match European economic performance became more and more obvious through the nineteenth and twentieth centuries. The resulting xenophobia exaggerated the initial problems, reinforced internal authoritarianism and fuelled resistance to external influences. The Communist takeover emphasized centralization while replacing stasis with deranged and contradictory directions. The extraordinary economic successes of Chinese people outside China itself – in Singapore, Hong Kong and Taiwan, and also as settlers in Britain, Canada and the United States – suggest that Chinese institutions were largely to blame for China's sustained economic failure.

From 1639 Japan was closed to external influence.[26] No foreigners could live there: trade was restricted to two ports. Internally, there was more pluralism than in China. Political organization was decentralized, and many features of European financial markets were developed independently. The exclusion of foreign innovations in institutions and technology was a crippling economic handicap, and this changed only after 1853. In that year Commodore Perry arrived to deliver the American business model, and he returned a year later, with the aid of American guns, to insist. Japan began to adopt Western technologies, but the import of Western institutions was slower. With the Meiji restoration came political centralization, leading to the obsessive militarism which in turn led to Pearl Harbor and ended at Hiroshima and Nagasaki. General Douglas MacArthur landed in Tokyo in 1945 to impose those elements of the American business model that Commodore Perry had overlooked.

MacArthur's objective was to reform Japanese institutions. The secularization of the role of the Emperor undermined the authoritarian state. Subsequent political leadership was fragmented and ineffectual, although the civil service remained powerful. The five *zaibatsu*,[27] which had controlled all large-scale economic activity in Japan, were dissolved. Japanese industry now focused on the production of high-quality consumer goods. Toyota transformed itself from a manufacturer of textile machinery into the principal competitor of Ford and General Motors. Matsushita – *zaibatsu* reinvented as conglomerate – became a leading producer of consumer electronics, under brand names such as Panasonic and JVC. Sony and Honda were creations of maverick individuals: Akio Morita, the man behind Sony, became Japan's best-known businessman. For forty years from 1950 Japan experienced the fastest growth of GDP ever seen in a major economy.

Japan's success was to be rivalled by the achievements of two former colonies – Korea and Formosa (Taiwan). Freed from Japanese control by the outcome of the Second World War, both countries found themselves on the fault line of the mutual suspicion of China and the United States. MacArthur moved to Korea, where a civil war widened into a conflict between China and the United States. In 1953 the country was divided at the 38th parallel. The difference between the subsequent economic performance of the two states then created is extraordinary – far greater even than the differences between East and West Germany or Finland and Estonia. South Korea will shortly become a rich state, barring accidents – or reunification. North Korea has both nuclear weapons and endemic famine.[28]

Taiwan was occupied by the nationalist forces defeated in the Communist takeover of mainland China in 1949. Like South Korea, it prospered through a mix of policies combining American and Japanese influences: protection against imports, strong export orientation, openness to external capital and technology, and competition between a small number of diversified industrial groups.

The two small island territories of Singapore and Hong Kong, with British institutions and Chinese populations, became rich states. Thailand, Malaysia and Indonesia, although still poor, have grown rapidly. Indo-China – Laos, Cambodia and Vietnam – ravaged by decades of war, is still one of the most economically blighted areas of the world; GDP per head is around $300 and little more than $1,000 at purchasing power parity exchange rates. But relative peace in the 1990s has been accompanied by rapid growth. The prospects for these countries look much better than for the similarly poor states of sub-Saharan Africa.

Is Asia a distinct model of economic development, or another Western offshoot?[29] There are many different structures of modern market economies and although all have common features, each development path is unique. Perhaps we should not be asking 'Why did economic development in east Asia progress so rapidly after the Second World War?' but 'Why did economic development in east Asia not progress more rapidly before the Second World War?'

Many of the key institutions and technologies of Western Europe were already present in Asia. Yet this potential was long frustrated by Chinese political structures. The Maoist regime inflicted even more economic damage. In other parts of the region, such as Japan and Hong Kong, American and British influence allowed the countries concerned to realize their own potential for economic development.

How It Happened

The history of the world, said Carlyle, is but the biography of great men. Perhaps, but the history of the market economy is not. There was no Paul Revere to summon the Industrial Revolution, no leaders to rank with George Washington and Thomas Jefferson. The few heroic figures in my account are inventors of new machinery, like John Kay. Who invented agriculture, insurance and banking, or corporations? No one did: they evolved. Adam Smith, the revered founder of modern economics, chronicled the market economy; he did not invent or design it.

The evolution of market institutions took place within the context of a range of other evolutions – in technology, in culture, in politics and the organization of society – and could not have occurred in their absence. But pluralism was common to all these processes. Modern scientific method generated and tested new hypotheses: the principles of science fed into new technologies. Intellectual life emphasized the claims of reason over traditional authority. Political systems made the transition from absolutism to democracy.

This was the common background to the emergence of productive economies and rich states. The lessons which emerge from it – the evolutionary development of market institutions, the need for them to be embedded in a social and political context, and the central role of pluralism in economic advance – will be repeated themes of this book.

Rich states are rich because of a process of institutional evolution which has taken place over centuries, even millennia. Differences in initial conditions, some of them quite small, explain why these countries, and not others, became rich. In the next chapter, I describe some of these institutions and trace the evolution of some of the most important: the institutions of agriculture, employment and limited liability.

5

Transactions and Rules

Going Home

At the end of the day, the Microsoft logo fades. Bill Bridges closes his Internet connection and shuts down his computer. He stops for a beer with colleagues, and takes the subway home. After an uncomfortable journey, he collects some groceries from the neighbourhood shop before entering his flat and watching a movie on television.

Bill's economic life is the result of a series of transactions within a framework of rules. Some of the transactions are contractual, some informal. Some of the rules are legal, others are expectations about behaviour. Bill has a contract with his employer. But most contracts of employment say little about the substantive content of the job. They describe procedural matters such as sickness and holiday entitlements, pension and termination arrangements. Bill's Dell computer uses a Microsoft operating system, and a site licence for Microsoft Office covers everyone in the building. The Internet service provider uses a British Telecom line on terms set out by Ofcom.[1] The Internet itself is governed by a nexus of formal agreements and informal understandings.

Bill and his friends understand the conventions of behaviour in the bar. But if they were joined by someone from a different culture, they would have to explain the rules. You buy the beer, but must return the glass. You can use the seats, the table and the other facilities of the pub, but you are expected to refresh yourself, and these rights, by purchasing more drink from time to time.

On the subway, Bill's season ticket opens a barrier and allows him access to part of London Underground's network. If a train comes,

Bill may or may not find a seat on it. The London Underground is owned and operated by London Underground Ltd., a company owned by central government. It functions within a complex regulatory and contractual relationship with Transport for London, responsible to the Greater London Authority.

Bill bought a Mars bar, a Granny Smith apple, and a bottle of Burgundy. Mars is a trademark of the Mars company. No one else can use the name Mars or produce an identical product. But the right to grow Granny Smith apples is not confined to Granny Smith. Anyone can produce or sell this variety of apples. The French *appellation contrôlée* regime governs what can be legally sold as Burgundy in the European Union; the grapes must be grown in a specified area, and production must conform to prescribed standards.

Bill tells people he owns his flat but, in fact, he has leased it for ninety-nine years. This complex legal structure is a solution to the tricky problem of how to give people rights of ownership over part of a building. There are different answers to this problem in other jurisdictions.[2]

Bill pays to watch television in three ways. Even to follow Bloomberg he must buy a licence. The proceeds of licence fees fund the BBC. The Independent Television Network is supported by advertising; cable and satellite services are available on subscription or pay per view. Tonight, he puts on a pre-recorded video tape. The first thing he sees is a description of the terms of his contract with the distributors and the applicable copyright legislation.

Contracts Within Rules

We acquire legal rights in a market economy by statute (a relationship between the individual and the state) or by contract (a relationship between two individuals). This distinction loosely parallels the distinction between property rights and exchanges, between rules and transactions. But most transactions in a market economy are governed by expectations and conventions, not the law. We are rarely conscious of making contracts. When Bill bought the Mars bar from the shopkeeper, the law inferred a contract. In many exchanges one party claims to impose a legal contract on the other. Microsoft asserts you have accepted its contract by breaking the seal on its software packs; your subway ticket tells you its use is subject to regulations made by London Underground Ltd. This unilateral imposition of contractual terms sometimes works, but the courts are not very sympathetic.[3]

In most everyday transactions, agreement is defined and enforced by expectations. We give money to the waiter because that is a social convention. These expectations are culturally specific: servers in US restaurants expect substantial tips; in Europe, a service charge is usually collected automatically as a percentage of the bill; in some countries – Japan, New Zealand – tipping is uncommon. Shops listen to complaints because they fear for their reputation, not because they fear court action. The costs of writing individual contracts, and using legal mechanisms to enforce them, are prohibitive for most transactions. And the law follows rather than leads the behaviour of buyers and sellers. It requires us to behave as would a prudent man: courts fill in contract terms to fulfil reasonable expectations.

The rules, laws and conventions that govern our economic lives have evolved over thousands of years, and they evolved in different ways in different places. The large overpopulated continent of Europe experienced a different coevolution from that of the isolated and sparsely inhabited island of Australia.

Australian Fish

Twenty or thirty years ago, Australian cuisine was among the dullest to be found. The recent influx of immigrants from Italy, Greece and Vietnam has filled Sydney and Melbourne with interesting restaurants. Yet one feature of Australian menus remains. A European visitor will be completely familiar with the meats – beef, lamb, pork and chicken – but not the fish: you will need advice on the relative merits of trevally, barracuda, orange roughy and yabbies.[4]

Farmers own animals but fishermen don't own fish. When European immigrants arrived in Australia, they brought useful animals – cows and sheep to breed for food, horses for transport, cats and dogs as pets. They shipped these animals because, both legally and practically, they could keep control over them. Cod or sole would have swum off into the Pacific Ocean, so they weren't brought. A few fish were exported from Europe to Australia. Trout are the most (to my mind, only) edible freshwater fish, and could be kept in the owner's lake. Carp also made the journey to Australia, and once technology made farming possible Tasmanian salmon appeared on Melbourne menus.

But this is only part of the story. Why was the export of species so heavily in one direction? Most food production in Australia today is of animals and crops of European origin, but there is no cultivation in Europe of animals and crops imported from Australia. We enjoy some Australian decorative plants, such as mimosa, but Australia's best known indigenous foodstuff is Vegemite.[5] Yali, a New Guinean, posed the question for his American visitor, Jared Diamond: 'Why did you offer us so much cargo and we offer you so little?' Diamond's remarkable book (1997) is his answer to that question.

Australia was probably not very well endowed with grasses and animals, but in any event native Australians had little reason to develop agriculture, and did not do so. Their sparsely populated environment allowed a nomadic lifestyle. The selective breeding of animals and grasses in Eurasia, which created the docile cow, the affectionate cat and the nourishing wheat grain, never happened in Australia. These European products followed Captain Cook to Australia. Different continents, different circumstances, different coevolutions.[6]

Labour and Wages

Agriculture developed from population pressure and new technology. The institution of employment developed for the same reasons. Most people in productive economies have jobs. We choose a career, and an employer. We work for agreed hours, we are told roughly what to do, and we receive a wage or a salary. We expect to hold this job for a longish period of time[7] – but not indefinitely. We are so accustomed to jobs that we rarely think about the nature of the institution.

Yet for most of economic history, jobs were unusual. And outside rich states, careers are still unusual. Few people have, or had, any choice about the work they perform. When I went to church as a boy,

I sang 'The rich man in his castle,/The poor man at his gate,/God made them high or lowly,/And ordered their estate' (a verse from 'All things bright and beautiful' that is now commonly omitted). We sniggered, but it described reality for most people who have ever lived. Their economic lives were – and are – almost completely determined by where they were born – geographically and socially – and by the traditions and conventions of the society in which they lived.

Farming for own use is, and always has been, the most common occupation. A farmer would usually share his crop with someone in a more elevated social position, or provide his superior with labour. Slavery and serfdom bound peasants to masters who fed them. Other workers were attached to noble households and both lived and worked within them. Apprentices learned from and might live with their masters, until they became independent craftsmen, able in turn to supervise apprentices. Social and economic institutions were linked in all these activities.

The enclosure of land deprived many small farmers of traditional cultivation rights but made wage labour available to landlords.[8] The social and economic status of wage labourers was lower than that of any other social group. Not until the end of the twentieth century were some wage earners – the senior executives of large corporations – the best paid people in the community, with high social status. Today, employment contracts in rich states are standardized and convention and law make it difficult to deviate far from the norm. Contracts can be neither too precarious nor too lengthy: efficiency and public opinion are against both casual labour and serfdom.

In a rich state, modern man and – mostly – woman goes to work and comes home from work. Working life can be separated from personal life as never before. Marx believed this would change the nature of politics and society, and he was right, though he did not anticipate that economic power at work would be exercised not by the owners of capital but by salaried managers. The separation of work and home makes conceivable the distinction of business and private values.

But – as I shall discuss in Chapter 26 – to make that separation conceivable does not make it real. While we can split our time between home and work, it is harder to split our personalities. Although we need not link our working lives and social lives, many people do, and the purely instrumental view of the nature of business – which reached its zenith in labour relations with the growth of mass production in factories like Henry Ford's automobile plant – has receded. The quality of work is influenced by the social context within which it takes place. Capitalism discovered that Marxian alienation was inefficient, and large manufacturing corporations no longer dominate the economy.

The Limited Liability Corporation

The process by which corporations came to exercise that dominance was lengthy. In antiquity and in the Middle Ages, business was conducted by individuals, or partnerships of people who knew each other well – who else would take on the risks? When larger partnerships were formed, speculation and fraud followed, and after the South Sea Bubble, large-scale commercial organization was prohibited in England. The objective was to restrict investment to ventures the participants might expect to understand. But throughout history, from the tulip mania of 1636 to the dot.com bubble of 1999, greed and gullibility have defeated that purpose.

The few exceptions to this prohibition were created under specific statutory authority. The most remarkable, and profitable, was the East India Company, which colonized areas larger than England itself. Canals and railways required not only substantial capital but authority to acquire the land through which they passed. Each railway required its own Act of Parliament. Some of these ventures were limited liability companies, and in the mid-nineteenth century this form of organization was opened to other businesses. Shareholders were responsible for the debts of the company only to the extent of the capital they had contributed. This protection allowed them to leave the management to salaried officers (who also normally had no liability for the company's debts).

The attractions of limited liability to shareholders and managers were obvious, but less compelling to those who wished to trade with them. Limited liability corporations became more common as new technologies created activities with larger capital requirements – electrifying cities, establishing new mass-production facilities.

Managers gained prestige. Isambard Kingdom Brunel was a great engineer, a visionary entrepreneur, and builder of the Great Western Railway, but he did not enjoy the status of the directors of the company. Even fifty years ago, social differentiation between directors and managers kept the latter out of the boardrooms of banks and insurance companies.

Alfred Sloan's General Motors, run by a cadre of trained and skilled executives, became the model for the modern corporation.[9] In the latter part of the twentieth century, companies such as Shell and General Electric took this professionalization of management to its highest degree. By 2000 most other forms of commercial organization – mutual companies, partnerships, and state-owned enterprises – had been converted into limited liability corporations.

And yet the relevance of this structure is less obvious in the twenty-first century. The distinction between the roles of shareholders and employees was clear when shareholders had bought the plant and employees worked in it. But the principal assets of the modern company are knowledge, brands and reputation, which are in the heads and hands of employees. What can it mean to say the shareholders 'own' these things?

The Internet and the Genome

Every generation must extend the rules of a market economy. In America and Australia, settlement demanded the creation of land rights. Larger-scale production made it necessary to invent corporate organization. Today, new rules are needed for the new technologies of the Internet and the genome.[10]

The architecture of the Internet was established by the US government and developed by the academic research community. Many businesses hoped to gain control of the Internet by dominating some component; the war between Netscape and Microsoft was bitter because both parties believed that browsers were that key component.[11] Microsoft won the war – by giving away free browsers – but did not gain the influence over the Internet that the company sought.

Nor did Excite, or Yahoo, or AOL or Cisco. Excite fell by the wayside; Yahoo became the leading portal; AOL established itself as chatroom host; Cisco was the biggest hardware supplier. But none of these companies achieved a position comparable to Microsoft's dominance of operating systems. Millions of websites vied to attract users. The new market for Internet services developed, like so many markets before it, from anarchic relationships between competing providers of complementary services.

Cheap copying and dissemination undermined existing market rules. Napster allowed web users to exchange collections of recorded music and seemed to threaten the conventional economics of record companies. Music publishers succeeded in closing Napster, but they cannot effectively prevent the electronic distribution of music. The challenge now is to find mechanisms to derive revenue from it.[12]

At Cambridge University in 1953, Francis Crick and James Watson identified the structure of DNA, the string of chromosomes which provides the blueprint for human life. By the early 1990s, further research – and the capacity of computers – had made it possible to identify the molecular structure of each individual chromosome. In 1992 the Wellcome Trust, a British medical charity, approved a ten-year project to map the human genome and established the International Human Genome Project in conjunction with four American research centres.[13] The identification of DNA was one of the scientific breakthroughs of the century but the sequencing of genes does not require exceptional intellectual gifts or scientific originality. It is a routine task for a competent researcher with a powerful computer.[14]

The process of academic research was leisurely, but private companies sought patents on gene sequences. It seems odd to many people that things which have existed naturally for hundreds of thousands of years should be patentable. Patents were devised to allow the inventors of new manufactured goods, like John Kay, to enjoy exclusive rights to their discoveries. This principle was naturally extended to chemical compounds in the modern pharmaceutical industry, and in recent decades pharmaceutical patents have been among the most valuable of all. In 1980, the US Supreme Court ruled that a living thing could be patented.[15] This proved a wide extension of the scope of the patent system. Companies claimed patents on many advances in genetic knowledge. It is not certain that many of these patents are valid, but the costs of infringing even a dubious patent are large.

Craig Venter, a medical entrepreneur, announced in 1999 his intention to decode the entire genome within three years. His company, Celera, subsequently filed tens of thousands of patents. In 2000, with rapid progress in gene sequencing in private and public sectors and on both sides of the Atlantic, President Clinton and Prime Minister Blair held a press conference to announce that the genome had been decoded and that the competing researchers would co-operate in making their knowledge publicly available.

The structure of rules which governs the relationship between the market and the genome and between the market and the Internet is today unresolved and incoherent. But the history recounted in the last chapter and the present demonstrates that neither central direction nor absence of direction will produce answers. Markets advance through the coevolution of technology and social institutions.

Framing the Rules

It was important to the development of agriculture to define and enforce new property rights in plants and animals. Once, a plant or animal was yours when you picked it or killed it: today it is yours when you seed it or brand it. This change was vital if farmers were to invest in crops and husbandry. But even this example makes clear that there are many different ways to define property rights; some are better than others, and the choice will change with technology and society.

Many economists talk about the rules of a market economy as a distribution of property rights. But the development of market institutions involved far more than the invention of property rights, and many modern market institutions are far too complex and subtle to be easily described in terms of property. The apples in my basket are mine and become yours when they are transferred to your basket. But where is the exchange of property when I turn on the television or use the subway?[16]

When someone smokes in a non-smoking area, we can say that they infringe the property rights of non-smokers. But it is easier, and shorter, to say they break the rules. And more illuminating, because it reminds us of the variety of ways – legal obligation, private action, social convention – in which the rule can be framed and enforced.

The emphasis on property has a conservative flavour: when we talk of defining and enforcing property rights, the picture in our minds is of a fence, a notice saying 'keep out' and a policeman standing guard. This conservatism is apparent in discussion of the Internet and the genome, where music publishers defend what they describe as their property and patentees of gene sequences say they are staking land claims. Market economies must constantly evolve new rules. The analogy with property is unhelpful: the best structures will give encouragement to investment and innovation in new technologies, just as dynamic societies of the past evolved new structures for ownership rights in living plants and animals, developed employment contracts and invented limited liability companies. These accompanied and allowed the historic development of agriculture, wage labour, and large-scale industrial organization.

The next part of this book describes the issues which the rules of the modern market economy evolved to handle. Rich states became productive by facilitating gains from trade and exchange and promoting innovation. The institutional reforms described in the two preceding chapters – agriculture, employment and corporations – brought about the transformation of economic systems from production for own use to the modern market economy in which we work for others and consume what others grow and make. This division of labour is the most important characteristic of a developed economic system.

Part Two

THE STRUCTURE OF
ECONOMIC SYSTEMS

6

Production and Exchange

Economics began for me on a dark winter morning over thirty years ago. An experiment set winter clocks an hour forward. It was still gloomy when Professor Youngson walked from the Adam Ferguson Building to the David Hume Tower to begin the first-year course in Political Economy.

Several Scottish traditions were being recognized. The names of the buildings acknowledged Adam Ferguson and David Hume, leading contemporaries of Adam Smith in the Scottish Enlightenment. Youngson was fulfilling a convention that the introductory course should be delivered by the senior professor. A tall, gowned figure, he was a gentleman scholar. His finest work was not about economics at all.[1] *The Making of Classical Edinburgh* expressed his love of the city's buildings.[2] Some architectural gems of classical Edinburgh had been demolished to make way for the hideous Adam Ferguson Building and David Hume Tower.

A nervous 17-year-old, I was sitting close to the front. Youngson began with a definition of economics – the allocation of scarce resources between competing ends.[3] This was not what I had expected. I had enrolled to learn about inflation, interest rates and foreign exchange – the economic events that filled newspapers and now feature on Bloomberg television. Youngson talked instead about the nature of economic systems. That seemed to me more interesting, and still does. The allocation of scarce resources between competing ends requires decisions about production, assignment and exchange. The system must determine what is made – the issue of production; and who gets it – the issue of assignment. And exchange establishes the link between production and assignment.

The shift by Cro-Magnons from production for own use to production for exchange was an institutional innovation to rank with technical innovations such as the manufacture of tools and the invention of the wheel. But only in today's rich states is most production for exchange. For most of history, and in much of the world even today, the main economic activity is the production of food for own use.

And throughout history, the allocation of scarce resources between competing ends was determined by custom, or by force. In a traditional society, decisions about what to produce, and the division of what was produced, were barely decisions at all. Each year followed the pattern of preceding years. The weather might vary, and with it the crop, but the outcome was distributed according to conventional rules. A customary economic system is an alternative to either a market economy or a planned society – but a static one. Customary economies had little capacity to deal with change and offered little encouragement to initiate change.

In modern society, we make decisions and choices, and the economic system is the framework within which we make them. It contains rules for assignment, production and exchange. In the late eighteenth and nineteenth centuries economists established a durable framework of analysis for understanding production for exchange. Adam Smith's principal work, *The Wealth of Nations*, described the division of labour. David Ricardo, an Anglo-Italian Jew who became a writer and Member of Parliament after successful speculation in bonds, laid out the principle of comparative advantage fifty years later. The effectiveness of an economic system is determined by its efficiency in exploiting comparative advantage and the division of labour.

The Colombe d'Or

For two hundred years European artists have been attracted to the bright light and brilliant scenery of the south of France. The walled village of Saint-Paul de Vence, in the hills to the north of Nice, still houses a community of artists.[4] Paul Roux, who bought a small hotel and restaurant at the entrance to the village in 1919, offered food and lodging to artists in return for examples of their work. Today, the

Colombe d'Or's collection of modern French art is the envy of many galleries.[5]

M. Roux was a talented cook and his visitors were talented painters. It therefore made sense for Paul Roux to cook and for Georges Braque, one of the artists he encouraged, to paint. The exchange of food for paintings benefited both parties. It is common to think of exchange as a process in which one party wins at the expense of another, and some exchanges are like that: one party tricks another, or one party makes a mistake.[6] But the exchange between Braque and Roux, like most economic exchanges, was characterized by mutual gains from trade.

The division of labour between Braque and Roux made these gains possible. By getting together each obtained a mixture of food and art. The two individuals had different capabilities. But these capabilities were, in themselves, insufficient for their needs. Braque needed to eat, and Roux did not wish to live by bread alone. Whenever there are differences in talent and a mutual desire for variety, there is the possibility of a division of labour and mutually beneficial exchange.

It seems obvious that if Roux was a good cook and Braque was a good painter, Roux should cook and Braque should paint. But Braque was a much better painter, relative to other painters, than Roux was relative to other cooks. Braque is one of the towering figures of French twentieth-century art. But even today, when the Colombe d'Or attracts well-heeled visitors from around the world, the Michelin guide will direct those who seek outstanding food to other restaurants in the area. (It gives the nearby Mas d'Artigny a star.)[7]

But even if Braque were a better cook than Roux, as well as a better painter (no evidence survives), it might be best for Roux to cook and Braque to paint. In the time he did not spend whisking mayonnaise by hand, Braque could produce a painting worth many, many meals. This benefit from exchange illustrates the principle of comparative advantage. Comparative advantage dictates that we should focus on what we do best, rather than on what we do better than other people. For exceptionally talented people like Braque, there may be more things they do better than other people than there are hours in the day. And for others, there may be little or nothing that they do better than other people. Comparative advantage requires us to look at our own relative performance in different activities. Both Braque and Roux benefit from following comparative advantage. Braque gets more time for his art, and Roux gets great pictures.

Comparative advantage is a subtle concept. Our instinct is always to ask 'Who is the best person for the job?' but it is a mistaken instinct. We need instead to ask 'Who should be doing this job, bearing in mind his or her productivity in a variety of other jobs, and also the productivity of other people who might be doing this job instead of the variety of other jobs that they currently are or might be doing?' Perfectly competitive markets make that calculation automatically. That claim – a principal cause of economists' fascination with perfectly competitive markets – is the subject of Part Three of this book.

Specialization and Capabilities in Business

Trade between individuals is possible, and mutually beneficial, because there are gains from specialization and differences in capabilities. These reinforce each other. Innate talent brought Braque to painting and Roux to cooking. Training and experience honed these talents.

Trade between firms emerged for the same reasons – gains from specialization, differences in capabilities. Modern firms extended the economic advantages of trade between individuals based on differences in capabilities and on specialization. The moneylender developed into the bank, the blacksmith became the iron works. Firms not only specialized themselves, but provided the opportunity for specialization in individual tasks by their employees. Adam Smith's famous example of the pin factory[8] described the – still novel – development of the division of labour within commercial organizations. If everyone focused on one operation, a group could produce many more pins than if each member fabricated a single pin from base metal to finished product.

In the early stages of modern business history, the organization of business was driven mostly by specialization. Large enterprises emerged in activities where economies of scale could be derived from the division of labour – Smith's pin factory – or where the activity required co-ordination of the specialist functions of many individuals – railroads and oil companies. The invention of steam power provoked a shift from workshop to factory organization in textiles because one engine could power many looms, and factory organization promoted many technical innovations. This is a particularly important example of the coevolution of technology and institutions.

The gains from specialization were believed to be limitless. At the end of the nineteenth century, it seemed that one company would dominate each major industry in each region of the world. That was certainly what business leaders like John D. Rockefeller intended.[9] Standard Oil, US Steel and American Tobacco were each dominant in the US market for their products.

The concentration of economic power in trusts, and the fear of an associated concentration of political power, provoked a reaction. The Sherman Act, passed in 1890, made it illegal to monopolize any line of business in the United States. When the complacently pro-business William McKinley was assassinated by an anarchist in 1901, Theodore Roosevelt became President and began a populist attack on the power of American trusts and the men who controlled them. Standard Oil and American Tobacco were broken up.

This was a decisive moment in the development of modern market economies. The attack on giant firms was never again to be as fierce. US Steel remained intact, only to experience a slow, sustained decline across the twentieth century. But no similar combinations would be proposed.[10] Firms which became dominant in any line of business would always find their ambitions checked. The US government used the anti-trust laws to launch cases against AT&T, the telephone monopoly, against IBM, and, in the closing years of the century, against Microsoft. The world's largest economy had chosen pluralism over monopoly in its market structure.

European business was necessarily more pluralist because there was no United States of Europe. But Imperial Tobacco, Imperial Chemical Industries, and IG Farben had similar ambitions in their sphere of influence. The scope of their aspirations can be seen from the titles which these companies adopted. Monopolies emerged later and so did policies to control them.

Britain adopted its first competition policy in 1948.[11] At the same time the occupying powers broke up concentrated industrial structures in Germany and Japan.[12] The founders of the European Union were clear that competition and pluralism, not consolidation, was to be the basis of economic integration. The Rome Treaty which established the Common Market in 1964 contains many provisions to this effect. In particular, Articles 81 and 82 made the restriction or distortion of competition or the abuse of a dominant position illegal. In 1989 the Commission acquired additional powers to block European mergers. In 2001, it was to be the European Union, not the US government, which checked the expansionist ambitions of General Electric,[13] America's largest business.

But it was not simply government action which prevented indefinite specialization. The division of labour, taken too far, produced organizational disadvantages. The epitome of specialization was the Ford Motor Company. Between 1908 and 1927, 15 million Model T Fords rolled off the company's production line at Highland Park near Detroit. Adam Smith's pin factory found its apogee in an assembly line on which each individual worker might undertake only a single operation.

But Ford had taken mass production too far. The company was overtaken by General Motors, which offered its customers choice of colour and variety of models. The tedious nature of assembly-line work meant that the motivation of those who worked on them was wholly instrumental. Labour disputes were common, and no one cared about the quality of the final product. Specialization had, by the 1950s, reduced the US automobile industry to three effective firms. But this was to be the high point of concentration and specialization. Competition from businesses that offered better quality and greater variety steadily reduced the share of the market leaders.[14]

Competitive Advantage

Firms came into existence to take advantage of the division of labour through specialization. But the scale of business today means that gains from specialization are largely exhausted. The structure of industry is today based on differences in the capabilities of companies. The success of the Coca-Cola Corporation is derived, in the first instance, from a distinctive capability – the still secret recipe for syrup patented by an Atlanta pharmacist in 1890.[15] But it is not really the fizzy sugared water. The company has exploited the division of labour through a

world-wide network of bottlers and franchisees. And, most import-
antly, it has developed an impressive marketing organization in support of the world's best-known brand. General Electric (GE) came
into existence as the vehicle for the inventive genius of Thomas Edison,
who found many more practical uses for electricity than anyone had
imagined possible. But the company gained its modern position by
developing the most powerful repository of general management skills
of any business. These capabilities – Coca-Cola's recipe and marketing
resources, GE's management school – are the commercial analogues
of Braque's talent as a painter and Roux's abilities in the kitchen.[16]

The automobile industry today displays the different capabilities of
twenty or more car manufacturers. Mercedes and BMW achieve high
standards of engineering in production line saloons. Hyundai benefits
from its low Korean cost base. Toyota achieves outstanding component reliability and short model cycles through close relationships
with subcontractors.

Firms in other industries build competitive advantages on their
different capabilities. Marlboro and McDonald's are brands comparable to Coca-Cola. Hotel chains and law and accountancy practices
also rely on distinctive capabilities based on name and reputation.
Some companies – such as Marks and Spencer and Benetton – have
created competitive advantages from distinctive capabilities in the
structure of their relationships with suppliers.

The competitive advantage of innovation is often transitory, because
successful innovation is easily copied. But some companies, such as
the pharmaceutical businesses Merck and Glaxo, are able to protect
their innovations legally. Others, like Sony, have an architecture that
generates a succession of innovations: and a reputation that wins ready
acceptance for everything – from transistor radios to Walkmans to
playstations – which they put into the marketplace. The legal protection which Merck and Glaxo obtain for their intellectual property
also gives other firms powerful strategic assets – such as Microsoft's
copyrights in its operating system, MS-DOS, and graphical user
interface, Windows. This variety of capabilities in firms provides the
basis for mutual gains from trade between firms, as the difference in
capabilities between individuals provided the basis of trade between
Braque and Roux.

International Trade

Economies from specialization, differences in capabilities: these are the factors which lead to mutual gains from trade between individuals and trade between businesses. They also lead to mutual gains from trade between countries. Trade between corporations was once mainly based on the benefits of specialization and today relates much more to differences in capabilities. Trade between countries seems to have evolved in the opposite direction.

Ricardo's analysis of international trade in the early nineteenth century emphasized differences in capabilities. Early trade flows were influenced by weather and natural resources. North-west Europe imported products which could not be grown at realistic cost in its own territory. Ricardo explained how Portugal, where the sun ripened the vines, exchanged wine for English textiles, which were manufactured in Lancashire where the damp climate prevented threads from snapping.[17]

Some modern trade is still like this. Countries with natural resources such as oil and minerals sell them to other countries which have none. Differences in soil and climate affect the production of crops and other agricultural products. But many rich countries have been reluctant to rely on such trade. Oil reserves have been developed at great cost in Alaska and the North Sea. The European Union would rather pay Sven to farm than import wheat more cheaply from Canada.

Specialization among countries has become more important than differences in intrinsic capabilities. Most international trade today is trade in manufactured goods between developed countries, and it is trade of this kind that has grown dramatically since the Second World War. Trade among the nineteen countries of Chapter 3 accounts for almost half of all world trade and that between these nineteen and poor states for less than a quarter.[18] Most of this trade is in goods which all other rich states have the capabilities to manufacture.

Like trade between individuals, trade between countries results from mutually reinforcing differences in capabilities and specialization. Differences in national capabilities today have very little to do with differences in resources or other natural factors: they have been acquired over time and are embedded in the cultures which gave rise to them. The world's most productive economy – Switzerland – relies on exports of precision engineering and speciality chemicals, which account for about 60 per cent of its exports and one quarter of its output.[19]

These have nothing to do with Swiss climate or terrain. Nor does Switzerland have favoured access to materials from which engineering and chemical products are made. Capabilities and specialization have reinforced each other in another process of coevolution. The choices made, almost by accident, by Swiss businessmen a century ago have a major influence on the structure of Swiss industry today. The Swiss education system influenced their choices of specialization. Heidi and her predecessors have instilled basic numerical skills of high order even in students who will be employed on production and assembly lines. The system developed further in response to the needs of Swiss business.

Since mutually reinforcing capabilities and specialisms depend on past choices, forgotten or now irrelevant historical events still influence the location of production today. Film producers in the 1920s sought the light of southern California. Films are rarely made in California any more, but Hollywood remains the centre of the world film industry. London is still a marketplace for shipbroking and marine insurance because of Britain's maritime past. Similar accidents of history – the site of Leland Stanford's university and Xerox Corporation's research facility – made Silicon Valley the centre of the international software industry.[20]

The competitive advantages of countries and regions – Switzerland, Hollywood, the City of London, Silicon Valley – are based on the competitive advantages of companies and of individuals. In Switzerland, each firm has a competitive advantage in its own particular line of business: and the common competitive advantages of all these firms are based on the competitive advantages that well-educated and trained Swiss workers themselves enjoy. The same is true in Silicon Valley. In both cases, the geographic proximity of businesses to each other reinforces these competitive advantages through the formal and informal sharing of knowledge, experience and people.

Hollywood and the City of London are slightly more complex. There is the same phenomenon of competing yet collaborating firms drawing on the same pool of talented individuals. But Hollywood and the City of London are also themselves marketplaces, and that is another source of competitive advantage. Business congregates in the largest marketplace, and that is why historic location remains so important even though its objective basis has disappeared.

Gains from trade are achieved by specialization and by taking advantage of the different capabilities of individuals, organizations, geographical areas, countries. The same principles govern the division of labour between people and companies, regions and states, with one exception. People, areas of the world, regions exist, and have rights and values, independently of their economic function. Businesses exist only for their economic function: and if they have no economic function they have no reason to exist. So households and countries must do what they are best at, whether or not they do it better than other households and countries. Businesses should only do what they can do better than others. So we speak of comparative advantage for people and for states, competitive advantage for companies. Comparative advantage is relative: competitive advantage is absolute. Production and exchange are governed by a division of labour based on the advantages of specialization and differences in capabilities. But production and exchange are not ends in themselves. Their purpose is to meet the needs of consumers. The next chapter is concerned with how economic systems find out what consumers want.

7

Assignment

Portrait of Dr Gachet[1]

One of the artists attracted by the light and scenery of southern France was a young Dutchman who rented a property at Arles, in Provence. The painter suffered acute bouts of depression, and was sent north to a physician in the village of Auvers-sur-Oise, near Paris, for treatment. Dr Gachet's ministrations were not successful and his patient committed suicide.[2]

The episode brought the doctor unexpected and undeserved immortality. After van Gogh's death, his *Portrait of Dr Gachet* was sold by his sister-in-law.[3] It was eventually auctioned in 1990 for $82.5 million, still the largest amount ever paid for a work of art.[4] In the last chapter I considered the first part of the allocation of scarce resources between competing ends, issues of production and exchange. This chapter reviews the second part: how the goods and services which are the result of production and exchange are assigned to individuals and households.

Portrait of Dr Gachet poses the economic problem of assigning a scarce resource in its simplest, starkest form. The painting is incomparable and unique (although van Gogh painted two portraits of Gachet; the other, thought to be inferior,[5] is in the Musée d'Orsay in Paris). There is one scarce resource, but there are many competing ends. Almost every gallery and art collector in the world would like the painting, and many could present strong arguments.

The most extensive collection of the painter's work is in the dedicated Van Gogh Museum in Amsterdam, where the visitor can best understand the development of the painter's talent. The Metropolitan

Museum in New York and the Musée d'Orsay have stunning collections of the greatest works of van Gogh's time. His achievement can be seen there in its proper historical context. Yet all these collections are already well endowed. Perhaps *Dr Gachet* should be hung in a museum in a provincial location or a poor country where there are no masterpieces at all.

How should we evaluate the claims of private collectors against those of national galleries? Art would not thrive without private patronage. There is far more good art than can be displayed in public galleries. These institutions have basements to which they consign currently unfashionable pieces. Still, there is a strong argument that great paintings should be on public display, not in private ownership. *Portrait of Dr Gachet* is now owned by a private collector and has disappeared. A recent exhibition in Boston, Paris and Amsterdam was specifically devoted to Dr Gachet's love of painting and painters and his association with van Gogh.[6] The Musée d'Orsay's portrait was at the centre of the show, but the world's most valuable picture was not there.

But state ownership does not emerge well from the story either. Van Gogh's talent was not recognized during his lifetime, or for some years after: decades elapsed before his work was accepted even for the basement of a public gallery. His work is preserved only because his sister-in-law had an eye to its commercial value. Private collectors were first to recognize his genius, and most of his pieces are in public collections because of the generosity of these patrons. *Portrait of Dr Gachet* was donated to the Städel Museum in Frankfurt by a local businessman. The reason it is not on public display now is that the German government disposed of it.

Portrait of Dr Gachet was condemned as decadent art by the Nazis and sold by Reichsmarschall Goering, who pocketed the proceeds. Fortunately Goering, who had a drug habit and was interested in developing his personal collection of tapestries, chose to sell the picture to a private collector – ironically, a Jewish refugee, Siegfried Kramarsky. 'Decadent' books were simply burned. After Kramarsky's death, his family asked Christie's to auction the painting. As the bidding in the New York saleroom reached its climax, eyes were focused on two people. One was Christie's Zurich representative, connected by telephone to her client. The other was a Japanese art dealer. The European bidder – probably a Greek shipping tycoon – offered $74 million, but that proved to be the limit of his willingness to pay. The portrait went to Japan, for $75 million. (The buyer's premium of 10 per cent took the total price to $82.5 million.)

Mechanisms of Allocation

The process of allocating the scarce resource – the *Portrait* – between competing ends involved no enquiry into these competing ends. We know what Mr Saito, the paper magnate represented by the Japanese dealer, did with the painting. But we do not know what use the contenders he outbid would have made of it, nor even, in most cases, who they were.

An alternative means of allocation would have asked these questions in some detail. Public galleries might be asked to disclose their plans; private individuals to explain why they were particularly appropriate owners of the portrait. There would need to be an International Art Committee to compare and evaluate these claims. We do not assign art or other valuable objects that way. But we do use such a procedure for allocating prized international sporting events.

The twenty-four-member executive of FIFA, the controlling body for international football, met to decide where the World Cup should be held in 2006. They chose Germany over South Africa by twelve votes to eleven. The missing vote was that of Charles Dempsey, a New Zealander who had been expected to support South Africa. If the vote had been tied, the chairman Sepp Blatter would have given his casting vote to South Africa. It is still unclear why Dempsey acted as he did. He spoke of great personal pressures, and resigned a week later. Letters offering money to executive members who cast votes for Germany were later shown to be a hoax, although Blatter himself is the subject of wide-ranging allegations of corruption.[7]

Where to hold the World Cup was a political decision. Where to hang *Portrait of Dr Gachet* was a decision made by the market. Where to hold the World Cup was decided by a process of voice – different people expressed conflicting views. Where to hang *Portrait of Dr*

Gachet was decided by a process of exit – there was no debate, no discussion, and the auction continued until all but one bidder had left the room.[8] Where to hold the World Cup was determined by a democratic process – of sorts. Where to hang *Portrait of Dr Gachet* was decided by the decentralized decisions of many people and institutions, all but one of whom concluded that they could not, or did not wish to, pay $82.5 million for the painting. Where to hold the World Cup was personalized, decided by named individuals, like Mr Blatter and Mr Dempsey. Where to hang *Portrait of Dr Gachet* was an anonymous decision. We know who the auctioneer was – Christopher Burge – but his identity played no significant role in the process. We know who the successful bidder was, although he was not there, and only because he chose to make a public announcement. We do not know who the under-bidder was.

These two types of mechanism define the ways in which goods can be assigned in an economic system. One type is political, hierarchical and personalized: the mechanism of complaint is voice. The other is market-based, decentralized, anonymous: the mechanism of complaint is exit.

Each of these approaches has merits and disadvantages. Some people regard the anonymity of the market as a virtue, others deplore the impersonality of market forces. Both processes are open to corruption. The squalor of international sporting bodies needs no further elaboration. Auction rings, in which dealers get together to allocate lots outside the saleroom, are frequent. Ten years after the *Dr Gachet* sale the Chairman of Sotheby's was sent to prison for illegal price-fixing and the Chairman of Christie's was unable to set foot in the United States for fear of arrest.

'From each according to his abilities, to each according to his needs.'[9] This traditional socialist slogan describes the objectives of any economic system. This requirement identifies the twin issues of information and incentives which any economic system must address. The problem of incentive compatibility is the problem of obtaining the information needed to make decisions about production and assignment. Market mechanisms and political mechanisms deal with incentive compatibility in quite different ways.

Incentive Compatibility in a Planned Economy

To allocate scarce resources between competing ends it is necessary to assess what abilities are – what it is possible to produce – and what needs are – the requirements of firms and the wants and desires of consumers. But almost all this information has to be obtained from the various proponents of the competing ends.

How can they be persuaded to assess it diligently and reveal it accurately? Most people are honest and well intentioned, and if you ask them for information they will give it. But they may discover that doing so is not to their advantage. If targets are set and resources allocated on the basis of information revealed, then it is better to be conservative about what is possible, pessimistic about what is needed, and optimistic about the benefits which will result. But the people to whom the information is supplied will realize what is going on, and calibrate their expectations accordingly. This process became known as 'plan bargaining' in socialist economies.

The submissions made by the various countries which hoped to host the 2006 World Cup were unashamedly propagandist, just as investment appraisals put to the senior managers of large businesses are always optimistic, and the business plans which utilities show their regulators are always gloomy. The hospitality offered to members of the FIFA executive committee who wished to inspect the alternative venues was lavish. No doubt some of these members managed to penetrate the haze of smoke and alcohol and find the information they needed to make an objective decision. Others found this difficult.

Obtaining the information needed to plan production encounters similar problems. No society in history offered such a wide range of rewards and punishments as the Soviet Union, from the economic and political privileges of the *nomenklatura* to the slave-camps of the Gulag. The Soviet economic problem was not an absence of incentives: incentives to conform to the dictates of the centre were very strong. The Soviet economic problem was that the planners did not have good information on which to base their directions to production units.

It was above all on these problems of information and incentives that the Soviet economy foundered. The information problem is the more fundamental. If a powerful state could accurately calibrate both abilities and needs, it could enforce production according to abilities and assignment according to needs. That is what the Soviet state sought, and failed, to do.

'Plan bargaining' was not confined to the Soviet Union, though it was endemic there. 'Plan bargaining' is found in any planning system: in government regulation of business, in the control of public services, and in the management of large private-sector organizations. When governments set targets for schools and hospitals, they face the same problem: the information needed to determine the targets appropriately is held by people in schools and hospitals, not people in government departments.

Lenin claimed to have found the answer to this problem: 'Seize the decisive link.'[10] Because the information required to control the system completely is extensive and impossible to obtain, the centre must focus on a few supposedly key variables. But these are subject to 'Goodhart's Law'[11] – any measure adopted as a target changes its meaning. If hospitals are judged by the number of people who wait more than twelve months for an operation, then the number of people who wait more than twelve months for an operation is likely to fall, but whether the service given to patients is better or worse is another matter altogether. If corporate executives receive bonuses related to earnings per share, then earnings per share will rise, but whether the business is better or more valuable is quite another question.

The inevitable result of these processes is the proliferation of targets. These become confusing and inconsistent, and undermine the authority and morale of those who engage in the activities which are being planned. Do markets manage the problems of incentive compatibility better?

Incentive Compatibility in Markets

People will only be honest in expressions of preference when we impose a cost to these expressions. This is how we tackle the problem in families and companies. There are children who must have everything they see, and dissolve into tears when they do not get everything they see. There are people in organizations whose every requirement is urgent and essential. We attach less weight to their claims and protests, and value expressions of wants and needs more highly when they are expressed rarely.

Some mechanism of price and cost is always present when we obtain subjective information about preferences, needs and abilities. In personal relationships, these prices are always implicit. When we put down our own tasks to help a colleague with an urgent project, we do not expect immediate reward. But both parties understand that a price is being paid. If our stock of goodwill is called on repeatedly without reciprocation, it will be exhausted. When I tell family and friends that there is something I badly need, and they defer their own needs, I play a card which loses its value if I play it often. These implicit prices, central to both personal and commercial lives, are called opportunity costs: the price of doing A is that it becomes more difficult to do B.

Among small groups of people who deal with each other frequently and know each other well – friends, families, close colleagues, the inhabitants of Sicelo's village – resource allocation occurs through these implicit price mechanisms. Market exchanges are needed when people deal outside these closed circles. Incentive compatibility is immediately more serious. We understand the real needs of our friends and family better than the needs of people we hardly know.

Market exchanges allow longer chains of wants. If I had to find a plumber who needed lessons in economics, my tap might drip for a long time. I might look for a bank needing economic advice which would offer the plumber a loan, but this would be complex to negotiate. With money, or some form of tokens, the coincidence of wants can be extended as required.

Money and prices have emerged whenever economic life has extended beyond a narrow community of people who interact with each other. Villages like Sicelo's may not need to keep score in a formal way. But larger communities need money. Small businesses like the farm on which Sven and Ingrid work use accountants only to deal with the bank and the tax authorities. Big businesses need accounts for internal control as well as external reporting. Money acts as medium of exchange, store of value, and unit of account.

These functions dictate the characteristics of a good money.[12] Money must be well defined – there should be no room for argument about whether a debt has been paid or not. Money must be storable. And money must have high value relative to its volume and weight, otherwise it will be difficult to carry it around. Many objects met these criteria in traditional societies. Some tribes kept score in cowrie shells. But scarce and decorative metals – gold and silver – were usually found to meet these requirements best. In concentration camps, where none of these was available, cigarettes became the medium of exchange and unit of account.[13] Long after money first emerged, it was realized that reliable promises to provide gold or silver – bank notes – were easier to carry than the metals themselves. I shall come back to the implications of this discovery in Chapter 13.

Strategic Behaviour in Politics

When FIFA assigned the 2006 World Cup to Germany, it did so in the last of a series of voting rounds. Three other contenders had already been eliminated. The design of voting mechanisms is complex when there are multiple choices. In the French presidential election of 2002, the incumbent, President Chirac, led the first round but with only 20 per cent of the vote. The far right Jean-Marie Le Pen won 17 per cent. The socialist Prime Minister, Lionel Jospin, obtained slightly less and was excluded from the final ballot. In that final ballot, Le Pen gained hardly any more support and Chirac was elected with 82 per cent of the vote. If supporters of other left-wing parties had backed Jospin in the first round, he would have been a candidate in the second round, and might well have defeated Chirac. It is not necessarily sensible to express our true preferences: but to vote strategically we must guess not just at the preferences of others, but at their own strategic behaviour. Voting mechanisms have their own problems of incentive compatibility. Condorcet demonstrated two hundred years ago that majorities can easily be assembled for inconsistent proposals. Kenneth Arrow – co-author of the Arrow–Debreu results of Chapter 14 – generalized this observation to an 'impossibility theorem': no voting mechanism can derive consistent social preferences from conflicting views about how society should be organized.[14]

Arrow, who lives in California, must have recognized the practical force of his impossibility theorem as the lights flickered and faded. The electricity blackouts in California in 2000 and 2001[15] occurred because there was no voting system which could prevent the Californian electorate from simultaneously demanding low electricity prices, no new generating plants and ever increasing amounts of electricity.[16]

This doesn't mean that politics is impossible. It does mean that political choices are sometimes incompatible and inconsistent. And it explains why we not only have, but need, the variety of devices through which political decisions are made – political parties, horse trading and log rolling, mediation in which concessions on one item are traded for favours on others.

Strategic Behaviour in Markets

But market mechanisms encounter similar problems. When the British government auctioned television franchises in 1993, Central Television won the exclusive right to broadcast programmes to Birmingham and the West Midlands for £2,000. They did not think the licence was only worth £2,000. It was worth much more, and the value of the company rose when the result was announced. Central guessed, correctly, that no one else would bid.

Suppose another potential bidder had understood Central's plan, and managed to keep its own intentions secret. It could have won the auction with a bid of £5,000. In bidding at auction, you are not just concerned to assess your own valuation. You are equally concerned with what others will bid. But their bids will in turn depend on their guesses about your bids. The bidding process becomes a game in which the bids bear only a weak relationship to underlying values.

Yet there is a variant of this procedure in which it is best to bid in line with your valuation. A judge reviews all the bids. The judge discards them all except the highest two, and gives the object to the highest bidder at the price offered by the second highest bidder. In that auction, you should bid whatever you think the object is worth. Suppose that amount is £100. If the highest bid from anyone else is £80, then you will get the object for £80. If the highest outside bid is

£110, you won't get the object, but you wouldn't have wanted to pay £110 for it anyway. A little time with pencil and paper will show that you can never lose by bidding your true valuation but you might lose out if you enter a false value. Alone among bidding procedures, this 'second-price auction' has the property of incentive compatibility: there is no benefit from strategic behaviour.

The mechanism sounds arcane and theoretical. It was proposed by an American economist, William Vickrey[N], who received the Nobel Prize in 1996 for his analysis of this and similar problems.[17] But the Vickrey scheme is, in essence, the allocation mechanism which was used to decide what should be done with *Portrait of Dr Gachet* when the Kramarsky family sold it in 1990. We do not know how much Mr Saito, the paper magnate represented by the Japanese dealer, would have been willing to pay, and nor did Christie's auctioneer. We only know that the maximum the second-highest bidder was ready to put on the table was $74 million. And Mr Saito won the painting for a 'nominal' $1 million more.[18]

It seems at first sight extraordinary that Mr Christie and Mr Sotheby should by chance have stumbled on the same device that Vickrey discovered two centuries later with the aid of clever mathematics. But it is not. Christie and Sotheby were inheritors of a long saleroom tradition which had tried different auction rules, abandoned some, and developed others. Social and economic institutions are adaptive: less appropriate institutions are displaced by more appropriate ones. Choices about the mechanisms of the market economy have been made, not by any conscious decisions, but from historical evolution through trial and error. Mr Christie and Mr Sotheby had never heard of incentive compatibility when they defined the rules for their salerooms – their successors have not heard of it yet. They developed, over time, the procedure which in their experience best satisfied their customers. These processes of adaptation and coevolution recur again and again in our search for the truth about markets.

Do Markets Work?

The auction of *Portrait of Dr Gachet* produced the right answer, in one sense. The bidders honestly revealed their assessments of the value of the painting; the auction assigned it to the person who valued it most. But this mechanism of assignment did not really solve the fundamental economic problem which Professor Youngson had posed – the allocation of a scarce resource between competing ends.

After Mr Saito bought the painting, it remained wrapped and stored in a high security warehouse until his death. We do not know why Saito purchased the painting. Or why he bought Renoir's *Moulin de la Galette* at Sotheby's a few days later for $78.5 million. Saito paid not only the highest sum ever paid for a work of art, but the second highest sum as well. Perhaps he hoped – wrongly – that *Dr Gachet* would appreciate in value. Maybe he derived satisfaction from the ownership of a masterpiece, or the world's most valuable painting. Still, this satisfaction was not based on any pleasure he or his friends or anyone else derived from looking at it.

If Mr Saito had been a great benefactor of mankind – if he had designed the operating system for the world's personal computers, or discovered an important new drug – we might feel that indulging his wishes, however eccentric, was a reasonable way to assign one of the world's great paintings. It would represent a just reward, and an encouragement to similar achievement by others. But Saito was an undistinguished Japanese industrialist, who nearly bankrupted the firm he inherited from his father and later received a prison sentence for corruption. *Portrait of Dr Gachet* was bought by a vain, silly, but very rich man.

Both political mechanisms and market mechanisms determined, at different times, the fate of *Dr Gachet*. Neither worked particularly well. Political voices required the painting to be removed from the wall of the Städel Museum. And they were probably reflective of majority public opinion at the time. The behaviour of the Nazis was extreme, but political authority in the arts has always threatened pluralism. Before the Reformation, the Catholic Church exercised control over the style and content of painting; arts administrators today exert power through the allocation of subsidies to arts and galleries.[19] Joanna van Gogh Bonger's speculation in the works of her brother-in-law brought his genius to the attention of the world as no central authority did or was likely to have done. But market forces did a poor job of allocating scarce resources between competing ends when they consigned *Portrait of Dr Gachet* to a sealed warehouse near Tokyo.

Choices between economic systems cannot be made on *a priori* grounds. Planners and social democrats think that only political mechanisms can deliver well-balanced solutions and legitimate outcomes. Supporters of the American business model believe that market outcomes are just and efficient simply because they are market outcomes. For both sides, there is much in the history of *Portrait of Dr Gachet* that needs to be explained away.

Political decisions suffer acute problems of incentive compatibility. These may not only produce bad answers to the assignment problem but also undermine the integrity of political decision-making itself. The consequences of market allocation depend on the origin and legitimacy of the distribution of property and other resources within which markets operate. *Dr Gachet* should not have gone to Tokyo, nor the World Cup to Germany. In the next two chapters, I consider other aspects of the choice between political direction and market forces as mechanisms for allocating scarce resources between competing ends.

8

Central Planning

Great Leaps Forward

In 1959 Nikita Khrushchev was General Secretary of the Communist Party and the most powerful man in the Soviet Union. Khrushchev had begun a process of liberalization following the death of Stalin. In a gesture of great significance, he paid a visit to the United States. He and his aides were dumbfounded when they visited a supermarket, and they went home believing the shelves had been specially stocked for their arrival.[1]

But a trip to Iowa made the greatest impression on Khrushchev. Khrushchev had long been enthusiastic about maize. As a young official he had made his reputation by expanding maize production. The American prairies were the world's largest source of maize. There was no faking the luxuriant fields that stretched as far as the eye could see. Khrushchev returned to Moscow convinced this was the future of Soviet agriculture. Large tracts of arable land were converted to maize. The experiment was not a success. Production fell. The economic setback which followed was one of the reasons why Khrushchev was toppled from power five years later.[2]

Russian agriculture did badly in this period, but experience in China, the other Communist superpower, was far worse. In 1957 Mao Zedong announced the Great Leap Forward. The creation of large people's communes would transform agriculture. The first, which covered 53,000 acres and embraced 44,000 people, was created in April 1958. By the autumn over 100 million peasant families lived in communes. They no longer produced food for themselves, and they ate in a communal facility. Every unit was encouraged to produce steel: backyard furnaces were the key to rapid industrialization. Mao declared war on the 'four pests': flies, mosquitoes, rats and sparrows. Much time and effort was devoted to collecting fuel for furnaces and to scaring sparrows from trees. The Great Leap Forward moved inexorably from farce to tragedy. Agricultural yields collapsed, and in the early 1960s famine spread across the country. Between 30 million and 40 million people died of starvation.[3]

Khrushchev and Mao made bad decisions. But they were not absurd decisions. Khrushchev simply made a mistake. Maize was not a more suitable crop than wheat in the Ukraine. Business people routinely make that kind of error. Mao was right to have concluded that Chinese agriculture should be rationalized into larger units, that China needed to expand its steel production, and that steel production should take place in small units rather than large facilities. The concentration of agricultural production and the growth of steel output have been features of development in most rich states. The world steel industry has been reorganized into smaller plants.

Yet the context of these mistakes turned them into disasters. The processes of decision-making were centralized and personalized and the outcomes were implemented on a huge scale.[4] Those who reported on the consequences did not wish either to hear or to deliver bad news. They were concerned to protect their own positions and to win approval from their superiors. And these powerful leaders were slowly, if at all, accountable for their failures.

More Great Leaps Forward

Anyone who has worked for a large organization will have similar experiences. The phenomenon of Khrushchev's maize is familiar. A senior executive returns from a trip, enthusiastic about a new idea. Subordinates implement the scheme, perhaps cynically, perhaps with enthusiasm. They congratulate their superiors on the wisdom of the strategy until enthusiasm wanes or the executive is fired or retires.

This was the case with William Morris (Lord Nuffield), the most important figure in the development of the British automobile industry. His bicycle shop in the centre of Oxford grew into the Cowley motor works. In the 1930s this was the largest industrial plant in Britain and Morris Motors was the leading producer of automobiles for the British Commonwealth. Morris was not an intellectual man. He was, however, a generous donor to Oxford University (largely for medical research, although he also endowed Nuffield College, where I was a postgraduate student). Morris wanted an institution that specialized in the useful business skills of engineering and accountancy. But a wily Vice-Chancellor, A. D. Lindsay, with a different view of the status of engineering and accountancy, persuaded him that economics and sociology were almost the same thing.

Morris's views were eagerly sought after – not just his views on the automobile industry, but also on world peace and the future of the economy. By schemers who hoped the Morris millions might endow their projects. By people who, like Morris himself, believed his extraordinary business achievements qualified him to pronounce with authority.

It is not recorded, and it is not likely, that Morris said anything prescient or novel about world peace or the future of the global economy. His views on the automobile industry were equally strongly held and of more moment. His position and his shareholding in Morris Motors required that these views be acted upon.

After Morris's elevation to fame and the peerage, his thinking became more idiosyncratic. There were many lapses of behaviour and judgement. Morris rejected the post-war opportunity to take over the Volkswagen plant at Wolfsburg – and with it designs for the most successful car of the post-war era. He thought there was nothing to be learned from German engineering. He insisted that the company's managers must win their positions by working up from the shop floor, as he had done.[5] Inept and insular management presided over steady decline. In 1974 the company Morris had created collapsed.

William Morris was Europe's greatest car maker. But Henry Ford was the greatest car maker in the world. The parallels are close. Ford was the most successful businessman of the twentieth century, but he died a sad and lonely figure, railing against Jews and tobacco, confiding only in his chief of security, insisting that his increasingly eccentric wishes be carried out. When Ford's son Edsel developed a six-cylinder model to compete with offerings from General Motors, Henry insisted on watching the destruction of the prototype.[6]

Professional management arrived in time – just – to save the Ford Motor Company. But even after the British government took over the remains of the Morris empire, it failed to find managers capable of running a modern automobile business.[7] Car production in Britain today continues under American and Japanese management.

People and Decisions

There are many similarities between the worlds of Khrushchev and Mao and those of Morris and Ford. Decision-making was centralized. Reporting was limited and sycophantic. Accountability for decisions was slow and indirect.

In all cases, the individuals who made decisions were people of ability and achievement. Khrushchev had demonstrated great administrative prowess in rising through the Soviet hierarchy during the Stalinist terror. Despite that experience he had retained integrity and humour. These qualities enabled him to begin the process of exposing and dismantling Stalinism. In doing so, he captured the imagination and even affection of a public outside his own country. If he had been born in the United States, Khrushchev would probably have been chief executive of a large corporation.

Mao, through extraordinary political and military skills, had successfully united the most populous country in the world under a single government after generations of havoc wreaked by competing warlords. This achievement ranks with those of Napoleon or Alexander the Great. If we do not today think of Mao in those terms it is because, unlike these two, he survived to exercise civil authority in China for twenty-seven years and made bad judgements with disastrous consequences.

Ford and Morris also exerted too much authority for too long. When Acton asserted that 'power tends to corrupt and absolute power corrupts absolutely', he did not principally mean financial corruption. People who have been right in the past cannot be blamed for thinking they are likely to be right in the future more than the average. The adulation that surrounds successful politicians and business people reinforces their understandable self-confidence.

Absolutism of authority is part of the problem. In Ford and Morris, in Soviet Russia and Communist China, decision-making was personalized and undemocratic. Would it not be better if wise men came together, in a single institution, to assemble the evidence, consider it dispassionately and set the direction for the industry?

British Electricity

That happened in British electricity. The industry developed as a series of local enterprises, many owned by municipalities, others by private companies. Some of these private companies were established by entrepreneurs who hoped to profit from the new technology, others by local dignitaries who wanted to bring to their local community the benefits of new technology. Over time, municipal ownership predominated.

In 1947 the electricity industry was nationalized. Nowadays, we tend to think of nationalization as meaning public ownership. But in electricity, the important change was not the substitution of public for private ownership, but the substitution of central government ownership and direction for local control. All the important consequences of nationalization followed from centralization.

After the dramatic end to the war against Japan, the peaceful use of nuclear energy was a symbol of a different future. In 1956, the Queen flicked a switch and the first nuclear electricity surged into British homes from the experimental Magnox reactor at Calder Hall. A decade later, several Magnox stations were producing power. But there had not been enough investment in new electricity-generating capacity. In the winter of 1964–5 power blackouts deprived homes and businesses of electricity. A Labour government had been elected in 1964 after a campaign which emphasized the 'white heat of technology'.[8] The government was committed to establishing a new national planning regime and decided on a large programme of investment in new power stations. Many options were debated, and it was concluded that five new gas-cooled reactors (AGRs) should be built on the lines of a small prototype. Fred Lee, a trade unionist who had reached the pinnacle of his career as Minister of Energy, announced the decision proudly. He emphasized not just the prospects of cheap power but the opportunity to develop a new technologically based export industry. 'I am quite sure we have hit the jackpot,' he declared.[9]

We had not hit the jackpot. Indeed, the construction of these reactors was probably the worst economic decision ever made by the government of a rich state. The average length of time to build a reactor was twenty years, and it was almost thirty years before their output matched their planned capacity. In the meantime total construction costs exceeded £50 billion (at 1996 prices).[10]

The AGRs were sold when British Energy was privatized in 1996. The proceeds were £1.9 billion, but the sale included a later reactor (Sizewell B) which had itself cost £3 billion to build. Moreover, the sale was possible only because the government agreed to a scheme to underwrite liabilities for future decommissioning costs. If the Central Electricity Generating Board had been a commercial company the write-off would have represented by far the largest loss made by any company, anywhere, in business history. For twenty years after Fred Lee's announcement, the right commercial decision would have been to forget the billions that had already been spent and abandon the project. It need hardly be said that no export order for this British technology ever materialized.

The Single Voice

It is obvious who made decisions in the Soviet Union and Communist China, in Ford and in Morris Motors. Yet it would be difficult to say that the decision to build AGRs was made by anyone at all. There were four groups involved – the Atomic Energy Authority, the Central Electricity Generating Board, civil servants and ministers. In a formal sense, the decision to go ahead was made by the hapless Fred Lee. But Lee had neither the capacity nor the authority to be the architect, rather than mouthpiece, of a decision of this magnitude. A powerful politician, faced with a mass of technical argument, can sometimes block a proposal if he or she has a sense that the conclusion is wrong. But Lee was not a man of that stature.

The Atomic Energy Authority was, naturally enough, in favour of the programme and the Central Electricity Generating Board mostly against. Among civil servants, there were two key figures. Burke (ultimately Lord) Trend was Cabinet Secretary. Edward (ultimately Lord) Plowden occupied a variety of Whitehall roles from the 1950s to the 1970s, including the chairmanship of the Atomic Energy Authority. One of the many influential committees Plowden chaired reviewed the structure of the state-owned electricity businesses. The problem, Plowden concluded, was that there was not enough centralization. The industry needed to 'speak with a single voice'.[11]

The industry did its best to speak with a single voice, and a voice that favoured the AGR programme. Those who expressed doubts found their career progression blocked or terminated. Others learned the lesson.[12] Anyone who provided negative feedback on the programme was treated in the same way. The concept of helpfulness is a deeply ingrained virtue – the primary virtue – of the British civil service. Helpfulness describes an individual's contribution to the orderly and consensual conduct of business. It does not relate to the nature and quality of decisions.[13]

The purge of those who were insufficiently helpful was far subtler than the Gulag, the Cultural Revolution, or the peremptory dismissal by Ford and Morris of those who disagreed with them. And it was even more successful, in its own terms. To this day there has been no inquiry into the AGR programme, no audit of the costs, no learning of the lessons. In contrast to the Great Leap Forward, or the random initiatives of Ford and Morris, decision-making for British electricity had the appearance of high rationality. But the consequences were the same: uniformity of opinion in the short run, economic failure in the long.

The Scale of Decision-making

Centralized economic decision-making is characterized by the single voice – the voice of an individual, such as Mao or Ford, the synthetic single voice of a process orchestrated and minuted by figures such as Burke Trend. The single voice makes decisions on a very large scale.

Khrushchev's experiment with maize was desirable and even beneficial. What distinguished the Soviet experiment was its size. An individual Russian farmer who had visited the United States might have been equally impressed by the productivity of the prairies, and might have brought back some seed. If yields had been disappointing, as they would have been, that would have been the end of the matter. If he had been successful, his rivals would have imitated. The scale of Mao's decisions was breathtaking. It is an extraordinary achievement that most of Chinese agriculture was converted to communal organization within a year. It is the kind of transformational change that the chief executives of large companies aspire to, but rarely achieve. But the scale of the change set the scene for the scale of the catastrophe.

No business leaders have ever enjoyed the wide-ranging political and economic authority of Mao and Khrushchev. But the size of the automobile industry enabled Morris and Ford to make momentous decisions. In the 1920s the output of the Ford Motor Company accounted for around 1 per cent of US GDP.

Fred Lee's plan was to build five power stations, more or less simultaneously, to an unproven design. With a single generating business for the whole of England and Wales, decisions of that magnitude have to be made. But nobody – however talented, however well-informed, however well-intentioned – had the ability to decide which technologies were appropriate for the British electricity industry for the next twenty years. The probability that *any* such decision would be badly awry is high. To stand any chance of success, a centralized decision-making process must be exceptionally sensitive to the consequences, and responsive to the changing environment.

This was not true in Russia, in China, in Ford or in Morris, or in British electricity. The process of centralization which established the single voice also stifled dissent. The feedback mechanisms in Ford and Morris were similar to the feedback mechanisms faced by Khrushchev and Mao, and equally ineffective. Even modest men rarely tire of the praise of loyal lieutenants. To point out the obvious failure of policy in British electricity was to label oneself as a disruptive influence in an organization which, by its own values, was performing more than satisfactorily.

That is not to say there was no feedback or accountability. Ford and Morris saw declining market share in competition with General Motors. This feedback – a crucial element in how markets work – is described more fully in the next chapter. It operated only slowly for Ford and for Morris because of market dominance created by their previous success. In Russia and China, the feedback came from popular discontent with economic performance, a mechanism which eventually toppled the Soviet Union and produced radical reform in China.

But these mechanisms were slow, and with that slowness went a lack of accountability on the part of the decision-makers. Morris and Ford were protected from outside criticism by their reputations and the large shareholdings they owned or controlled. The most accountable of these leaders was Khrushchev, ousted by his fellow *politburo* members. Morris was gradually pushed out of his automobile business after it merged with its rival, Austin, but Ford and Mao continued in office until death and their only accountability is to the jaundiced eyes of history.

Feedback and accountability were almost completely absent in British electricity. The few critics were ignored or disparaged and Trend and Plowden, elevated to the peerage, continued to chair committees to the end of their lives. The stream of misleading information about nuclear electricity only ended when the privatization of electricity companies in 1990 made ministers and directors personally liable for statements made to investors. The AGRs were withdrawn from sale and the construction of further nuclear power stations abandoned. Since these nuclear decisions were in principle more subject to democratic scrutiny and control than those of Ford and Morris, Mao or Khrushchev, the failure of accountability is particularly striking.

9

Pluralism

In the declining years of their founders, Ford and Morris were particularly badly managed companies. It is time to look at a well-run private sector business.

General Electric (GE) was the most successful corporation of the twentieth century. Of the dozen largest companies in 1900, only three – Shell, Exxon (the modern name for Standard Oil of New Jersey, the largest component of Rockefeller's Standard Oil) and GE were still in that group at the end. GE is the world's most valuable company, having regained the status it briefly lost in the bubble – first to Microsoft and then, absurdly, to Cisco, a manufacturer of Internet routers.

America's leading electrical company in 1900 was bound to do well in the hundred years that followed. The nature of its success, however, is surprising. GE sold its computer business in 1970, after being consistently outpaced by IBM. GE made little impact in consumer electronics in the face of Japanese competition, and its most important activities today are in aero engines, financial services and medical equipment. The history of GE is one of strong management applied to a diverse and changing range of businesses. In consequence, it is not only the best-managed company in the world but also the most studied, and its chief executive has almost always been the most respected business leader in the United States. From 1981 to 2001, that position was occupied by Jack Welch.[1]

The facts about GE are buried in a welter of management-speak. But Welch's most famous initiative, 'workout at GE', represented, above all, an attack on the single voice. The structure which Welch inherited at GE represented centralized planning at its most sophisticated and effective. Reg Jones, Welch's predecessor, had developed systems with the aim of understanding and controlling all areas of the world's largest business. 'I could look at six planning books and understand them well enough to ask the right questions.' The US Defense Department undertook a survey and concluded that the new man in charge at GE 'was probably inheriting the world's most effective strategic planning system and that Number Two was pretty far behind'.[2]

Welch set out to dismantle this structure. He described as 'superficial congeniality'[3] what the British civil service calls helpfulness. He set out to replace GE's 'superficial congeniality' by a process of substantive debate and argument. The contradictions raised are apparent in a 1982 interview with GE's chief planner, W. G. Rothschild. In the spirit of GE's earlier tradition, Rothschild asserts: 'I can assure you that a guy who doesn't implement the strategy is in big trouble . . . we tell the CEO when a manager is not on plan.' Yet Rothschild goes on: 'I like being challenged, and I like people to argue with me. By the way, that happens to be what our new chairman likes too. The new buzz-word here is contention management. I'd say that's where we are and where we're going.'[4] In that, at least, Rothschild was right. Within a short time, Rothschild himself and much of GE's central planning staff had disappeared.[5]

The opposite of 'superficial congeniality' was 'facing reality' – performance judged by externally measured achievement rather than contribution to internal culture. 'Facing reality was not one of the company's strong points. Its superficial congeniality made candor extremely difficult to come by.'[6] Welch would illustrate 'facing reality' with GE's nuclear power plant division. Its managers could not accept that both economics and politics had turned against nuclear power. By attacking helpfulness, and abandoning superficial congeniality, GE recognized these realities – as Britain's centrally planned electricity industry never did.[7] GE's nuclear power plant business was turned into a profitable sales and support operation.

But the most important part of GE's reorganization was the systematic decentralization of authority. 'I did away with that (approval and appropriation) process and haven't signed an appropriation approach in at least eighteen years. Each business leader has the same delegation of authority that the board gave me. . . . The people closest to the work know the work best.'[8] To advance, GE had to embrace pluralism – to replace 'superficial congeniality' by open debate, to dismember the central planning and decentralize authority. Welch attempted to tackle some of the key problems identified of central planning – in particular, decision-making on too large a scale, and the lack of effective processes of feedback and accountability.

Yet centralization, conformity to internally generated values, too much authority seized by leaders whose adjutants derive no advantage from telling the truth, are inescapable in very large organizations. Welch was a more intelligent man than either Ford or Morris, and he did not outstay his effective tenure as long as Ford or Morris did. But he did outstay it. In his autobiography, the engaging character who takes charge of GE in 1981 becomes less attractive as self-confidence is reinforced by success. The word 'I' appears more often.

Welch extended his tenure as CEO of GE to see through a planned merger with Honeywell. His embarrassing account of his failure to gain European Commission approval demonstrates the same isolation from honest criticism that crippled Ford and Morris – and Mao and Khrushchev. Welch could not understand the fear that one company might enjoy too much influence over the development of the aircraft industry by its dominance across a whole range of aircraft components. The Commission valued pluralism.[9]

Pluralism in Pharmaceuticals

An adverse effect of the AGR programme was that many talented applied scientists in Britain were employed in trying to make these reactors work – an activity which yielded no direct economic benefit and no spin-offs. The pharmaceutical industry illustrates how they might have been better employed.

ICI was once Britain's most respected business. Its reach was always global. Competition was muted by tacit agreements which divided the world into spheres of influence – Du Pont held sway in the Americas, ICI in the British Empire and Commonwealth, IG Farben in continental Europe. The heavy chemical business remains prone to price-fixing agreements even now.[10] But ICI operated in a competitive marketplace.

Its management training and development were exemplary. While Morris emphasized dirty hands, ICI's recruitment policies were unequivocally meritocratic. Succession arrangements were designed to prevent the emergence of any single dominant figure.[11]

Eventually, this created problems. After forty years, the company was managed by a cadre of able bureaucrats whose entire working career had been spent in ICI. Helpfulness was never prized at ICI as in the civil service, but it helped to be helpful. Only in the 1980s did the company break with this tradition by appointing as chief executive a flamboyant figure with a large moustache and lurid ties, and, under John Harvey-Jones, begin a process of internal reform and reconstruction.

But for decades the ICI management system served the company well and, in a period when few able British graduates entered industry, the calibre of its managers stood out. After the Second World War, the company realized that the growth of the chemical industry would be in pharmaceuticals rather than the traditional businesses of dye-stuffs and explosives.[12] That was a correct judgement, but one that took a long time to be vindicated. When the ICI pharmaceutical division became Zeneca in 1993, its stock market value was greater than, and soon far greater than, the traditional chemicals business which remained. But all that was far in the future. In the post-war period, ICI recruited a fine team of able young scientists but the pharmaceutical division lost money for almost twenty years before beta-blockers, the first drugs effective against hypertension, brought in large revenues.

The chemist principally responsible for beta-blockers was James Black, a Scot who had been attracted to ICI by the combination of freedom in research and large corporate resources. Black believed that the therapeutic principles behind beta-blockers had wider application. The senior management of ICI pharmaceuticals, relieved to have a profitable product, was less certain. Black was encouraged to focus on existing developments and the promotion of beta-blockers. Frustrated, he left ICI and joined Smith Kline, a competitor. Black was right and ICI wrong. The principle of blocking receptors was the basis for Tagamet, an anti-ulcerant which became one of the best-selling drugs in the history of the pharmaceutical industry, and Black won the Nobel

Prize for his discoveries. Tagamet was outsold only by Zantac, a similar product manufactured by another British company, Glaxo.

Through the growth of ICI Pharmaceuticals, Smith Kline, and Glaxo, Britain developed a world-class pharmaceutical industry. It was vital that there were many companies. Other British drug companies had grown reliant on steady profits from patent medicines. Beecham's Pills had made a fortune for the company's founders, funded Sir Thomas Beecham's musical aspirations, and enabled the company to develop other consumer products, such as Ribena and Lucozade. But the development of a modern science-based industry required a new entrant, ICI, with skills in science rather than in marketing.

Who could have known whether Black's enthusiasm for his own ideas was well founded? As it happens, ICI managers made the wrong decision. It did not matter to the future of the industry – although it certainly mattered to ICI – because Black was able to go to Smith Kline. But Smith Kline did not have the new marketing skills needed to penetrate the American drugs market. Glaxo first bought these skills from Hoffman la Roche and gradually developed them internally.

All contenders in the British pharmaceutical industry were competent businesses. None displayed the stubborn insularity of Morris Motors (and its successors the British Motor Corporation and British Leyland). The case for a national champion, talking with a single voice, was also made in the pharmaceutical industry. In 1972 Beecham attempted to take over Glaxo, which itself proposed a merger with Boots.[13] The Monopolies Commission rejected all the plans, and was vindicated when Glaxo went on to become the world's largest pharmaceutical business. The key to the success of the industry was that no one – not Beecham, not ICI, not Smith Kline, not Glaxo – had the power to control its development.[14] The same pluralist process gave the world photocopiers and personal computers.

Xerox Parc

Photocopying was invented by a lawyer, Chester Carlson, who had tired of the problem of obtaining good copies of documents. Carlson had difficulty finding a backer. It is claimed that IBM, GE and RCA investigated the proposal, and all turned it down. Incredible though it seems to us now, they thought there would not be sufficient demand to justify the costs and risks of development.[15] Eventually a small firm, the Haloid Company, decided to risk everything on Carlson's invention.

After fifteen years of development, the company launched the first commercial photocopier. Haloid called the patented process Xerography and changed the company name to the Xerox Corporation. Even at this point, other office equipment manufacturers were sceptical, and the Xerox Corporation did not have the resources to market photocopiers world-wide. A British film studio, the Rank Organization, took the rights to develop and distribute machines in most markets outside the USA. (The Rank Organization's trademark of a man striking a gong still introduces many classic movies.)[16] Rank's film production was quickly dwarfed by its photocopier business.

Early machines were large, slow and broke down frequently. Office activities were frequently halted as secretaries waited for the Xerox engineer. Xerox's equipment got better, but not sufficiently better, and when Xerox patents expired market leadership switched to the Japanese optical company Canon. Conscious that revenues from its initial monopoly would not continue indefinitely, the Xerox Corporation sought to diversify into other high technology office products. A research centre was established at Palo Alto, in the centre of what was to become Silicon Valley.

Xerox Parc was a fertile source of innovation.[17] The fax machine was pioneered there, as was the laser printer, the Ethernet and the graphical user interface (the icons and pointers which make modern computers easy to use). Yet, despite the company's stunning achievement with photocopiers, Xerox never succeeded in turning its innovative capability into corresponding commercial success.[18] It would be left to others to exploit the most revolutionary product of Xerox Parc – the personal computer. Xerography had come into being because no single voice controlled the office equipment industry. A cacophony of voices was to be heard in personal computers.

The Personal Computer

For many years, most experts thought that computing power would be like electric power, and, if Lord Plowden had been in charge, it probably would have been. A few gigantic facilities would maximize economies of scale. Everyone would plug into these super computers. In the 1970s a university, or a business, would typically have one computer. The computer industry might also have developed through an extensive range of application-specific machines – the word processor, the games console, specialist calculators for engineers and accountants.

A process of diversity and experiment produced a very different answer. In 1971 Intel developed a general purpose chip – the microprocessor. The logic of applications was found, not on the chip, but in the memory. This paved the way for the general purpose minicomputer. In 1973 scientists at Xerox Parc built the first functioning personal computer, the Alto. It was eight years before they unveiled a commercial version. The new product impressed the trade press with its sophistication, but it was by then too idiosyncratic and expensive for the market.

While Xerox was perfecting the Alto, personal computers were developed by hobbyists. The Altair minicomputer was advertised in *Popular Electronics* magazine in December 1974, a self-assembly kit with a price of $400. Two young Harvard students, Paul Allen and Bill Gates, devised a simple programming language, BASIC, for the Altair.

Toy computers were next. The BBC micro, produced by Acorn, was linked to schools broadcasting and designed to introduce children to the world of computing. Clive Sinclair – whose appearance and personality matched the stereotype of the madcap inventor – sold home computers. Cassette tape recorders provided memory. Sinclair was seen long-jumping in television advertisements to illustrate the quantum leap in capability provided by his QL machine.

By now, some large companies, such as AT&T and Sony, had recognized the potential of small computers for small businesses. The first desktop computer I used, in 1981, was made by Sirius, an Exxon subsidiary. But then IBM launched a range of personal computers – the PC. A machine with an IBM label was not a toy. IBM's reputation and market presence were such that whatever they supported would command wide acceptance. It didn't matter that the PC's performance was inferior to that of other machines on the market. IBM's was the system for which people would write software. Within months, 'PC' had become the generic term for a small computer.

For the operating system IBM had turned to a small company, Microsoft, run by Gates and Allen. Microsoft in turn bought the operating system, which it renamed MS-DOS, for $50,000. But IBM did not take exclusive rights. The computer giant had no real sense of the revolution it had launched. When IBM attempted to regain control with a new and more sophisticated operating system, OS2, it was too late: MS-DOS was everywhere. IBM had other competitors. In 1983 a group of Japanese manufacturers attempted to extend their dominance of consumer electronics by agreeing a standard, MSX, for cheap home computers. But the market was not ready for gadgets that were more than toys but less than business machines, and MSX vanished.

The choice of the enthusiast was Apple. Apple machines were more fun. Gates and Microsoft had understood that commercial success depended on ease of use rather than technical sophistication. Steve Jobs, founder of Apple, extended this vision further – a computer that did not need an understanding of computers. To achieve this, Jobs drew on another invention from Xerox Parc: the graphical user interface. Apple machines had screens which resembled a desktop, and friendly aids such as a mouse and recycle bin.

You could access these capabilities only by buying Apple's integrated software and hardware. Apple's determination to maintain its proprietary system lost out to widespread adoption of the open standard of the IBM PC – just as Sony's restricted Betamax standard lost out to JVC's open VHS in the video cassette recorder business (Chapter 21). The combination of Apple's graphical user interface with Microsoft's ubiquitous MS-DOS operating system was bound to succeed. Microsoft launched an early version in 1988 and an effective version of Windows two years later. The rest – Microsoft's domination of the personal computer industry and Gates's rise to become the world's richest man – is history.[19]

The Process of Pluralism

Nikita Khrushchev, or Lord Plowden, might have asked: 'Who was in charge of the successful development of the personal computer industry?' There is no doubt that whoever was in charge of the development of computers in the Soviet Union would have had much to learn from that person. But nobody was 'in charge'. If Khrushchev's hosts had introduced him to the Chairman of IBM, or Bill Gates, they would have ensured that their visitor completely missed the point. Markets work because there is never a single voice.

No one saw for more than a few months ahead how the personal computer industry would evolve. Gates and Jobs believed that the future lay with small machines that were very easy to use – a widely held though not, for many years, a majority view. But Jobs's strategy for his company did not work, and Gates's success derives directly from one particular event – his association with IBM. The majority of initiatives failed. And not just initiatives, such as Sinclair's QL or the Japanese MSX, which proved dead ends. Most initiatives which were crucial to the development of the industry were ultimately commercially unsuccessful.

This is how new industries develop and new products emerge. There were many contenders in the race to determine the shape of the world car industry: the race which Henry Ford joined just after the turn of the century and William Morris entered after the First World War. Would cars be steam-driven, or electric, or powered by an internal combustion engine? Would automobiles remain for ever the province of rich men who could employ chauffeurs, or become available to a mass market? As late as 1927, the economist Edward Cannan, watching from his Oxford home as the Cowley motor works rose on the edge of the city, wrote that he could not imagine where the demand for Morris's products would come from.[20] But the key point is that there was a race. Many people had an opportunity to back their own judgement. Through some mix of luck and judgement – and it is likely that luck was as important as judgement – Ford and Morris and those who supported them backed the winners.

But the race never ends, and that is why Ford and Morris were penalized for their errors. Ford's global leadership was overtaken by General Motors. British Leyland, the successor company to Morris Motors, disintegrated in the face of international competition. Feedback mechanisms within these organizations failed, but the broader feedback mechanisms of the market economy ultimately succeeded in promoting managerial reorganization at Ford, and in taking responsibility for car production out of the hands of the duffers at Leyland.

Most decisions are wrong. Most experiments fail. It is tempting to believe that if we entrusted the future of our companies, our industries, our countries, to the right people, they would lead us unerringly to the promised land. Such hopes are always disappointed. Most of Thomas Edison's inventions did not work, Ford, Morris and Mao ended their careers as sad, even risible figures. Bill Gates missed the significance of the Internet, Mrs Thatcher introduced the poll tax, and Napoleon died in exile on St Helena. Even extraordinarily talented people make big mistakes.

But because most decisions are wrong and most experiments fail, it is also tempting to believe that we could manage businesses and states much better if only we assembled sufficient information and cleverer people, and debated the issues at length. This is how decision-making is supposed to be in the public sector and in many large organizations.

What would Lord Plowden, chairing a committee in the 1970s to determine the future of the computer industry, have done? He would have deplored the failure of the industry to speak 'with a single voice', but would have found the best approximation to that voice in the chief executive of IBM. He would have consulted widely in the industry, certainly discussing with Intel what they thought might happen, and commending them on their co-operation with IBM. He might even have gone so far as to hold discussions with Xerox, even though they were not actually making computers at the time of his report. If he had received submissions from the young Bill Gates and Steve Jobs, he would have smiled gently and passed them to the secretary of his committee to file.

This picture is not fanciful. It is more or less how the computer industry developed, or failed to develop, in the Soviet Union. It is more or less how IBM developed its policies and strategy for the future of its industry. And even in the 1990s, after Mrs Thatcher's market revolution, the British government established 'foresight committees', chaired by figures with Plowden-like skills, to advise on the future of science-based industries.

But nobody has such foresight. And these structures would fail even if the people who staffed them were infinitely intelligent and far-seeing. What would an omniscient planner, blessed with the advantages of hindsight, have said when faced with the numerous business strategies described above? He would have told Xerox that they could not develop commercially successful products from the PC and the graphical user interface. He would have explained to IBM that the company's strategy would destroy its core business. He would have foreseen the failures of MSX and QL. He would have told Apple that its policy would take the company to the edge of collapse. And he would have said many of the same things to the people who developed the automobile industry or commercial aviation.

There are always well-founded objections to any new proposed course of action. There is always a proposal which might be better than the one currently being considered. As a result, these apparently rational processes frequently fail to make decisions at all and, when they do, often make worse decisions than those which emerge from more intuitive, and certainly speedier, processes.

Failures of Discipline

Pluralism is the key to the success of a market economy. But pluralism must also be disciplined. A consequence of the extraordinary success of pluralism in promoting innovation in personal computers was the collapse of market discipline in the 1990s.

By the mid-1990s it was apparent that the Internet was an innovation of major significance. The key to giving access to the Internet to a wide public was the development of easy-to-use browser software. The best browser had been created by students at the University of Illinois. Jim Clark, who had become rich by developing and selling an earlier software business, Silicon Graphics, hired the team who had created it, settled the inevitable lawsuit with the University of Illinois, and launched Netscape Navigator. Within a few months Navigator had achieved market dominance, a result not only of its usefulness but its price: it was usually given away, and when shares in Netscape were sold to investors in 1995 the company's sales revenues to date had been less than $20 million.

The demand for Netscape shares was such that the shares closed on the first day at $58, valuing the company at $2.2 billion. These figures were eclipsed as Internet enthusiasm grew: the shares quickly rose to $170, which made Clark a billionaire. Microsoft developed its own browser, Internet Explorer, with very similar capabilities, which it provided free with Windows, and this quickly overtook Navigator. In 1999 Netscape was acquired by AOL at a price which still gave early investors a profit. No doubt it seemed a good idea at the time. Today Navigator's market share is below 10 per cent.

Although Netscape never became a successful business, the company did have a proven chief executive, a good product and a strong market position. As the decade progressed, an increasing number of companies were launched by individuals with no management or commercial experience, no realistic business plan and no identifiable product.

Boo.com was launched in 1998 by a glamorous Swedish couple, Ernst Malmsten and Kajsa Leander. Its objective was to sell the coolest fashions on the Internet through a virtual sales assistant, Miss Boo. By 1999 the company's operating expenditure was around $20 million per month, of which significant amounts were spent in chic London venues – the Ivy restaurant, the bar of the Metropolitan Hotel. The money was raised by J. P. Morgan, once the most staid of investment banks. It mostly came from rich individuals – the Benetton family, Bernard Arnault and Middle Eastern investors. The home page of the company's website, which was finally launched in November 1999, took eight minutes to download on a standard modem. In May 2000 Boo.com went into liquidation, having spent over $100 million and sold almost nothing.[21]

The ease with which money could be raised to fund businesses such as these, particularly in the United States, was widely applauded as a demonstration of the vitality of financial markets.[22] In reality, it represented a collapse of market discipline. Investors failed to discriminate between proposals, believing that any stake they held in an

Internet-related company could soon be sold to someone else at a higher price. Noise traders – people whose purchases and sales were related to knowledge of the fundamental values of securities – came to dominate. Venture capital managers and investment banks received fees for promoting investments in these businesses, yet it required only common sense, not professional expertise, to see that such companies had no chance of success.

In early 2000 the valuation of technology stocks in general, and Internet stocks in particular, reached a peak and then crashed. The supply of venture capital to new Internet businesses dried up almost immediately. From the Netscape flotation to the market crash, the collapse of market discipline had lasted five years.[23]

Because the world is complicated and the future uncertain, decision-making in organizations and economic systems is best made through a series of small-scale experiments, frequently reviewed, and in a structure in which success is followed up and failure recognized but not blamed: the mechanisms of disciplined pluralism. Welch's reputation as the greatest manager of his generation is not based on the big calls which he got right, on his Napoleonic vision, his Fordist determination, or his Edisonian invention. Welch understood that the principal function of the managing director of the world's largest commercial organization was to appoint good people and trust them to do the job; it was to introduce pluralism, and at the same time to impose discipline, through audit and accountability. Both within organizations and outside them, it is in the combination of pluralism and discipline that we find the truth about markets.

10

Spontaneous Order

Order Without Design

'Who designed the market economy?' No one did. It is the result of the simultaneous evolution of social, political and economic institutions over hundreds, even thousands of years. 'Who developed the personal computer?' The answer, again, is that no one did. The industry has emerged from an unplanned process of trial and error within a framework of disciplined pluralism. There is a deep human need to find ordered, personalized explanations of the complexities and vicissitudes of life. Almost all religions have an account of the creation of the world. Most primitive cultures believe that drought or bad weather are expressions of some human emotion, such as anger or revenge.

Similar instincts lead modern men and women to personalize large corporations (and to seek someone to blame for floods and rail accidents). We lionize Jack Welch because it is hard to believe that an organization like General Electric achieves so much through decentralized decision-making and negotiation between thousands of autonomous individuals. It is easier to think it is the expression of the will of one man.

For centuries, theologians argued that the complexity of nature was evidence of the existence of God. William Paley drew a famous analogy: if we found a perfectly engineered watch at our feet, then there must be a watchmaker. But the analogy is misleading. The thinkers of the Scottish Enlightenment, whose names graced those Edinburgh University buildings, were among the first to grasp one of the most powerful, wide-ranging and elusive intellectual ideas of the last two centuries.[1] Structures and systems can have the characteristics of elaborate design without a designer. David Hume anticipated and refuted Paley's theological argument.[2] Adam Ferguson applied the same thought to social institutions: 'Nations stumble upon establishments, which are indeed the results of human action but not the result of human design.'[3] A century later, Darwin was to throw back Paley's example with his own metaphor of the 'blind watchmaker'.[4] And today we understand that evolution has produced organisms whose complexity far exceeds the capacity of any human mind – organisms such as human beings, General Electric and the international division of labour.

The success of Darwin's theory has led to attempts at too literal an analogy.[5] Genetic selection is only one type of evolutionary process. Black parents have black children, and French-speaking parents have French-speaking children, but for different reasons.[6] The transmission of acquired skills – impossible in genetic selection – is central to business and economic life. Evolutionary mechanisms themselves are in any case only one example of processes which create order without design – others will be described in the course of this chapter. The importance of Darwin's theory outside biology is that it demonstrates the extraordinary potential of spontaneous order. No one who has fully understood it ever thinks the same way again.

Co-ordination in Market Economies

Adam Smith was the great economist of that Scottish enlightenment. And his metaphor of the invisible hand is the most famous expression of order without design. Smith described how the division of labour had fuelled economic growth, 'the natural progress of opulence'. But how was that division of labour organized and co-ordinated? The answer was the invisible hand. As I shall discuss in Chapter 16, I am not sure this interpretation of Smith is right.

But whether or not it was Smith's answer, it is a good question. We can imagine Khrushchev in the supermarket posing his own version: 'Who is in charge of the supply of groceries to California?' To anyone unfamiliar with the institutions of the market economy, it seems bizarre that this question has no answer. In the striking phrase of Ken Arrow[N] and Frank Hahn, two of the economists who have framed these issues, 'The immediate "common sense" answer to the question "What will an economy motivated by individual greed and controlled by a very large number of different agents look like?" is probably: "There will be chaos".'[7] And yet there is not chaos. In rich states, we are so accustomed to the absence of surpluses and shortages that we feel angry when we encounter them – when a shop does not have the size or colour we want, when we cannot find a taxi or a bus late at night, and certainly when California cannot maintain consistent supplies of electricity.

Market economies solved the co-ordination problem more successfully than centrally planned ones. This discovery astonished Khrushchev, and it should astonish us. Many of the failures of centrally planned economies were failures of innovation. The pluralist programme of experiment, failure and fresh experiment did not occur in the Soviet Union, and so that country did not produce new drugs, modern automobiles or personal computers.

But the greatest failures of centrally planned economies were in co-ordination.[8] Queues formed in pursuit of erratic supplies of consumer goods. Factories failed to meet targets because they could not obtain the necessary raw materials. Other industrial goods were in excess supply. The Soviet Union had more steel-making capacity than the United States,[9] and it is hard to understand where all the steel went. Some of it was simply left to rust. For the casual visitor, failures of co-ordination are one of the most obvious differences between rich and poor countries. The electricity supply is often unreliable, some essential goods are not available. This is sometimes the result of poverty, but also a cause.

So how do rich states do it? Khrushchev might have been introduced to Sam Walton, America's largest retailer,[10] but Walton would have told him that he was only one of several people in charge of the supply of groceries in California. 'And who liaises between them?' Lord Plowden would have asked: 'Which committee orchestrates the single voice?' Not only is there no such committee: to form it would violate US law.

And who co-ordinates relationships of firms in the supply chain?

Who ensures that goods are produced to fill the shelves? Khrushchev might have speculated on the answer: in market economies prices rise or fall when there is a physical shortage or surplus, so there are no empty shelves or unsold produce. This is indeed the mechanism which emerged in Russia when centralized supply chains broke down after the collapse of the Soviet Union.[11]

But raising prices to deal with temporary shortages is so unpopular with consumers that retailers are reluctant to do it. Shoppers accept price fluctuations of seasonal products, but not price fluctuations from co-ordination failures.[12] When the failure of Californian electricity supplies did lead to price spikes there was the same political outcry that would have been expected in the Soviet Union.[13] The answer Sam Walton would have given to the question 'How do supermarkets deal with shortages and surpluses?' is that the problem rarely arises.

Rich states are not free of co-ordination failures. Co-ordination in electricity supply is a powerful example, which is why it will recur often: the consequences of even a small and short-lived co-ordination failure are so obvious – the lights go out, as they did in Auckland in 1998, in California in 2000, and routinely in poor states. Perhaps the most serious co-ordination failure in productive economies is unemployment, a co-ordination failure that planned economies have largely avoided, although at the price of other co-ordination failures elsewhere. How market systems achieve co-ordination is the subject of Part Three of this book.

At the Supermarket

Khrushchev did not have to worry about which queue to join at the supermarket checkout, but we do. We can look at the characteristics of the queues: how many people, how full are their trolleys? Will those ahead unload their baskets quickly? Or engage in extended discussion with the cashier? Or we can simply join the nearest queue. So long as some people – it need not be very many – are scanning the store to find the shortest queue, we can expect that the time we spend in each queue will be much the same. If any queue looks short, these activists will join it. The activists probably wait slightly less than we do, but not much – enough, however, to give them some return on their socially beneficial activity.

This is a simple and banal example of a system of spontaneous order. It is organized, and in some respects efficient, but it is not directed. It is probably more effective at keeping down waiting-times than direction by a bossy store manager. The manager would not be able to keep pace sufficiently well with the constantly changing progress at the checkouts, nor would he always find people ready to follow his instructions – the twin problems of information and incentives that confront planners everywhere.

The outcome of this self-organizing system emerges from the individual decisions of shoppers. They are not pursuing a collective goal of short and uniform waiting-times, although their actions have this effect. Their actions are self-regarding, but not purely self-interested: if the supermarket were full of people whose only objective was to get through the till as quickly as possible it would not be possible to operate any queuing system at all. The orderly process is the product of limited self-interest and social convention.

Although nobody designed this system, design might improve it. Many customers are willing to allow other shoppers with few purchases to jump the queue. To facilitate this, some supermarkets have responded with separate queues for those with small amounts to buy. A system that works well in one environment may fail in another. In a supermarket, we can see how much is in everyone else's trolley. But in an airline ticket queue, the person in front may be booking a round-the-world itinerary or simply asking the way to the gate. A single queue feeds several agents.

Our everyday supermarket experience demonstrates two different kinds of process. Individual shoppers are led 'as if by an invisible hand', to keep down overall waiting-times. No one consciously intended to bring this about and it might be more difficult to bring it about by conscious intention. The process is dynamic but not evolutionary. But there is also an evolutionary mechanism at work. In competition with each other, supermarkets adopt mechanisms which efficiently serve the needs of their customers. This combination of processes illustrates in microcosm how market economies evolved – and evolve.

Chaos and Path-dependency

We could develop a mathematical model of supermarket queues. Such a model would be dynamic – the length of queues constantly changes. It would display feedback – the number of people who join a queue will depend on the number of people already in it. I suspect most readers will be sceptical of the value of doing this. But there really is a branch of mathematics called queue theory,[14] and it has practical implications. Much of it was developed to assist engineers in the design of telephone exchanges. Related models are widely used in business today, to plan stockholding and even to manage checkouts.

For two centuries now, the social sciences – indeed most sciences – have been overshadowed by the successes of physics. The great physicist Max Planck reportedly said that he had been tempted to take up economics but had concluded it was too hard.[15] What could Planck have meant? The most remarkable achievements of physics have been with simple systems, such as planetary motion, which can be comprehensively described by two or three variables. The natural sciences have also made great progress in understanding systems where the number of units – such as molecules or electrons – is very large, but where these units behave independently or with interactions which can be described by simple rules. The motion of gases and liquids has this character – and so do queues in large supermarkets. But models based on statistical mechanics don't help with the village post office, where the particular behaviour of individual customers matters, or with the development of the personal computer industry, where the interactions between firms are complex. These are not simple systems which can be solved analytically. Nor are they characterized by the random complexity which is tractable by statistics. Firms and households interact with each other frequently, and in different and complicated ways. They are not so large that a model can describe and incorporate their individual idiosyncrasies, nor so small that these idiosyncrasies can be treated as random. The study of economics and business shares these characteristics with other sciences which seem 'too hard' – weather systems, movements of the earth's crust, much of biology and medicine. Our knowledge of all these areas of study is still piecemeal and inadequate. Organized complexity[16] is that intermediate area between simple systems and the statistics of random individual behaviour.

Meteorologists, biologists, seismologists and economists have all developed mathematical models of their processes. All have shared the hope that they could use their models to see the future. But meteorological, geological, biological and economic systems develop in ways that are very sensitive to initial conditions.[17] This property has today entered popular discourse under the label 'chaos theory'. The idea has been familiar for a long time: 'For want of a nail the shoe was lost.' In the film *Sliding Doors*, Gwyneth Paltrow experiences two quite different lives depending on whether or not she succeeds in entering a subway train before the doors close. Tom Stoppard has the cast of his play *Arcadia* debate and experience alternative futures. In the most famous metaphor of chaos theory, a butterfly flapping its wings provokes a tornado thousands of miles away and days later.[18]

Systems in which initial conditions affect subsequent behaviour indefinitely are path-dependent.[19] Path-dependency is why the film industry is still based in Hollywood and maritime insurance in London. The design of our computer keyboards is path-dependent: the qwerty layout was devised in the earliest days of typewriting and although it is ergonomically inefficient users are familiar with it and the number of qwerty keyboards and typists is too large to make any change possible.[20] The coevolution of technology and institutions – the development of the social and economic infrastructure of rich states – has been a path-dependent process.

But path-dependency in which outcomes are sensitive to small details – the problem of the butterfly and the tornado – is fatal to forecasting. The hopes that were placed in the development of computers and mathematical modelling have been disappointed. Scientists have not been successful in developing models that predict the weather, or volcanic eruptions, more than a few days in advance. They cannot predict earthquakes at all, nor tell us how soon we will shake off a cold. Nor can we anticipate the development of the economy, or the performance of business for more than a short time ahead.

Successful long-range weather forecasting is almost certainly impossible – we will *never* be able to answer questions like 'What will the weather be on 4 June next year?' – and the same is true of economic and business forecasting. That is why much less resource is now devoted to this kind of meteorology, or to economic forecasting models, and why the talking heads of Bloomberg television simply cannot know the things they claim to predict.

Some scientists have attempted to establish general principles that might be relevant to all problems of organized complexity. The world centre for this research is a spin off from the US nuclear research establishment at Los Alamos, located at Santa Fe in the mountains of New Mexico, and analysis undertaken there goes under the heading of complexity theory.[21] The hope is not to predict the future, but to gain a better understanding of the general properties of complex systems.

We cannot know what the weather will be like next 4 June. But meteorologists can give an indication of the average temperature to be expected and the likely range. They can assess the probability of rain, and make contingent predictions – it is more likely to be sunny on 4 June if it is sunny on 3 June. All this is useful if we are planning a wedding reception on 4 June. And that knowledge is considerably more useful than the confident assertion – it will be sunny and the temperature will be 23 °C – which people expect, even demand, from a talking head.

Business people, politicians and consumers can have the same kind of knowledge – averages, probabilities, contingent predictions – about how the economy will evolve. And this is the only kind of knowledge they can have about how the economy will evolve. People who purport to forecast the level of the stock market next year, or what the demand for air transport will be in 2015, are charlatans.

The Search for Spontaneous Order

Darwin described the behaviour of social insects as 'by far the most serious special difficulty' for his thesis.[22] Ant colonies co-operate to build nests. They send expeditions to collect and retrieve food with an efficiency which is closer to Sam Walton's Wal-Mart than Khrushchev's Soviet Union. The chemical signals by which ants communicate with each other, and the evolutionary biology which explains their co-operative instincts, are today largely understood.[23]

It is probably not an accident that during the bubble films were made – such as *Antz* and *A Bug's Life* – which anthropomorphized social insects. The Disney Corporation imposed on nature its perception of how the Disney Corporation is run. But insect colonies are not like these films. There are no boss ants and no supervisory ants. The queens of colonies do not sit above them directing their activities. They sit below them waiting to be generously fed.[24]

But perhaps the reality of the Disney Corporation has some resemblance to the ant colony. The philosopher Alasdair MacIntyre, whom we shall meet again, likens the presidents of large corporations to clergymen praying for rain.[25] The reverse analysis really may be the more interesting. What can we learn about human organization – such as the co-ordination of the division of labour in an unplanned economy – from the emergence of spontaneous order in nature?

Imagine a population trying to find higher points in a large, uneven and unexplored landscape. There are several possible approaches.

One is for everyone to congregate at the highest point yet discovered, and to move in a group when plausible evidence of a yet higher point is obtained. This procedure has much in common with central planning. And, as with central planning, there is a possibility that a good result is chosen relatively quickly. But it is not a very large possibility. A more probable outcome is long periods of stasis followed by occasional violent disruptions, and because there is only analysis, not experiment, the process does not naturally generate much information about the scope and scale of the unknown landscape.

Another possible approach is purely individualistic. Everyone searches for higher points in their own immediate locality. This is close to the mechanism of evolution. Steps are chosen at random: if they lead upwards, they are maintained, if they lead downwards, retraced. No common knowledge is generated, only individual experiences.

Yet another way of dealing with the problem is neither intentionally co-operative nor strictly individualistic. The general aim is to find patches of higher ground. Groups which succeed encourage others to join them. This is in the interests of both the group and the individuals it attracts: the former gains from more intensive searching, the latter benefit from the experience of the successful group. This mechanism has a good chance of achieving better results than either of the others, because it strikes a balance between decentralization and co-ordination. Yet it requires no direction: it is a mechanism which would be very likely to develop spontaneously.

This account follows a model developed by Herbert Simon[N], who studied theories of decision-making. Simon's career was devoted to an attack on the picture of rational action in which households and firms define objectives and compute the best means of achieving them. Even if we had such clear objectives, the world is too complex to allow us to achieve them. An instruction to 'find the best allocation of scarce resources between competing ends' is, like an instruction to 'find the highest point in California', simply not capable of being implemented.[26] The information required to find the highest point on a static landscape is immense: we can do it only because generations of surveyors mapped it. If topography is constantly changing, like the business and economic landscape, the informational task is impossible. Simon asserts that we do not maximize, we satisfice – we follow rules and procedures, like the organization of supermarket queues, which produce results that are good enough.

Simon's example parallels complexity theorist Stuart Kauffman's description of what he calls fitness landscapes.[27] Kauffman is interested in the general mathematical structure of complex systems. Height above sea level in Simon's example might equally be a measure of how well a species is adapted to its environment, or how effectively scarce resources are allocated between competing ends. Kauffman's conjecture is that there are common models and principles of self-organization which describe phenomena as diverse as the emergence of life and the construction of social order.

Complexity theory occupies today a strange, perhaps unique, position within the scientific canon. It has attracted the attention of scientists of exceptional distinction and creativity, and yet stands somewhat outside the mainstream of professional knowledge. Economists are particularly sceptical.[28] Many economists would like to be physicists. The most widely used model of spontaneous order in economics follows the structure of 'simple system' physical models. But, like the simple system models of modern physicists, it includes many variables and its mathematics is far from simple. This is the model of competitive equilibrium associated with Arrow and Debreu. Part Three of this book is devoted to the development of this theory. In Part Four I shall come back to a wider range of ideas about the nature of spontaneous order.

Part Three

PERFECTLY COMPETITIVE
MARKETS

II

Competitive Markets

In a perfectly competitive market there are enough buyers and sellers of each commodity for none to have much influence over the price. Supply and demand are constructed from the independent decisions of many consumers and many producers. The co-ordination of these decisions is the extraordinary achievement of market economies.

Perfectly competitive markets require homogeneous commodities. There cannot be a competitive market for *Portrait of Dr Gachet* because there is only one original version of it (or arguably two). So there can only be one buyer, and one seller. There is not even a competitive market for van Goghs, or master paintings, because there can never be many sellers.

The Colombe d'Or has a unique location. What was offered reflected the particularities, culinary and organizational, of M. Roux. Coca-Cola has a unique recipe and an unsurpassed brand. Swiss engineering and chemical businesses command high prices for their products because very few companies can match their technical skills. These products all face competition, but they are not sold in perfectly competitive markets.

As economies evolve, more and more of the goods and services that are exchanged are idiosyncratic. A little bit of differentiation will not affect the issue very much. The Colombe d'Or is unique but there are enough restaurants like it for the prices on its menu not to differ very much from others in the neighbourhood. How much substitution makes a market competitive is a matter of fine judgement. And costly judgement: argument over market definition in anti-trust cases has become a lucrative source of employment for economists.[1] But, even now, many exchanges are of commodity products – goods whose annual production is millions of units which differ little from each other. Like oil, milk, electricity and video cassette recorders.

Supply

Oil

Oil was first exploited on a commercial scale in the nineteenth century. Deposits that were easy to find and close to major population centres, such as the oilfields of Ohio, were small and quickly depleted, but much larger quantities of oil were found further underground. Texas became rich on the productive fields of Spindletop and Corsicana.

The largest accessible deposits of oil today are in the Middle East, particularly Saudi Arabia; there are also major supplies in Venezuela, Iran and Russia. The fields there are generally smaller and development more costly, but the methods of exploration and production are mostly routine. The politics may be harder to manage.

The limits of exploration technologies have been extended in Alaska and the North Sea. Alaskan temperatures are so low that the ground is permanently frozen and oil cannot easily be piped. The North Sea has deep water and rough surfaces. The costs of finding and extracting this oil are much higher.

Other oil deposits are even more difficult to tap. There is oil beneath the major oceans, beyond the reach of existing drilling capabilities: at great cost, these capabilities could be extended to make exploration possible. In the tar sands in Venezuela and at Athabasca in Canada, there is enough oil to satisfy the demands of motorists, airlines and power stations for decades, even centuries; but the cost of extracting it is well above current oil prices.[2] The availability of oil is a commercial rather than a technological question. The reserves of oil which are available at $100 a barrel are many times the reserves available at $10 a barrel. And the more oil is needed, the more of these different sources of supply are required. If the demand for oil were lower, it would be met entirely from the Middle East. As things are, we draw on Alaska and the North Sea, but not the ocean beds or the Athabascan tar sands.[3]

Milk

New Zealand has a wet, temperate climate and more than enough land for 4 million people. There were no cows in New Zealand until European settlers arrived just over 150 years ago. But today there are more cows than people. New Zealand is ideal dairying country. The lush grass on which cows thrive is also found in Argentina and Ireland. But costs in these locations are not as low as in New Zealand. Argentina has good dairy land, but it is even better for beef cattle. Ireland's butter is expensive because the protectionist Common Agricultural Policy means that Irish production is intensive and in small units.[4]

For both oil and milk, we can illustrate how much oil or milk can be produced and at what price. If prices are very low, only the most accessible oil will be drilled and the best dairy land farmed – Arabian oil, New Zealand dairying. The higher the price, the more extensive the range of products that will be required.

Electricity

Nuclear power stations are extremely costly to construct and to shut down. But once they have 'gone critical' – the nuclear reaction in the core of the plant has begun– they can generate heat and hence electricity more or less continuously with only small additions of uranium. Their operating costs are very low. Gas and oil stations are much cheaper to build, but since they must constantly be supplied with fuel their running costs are higher than those of nuclear plant. In general, newer stations are more efficient, and older plant is used sparingly. Plant can be labelled according to a merit order – the plant with the lowest running costs at the top, the plant with the highest running costs at the bottom. The more electricity is required, the higher the costs of the plant from which it is generated.[5]

Video Cassette Recorders

For oil, milk and electricity, higher production entails higher cost. The supply curve for a manufactured good like a VCR is different. The first domestic video recorders were manufactured and distributed by an American company, Ampex, in 1963. They cost $30,000 in Niemann Marcus (Texas' most expensive department store) and after five years around 500 had been sold. In the 1970s Japanese manufacturers established a consumer market for video cassette recorders.[6]

The more oil or milk is required, the more it costs per litre, because higher-cost production must be employed. But the cost of making video recorders falls as the rate of output increases. It falls because there are economies of scale in their assembly and in the production of components. The cost of making video recorders has also fallen because so many video recorders have been made. Most of the things that could go wrong with video recorders, or in the process of making video recorders, have by now gone wrong and been fixed. The accumulated experience of video recorder manufacturers has lowered the cost of production, and steady technological advance has reduced the cost of both components and assembly. These three sources of falling costs – greater annual output, greater cumulative output, and technological advance – can all operate independently of each other, but in practice they have been closely linked.[7]

Demand

Oil

There is a hierarchy of uses and substitution options in the oil business. Aeroplanes require high quality kerosene. Automobiles run on gasoline, though we can choose between gas guzzlers and superminis. Cars could run on gas, and less easily on electricity. Electricity generation is a major user of oil, but electricity can also be produced from gas, coal or nuclear fission. The lower the cost of oil, the further down the list of uses and substitution options consumers go.

Milk

Like oil, milk has a hierarchy of uses. We can do a lot with milk. We can drink it fresh. We can subject it to heat treatment that will keep liquid milk pure, though not nice to drink, for several months. We can make it into butter or cheese. We can turn it into powder, which is cheap and easy to transport. We can turn it into caseinate, which is a form of plastic – shirt buttons may be made of milk.

And the more milk we have, the more of these things we shall do. But there are many decreasingly valuable uses for milk. Fresh milk really has no substitute. Milk products, like butter and cheese, do. Milk is turned into powder for animal feedstuffs or industrial uses only when there is major oversupply.

Electricity

It takes a power cut to remind us of the myriad ways we use electricity. It costs 2p–3p per hour to power a personal computer. Not many people would prefer a clockwork PC, or switch off their computer to economize on electricity. Computers, televisions, vacuum cleaners are high value uses for electricity – the cost of the electricity is small relative to the value of the output. But there are plenty of dispensable uses for electricity – there are many alternatives to electric space heating, and we really ought to turn off that light.

Video Cassette Recorders

Domestic video cassette recorders were introduced in the UK in 1971. A machine cost around £2,500 at 2002 prices, and they were bought by rich people and the gadget-conscious. The evolution of demand followed a common pattern for consumer goods. Prices gradually fell, and the market for the product grew steadily. Demand increased for a bit, but eventually most of those who might ever want to buy a machine had one. Sales actually declined, sustained only by replacement demand and second purchases.

Matching Supply and Demand for Electricity

Until 1990, the control room of the National Grid received full details of the availability and running costs of all the power stations in England

and Wales, which were linked in a single network. Operators were constantly provided with information about actual and expected demand for electricity. As demand varied, they would instruct stations to produce power, or to stop doing so.

Demand for electricity is very low during the night. Only nuclear stations operate then. As morning approaches other plant is put on standby. In Britain, demand for electricity is usually at its highest in the early morning, when households prepare to go to work at the same time as offices and factories prepare to receive them. As this process builds up, more stations are called on to produce. Peak demand for electricity each year usually falls on a cold winter's morning, when users rise reluctantly from bed and additionally turn on a fan heater. There are also freak spikes in demand, as when half-time in the World Cup final prompts 5 million households to switch on kettles.

Demand for commodities often has a time dimension. Fresh milk needs to be drunk within a few days, and demand for it is stable through the year. But the lactation of cows is not stable. The plentiful milk supplies that are available in spring and summer are used to make butter and cheese, and, if need be, powder and caseinate.

Storing milk is problematic – the EU had butter and powder mountains because this was the cheapest means of storing milk. Storing electricity is almost impossible. A century's technological advance has not come up with a cost-effective battery, and the best way of storing electricity today is to pump water up a hill and let it run down again when you want the power.

The National Grid represented successful central planning. The system which failed so badly in determining the overall direction of the industry worked well at this detailed operational level. There were occasional attempts by interest groups and government to interfere with the merit order – in particular to persuade the Central Electricity Generating Board to burn more coal – but these were mostly rebuffed. This planning system worked because the engineers who controlled it were competent and honest, and were supplied with accurate information about operating conditions in all the fifty or so power stations. It helped that the whole network was under the single ownership of the British government.[8] Problems of incentive compatibility had largely been solved.

In 1987 the government decided that it would sell the power stations, and end unified ownership and control. This decision seemed perverse to many people in the electricity industry, and risked the loss of efficiencies which came from the operation of the merit order. Could another scheme be devised which would do the same job? The government's objective was to find a market mechanism that would preserve the efficiency characteristic of the merit order. The answer was to establish an electricity pool. The owners of each power station would make bids into the pool. Their bid would state the generating capacity they offered, and the price at which they would sell. The engineers of the central control room were replaced by traders, who reviewed the bids. As demand fluctuated, the traders bought supplies just sufficient to meet demand. The highest bid they accepted was called the pool price, and all successful bidders received the pool price.[9]

At first sight, it might seem more appropriate – and cheaper – to pay bidders only the price they had quoted. But the designers of the pool had thought carefully about the issue of incentive compatibility. If the pool paid each bidder their asking price, then the owner of each station would try to guess the maximum the pool would be prepared to pay, and pitch their bid at around that level. Sometimes their guesses would be right, sometimes wrong. On average, the bids would be higher than those made under the pool system. The problem of pool design is very similar to the problem of auction design at Christie's and Sotheby's. Under the pool arrangements, it made sense for each station to bid its actual costs. A moment with pencil and paper confirms this property. It is also true, but harder to show, that the pool mechanism is the only system which is incentive compatible.

The Market for Oil

There is a 'merit order' for oil, just as there is a merit order for electricity. Electricity is a very special commodity, because even a transitory imbalance between supply and demand is intolerable. But small differences in the supply and demand for oil can be accommodated for a time without great inconvenience. There is always oil in transit at sea and it can be stored in tanks and refineries.

So there does not need to be a mechanism in the oil market like the central control room of the National Grid,[10] and there is none. In Europe, the largest market is at Rotterdam. There are other oil markets at the International Petroleum Exchange, just by the Tower of London, or in the New York Mercantile Exchange (NYMEX), in the World Financial Center in Manhattan. Most oil trading does not take place on any of these exchanges. Oil companies make contracts with each other, and their own subsidiaries, and long-term agreements with producers and customers. But the price in active markets such as Rotterdam or NYMEX is the principal influence on the terms of these trades. The price of oil varies according to quality and its location. Brent (North Sea) crude commands a higher price than oil at Dubai. The market equivalent of leaving a long queue to join a shorter one is called arbitrage: the speculative activity of buying in one market while selling the same commodity in another at a slightly higher price. Where there is more than one market in the same commodity, as for petroleum, arbitrage ensures that prices in all markets are similar, just as activism in the supermarket equalizes waiting-times.

In 1973 the Organization of Petroleum Exporting Countries (OPEC) decided to refuse to supply oil except at a much higher price than previously. This disrupted the oil industry's merit order. It stimulated supplies from areas – such as Alaska and the North Sea – outside OPEC's control and, in the end, probably brought little benefit to the countries that had provoked the refusal.[11] In the meantime it reduced the efficiency of world oil supply.

The pool price in electricity was the price needed to bring forward enough supply to meet demand: the world oil price is also the price needed to bring forward enough supply to meet demand. If the world oil price is $25 per barrel, that is because it needs to be high enough to make exploration in Alaska and the North Sea worthwhile – we need that oil – but not so high that it makes production in Athabasca profitable – we don't need oil costing that much. At $25 per barrel, however, low-cost supplies – such as those of the Middle East – are very profitable.

The competitive oil market has, without any intervention, the property of incentive compatibility that the government was anxious to create in the electricity pool. The market price – $25 per barrel – is a single price, paid by all buyers and received by all sellers. That common price is less than some buyers would be willing to pay. Most sellers would still be willing to sell their oil at a lower price. The difference between the maximum price a buyer might pay and the market price is called consumer surplus – the buyer's gain from trade. The difference between the minimum price a seller would accept and the market price is called economic rent. It is consumer surplus that makes us happy, and economic rent that makes us rich. I shall return to consumer surplus in Chapter 18, and economic rent in Chapter 24.

The trading arrangements in the electricity market were invented by a government which set out to create a market structure where none had existed before. It is rare for markets to develop in this way. The oil market was not invented: it emerged as the world oil business evolved. Most markets emerged spontaneously to match scarce resource to competing ends. Some emerged centuries ago.

The Market for Flowers

Just over the border into Italy from the French Riviera is the Autostrada dei Fiori – the motorway of flowers. The hillsides along the Ligurian coast are covered with plastic and glass. The flowers are transported each morning to the market at San Remo, and the market is a stunning spectacle. Full of colour and the babble of excited Italian traders. Tens of thousands of blooms change hands every day. The price of each kind of flower can change in the course of the morning if there is an imbalance between supply and demand. Prices vary as particular flowers move in and out of season. At periods of exceptional demand, like Christmas and Easter, prices rise across the board.

If no one has much influence over the price in a competitive market, how is the price determined? In one sense, prices are not fixed at all; no co-ordinating mechanism, like the control room of the National Grid, balances supply and demand in the San Remo flower market, nor does any agency determine the price of different blooms. The municipal market rents space to traders and regulates their behaviour, but that is all – just as in the public marketplaces of ancient Athens.

Within the apparent chaos, noise and bustle of the San Remo market, a spontaneous order is formed every day. At the beginning of the morning flowers arrive from a thousand locations along the coast. At its end, they are on their way to an even larger number of destinations across Europe. The assortment in arriving trucks matches the production of individual growers. The assortment in leaving trucks matches the requirements of individual florists.

There are only prices for individual transactions, and yet there is a typical price, a market price that equates supply and demand. In the oil market, the reports of the Petroleum Argus are regarded as definitive of oil prices. San Remo does not have even that degree of formality. Traders in similar products are generally grouped together. This enables them to keep an eye on each other's prices and each other's stocks. They know that they will not sell much if their prices are above their competitors, and they also know that they must dispose of their stock by the end of the morning.

Most traders attend the market every day, and use their experience to judge the level of stocks and the strength of demand. They judge each other, too: some traders will be particularly influential. A market price for each bloom emerges from the balance of supply and demand, but an experienced trader will leave with a slightly higher average payment for his flowers, and a skilled buyer will pay slightly less. Knowledge of other flower markets will be helpful, but not very helpful. It is local experience that is really valuable.

Yet a first-time trader in San Remo will not do badly if he simply keeps an eye on what other people are doing and buys or sells at the going price. Others will nudge the price up, or down, in response to supply and demand. These more experienced traders will do better, but not much. The spontaneous order of the San Remo market is similar to the spontaneous order of the supermarket queue. In the supermarket, a few activists who watch the length of neighbouring queues determine waiting-times. At San Remo, similar activism by skilled traders determines the price. Their skill and experience are specific to the San Remo flower market. None of them has any extensive knowledge of the factors that determine supply and demand in European horticulture, or even of other flower markets, such as those in Holland.[12]

Many other markets function like this. In some – such as markets for aeroplanes or ships – there are brokers. Brokers are professional watchers of the market. They advise a buyer or a seller about the price to expect. They will put buyers and sellers in touch with each other. Brokers normally live by charging commissions on deals they facilitate. Sometimes brokers become market makers, who risk their own capital by buying in the expectation of selling on later at a profit, as in the used-car market.[13]

Trading at San Remo is about as close to a perfectly competitive market as we find. No individual buyer or seller has much influence over the price. And trading at San Remo is also close to being incentive compatible. There is rarely much to be gained by strategic behaviour. A person wanting to buy a lot of flowers would be unwise to walk into the market and announce it. But subtle ways of beating the market are hard to devise and likely to backfire. And concern for reputation with fellow traders also encourages incentive compatibility.

Virtual Markets

Once, almost all competitive markets had physical locations, like the San Remo flower market. There are still many markets like this. In London, Covent Garden is the trading centre for fruit and vegetables, Smithfield for meat, Billingsgate for fish.[14] Used cars are bought and sold in auctions around the country. Local cattle and grain markets have existed for centuries. In Thomas Hardy's *Far From the Madding Crowd* Bathsheba Everdene hires her shepherd, Gabriel Oak, at a country market.

These markets were social as well as economic events. The social context of the market supported its economic function by establishing personal relationships and facilitating the exchange of information. Less than fifty years ago, dock workers would be hired on a daily basis by employers who matched the supply of labour to the number of ships in port. But with decasualization of dock labour the last markets in which workers were bought and sold like physical commodities were closed. Spot markets in labour are now more or less dead, although, as at Casterbridge, the annual meetings of the American Economic Association incorporate a hiring fair at which young Ph.D.s parade before their prospective Bathshebas.

Many markets are securities markets; traders buy and sell paper which confers the right to physical commodities, rather than the commodities themselves. So people can trade even if they do not actually own the oil they sell, or want the oil they buy. Trade on these exchanges is in standard contracts, such as 'a barrel of Brent crude'.

Many markets, including most securities markets, had physical locations even if the commodities traded were not on display. People would buy and sell ships on the floor of the Baltic Exchange. Shares were traded on the floors of the New York and London Stock Exchanges. The large Room at Lloyd's was the centre of the London – and for long the world – insurance market. The expectation that markets would have a physical location changed with the invention of the telephone, which made it easy for people who were not in the same place to negotiate deals. But communication by telephone was one-to-one. Only with the development of modern electronic systems was it possible to secure access to information about other trades and other traders – the access which San Remo traders enjoy by watching each other – without an actual physical meeting-place.

The inside pages of the *Financial Times* or *Wall Street Journal* contain lists of prices in literally hundreds of markets – electricity, milk and oil; coffee, copper and pork bellies; securities markets, bonds and foreign currencies. Even the risk of a cold winter or a Japanese earthquake can be traded.[15]

Today, electronic trading has taken over most of these markets. What were once busy, jostling, trading floors are now eerie, empty museum pieces. A 'trading floor' is no longer an exchange in which buyers and sellers clamour for each other's attention. It is home to rows of screens on which traders place their orders. The habit of dealing in big rooms remains – because the marketplace still requires the exchange of information as well as the exchange of commodities. But today these big rooms are the private property of organizations such as Goldman Sachs and Morgan Stanley, not the collective property of NYMEX or the London Stock Exchange. These traders deal with their counterparts in other, similar, rooms. At the height of Internet mania, it was widely asserted that most trading would soon be electronic. Electronic trading works well for standardized commodities in perfectly competitive markets. One dollar is much the same as any other dollar. But to trade remotely it is necessary to know exactly what is for sale and that the reputation of the other party is good, or that some exchange or intermediary will guarantee performance.

So it is hard to imagine that San Remo will go electronic. Wholesale buyers of flowers, or meat or fish, will want to see what they are buying, because making these assessments is a key business skill. It was possible, if demeaning, to buy and sell dock labour in a market-place because what was bought and sold was – literally – a pair of hands. But even there employers knew that some workers were stronger or more reliable and branded others as troublemakers. Almost every technological and institutional development in a modern econ-omy is towards greater differentiation of products. In Chapter 18, I shall discuss how this changes things.

Rigging Competitive Markets

No trader has significant influence on price in a perfectly competitive market. All traders wish they could have significant influence on price. In 1979 a fabulously rich Texan family, the Hunts, tried to take control of the world market for silver. For a time, they succeeded in raising the price substantially, and people queued to melt down their family heirlooms. But in the end billions of Hunt dollars were not enough to establish a monopoly, and the price of silver (and the Hunt family fortune) collapsed.[16]

Governments frequently intervene in securities markets, to try to influence the price of their own bonds or their country's exchange rate. Since central banks can print money it might seem that their influence on markets would always be decisive. If politicians were willing to make absolute and unlimited commitments, this might be true. But they rarely are. The International Tin Council was established by governments of tin-producing and -consuming countries with the good intention of aiding poor tin producers and stabilizing their receipts.[17] The Council ran out of money with which to buy tin, and entered into forward commitments[18] to buy still more tin. Seeing a growing black hole, the member governments refused to provide money to enable the Council to honour its contracts and the Council and the tin price collapsed. The diamond market, managed by de Beers for decades, is almost the only commodity market in which a trader has successfully influenced the price over an extended period.[19]

On 'Black Wednesday' in 1992, the financier George Soros gambled that he could borrow more sterling to exchange for foreign currencies than the British government would be willing to buy to support its own exchange rate. Soros won his bet, and Britain was forced to leave the European Monetary System. The reputation of the Prime Minister, John Major, and the Chancellor of the Exchequer, Norman Lamont, never recovered from this debacle.[20]

Not all government interventions fail. The Asian crisis hit all securities markets in 1997. The Hong Kong Monetary Authority knew that its financial system was stronger than those of its neighbours and bought shares on the Hong Kong stock exchange. The Authority sold these shares subsequently at a substantial profit, much of it derived from Soros and another speculator, Julian Robertson. After this debacle, Soros and Robertson announced their retirements from fund management and returned money to their investors.[21] But even the Chinese government blinked. It decided it had risked enough, withdrew market support, and allowed prices (temporarily) to fall.[22]

The complex structure of the electricity pool was intended to reproduce the efficiencies of the Central Electricity Generating Board's planning system – the merit order – by an incentive-compatible mechanism in a competitive market. The scheme would probably have worked if each of the fifty or so power stations had been under separate ownership. But the government's restructuring of the industry did not go so far. Most of the key stations were owned by two firms – National Power or Powergen. These generators quickly discovered that they could keep prices high by putting in bids above the cost of production. The outcomes were not incentive compatible or efficient, and electricity prices rose higher than they need have done. In 2001 the pool was scrapped and replaced by arrangements much more similar to those of the world oil market.[23]

Incentive compatibility is a key objective of a market economy and a specific objective of the electricity pool. But it is only perfectly competitive markets that achieve full incentive compatibility. Once sellers or buyers are sufficiently large for their behaviour to influence the price, they begin to behave strategically.

EasyJet

In perfectly competitive markets, the price that equates supply and demand emerges through spontaneous order, as at San Remo. In markets that are less than perfectly competitive, a seller decides what price to charge. Balancing supply and demand becomes a business objective, rather than the outcome of a decentralized process. One of the most sophisticated such markets is the market for airline seats.

The Boeing 737 is the most widely used commercial airliner. It can seat between 100 and 140 passengers, depending on how much legroom is allowed. The low-cost airline EasyJet flies only Boeing 737 aircraft with 137 seats. EasyJet, and other airlines, have more or less the same number of planes and seats available every day. Once they have decided the size of their fleet, their capacity is essentially fixed. But demand varies widely. Many people want to fly to Nice on the Thursday evening before Easter. Very few want to do so at midday on a Tuesday in November. So EasyJet sets the price according to the level of anticipated demand. I myself have paid £180 for the first of these flights and £17.50 for the second.

At first sight, the problem which EasyJet faces looks very similar to the problem of the San Remo flower-seller. Empty seats on planes are as useless and as unprofitable as flowers left wilting when the San Remo market is closed. But San Remo is a competitive market, in which no one fixes the price. EasyJet faces only a few competitors, and although it monitors their actions carefully, the services they offer are not identical.

So EasyJet and all other airlines have sophisticated computer packages – yield-management systems – designed to enable them to monitor the balance between supply and demand. These systems are fed basic information – when Easter falls, the date of the Monaco Grand Prix, what happened last year. The objective is not to fill the plane, but to maximize revenues from the flight. An airline would rather have some empty seats than a planeful of passengers all on discounted tickets. It hopes to sell seats at high prices to business passengers in a hurry and at lower prices to price-sensitive tourists. Many cheap fares require passengers to stay for a Saturday night. The airline does not care where you spend your Saturday, but business travellers would usually prefer to spend it at home and tourists at their holiday destination.

Spontaneous order – the disciplined and effective matching of buyers and sellers which emerges from the apparent chaos of the San Remo flower market – is often found in competitive markets, in which products are homogeneous and market trading is fragmented. Once products become differentiated, and sellers have sufficient market share to influence price, the problem of setting price and managing demand is very different, and more complex. And co-ordination may actually be more difficult to achieve, as anyone who has experienced an overbooked flight knows.

Oil and milk, electricity and VCRs, flowers and airlines seats, are typical commodities bought and sold in competitive markets. But these are not what Bloomberg television means by 'the markets'. The traders whom they serve deal in risk and in money. The very particular markets for these commodities are the subject of the next two chapters.

12

Markets in Risk

From the Rialto to the North Sea

The Merchant of Venice stood on the Rialto, waiting nervously for his ships to return to Venice. In the city Shylock sharpened his knife in anticipation of a pound of Antonio's flesh. Only later in the Venetian Republic was marine insurance invented. This enabled the risks faced by merchants to be spread over many individuals. All could sleep easily in their beds, knowing that no single event could expose them to perils as grave as Antonio's. The market was developed further in Edward Lloyd's coffee house in the City of London. Lloyd's of London is still a centre of the marine insurance market today.

In 1988, a gas explosion destroyed Piper Alpha, a North Sea oil rig. One hundred and sixty-seven men were killed. Others were plucked by helicopter from the freezing sea. An emergency clean-up limited pollution, but when the costs of the destruction of the rig, compensation paid to victims, and production losses were added together, the total exceeded £1 billion. The rig operators, Occidental Petroleum, made one of the largest insurance claims related to a single incident. Much of this insurance was placed at Lloyd's. As had been traditional since the gatherings in Edward's coffee house, many different Lloyd's insurers (underwriting syndicates) had agreed to meet a share of the claim. But the market had grown more complex and sophisticated in the intervening centuries. Some syndicates had reinsured their risks. Reinsurance means that another insurer agrees to meet a share of a claim when it exceeds an agreed sum. The reinsurer acts as insurer of an insurer. A different form of reinsurance was known as an excess-of-loss policy. If the total losses of a syndicate from all claims, whatever their origins, became too great another syndicate would pay the balance.

The size of the Piper Alpha loss meant that it cascaded round the market. The first claims were directly related to reimbursing Occidental. But then, through reinsurance and excess-of-loss policies, many more insurance claims at Lloyd's were triggered by the losses of the primary insurers. The total value of claims at Lloyd's arising from the Piper Alpha disaster was £16 billion, and the vast majority of these were claims by one insurer against another. Syndicates which had written excess-of-loss policies for other syndicates had, without knowing it, insured Piper Alpha over and over again. Far from spreading risks over many people, the insurance market had concentrated them on a few. Piper Alpha was the beginning of a process which cost some members of Lloyd's their wealth – even their lives and sanity. The process brought the market close to collapse, and ended the system of insurance underwriting by well-off individuals (Lloyd's 'Names').[1]

There is something very odd about this story. Early markets in risk – marine insurance – enabled vulnerable individuals to spread and share their risks.[2] Centuries later, when markets had become more developed, more sophisticated and more costly, they operated in just the opposite way. The risk associated with the Piper Alpha disaster was transferred from an organization well able to assess and bear it – a $1 billion loss would leave only a small hole in Occidental Petroleum's balance sheet – to vulnerable individuals who were quite incapable of knowing what the risks were or dealing with them when they hit. In Chapter 19, I shall try to resolve the puzzle.

Markets in Risk

The economic approach to uncertainty sees risk as a commodity like any other. There are natural calamities, whose consequences cannot easily be avoided – events like adverse weather or the onset of disease. But our economic and social organization manufactures risks, as it manufactures other commodities. Business necessarily involves the risk of accident at work, the risk of unemployment, the risk that a venture will fail. Risks can be bought and sold, so that every risk has its market and its market price. Trading risks may yield gains from exchange, for the same reasons as other trades yield gains from exchange – differences in preferences associated with differences in capabilities and benefits from specialization.

Some people like taking risks and others don't, just as some people like apples and others don't. The risks in our lives may not be risks we want to hold, as the apples that fall in our orchards may not be the fruit we want to eat. Capacity to bear risk varies. The richer we are, the better placed we are to face the risk of a given loss. These differences in appetite for risk are differences in capabilities. Some people have professional skills in the measurement and evaluation of risk – benefits from specialization.

The gentlemen in Edward Lloyd's coffee house probably fell into all these categories. They enjoyed the gamble. They were affluent and did not expect to be greatly incommoded if the ships they had insured did not return; they spent agreeable days studying ship movements and tides. The merchants whose risks they bought felt differently. Insurance is partly a matter of transferring risks to those who would prefer to carry them. But its most important function is risk-spreading. A risk that is large in relation to the wealth of the individual or organization concerned – the loss of a ship, damage to a house – can be borne with equanimity if it is widely shared. The value of my house is a large proportion of my own wealth but a tiny fraction of the total wealth of the shareholders of an insurance company.

Michel Albert has caricatured the twin origins of the modern insurance industry.[3] English gentlemen met at Lloyd's to speculate on the fate of ships; Swiss villagers gathered together to agree to help each other if their cow died (and it is true that even today England and Switzerland are major insurance centres). Between them they had discovered risk-preference and risk-spreading as reasons for risk trading.

It may also make sense to buy and sell risks if the risk you buy offsets a risk which you already hold. In the summer of 2000 Corney and Barrow, who operate a chain of wine bars in the City of London, made a contract with Enron: the company agreed to pay £15,000 on each Thursday or Friday between June and September on which the temperature in London did not rise above 24 °C.[4] If the weather was cold, fewer City office workers would linger after work to enjoy Corney and Barrow's wine. But, when they went home and switched on their heating, the demand for Enron's gas would increase. The two risks offset each other. By exchanging risks each company might add stability to its earnings.

Trading on Differences in Risk Assessment

But most of the trades in risk markets are not the result of different tolerances for risk, the need to spread a risk, or the opportunity to hedge. Most people who trade risks do so because they think they have made a better assessment of the risk than others.

Punters at a betting shop perusing *Racing Post* bet when they think the odds are in their favour. Bookmakers, as the name suggests, make a book on the basis of the different opinions of their customers. They establish a market in guesses about the outcome of the race. They vary the odds on each horse according to the weight of money placed. If one horse attracts support, bookmakers shorten its odds and lengthen odds on others, hoping to attract a wider variety of bets. This is the process by which the odds constantly change in the minutes before the start of the race. The bookmaker's ideal is to establish a position in which he will win regardless of the outcome of the race.[5]

The 'market' in bets on horses is one in which risks are traded between people with different assessments of the same uncertain event – the result of the five o'clock race at Ascot. The 'market price' – the odds on each horse – is an average of the assessments by many different punters of the likelihood that the horse will win. The more money people are willing to place, the more their views contribute to the average.

Stock markets and other securities markets, such as the foreign exchange market, function in the same way. Prospects for any particular company or currency are always uncertain. Some people rate the company or country more highly than others. The market price is the average of everyone's valuations, weighted by the amount of money that players are able to mobilize behind their views. Just as the bookmaker determines the odds when he sets his book, market makers determine the price by balancing the supply and demand of buyers and sellers who each make different assessments of the same risks.

Bookmakers try to avoid taking positions on the races they cover because they know, even if their punters do not, that backing horses is usually a mug's game. In financial markets, it is much more common for the banks, securities houses and others who make markets to form their own views on the likely movements in the assets in which they deal. Most financial institutions believe this activity is profitable for them, even after estimating the costs of the exposures they run, and perhaps this is true.

Enron began as market maker but became an increasingly important energy trader. But profits from this source were harder to earn than Enron executives had hoped or their shareholders wanted to believe. Failing to make profits in its business, the company adopted complex accounting devices to manufacture them. The collapse of the company in November 2001 was the largest corporate bankruptcy in history.

When people trade because one has a greater ability to bear the risk than the other, the exchange is mutually beneficial – as it was for Braque and Roux, or for the San Remo flower-traders or those who bought and sold in the electricity pool. But transactions in markets based on differences in the perception of the same situation by different people are not like that. One party's gain is the other's loss. We never know in advance who loses and who gains. The answer will be clearer, though not always certain, with hindsight.[6]

Efficient Markets

The efficiency of perfectly competitive markets is the subject of Chapter 15. In risk markets the term 'market efficiency' has a specific, and narrow, technical meaning. Efficiency describes how the market assimilates information about the risks which are being traded. Horses have 'form', which is reported in detail in the sporting press. Punters often believe they have special knowledge about particular horses: sometimes this is true, mostly it is not.

Companies file accounting records, and their share price histories are available from services like Bloomberg and Reuters. Analysts report on the outlook for individual shares. Economic prospects for different countries are described in many public documents. Some traders believe they are particularly well informed about the activities of other traders. Some analysts believe they have insights into businesses or economies which are denied to others. Sometimes this is true, mostly it is not.

The efficient market hypothesis is that all this information forms the background to the risk assessment of market traders, and all these assessments are weighted and incorporated in the market price of an uncertain event. All available information about a risk is already reflected in the price of the associated security. In an efficient market it is pointless to act on the basis of information such as 'Lochnagel put in a strong finish in the last race', 'General Electric has excellent management', 'Demand for mobile phones will continue to grow' or 'Dr Greenspan is an outstanding chairman of the Federal Reserve Board'. These observations are well known, have influenced other people's assessments and are 'in the price'. They are the reasons why the odds on Lochnagel are short, the price of General Electric shares is high, mobile phone companies trade at large multiples of their current earnings and the dollar is strong.

There is powerful evidence to support the efficient market hypothesis. The theory predicts that the prices of risks will follow a 'random walk'. This is a process in which the next step is equally likely to be in any direction. Many physical processes have these characteristics, such as the movements of particles in liquids. This is an area where models derived from statistical mechanics seem to work – the Black–Scholes model described below is grounded in the analysis of physical systems. And numerous statistical analyses of prices in markets for securities and commodities have confirmed that they display the characteristics of a random walk. In an early test of the theory, the statistician Maurice Kendall discovered that all but one of the series he studied fitted the random-walk prediction.[7] It emerged that the one which did not was not in fact a series of actual market transactions but had been prepared as an average of estimated market prices. This is the kind of satisfying confirmation of a theory which physicists often experience but is rarely available in the social sciences.

The efficient market hypothesis invites a sceptical view of claims of the ability of experts to make money themselves – and even more, perhaps, of their ability to make money for other people – by trading risks. This scepticism is more readily applied to racing tipsters than to professional investment managers, but there are grounds for applying it to both. On average, investment managers do not outperform a random choice of stocks and the past outperformance of such managers is a poor guide to their future success.[8]

Derivatives

In insurance markets, securities exchanges, betting shops, one person sells a risk to another. Derivative markets enable risks to be divided, packaged and repackaged. If Antonio's ship was loaded with a cargo of cloves, Antonio incurred at least three risks – loss of the ship, delay to the ship and fluctuations in the price of cloves. Different people might be better placed to assess and assume these different components of Antonio's overall risk. A marine engineer might assess the stability of the hull, a meteorologist could calculate the state of the tides, and a spice merchant would be well informed about supply and demand for cloves.

Or there might be a market in participations in Antonio's venture. This would give the holder a share in the overall profit or loss. The value of this share would be determined by external events as well as Antonio's shrewdness as a businessman. But this primary market could also give rise to many derivative markets. There might be separate markets for insurance against loss and insurance against delay. Antonio might agree to sell his cloves, when they arrive in three months' time, at a price agreed today. This is a forward contract, of the type which the International Tin Council failed to honour. Or Antonio might make a contract under which he will receive a minimum price for his cloves even if the market price has fallen (a put option). If only he had bought such insurance, and a forward contract or a put, he could have slept comfortably at night knowing that he had secured the certain ability to repay Shylock's bond.

Excess-of-loss insurers of Piper Alpha had given a put option to the primary syndicates, which would cap their losses at a fixed sum. A call option gives the right, but not the obligation, to buy something in future at a price fixed in the contract today. If you buy a call, you benefit from price rises but are not exposed to price falls. Of course, you pay a price for either a put or a call option.

Modern portfolio theory – the mathematical analysis of risk markets – was developed at the University of Chicago from the 1950s to the 1970s. In 1973 Fischer Black and Myron Scholes[N] developed a model which allowed derivatives to be precisely valued.[9] The theory was quickly adopted on Wall Street, and the range of derivative securities grew in range and complexity. Derivative markets allow risks to be packaged and repackaged. They enable people to assemble portfolios of risks which meet their own specializations, differences in preferences and differences in capabilities. They also allow people to gamble on the belief that their own assessments of risks, different from the market average, are correct.

Financial market theory – the theory of risk markets – is the jewel in the crown of business economics. 'There is no other proposition in economics which has more solid empirical evidence supporting it than the Efficient Market Hypothesis.'[10] The theory combines technical sophistication with immediate practical application. In the 1990s its practitioners – often described as rocket scientists – were sought after for highly paid jobs in securities houses. Yet all is not entirely well with this theory, and the self-confidence of its practitioners is diminishing. I shall return to this in Chapter 19.

13

Markets in Money

Market economies trade flowers. They trade electricity. They trade risks. They also trade money itself. Money is different from these other commodities because it has no intrinsic worth. Money is the unit of account in which Lester Thurow keeps score: the medium of exchange by which we measure the price of everything else.

But there are many different units of account and mediums of exchange: dollars and euros, Australian dollars and Singapore dollars, pesos and złotys. So we trade one money against another – dollars for euros. Money is also a store of value: we need money tomorrow as well as money today. We buy and sell different currencies in foreign exchange markets; we exchange money at different dates in money markets. These markets are regularly featured on Bloomberg television.

Foreign Exchange Markets

Man in Red Braces (MIRB): Great to have you on the show. What determines the rate of exchange between dollars and euros?

Salomon Merrill (SM): Supply and demand, demand and supply. In the short run, speculative supply and demand from losers like the people watching this programme. But in the long run, noise trading cancels out. What matters is supply and demand for goods and services sold in dollars relative to supply and demand for goods and services sold in euros.

MIRB: You mean, the relative economic performance of the US and Europe?

SM: To a degree. You and I can choose where we take our holidays, or even buy our books and CDs. On a much larger scale, businesses can choose where they buy goods and services and where they sell them. And businesses can arbitrage between alternative sources of supply.

MIRB: Arbitrage – that's a long word for our viewers.

SM: Arbitrage is buying cheap in one market and selling dear in another. Like moving to the shortest queue in the supermarket. Arbitrage prevents the prices of portable goods varying much.

MIRB: What about things like houses, or subway rides? You can't shift them across the Atlantic.

SM: No, and that's why purchasing power parity exchange rates can differ from official exchange rates. But there is a limit to how much they can differ. That's why the principal influence on the movements of different currencies in the long run is differences between countries in the rate of inflation.

MIRB: Purchasing power parity – that's a real mouthful. You can find an explanation in Chapter 3 of *The Truth About Markets*, but we're not allowed to mention that book on Bloomberg television. Do you have some tips for the good business folk watching?

SM: No, but their activities have a large effect on exchange rates. They arbitrage between assets. They can't simply lift a factory and locate it in another country. But businesses decide where to expand, where to locate. These choices create demands and supplies of currency. And treasurers – the people who buy and sell overnight money – decide whether to hold deposits in one currency or another.

MIRB: Aw, I thought they were just trying to make a buck.

SM: Yes, they look at the expected rate of return on the investment or the deposit. When businesses decide where to put their plants, they look at the level of prices and wages and assess the political, social and economic infrastructure. When treasurers decide where to hold liquid assets (or liabilities) they look at interest rate differentials and what they expect to happen to exchange rates over the next few months.

MIRB: So your recommendation is turn on, tune in . . .

SM: The exchange rate at any time is an average of all views in the market, just as the odds on a horse are the average of all assessments of its chances.

MIRB: You're not seriously comparing the markets with a horse race?
That was Salomon Merrill, foreign exchange economist at Lynch
J. P. Morgan.

Money Markets

Antonio was waiting nervously because he had guaranteed Shylock's
loan to Bassanio. The purpose of the most famous of all loans was
to finance Bassanio's profligacy rather than Antonio's business. In
Shakespeare's time the normal purpose of lending was to allow such
overspending. Antonio draws a sharp distinction between participat-
ing in a venture and lending at interest.[1] That distinction lay behind
the Christian prohibition of interest, which survives in other religions,
and restricted money-lending to excluded groups, such as Jews. In time
governments became the main profligates.

The substantive loan was from Tubal, a rich co-religionist of Shylock's, to Bassanio, a friend of Antonio. Bassanio could not borrow
directly because his credit was poor. Tubal did not lend directly because
he was not in the business of identifying and assessing credits. Interme-
diation was essential. Transactions between Antonio and Bassanio,
and between Shylock and Tubal, were relatively straightforward
because of their social relationships. The transaction between Antonio
and Shylock required notarization and security, and that was what
caused all the trouble.

In a money market, traders buy and sell money tomorrow, money
in five years' time, money in twenty-five years' time. The price of future
money is generally expressed as an annual rate of return. On the day
I am writing this the price of £1 tomorrow is 99.986 pence today. This
is an annual rate of interest of just over 5 per cent. At the same rate,
the price today of £1 in twenty-five years' time is 29p.

As in any other market, price is determined by supply and demand.
The overnight rate is volatile. Who borrows money tonight for repayment tomorrow? Mostly banks and businesses, which daily undertake
large numbers of financial transactions and need to balance their
books. But long-term interest rates are much more stable. Borrowers
for five or twenty-five years are households buying long-lived assets,

like cars or houses, and companies which need to finance working capital or new investment.

The supply of capital comes from people who have more money than they need, or who want to save for their retirement, their descendants, or a rainy day. The activities of intermediaries obscure this. We see Shylock trade with Antonio, but the underlying transaction is between Tubal and Bassanio. And as with Tubal, the supply comes from individual savings: as with Bassanio, demand comes from overspending and investment by households, businesses and governments.

The supply of capital is not very sensitive to its price. Interest rates do not have a large effect on how much we want or need to save: they may have more effect on how much we are *able* to save, or spend, because the cost of long-term borrowing such as mortgages varies.

Demand is very different. Much investment is insensitive to interest rates. But many households, most businesses and all governments have a supply of long-term projects which they could undertake if capital were sufficiently plentiful. Keynes once looked forward to an era in which more or less everything that could be built had been built.[2] But this seems fantasy. New technology creates new investment opportunities. We pull down the old and build anew. Many offices built in the 1960s have already been demolished. As a result, the price of capital – its long-term rate of return – never goes much below 2 per cent, or much above 4 per cent or so. I explain below what these figures mean and how they are calculated.

Banks

Capital markets match people who have money, like Tubal, with people who need it, like Bassanio. This matching is like dating, but riskier. If we want to lend, we must find a borrower; if we want to borrow, we must find a lender. We must judge the quality of our partner – more important for lenders than borrowers. And we have to explore whether both borrower and lender are willing to commit for the same period of time.

Banks solve all these problems. We don't have to seek a rich lender, or an indigent borrower: we go to the bank. The bank judges the credit-worthiness of its borrowers. As Tubal, we lend to Shylock rather than Bassanio and rely on Shylock's credit rather than Bassanio's. Since the bank has many borrowers and many lenders, it can allow us to withdraw our money without having to call in a loan ahead of time.

The first banks were established by rich individuals and the bank's reputation reflected their personal wealth and standing. In time, the credit of the bank reflected the reputation of the institution rather than that of its partners. Even today banks bear names that preserve the memory of their affluent founders – Barclays, Lloyds – or the grandeur of their pretensions – the Bank of America, the Royal Bank of Scotland – and have extravagant banking halls. They want to convince you that they will be there when you want your money back.

Banks discovered that if their credit was sufficiently strong, they could issue promises in excess of their readily available resources (or even their total resources). Antonio did not lend Bassanio the money himself because he did not have it. His ships were at sea or, as he subsequently discovered, at the bottom of it. Antonio instead gave Shylock a guarantee. Banks could issue guarantees without expecting more than a proportion of them to be called.

The banknote originated as a bank's promise to pay. And since people were confident of the bank's promise, its notes, as valuable as gold or silver but more convenient, circulated widely. Every aspect of economic life came to depend on these promises being honoured. From the earliest days of market economies, governments monitored the solvency and integrity of banks and limited their power to issue notes. The right to issue notes was very profitable and the risks of unregulated issue were large. Eventually note issue became a state monopoly.

With government as the only supplier of money came the ability to influence, even determine, the price of money. This power to fix interest rates was so central to economic life that it seemed it must be brought under political control. Central banks became agencies of government. The Bank of England was once the government's bank; the US Federal Reserve Board emerged from bodies established to support and supervise commercial banks; the Deutsche Bundesbank succeeded the currency board which was established in the British and American zones of Germany in 1948. In 1999 the newly established European Central Bank took on a similar role within the Eurozone.[3]

But even government cannot be trusted with the power to print money. The deliberate destruction of the German monetary system in 1923–4 wiped out the savings of many middle-class Germans and helped pave the road for Hitler.[4] The most successful central banks – the Federal Reserve Board and Bundesbank – have had considerable independence, and this lesson has been learned elsewhere. The Bank of England was given power to set interest rates in 1997, and the European Central Bank has similar freedom.

Central banks control the supply of money and the level of short-term interest rates. But long-term rates of return are still determined by the balance between the supply and demand for capital. Someone needs to own all the houses, offices and other buildings in the world, and all the assets of global businesses. And these assets are ultimately the total wealth of private individuals – the property companies, insurance companies and other institutions which appear on the ownership registers are all really all of us (plus Bill Gates and a few others). Long-term interest rates equate the supply and demand for all these assets. In this context, even the US government is small. When the Federal Reserve Board cut short-term interest rates from 6 per cent to 1.75 per cent in 2001, one of the most dramatic cuts in history, long-term interest rates moved hardly at all.

Bonds

Short-term interest rates are largely determined by the world's govern-ments. Long-term interest rates are determined by the underlying supply and demand for capital. The link between short and long rates is called the term structure of interest rates (Fig. 13.1). It is compiled by looking at rates of interest in the bond market.

Banks match borrowers and lenders, and allow lenders to get their money back before the borrowers repay. Bonds are another means of handling the same problem. The bond market is a secondary market, in which the right to receive payment of a loan can be sold to someone else. The price of a bond in this secondary market will not necessarily be the same as the original amount of the loan. The credit risk may have changed. As I write this, the debt of many telecoms companies

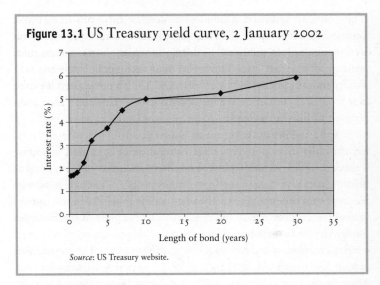

Figure 13.1 US Treasury yield curve, 2 January 2002

Source: US Treasury website.

can be bought for less than half its repayment value: these companies borrowed extravagantly and many people are now sceptical of their ability to repay.

A bond gets younger every day. A twenty-year bond, sold after fifteen years, is effectively a five-year bond. Its price will be similar to the price of new five-year bonds. If it is not, then arbitrage between the two types of bond will bring prices into line. If interest rates fall, existing bonds become more valuable; if interest rates rise, they fall in price.

In the nineteenth century, Bloomberg television would have been mainly concerned with the price of government bonds. These movements were tiny by modern standards, except in times of extreme instability – Bloomberg would have reported from Gettysburg and employed military strategists as talking heads. Holders of Confederate securities did as badly as holders of dot.com stocks.[5]

People buy bonds, or make deposits, because they want money tomorrow rather than today. But what they really want tomorrow is not money but the things which money can buy. If the value of money can change, that will influence the terms on which they buy bonds.

The nominal return on a bond or deposit is the extra money you receive when it is repaid. The real return is the extra value which you can obtain with that money. In Britain in August 1974 interest rates were around 12 per cent. This return may seem high, but in the next twelve months prices rose by 27 per cent. The £112 received for each £100 invested would only have bought goods that could have been had for £82 a year before.

In 1982 the British government issued bonds which offered a real return rather than a nominal one. Several other countries, including France, Sweden and the United States, have followed suit. No government can exactly guarantee to maintain people's purchasing power, because that depends on exactly what people think they want to buy. These bonds link interest and repayment to the price of commodities bought by an average household.

The creation of indexed stock was the decision of a government which had promised to reduce inflation and was backing its own rhetoric. Its confidence was vindicated by its performance. Over the following twenty years investors earned (and the government paid) 8.4 per cent per year on long-dated government bonds, and 4.7 per cent on Treasury bills (which have a maturity of ninety days). The return on indexed stock was only 3.4 per cent.[6]

Over the twenty years since indexed bonds were launched, the expected rate of return on them has been in the range 2–4 per cent. This figure is typical of the difference between inflation and nominal bond rates over a much longer period,[7] and indexed bonds issued by the governments of rich states are the safest investments available.

Selling Risk, Buying Capital

If a higher return is sought, with more risk, we go to the stock market. Over time, the distinction between lending and interest and sharing business risks became blurred. Businesses needed to trade in both risk and capital. They sold risk to spread and diversify the results of business ventures. They bought capital to finance plant, buildings and stocks of commodities.

Buying risk and selling capital are different functions, but there is logic in asking the same people to do both. Anyone who assumes the risks of a business will be expected to pay up if things go wrong. The Lloyd's insurance market, which covered Piper Alpha, separated the acceptance of risk from the provision of capital. The 'Names' did not have to put up much money, simply to show that, as wealthy gentlemen (or women), they had means to do so if required. After Piper Alpha, and other disasters at Lloyd's, the money proved difficult to collect. Some Names did not have it, and others were slow to pay, or hired lawyers to explain why they should not pay. Today Lloyd's, like other businesses, covers its risks from money subscribed in advance: capital must be sold when risk is bought.

Still, different people have different appetites for buying risk and selling capital. Some may have little capital, but be willing to take high risks. Others want to sell capital, but do not want to buy risks. Financial intermediaries repackage securities to establish different combinations of risk and return. Some repackaging meets consumer demand. Much is smoke and mirrors, designed to encourage people to buy things they would not buy if they understood them, as with the Lloyd's spiral.[8]

Originally a shareholder would provide a proportion of the outlays of a venture and receive a share of the returns. Shareholders bought the risk and supplied the capital in equal proportions. Profit was both a reward for risk and a return on capital. As business became more complex, investors knew less about businesses in which they had placed money. Business speculation without ruin became attainable with the invention of limited liability. The scene was set for the development of modern stock markets.

The Changing Role of Stock Markets

The modern shareholder is very different from a participant in a venture like Antonio's, who put up a share of the outlays and received a share of the revenues. The stock market today, like the bond market, is principally a secondary market. This enables investors to withdraw their money without obliging the company to repay it. An initial public offering – the introduction of a new company to the stock exchange – usually raises some fresh capital from new shares, but its main function is to establish a market in these secondary participations. Because there is a secondary market, businesses can expand and grow: they do not have to return funds to investors whenever their ship comes in. Modern companies can expect to have an indefinite life. Their shareholders receive dividends, regular distributions of the company's profits. The value of a share rests on the dividends they can expect to receive, just as the value of a bond is the flow of interest payments.

However, many companies, especially in the United States, pay no dividends.[9] Even though Microsoft is one of the most profitable and valuable companies in the world, it has never paid a dividend. Why would anyone buy its shares? The company has earnings and assets. This gives value to the shares even if the company does not pass any of that value on to its shareholders. This argument may not convince us. But so long as a large group of people do believe it, we can expect to be able to sell our Microsoft shares to them. People buy Microsoft shares because they think they can sell them at a higher price to someone else, and history shows that they have often been right. Since 2000 they have less often been right, and markets will probably again attach more weight to dividends.

Some companies which do not pay dividends, including Microsoft, buy their own shares in the stock market. This increases their share price. It also benefits executives who own call options in the company's stock. If the company pays a dividend, only shareholders benefit. If the share price rises, option holders profit as well.

A Guide to Bloomberg Television

The talking heads who appear on Bloomberg television and claim to predict share price movements may be fundamental or technical analysts. Fundamental analysis looks at expectations of future earnings and dividends. Technical analysis identifies trends in share prices which will help to predict future movements. Technical analysts talk of support levels and resistance levels. They scrutinize charts in the hope of identifying patterns, such as 'head and shoulders' or 'double bottoms'.[10]

The efficient market hypothesis suggests that both fundamental analysis and technical analysis will fail, because any public information about shares and companies is already reflected in the price. Technical analysis cannot work – everyone can scrutinize the charts – and fundamental analysis only if it draws on private information, which would usually be illegal.[11] Chartists (as technical analysts are often called) are the astrologers of the business world: they use arcane language, comprehensible only to themselves, and couch predictions in ambiguous terms which can rarely be falsified.

The case for fundamental analysis is rather stronger. There is a problem with extreme versions of the efficient market hypothesis. If acting on publicly available information is not worthwhile, because it is already in the price, no one will act on it, and therefore it will not be in the price. A small amount of market imperfection overcomes this objection. The people who move from queue to queue at the supermarket wait very slightly less long. Since the stock market is large, picking up a little bit of advantage sufficiently often can yield larger profits.

And there do seem to be some – though not many – cases of investors who have outperformed the stock market through fundamental analysis by a sufficient amount and for sufficiently long that their success cannot be explained by chance. In Chapter 19 I shall review evidence against the efficient market hypothesis and in Chapter 24 introduce Warren Buffett, the man who seems to be its living refutation.

Intangible Capital

Investment is present sacrifice for future gain, and anything that may yield a prospective return is an asset. Our assets constitute our wealth or our capital. Our capacity to earn wages and salaries is sometimes called our human capital. We are born with human capital. We can increase our human capital through education and training and depreciate it through idleness, drinking too much, or old age. It is possible to estimate returns on human capital – the value of additional earnings which people can expect from an investment in schooling or an MBA.[12]

Successful businesses – businesses with competitive advantages from distinctive capabilities – are worth more than the value of their buildings, their plant and their stocks. Accountants used to call this the goodwill of the business. For the shop, the pub or the small manufacturer, that was an appropriate term. The intangible asset was the loyalty of satisfied customers.

There are many different kinds of distinctive capability in the modern economy and therefore many different kinds of intangible assets: competitive advantages based on brands or reputations with groups of customers; strategic assets such as patents and copyrights or local monopolies; structures of relationships with suppliers or employees. 'Our people are our greatest asset' is a cliché of company reports, but there is a lot in it. All these factors explain why the value of companies is greater than the value of their tangible assets.[13]

Most recently, the sociologist Robert Putnam has written of social capital.[14] Putnam's thesis – encapsulated in the striking title of his book, *Bowling Alone* – is that group social activity in the United States has declined. Almost two centuries ago Tocqueville wrote of the desire for association as a feature of American life.[15] Perhaps that association, which was not only the basis for America's civil society but an element in its economic success, has been eroded in recent decades.

Market economies, and market societies, are embedded in social institutions. Chapters 17 to 22 will describe many of these. Putnam is right to worry that the institutions which are the basis not just of civil society but of economic life are being eroded. But there is desperation in the term 'social capital'. Putnam fears he can attract the attention of his audience only by expressing himself in economic terms.

There is much to be said for reserving the term 'capital' for what can be bought and sold in the market for capital. Some, but not many, intangible assets meet this test: human capital does not, and social capital certainly not. Education and skills are an asset, and so is the glue that holds society together, but they are not in this sense capital.

14

General Equilibrium

The Co-ordination Problem Revisited

It is now time to go back to the problem posed in Chapter 10. How is it that market economies solved the co-ordination problems of production, exchange and assignment so much more effectively than planned ones? The concept of spontaneous order – the idea that complex systems may have properties of self-organization – is powerful: but the knowledge that self-organization is possible falls a long way short of either demonstrating that co-ordination happens spontaneously or explaining how it might happen spontaneously.

Competitive markets – whether for electricity or for flowers, for oil or for milk, for risk or for money – produce their own local equilibrium which equates supply and demand. The lights stay on, the flowers that arrive at San Remo at the beginning of the morning leave it at the end. This solves part of the co-ordination problem, but only part. The remarkable feature of the market economy is that it seems to solve a large variety of co-ordination problems simultaneously. The flower market clears, and electricity demand matches supply. There are enough trucks at the market, but not too many; enough gas for power stations, but not too much.

Central planners always found it easy to deal with any particular co-ordination failure. By switching resources we can always relieve a shortage or a surplus: this is what we do when we plan our households or our businesses, and it is what the people who ran the Soviet economy did all the time. The trouble is that there are always knock-on consequences. When we solve one problem, we almost always create another elsewhere. We face this same issue in co-ordinating our muscles, or assembling IKEA furniture. It is easy to make one piece fit. The tricky thing is to make them all fit at the same time. General equilibrium is the problem of making everything fit at once.

With IKEA furniture, we can be reasonably confident that it is possible to make everything fit at once. Someone at IKEA has already tried. Producers in traditional, pre-market societies were also confident the co-ordination problem could be solved, because they too had done it before. The general equilibrium of the system was assured by experience over many generations in which each year was very much like another. But neither of these answers applies in a complex modern economy. There can be no designer: the problem of incentive compatibility demonstrates that no central planner could ever assemble the combination of information and incentives needed to dictate general equilibrium from the centre. The economic lives of the citizens of rich states are constantly changing. We can't simply rely, as traditional societies could, on the order of the past producing order today.

Still, history is important. What happens today at San Remo, or in the National Grid's control room, is different from what happened yesterday, or will happen tomorrow. But it is not completely different. The mechanisms by which the flower market or the electricity market function change only slowly, even though the results of the mechanisms change every day. Institutions like these did not come into being instantly: like other complex social or biological organisms, they evolved from simpler versions. That is part of the reason why it is so difficult to create sophisticated market institutions where none existed before.

So how do the different bits of a market economy fit together? This question cries out for a mathematical approach. The first mathematical economists were found in nineteenth-century France. Jean-Baptiste Say formulated the idea of general equilibrium in 'Say's Law': supply creates its own demand. Say was one of the best economists before Larry Summers to become Minister of Finance. But the most important contribution came from a young colleague, Léon Walras, with whom Say had established an unsuccessful co-operative bank. After the failure of the bank, Walras retreated to a chair at the University of Lausanne where he set out, in his *Principles of Political Economy*, the mathematics of a general equilibrium system.

Adding Up

When we assemble IKEA furniture, we should find that, if we have successfully put together all the bits except one, the last component automatically fits into place. This often doesn't happen! Usually this means we have assembled it incorrectly. In a co-ordinated system, the position of the last piece is predetermined by the position of all the others.[1] The economic analogue is Walras' Law.

Walras' Law is an economic application of bookkeeping principles. Double-entry bookkeeping is not as exciting an invention as railways or the Internet. But double-entry bookkeeping was as important as these innovations to the development of modern market economies. Every expenditure must be matched by a receipt. By keeping track of all entries in a ledger, the activities of a household or business can be regulated and controlled. Double-entry bookkeeping put the discipline in disciplined pluralism.

Double-entry bookkeeping is to economic and commercial life what the second law of thermodynamics is to the physical world, and it has the same role in deflating the pretensions of dreamers and fantasists. The claims made by Enron and for the Internet boom were impossible for the same reasons that alchemy and perpetual-motion machines were impossible. Woolly minded people, and fraudsters who prey on them, assert economic equivalents of alchemy and perpetual motion. But sadly, for an individual or household:

spending must (more or less) match earnings

and for firms or institutions (including the government):

assets must match liabilities.

For the economy as a whole, there are similar 'adding up' constraints. The most important are:

production must (more or less) equal consumption
exports must (more or less) equal imports
the total value of production must (more or less) be equal to the total value of consumption

and

> all net assets and liabilities of corporations and of governments are ultimately net assets and liabilities of individuals or households.

Because of these bookkeeping constraints, we can't measure the overall consequence of a change to an economic system by simply adding up immediate individual effects. If we alter one component, every other one will have to change, a little, in order to ensure that the requirements of a double-entry system still hold.

DIY Economics

David Henderson was head of economics and statistics at the Organization for Economic Co-operation and Development (OECD), located near to the Bois de Boulogne in Paris's leafy 16th arrondissement. The OECD is often described as the club of rich states – its membership more or less coincides with the rich states identified in Chapter 3. In 1985 Henderson delivered the annual BBC Reith Lectures.[2]

The theme of Henderson's lectures – born of frustration with economic pronouncements of politicians – was what he called 'DIY economics': the false propositions which people who have not studied economics know instinctively are true. Sir Samuel Brittan, whose experience as an economic journalist is somewhat different, calls the same phenomenon and propositions 'businessman's economics'.[3] Anyone who claimed expertise in 'practical physics' derived from their experience of driving a car or boarding an aeroplane would immediately reveal themselves as a fool. It is a measure of the failure of economists to persuade the public of the value of what they do that there are no such reactions to those who claim practical knowledge of economics.[4] There is almost no DIY dentistry, little DIY history or law, rather more DIY medicine. There is much DIY economics.

The most common weakness in DIY economics is failure to understand general equilibrium issues, often a result of a lack of appreciation of the role of bookkeeping constraints. These constraints mean that what is true at the level of the individual household or firm may not be true at the level of the economy as a whole. This is a subtle source of misunderstanding, because economic lives are conducted in households and firms: we do not see the abstractions of general equilibrium. This misunderstanding is expressed in Margaret Thatcher's claim that household budgeting had prepared her for the management of the national economy.[5] The advocates of DIY economies 'know' the truth of what they say from their own experience.

If a firm increases its sales without any reduction in price or rise in costs, the outcome is good for its shareholders and those who work for it. Conversely, if the firm loses market share to a competitor, everyone associated with it is worse off. Applying this simple wisdom to the economy as a whole, we should try to increase national sales – our exports – and diminish national purchases – our inputs – and the more successful we are in this endeavour the better off we shall be. This theory – mercantilism – was believed by most economists before Smith and his contemporaries, and expounded in books with titles such as *England's Treasure by Foreign Trade*.[6] It is a widely held thesis in DIY economics today although it enjoys broadly the same scientific status as the phlogiston theory of heat or the Ptolemaic explanation of how the sun orbits the Earth.

The weakness of the argument is the failure to recognize the bookkeeping constraint. The balance of payments must, in the long run, balance. This applies to the national economy, but there is no corresponding constraint at the level of the individual firm. An increase in exports by one firm will be matched either by an increase in imports or by a reduction in exports by some other firm. What is true for an individual company is not true for Great Britain plc.

The John Kay who invented the flying shuttle was forced to flee to France by Luddites who feared his ingenuity would destroy their jobs.[7] The Luddites had good cause to be afraid for their jobs, many of which disappeared. There are many fewer jobs for bank clerks now that mechanical record-keeping is undertaken by computers, but there are not fewer jobs overall. In both these industries employment ultimately increased, because the new technology that displaced the Luddites and the bank clerks led to increased demand for textiles and for financial services. The effect of this increase in demand more than offset the immediate job losses. (This was not necessarily consoling for the individuals concerned.) The adding up constraints of general equilibrium require this. Lower costs from new technology must lead to lower prices, or increased profits, or both. Even if there is no increase in spending on the products of industries directly affected – and there often will be – there will be more expenditure on the products of some other industries and additional opportunities will be generated there. Over the two centuries since the Luddites first wrecked machinery, productivity has increased more than fifty-fold. But instead of having 98 per cent unemployment, we produce fifty times as much.

Current technological changes are no different. In some instances, increasing exports may yield benefits to the national economy (and not just to those who actually export), and new technology will reduce overall employment (and not just the employment of those who are displaced by new technology). But these results are not generally true, and cannot be deduced for the economy as a whole from the hard-earned experience of individual businesses and the people who run them.

Economic Theory Advancing

Adam Smith and David Ricardo demonstrated the fallacies in the arguments of mercantilists and Luddites. Walras elaborated the implications of these bookkeeping constraints for the economic system as a whole and set out the framework of the general equilibrium issue. But this is far short of demonstrating a solution to the co-ordination problem. And after Walras, the theory of general equilibrium stalled under the towering influence of the Cambridge economist Alfred Marshall. Although himself a capable mathematician, Marshall derided the use of mathematics in economics. His discourse *Principles of Economics*, published in 1890, follows his injunction to 'burn the mathematics'.[8]

John Hicks[N] was to play the largest European role in setting foundations for the further development of economics. Hicks studied and taught at Oxford, Manchester and London rather than Cambridge. *Value and Capital*, which Hicks published in 1939, was followed in 1947 by *Foundations of Economic Analysis*, the doctoral dissertation of a young American economist, Paul Samuelson[N].

No modest man calls his doctoral thesis *Foundations of Economic Analysis*, but Samuelson was to become the leading economist of his generation. *Foundations of Economic Analysis* (which should not be confused with Samuelson's best-selling textbook, *Economics*) joins Keynes's *General Theory of Employment, Interest and Money* as the most important works in economics of the twentieth century. But although only ten years (and a world war) separated their appearance, comparison of the two volumes demonstrates a sea change. The *General Theory* is discursive and opaque and glitters with literary brilliance. *Foundations* is mathematical and precise, and any pleasure it gives the reader comes from its content, not its prose. The transition marked a change in the style of economics, and a shift in hegemony in economic theory from Cambridge, England to Cambridge, Massachusetts,[9] and more generally from Europe to the United States.

Hicks and Samuelson defined the basis for a new mathematical economics. Soon after, Kenneth Arrow[N] and Gerard Debreu[N] set out the theory of general equilibrium, and the Arrow–Debreu model has been central to modern economics ever since.[10] One reason why Smith and his polymathic contemporaries could not give formal content to their descriptions of spontaneous order was that the relevant mathematics had not been invented. It had not been invented even in the time of Say and Walras. The discovery of algebraic topology in the twentieth century gave Arrow and Debreu the tools they needed. Fixed-point theorems[11] describe properties of convex sets. A detour is required to explain the economic implications of the mathematical property of convexity.

Convexity

A convex set has the property that a collection which contains two items also contains an average of these two items.[12] If the collection is 'things I like', then convexity implies that I also like a combination of 'things I like'. The averaging process tends to make things better rather than worse.

Addiction violates convexity. Not many people want just a little heroin. And there is a problem with convexity when goods are indivisible. No one wants half a car. But we can see addiction as pathological behaviour, and our instincts and our social attitudes commend convexity. We applaud moderation in all things, say that a little of what you fancy does you good, and admire well-balanced, well-rounded, individuals.

The desire for convexity seems to run deep in human attitudes. Herrick wrote that 'Beauty is a golden mean,/'Twixt the middle and extreme.' This is a good definition of convexity, and modern psychologists have confirmed that Herrick was right. The collection 'faces I find attractive' is convex. If the faces of two beautiful women are merged using computer technology, most people like the result.[13]

It probably isn't an exaggeration to say that the behaviour of market economies depends on how convex the world is. To get a sense of why this is so, imagine dropping a ball into a bowl: it circles round, slows down and eventually arrives at some sort of equilibrium. This happens because the collection of 'points inside the bowl' is convex. Now turn the bowl upside down. The set of positions the ball can take is no longer convex: the ball gathers speed and runs away in an unpredictable direction. The shape of the space governs the dynamics of the process.[14]

In a convex environment, minor adjustments, trial and error, piecemeal improvements, tend to make things better. There are many objectives, which partly conflict, and variety is prized. It is in this world that the processes of disciplined pluralism perform well. Market economies don't seem to cope very well with urban transport systems, where it probably really is better to focus than to have a little of everything, which is what the market tends to generate.

If specialization pays, the set of 'things which I can make' is not convex. Suppose M. Roux could cook a hundred meals if he cooked all day, and copy four of Braque's sketches in the same time. Convexity would require that if he cooked for half the day and sketched for the remainder, he could cook fifty meals and produce two drawings. But he probably can't. Convexity implies that there are no benefits from specialization, and no economies of scale. If 'things which I can make' formed a convex set, then it would be possible, and even desirable, for everyone to be self-sufficient.

The division of labour is rewarding because the world is not completely convex. But it needs to be somewhat convex. If the collection of 'things the world economy can make' were not convex, then the likely outcome would be extreme specialization and extreme instability. The market economy would fail to produce the variety of goods and services that people want, and a planned economy would also find it difficult to find a good solution. We need some departure from convexity, but not too much: some gains from specialization, but not gains without limit.

And this seems to be what we see. There are benefits to specialization but they run out, because every specialist has limited capacity. If Picasso was the greatest artist of the twentieth century, why were not all paintings Picassos? Partly because of convexity of preferences: even if we think that Picasso's paintings are the best, we might like to see a mixture of Picassos and Braques. But also because Picasso could not have painted all the paintings in the world, even if he had painted all day and all night; and if he had, many of his works would not have been very good. So there is also employment for slightly less talented painters, like Braque; and even employment for the much less talented people who hang their works on park railings.

Gains from specialization also run out because too extensive specialization is boring. There are almost always technical economies of scale to be found; ultimately, they are almost always offset by human diseconomies of scale. It is that balance that gives us the small-scale non-convexity and large-scale convexity we need.[15]

The Existence of General Equilibrium

Arrow and Debreu established precisely the way in which individual decision-making by households and competitive firms might produce consistent outcomes. The conjecture of the 'invisible hand' became an exact mathematical result.

Arrow and Debreu worked in the context of a specific, simplified model of the economy in which both the sets of 'things which I like' and 'things which can be made' are convex. All markets are perfectly competitive and the households and firms which trade in them are materialistic and self-regarding. Their preferences and choices are independent of those of other households and firms. Each household decides what to consume, independently of the choices of others. Not only does each firm make its decisions about what to produce independently of those of others, its technology and methods of production are not affected by what other firms do. It is not possible, for example, that your purchases might influence mine. Or that pollution from one factory might affect the output of other firms or the welfare of households.

The Arrow–Debreu theorem shows that, if these conditions hold, there is a set of prices such that aggregate supplies will equal aggregate demands for every commodity in the economy. There will be no surpluses and no shortages. A co-ordinator is not necessary to achieve a co-ordinated outcome. The manufacture of a car requires the contributions of thousands of resources and thousands of people. But it isn't necessary for anyone to oversee the whole of that process. It is sufficient that people make decisions on the basis of the prices they see and the knowledge of their own preferences and production possibilities.

Each individual household wants food, housing, clothing, transport. But in a perfectly competitive market no overall co-ordination is required to ensure that the way in which households, in aggregate, split their budgets between food, housing, clothing and transport matches the quantities in which producers make food, housing, clothing, transport. Here, too, it is enough that people make decisions on the basis of their own limited knowledge. If we don't find these things amazing, it is because we are so accustomed to the idea that market economies do mostly achieve co-ordination. But we should recall how difficult it proved to achieve the same results in a planned economy which sought co-ordinated outcomes through central oversight.

The abstract nature of the model must give many people pause. This arcane mathematics seems far removed from the basic questions that motivate the study of economics. Why is Heidi rich? Why is Sicelo poor? The assumptions of the theory are obviously unrealistic. Our preferences are influenced by those of other people, different production processes interfere with each other, economies of scale are widespread. But this is not criticism enough. Because economic systems are very complex, *any* model we specify involves extensive simplifying assumptions.

A model like that of Arrow–Debreu demonstrates the possibility of spontaneous order in economic systems. It does not necessarily follow that there *will* be spontaneous order. Nor does it follow that if there is co-ordination, or spontaneous order, the Arrow–Debreu model explains it. But some approximation to spontaneous order does seem to be a feature of real market economies, and the Arrow–Debreu model offers one coherent explanation of how such spontaneous order might come about. In the next chapter, I review a further claim for the Arrow–Debreu model of perfectly competitive equilibrium: the claim that the outcome is not only co-ordinated, but also efficient.

15

Efficiency

The History of Light

It is dark for half our lives. For most of history, artificial lighting has been too costly for widespread application in either our work or our social lives. Cro-Magnon man could not have painted in the caves of Lascaux without artificial lighting, so lamps have a long history. But the candle was the only revolutionary improvement in lighting technology before the end of the eighteenth century.

Energy technology changed fundamentally in the nineteenth century. Gas and electricity were produced centrally and distributed locally, and good quality domestic lighting became affordable. When Thomas Edison demonstrated electric lighting at Menlo Park in 1880, huge crowds of New Yorkers gathered to see. In the twentieth century the cost of light has fallen much more rapidly than the cost of energy. Without these improvements in the efficiency of lighting technology, we would not be able to live the lives we now do; there would not be enough energy. But what exactly do we mean by efficiency improvements? And how do we measure them?

For physicists, the amount of light (which they measure in lumens) produced per unit of energy consumed would seem a natural way to measure efficiency. Many improvements in lighting technology focused on this factor – essentially the ratio of light to heat. Light was once an incidental by-product of combustion – the flicker of a flame. Modern low energy fittings provide light and almost no heat.

Much of the gain in efficiency has come from better ways of distributing energy. Petroleum exploration and development have enabled us to substitute mineral oil for whale blubber (which was once an important source of light). Gas is delivered along pipes, and houses are lit with electricity: gas, oil or coal is burnt in a central power station and electricity is sent along wires to our houses. Energy losses in electricity generation and transmission are more than offset by the greater efficiency with which households can use electrical energy.

We use more of some resources to use less of others, and this extends beyond improvements in energy efficiency. Lamps had a better light to heat ratio than open fires, and candles a better light to heat ratio than lamps. But this gain in physical efficiency had a cost. More effort was needed to find these more efficient fuels and process them.

Table 15.1 Lighting efficiency

Year	Source	Physical efficiency (lumens/watt)	Economic efficiency*
500,000 BC	Open wood fire	0.002	70
30,000 BC	Cro-Magnon lamp (animal fat)	0.015	15
1800 BC	Babylonian lamp (vegetable oil)	0.06	4
AD 1800	Candle (tallow or whale blubber)	0.01	0.7
1870	Early gas lamp	0.25	0.03
1890	Early electric lamp†	2.6	0.08
1990	Modern electric lamp	14.2	0.00006
2000	Low energy fluorescent lamp	70	0.00001

*Hours of work needed to keep a 100 watt bulb on for an hour.
†Economic efficiency falls because of the cost of electricity relative to gas.
Source: derived from Nordhaus (1997).

We can write down a list of the resources we use today to produce light, and lists of the resources we would have used a century or a millennium ago. All these lists are different: in length, in the items they contain. To compare their efficiency, we need to make precise the instinct that today's list is smaller, even if it is not shorter. The obvious means is to translate all items into a single unit, such as the hours of work needed to produce them. Table 15.1 shows the result of this calculation. A modern 100 watt bulb produces about 1,400 lumens. Cro-Magnons would have had to work for twelve hours gathering fuel to sustain that level of lighting for ten minutes. It is easy to see why Braque produced many more paintings than the cave people of Lascaux.

Comparing Vectors

A vector is simply a mathematician's term for a list of numbers. If every number in one list is larger than every number in another list, the corresponding vector is larger. If some numbers are larger in one list and some larger in the other, we need to make judgements. Only a weighting scheme can allow us to rank the two vectors.

We face this problem every time we choose between alternative purchases. Consumer reports help us approach this problem in a systematic way. So when the British magazine *Which?* looked at digital widescreen televisions, it rated the sets as shown in Table 15.2. So which set is best? The answer isn't immediately obvious. But the answer cannot be the Sony or the Thomson. If you like the Sony, the Panasonic is just as good but has more features. And if you like the Thomson, the Philips is just as good but has more features. But is the Panasonic better than the Philips? It depends whether you want lots of features or good picture and sound quality. I can't advise you on that, but readers expect that *Which?* might. So *Which?* weights the different characteristics. It gives 43 per cent weighting to sound and picture, 20 per cent to features, and 20 per cent to ease of use. These judgements allow it to rank all the sets. They conclude that the Panasonic is best. Under their weighting system, the Sony is also better than the Philips. Once weights are introduced, you can not only choose the best, you can also rank all the alternatives.

The weights reflect the opinions of people at the Consumers' Association about what we should value in a television set. No doubt they are well informed and objective. However, you may think picture quality is more or less important than the Consumers' Association does. Each of us has our own personal weighting system to apply to the

Table 15.2 Choosing a television

Characteristics	Manufacturer			
	Panasonic	Philips	Sony	Thomson
Features	Many	Most	Fewest	Very many
Picture quality	Good	Good	Good	Good
Sound quality	Good	Acceptable	Good	Acceptable
Ease of use	Good	Poor	Good	Poor

Source: *Which: Widescreen TVs* (February 2002).

characteristic vectors. That is why we don't all buy the same set, even the one the Consumers' Association recommends, and why even the Consumers' Association is hesitant about identifying one as best buy.

But not everything is commensurable. When Charles Darwin, that most rational of men, contemplated marriage, he compiled a careful list of pros and cons. It might be expected that the cons would come out on top: there are more of them and they are strongly expressed. But Darwin married, and had ten children. He disregarded the list, and decided he couldn't contemplate a life alone.[1]

An Evening in Küssnacht

Heidi: You insist on looking at everything in financial terms, Hermann. Can't you understand that some things are more important than money? Health, the environment, life itself. How can you put a price on a person, or a species?

Hermann: Of course there are more important things than money. Life, children, relationships. And in Switzerland most people have as many material goods as anyone could reasonably want. That's precisely why we can be concerned about the environment – and why it's important that we protect it.

Heidi: So why do you reduce everything to money?

Hermann: When I 'reduce things to money', I'm not saying that money is the goal. I'm simply using money as a means of comparison. Remember when we bought our holiday place in Umbria.

We calculated what it would cost us and what we would save on hotel costs.

Heidi: Well, you did, Hermann.

Hermann: That's true. But we went over the sums together. That doesn't mean we go on holiday to save money. Money is just a measuring rod for costs and benefits.

Heidi: But you can't apply that kind of calculus to the environment, or to human life.

Hermann: Why not? Take your recycling scheme. It conserves some resources, it uses others. How can you balance one against the other except in financial terms?

Heidi: You're missing the point. The environment is too important to be reduced to financial terms.

Hermann: But you don't really believe that. We both hate the way electricity pylons sprout from the woods on the slopes above the lake. But even in Switzerland, it's too expensive to lay all cables underground. Life always involves choices – allocating scarce resources between competing ends. And no society is so well endowed that it can avoid choices.

Heidi: But you can't make all choices in this way. Some things are more important than money. How do you value a human life?

Hermann: But we trade off money against safety every day. The cheapest way of saving lives is to invest in road improvements. Remember that bend on the road to Davos where we nearly had an accident. Five people have died there in the last ten years. They're building a tunnel to reduce the bend and the gradient. And you know you could have a safer car than the Micra, if you spent more.

Heidi: You're incorrigible, Hermann. Only an economist could think in that way.

Hermann: But economists must, and so should policy-makers. When your friend Mieke from Novartis came round to dinner, she explained how we kill more people by delaying new drugs than we save by testing them exhaustively. And her partner Fritz works for the Swiss nuclear safety inspectorate. There have been no accidents in Switzerland, far less a Chernobyl. And that's a good thing, of course. But he argued that what we spend on precautions and security is excessive. We might do more for health and longevity if we spent the money on gym equipment and propaganda against eating and drinking too much.

Heidi: Go and work out on the exercise machine while I see to supper.

Commensurability

The discussion between Heidi and Hermann raises two distinct issues. Can different objectives be treated as commensurable? If they are commensurable, what are the terms – money, cost, fuel efficiency or some other yardstick altogether – by which commensurability is to be measured? These issues are often muddled, because people who want to make sweeping claims for commensurability typically use money as their metric, and those who wish to deny commensurability often choose to attack the use of money as measuring rod.[2]

For some economists, all goals are commensurable. America's leading law and economics scholar, Richard Posner, takes a far more extreme position than Hermann. Posner asserts that there is no difference between justice and economic efficiency – 'when people describe as "unjust" convicting a person without a trial, taking property without just compensation . . . they can be interpreted as meaning nothing more pretentious than that the conduct in question wastes resources.' Even the sympathetic Todd Buchholz describes this as a 'dim observation by a brilliant man' and notes that it was watered down by the third edition of Posner's treatise.[3] This illustrates the problems of defining property rights in too general a way (see Chapter 5).

The right to be free of racial discrimination, or sexual harassment, is not a property right. Those who benefit from such a right do not have the option to sell it or transfer it; someone who proposed to give up the right not to be harassed, or discriminated against, in return for a sum of money would have misunderstood what was intended. Conversely, the right not to be harassed, or discriminated against, is not an entitlement to receive large sums of money if one does suffer harassment or discrimination. 'Rights are trumps,' in Ronald Dworkin's striking phrase[4] and the essence of a trump card is that it is not commensurable.

There are values in society which are not commensurable in financial terms, and may not be commensurable at all. The value pluralism of Isaiah Berlin[5] asserts that conceptions of what is good in society almost invariably include incompatible goals. This is not relativism: Berlin does not believe that all conceptions of the good are equally valid. His position provides the middle ground that both Heidi and Hermann are right to seek. It is not unreasonable to refuse to measure human life in terms of forgone video recorders.[6] Such refusal may lead to apparently inconsistent choices – as when we spend more to rescue someone in distress at sea than on life-saving road improvements. This is disturbing, but not necessarily irrational, in any ordinary sense of the word.

At Heidi's end of the spectrum, claims of incommensurability are often made by people who wish to deny that choices in the allocation of scarce resources between competing ends have to be made, or simply to assert the primacy of their own values – what is important to you is never commensurable with what is important to me. The more assertions of incommensurability are made, the more arguments – like that between Hermann and Heidi – are necessarily inconclusive. This leads to the incoherent discourse that follows from the assertion of a multiplicity of rights. The conflicting assertions of 'right to life' and 'right to choose' find no common ground, and the proponents of these conflicting rights can, and do, conduct their debate only by shouting at each other or even killing each other.

If rights are trumps, only a few suits can be trumps. This makes it important to resist the designation of a wide range of desirable outcomes – paternity leave, or disabled access – as 'rights' which therefore have to be implemented regardless of cost. Choices in the allocation of scarce resources between competing ends have to be made. Recycling glass or paper is not a worthwhile objective in itself, and it is reasonable to ask proponents to justify it in terms of specific costs and benefits. Environmentalists are particularly prone to sweeping claims of incommensurability. There may be environmental goals which are, in Berlin's terms, incommensurable with materialist goals: but that does not imply that environmental policies should not be assessed in consequentialist terms. Those who claim that biodiversity should be maintained regardless of cost cannot simultaneously justify biodiversity by reference to its economic benefits.

The Terms of Commensurability

Measures of efficiency require the comparison of vectors of inputs and outputs. A larger output vector from the same input is more efficient. A smaller input vector for the same output is also more efficient. This is how we could conclude that the Panasonic was a better set than the Sony, the Philips better than the Thomson. But it did not enable us to compare the Panasonic and the Philips, or even to say that a modern low energy light bulb is more efficient than the lanterns the Cro-Magnons used.

Which? magazine resolved the comparison between television sets by weighting the characteristics of sets. The weights were based on the value they thought buyers would attach to these different features. In a perfectly competitive market, the price of the goods and the features of goods will correspond to the value buyers attach to them. This is the basis for using market prices to achieve commensurability, and using GDP to make comparisons of vectors of outputs between countries and over time.

The obvious problem is that the value people attach to particular goods or services is the result not just of how much they want those goods or services, but also how much money they have. Mr Saito did not put the extraordinary value of $82.5 million on *Portrait of Dr Gachet* because he was uniquely devoted to great art but because he was extraordinarily rich. The legitimacy of market values as weights depends on the legitimacy of the income distribution that gives rise to it.

Another way of approaching this issue tackles the problem directly. The purpose of an economic system is not to produce physical output, but to enhance the welfare of the households that live in it. Surely we should judge the efficiency of an economy by its contribution to the welfare of its citizens? But how would we measure their welfare? For nineteenth-century polymath John Stuart Mill, and the first British mathematical economist, F. Y. Edgeworth, the welfare of society was based on the welfare – the utility – of its individual members. Inspired by Jeremy Bentham (whose stuffed body can still be seen in a glass case at University College London), they looked forward to a felicific calculus, which would measure progress towards their objective, the greatest happiness of the greatest number, in an objective manner.

The felicific calculus was designed to solve the knotty problem of commensurability – how to weight my utility against yours, how to decide whether greater aggregate happiness had been achieved. Sadly, progress towards the felicific calculus remains elusive, and utilitarianism fell out of fashion amongst philosophers many years ago.

Pareto Efficiency

Vilfredo Pareto, Walras's successor at Lausanne, believed, like the utilitarians, that the welfare of society could be defined in terms of the individual utilities of individual citizens or households. He was content simply to list the utilities they achieved as a vector. So instead of a vector that described picture quality, sound quality, etc., a vector would list the welfare of the Smiths, the welfare of the Joneses, and so on for all the households in the economy.

It is sometimes possible to make comparisons of televisions without attaching any weights to the components of the vector. The Panasonic was better than the Sony because it had more features, and all other characteristics were equally good. In a precisely analogous way, we would have a better policy, or a better allocation of resources, if we could make the Smiths or the Joneses better off without making anyone else worse off. This is described as a Pareto improvement.

In other cases, no such comparison of vectors is possible. Whether the Panasonic was better or worse than the Philips was a matter of judgement and opinion. The Philips was better in some aspects – it had more features – but the Panasonic had a better picture. Similarly, if the Joneses are better off and the Smiths are worse off, an evaluation requires a weighting of the welfare of the Joneses and the Smiths. We have to judge whether the gain to the Joneses exceeds the loss to the Smiths. Ideally, we need the felicific calculus. If we use money to make the comparison, then we employ an implicit felicific calculus which attaches a weighting to the welfare of the households concerned based on the amount of money they have.

Pareto's claim is that it is often – not always, but often – possible to avoid these judgements. He developed a further twist to this argument. If no Pareto improvement is possible – if it is not possible to make the Joneses better off without making the Smiths worse off, or vice versa, then the outcome is described as Pareto efficient.[7] An allocation of scarce resources between competing ends is Pareto efficient if it is impossible to make one household better off without making another household worse off.

It is hard not to be in favour of Pareto efficiency. A Pareto improvement is the politician's dream – a policy from which there are only winners. If we could make someone better off without making anyone worse off, wouldn't we do it? And yet you may already have a sense that Pareto is about to lead us somewhere you may not wish to go. A state of affairs might be Pareto efficient, and yet deplorable. A sadist is torturing his victims. But this outcome could still be Pareto efficient – we can only stop the torture by making the sadist worse off.

The Fundamental Theorems of Welfare Economics

Any exchange which benefits both parties and has no adverse effect on anyone else is a Pareto improvement. So an economic system can be Pareto efficient only if every possible mutually beneficial trade has occurred. This seems to link Pareto efficiency with free, competitive markets. Allowing the market economy to function freely will have the result that people will trade with each other until Pareto efficiency is achieved. For many supporters of the market economy, the argument is as simple as that – I've heard it often from practitioners of DIY economics.

It isn't as simple as that. Voluntary trade between two individuals benefits them, but it will only be a Pareto improvement if it has no adverse consequences for other people. If my purchase, or your production, affects others, it will not lead to a Pareto improvement, and it often will affect others, because others want to buy the same goods as I do, or your output raises the costs of a third party.

Further – and the problem turns out to be fundamental – there is an issue of incentive compatibility. A trade which benefits the parties involved will have consequences for others if it affects the terms on which other people can trade. This is very often true. When a plane is about to depart with an empty seat, it would be a Pareto improvement if the seat were filled by a passenger willing to pay anything at all. But the airline won't do this, because if seats were regularly available for next to nothing whenever one was empty, there would be effects on the behaviour of full-fare-paying passengers. Airlines have the sophisticated yield-management systems of Chapter 11 to handle precisely this problem. Their aim is not to fill the plane, but to strike a balance between filling seats and obtaining good prices for seats. If they could read minds and gauge exactly how much each passenger would be willing to pay, they could engage in perfect price discrimination[8] and achieve Pareto efficiency; but of course they can't.

So free trade leads to Pareto efficiency only in perfectly competitive markets, because only perfectly competitive markets are free of these incentive-compatibility problems. Market economies that are competitive but not perfectly competitive, offer many opportunities for Pareto improvements.

But for the perfectly competitive markets described in the Arrow–Debreu framework[9] we have the fundamental theorems of welfare economics:

> every competitive equilibrium is Pareto efficient
> any allocation of scarce resources between competing ends that is Pareto efficient can be achieved by a competitive equilibrium.

Don't worry: the book gets easier from here. But there is no escaping the fundamental theorems of welfare economics if we are to examine the claim that competitive markets necessarily lead to efficient outcomes. These claims are made not just by theoretical economists but by practical politicians. Ronald Reagan was not much interested in algebraic topology: but the intellectual influences on him, when finally disentangled, can be traced back to those fixed-point theorems.

Part Four

THE TRUTH ABOUT MARKETS

Neoclassical Economics and After

Smith and Hayek

Some economists regard the Arrow–Debreu results and the fundamental theorems of welfare economics as the modern expression of Smith's invisible hand.[1] But Smith would be surprised at what is attributed to him today. Politicians and business people vie in admiration for what they believe to be his doctrines. Keith Joseph, generally regarded as Margaret Thatcher's economic mentor, was appointed Secretary of State for Trade and Industry in 1979. He presented his civil servants with a reading list headed by *The Wealth of Nations*.[2] Yergin and Stanislaw's description of the revival of market economics makes frequent reference to Smith and sums up his 'argument for self-interest': 'the pursuit of individual interest cumulatively adds up to the overall betterment of society'.[3]

This reverence for Smith even extends to hymns.

> 'Adam, Adam, Adam Smith
> Listen what I charge you with
> Didn't you say
> In the class one day
> That selfishness was bound to pay?
> Of all doctrines that was the Pith
> Wasn't it, wasn't it, wasn't it, Smith?'[4]

Was this really the Pith of Smith's doctrines? The widely quoted passage is: 'by directing that industry in such a manner as its produce may be of the greatest value, he intends only his own gain, and he is in this, as in many other cases, led by an invisible hand to promote an end which was no part of his intention'. On careful reading Smith does not say that selfish behaviour is praiseworthy, is bound to pay, or necessarily promotes the best interests of society. When we join the shortest queue at the supermarket, we intend only our own gain and promote an end which is not part of our intention. It does not follow that our behaviour is governed by self-regarding materialism, or that such behaviour leads, cumulatively or otherwise, to the overall betterment of society.

The passage containing the invisible hand metaphor is not about general equilibrium theory: its purpose is to explain why merchants would continue to buy British products even if tariffs were removed. The metaphor itself originates in Shakespeare's Scottish play, *Macbeth*, and seems to have intrigued Smith. In his other major work, *The Theory of Moral Sentiments*, in which what Smith calls sympathy plays a central role, Smith wrote: 'They [the rich] are led by an invisible hand to make the same distribution of the necessities of life, which would have been made, had the earth been divided into equal portions amongst all its inhabitants.'[5] While it is unlikely that Smith held the views popularly attributed to him, speculation as to what exactly he did think is not helpful in arriving at the truth about markets. Our purpose now is to explain economic systems which Adam Smith could not conceivably have imagined. And for this reason it is no more likely that *The Wealth of Nations* would be useful in the day-to-day work of civil servants at the Department of Trade and Industry than that the works of Newton would be useful to a modern physicist or engineer.[6] Smith's important insights – such as the division of labour and the loose but prescient notion that co-ordination might be achieved through spontaneous order – have been absorbed and developed in the corpus of current knowledge.

Friedrich von Hayek[N] was largely neglected in modern economic thought until he was an unexpected recipient of the Nobel Prize in 1974. In the last years of his life, he was lionized by business and political leaders. It is hard to imagine many of them had read his works. Hayek also appears on Keith Joseph's reading list. The citation is *The Road to Serfdom*, written in 1944 as a commentary on the introduction of a welfare state in post-war Britain. As the extravagant title suggests, Hayek's style is at once Delphic and dogmatic. In Hayek's mind his opponents are usually not just wrong, but mentally and morally defective, but he articulated more clearly than any other twentieth-century economist the concept of spontaneous order.

Along with a fellow Austrian, Ludwig von Mises, Hayek was one of the first to see that the information problems of planned economies were intractable. For many inside and outside the Soviet Union, central planning could be made to work with sufficiently powerful computers. Hayek understood this would never be so. Problems of incentive compatibility, and the absence of the collective knowledge created by the trials and errors of disciplined pluralism, would inevitably lead to failure.

Hayek, von Mises and some other Central European economists of the early to mid-twentieth century are sometimes described as 'the Austrian school'.[7] Hayek was actually an isolated figure, and the Nazi destruction of the intellectual life of Central Europe prevented the development of any continuing tradition. More recently, the conservative baton has transferred to Chicago.

The Chicago School

Almost from its foundation by John D. Rockefeller, the University of Chicago was a centre of conservative economic thought.[8] Gary Becker[N] encapsulates the philosophy: 'The combined assumptions of maximizing behavior, market equilibrium, and stable preferences, used relentlessly and unflinchingly, form the heart of the economic approach.'[9] As well as Becker and Friedman, Chicago figures such as George Stigler[N] and Richard Posner have played an active part in policy debates. Chicago is held responsible for various neo-liberal experiments in South America and New Zealand.[10]

The centrepiece of Chicago economics is the insistence on rationality captured in Becker's statement. Becker's own most celebrated work is an economic analysis of family behaviour[11] and his Nobel citation congratulates him for 'having extended the domain of microeconomic analysis to a wide range of human behaviour'.[12] Becker sees few, perhaps no limits to this extension. In his Nobel lecture he writes:

In the early stages of my work on crime, I was puzzled by why theft is socially harmful, since it appears merely to redistribute resources, usually from richer to poorer individuals. I resolved the puzzle by pointing out that criminals spend on weapons and on the value of their time in planning and carrying out their crimes and that such spending is socially unproductive.[13]

The *Journal of Political Economy*, published from Chicago, has included articles on the economics of suicide and of language – and an exasperated response on the economics of brushing teeth.[14] But no parody is required.

Chicago was also the base for attacks on the post-war Keynesian orthodoxy of monetary and fiscal policy. Milton Friedman's counter-revolution emphasized the role of central banks controlling the supply of money relative to the importance of government adjusting levels of taxation and public expenditure. Another Chicago economist, Robert Lucas[N], applied 'the combined assumptions of maximizing behavior, market equilibrium, and stable preferences' to macroeconomic issues 'relentlessly and unflinchingly'. Most theories of boom and bust – the business cycle – base their explanation on mistakes by firms or households, or on market imperfections. Perhaps there are speculative bubbles, or excess inventories; perhaps prices and wages fail to respond to supply and demand. But Chicago is unwilling to believe that markets make mistakes or fail to succeed in balancing supply and demand. Real business-cycle theory dismisses market imperfections, and assumes 'rational expectations' – consumers and businesses behave as if they had access to all available knowledge and infinite calculating power. Real business-cycle theory takes the assumptions of rationality in business decisions to the same extremes as Becker's description of family life.[15]

The Chicago School also recognizes the merits of the market system as a pluralist process of experiment and discovery. Some of the most compelling formulations of the arguments of Chapters 8 and 9 have been presented by Chicago economists such as F. H. Knight and more recently by Almar Alchian.[16] But the much stronger claim of the Chicago School is that competitive markets have efficiency properties unattainable under any other form of economic organization. The intellectual basis for this assertion is provided by a combination of the rationality postulates of Becker, the Arrow–Debreu framework of general equilibrium, the fundamental theorems of welfare economics, and a dose of individualistic political philosophy. It is time to place this last piece of the jigsaw.

Nozick and Rawls

John Rawls's *A Theory of Justice*, published in 1972, and Robert Nozick's *Anarchy, State and Utopia*, which appeared in 1974, are among the most influential works of modern political theory. Neither of these Harvard philosophers was a proselytizing figure in the manner of Chicago economists. Indeed, the gulf between the dialogue of political philosophers and practising politicians has perhaps never been wider than today. Both Rawls and Nozick were, however, influential among economists, Rawls for those whose political leanings were to the left and Nozick for those who inclined right. There is a natural affinity between their frame of reasoning and the fundamental theorems of welfare economics.

For Nozick, it is illegitimate to use the coercive power of the state to make some better off at the expense of others; his concept of justice requires the protection of property rights legitimately acquired or legitimately transferred. Nozick's government must achieve Pareto efficiency, but may not choose between alternative allocations which are Pareto efficient. The first of the fundamental theorems of welfare economics – every competitive equilibrium is Pareto efficient – could have been written for Nozick. The economic policy suggested is the creation of a framework that will permit competitive equilibrium to be achieved: no more, no less.

Rawls invites us to stand behind a 'veil of ignorance', and order states of the world without knowing our role in them. The world economic system encompasses the different economic lives of Heidi and Ivan, Ravi and Sicelo, but we are not aware which of these people we ourselves will be. Rawls invokes what he calls the 'maximin principle' – since we fear we may be Sicelo, we favour policies which will make Sicelo as well off as possible. The Rawlsian approach not only justifies substantial redistribution, but requires it.

If the first fundamental theorem of welfare economics was written for Nozick, the second was written for Rawls. We stand behind the veil of ignorance, in search of a just mechanism for allocating scarce resources between competing ends. We are bound to choose a Pareto-efficient outcome. The choice between Pareto-efficient outcomes will be determined by the maximin principle. The second fundamental theorem of welfare economics – any Pareto-efficient outcome can be achieved by an appropriate allocation of resources – tells us that all we need do is get the initial distribution right. Competitive equilibrium will take care of the rest. A free market economy, with income redistribution, meets the requirements of Rawls's *A Theory of Justice*. Fukuyama, searching for the end of history, meets Rawls emerging from behind the veil of ignorance. We find them both in the United States at the end of the millennium.

Nozick and the first fundamental theorem argue for the justice and efficiency of the American business model. A competitive market equilibrium is just simply by virtue of being a competitive market equilibrium. And Rawls and the second fundamental theorem argue for a more moderate version of political economy – redistributive market liberalism – to which I shall return in Chapter 27. With appropriate redistribution, a competitive market system will bring about a just and efficient outcome. Rawlsian justice need involve no discussion of how the economy operates, so long as we are satisfied that it is perfectly competitive. If society will only wind up the mechanism the market will direct us towards the desired result.

The Half-way Mark

The fundamental theorems of welfare economics rest on the assumptions of the Arrow–Debreu model, and if that model were a correct description of how markets work, this book would end here. In Chapter 6, I explained the mechanisms of production and exchange – gains from trade through specialization and competitive and comparative advantage – which have made modern economic systems so much more productive than subsistence economies. In Chapters 7 and 8, I described the incentive-compatibility problem, and explained why central-planning systems had struggled while market economies had, at least sometimes, evolved solutions. In Chapters 8 and 9, I explained how central planning – 'the single voice' – had stifled innovation, and illustrated the mechanisms of disciplined pluralism which made market economies so innovative. These mechanisms have driven the coevolution of institutions and technology which, as we saw in Chapters 4 and 5, characterized the emergence of rich states.

The co-ordination problem remained. How does a decentralized market economy succeed in organizing the division of labour, specialization and competitive advantage? Why does uncoordinated individual behaviour not end in chaos? Chapter 10 considered that question, possibly revealing glimpses of the answer, but ending inconclusively. In Part Three, I described the best-articulated response – the theory of perfectly competitive markets. Chapter 11 described the general functioning of competitive markets, and Chapters 12 and 13 the workings of the markets for two peculiar but central commodities in the modern economy – the markets for risk and capital. In Chapter 14, I explained the theory of general equilibrium, how it all fits together, and in Chapter 15 how general equilibrium theory laid the foundations for the claim that the outcome of competitive markets is not only co-ordinated, but efficient.

The Arrow–Debreu results are the culmination of a long tradition in economics which emphasizes supply and demand, perfectly competitive markets and the search for market equilibrium, conducted by independent, self-regarding agents. This framework is today known as 'neoclassical economics'.

The very term 'neoclassical economics' provokes hostile reaction. Neoclassical economics focuses on individuals, who are assumed to be self-regarding materialists, and that is unattractive. Neoclassical economics is imperialist:[17] many of its practitioners are openly contemptuous of other social scientists, and believe the job could be better done by economists. The contempt is often reciprocated. Neoclassical economics is mathematical, and it is difficult. Students would like something easier, and there is always a sympathetic audience for those who say that what is hard to understand is not worth understanding. In the 1970s economics became one of the most sought-after subjects in schools and universities, but its popularity has waned. Students expected material that would help them in business, and they didn't find it.[18]

This neoclassical theory is elegant and in a sense comprehensive. But it cannot be the end of our search for the truth about markets. It is not that it is wrong, or even irrelevant: many practical insights into how markets work emerge both from the analysis of individual markets and from the theory of general equilibrium. It is just that it is not enough. Some markets are perfectly competitive: but most are not, and even the small modifications needed to cope with EasyJet seemed to change quite a lot. No one could believe that the full panoply of assumptions needed to prove the Arrow–Debreu theorems hold. The analysis of perfectly competitive markets for risk and for capital is instructive, but the extraordinary behaviour in risk and capital markets in the last decade demands explanation. To say that such behaviour must have been rational otherwise it would not have occurred is completely uninteresting.

Becker's assertion that 'the combined assumptions of maximizing behavior, market equilibrium, and stable preferences, used relentlessly and unflinchingly, form the heart of the economic approach' is, on reflection, extraordinary. Why should 'the economic approach' rest on specific empirical assumptions about behaviour, especially when these assumptions are at best partially true? The thoughtful economist, like the trained physicist or skilled doctor, will use whatever techniques and assumptions are appropriate to the task at hand, and expect different assumptions and techniques to be appropriate to different tasks. Economics is not theology, but a means of understanding the economic lives of Heidi and Ravi.

That is why you are only half-way through this book. The truth about markets is much more complex, more interesting and less well understood.

The Enlightenment and Modernity

The failure of socialism, as both doctrine and applied political system, leaves intellectual confusion behind it. This uncertainty threatens the whole Enlightenment project of which Adam Smith and Adam

Ferguson were founders. These eighteenth-century scholars were concerned not just to describe the emergence of spontaneous order in social and economic affairs, but to prescribe for a better society. *The Wealth of Nations* was published in 1776, just after Massachusetts colonists had thrown tea into Boston harbour. The architects of the American and French republics hoped to design ideal social and political institutions on scientific lines. That rationalist vision has dominated the social sciences ever since.

The Enlightenment was to become modernity, and to influence not just economics, politics and sociology, but all areas of cultural and intellectual life. The rise and fall of modernity – the attempt to reassess knowledge from first principles on a rationalist basis – is most clearly exemplified in architecture. From the 1920s, modernist architects – freed by technology from the constraints of conventional building design – set their classical traditions aside. This enabled them to rethink the relationship of buildings to function. In Le Corbusier's famous phrase, 'a house is a machine for living in'. In this spirit, he designed the first tower blocks in Marseilles in 1952. Modernist architecture swept across the world.

It was all a terrible mistake. The architectural commentator Charles Jencks famously announced that the modernist era ended on 15 July 1972, when the Pruitt–Igoe housing scheme at St Louis was demolished.[19] The estate, constructed less than twenty years earlier, had won many architectural awards as a pointer to modernist urban living. But a house is not a machine for living in. The scheme failed to meet the social needs of its residents, and fell victim to crime and vandalism. Its emphasis on functionality proved, in the end, not to be functional.[20] Postmodern architecture is eclectic, drawing on many historical traditions, and offering multiple interpretations of function and appearance. In the last century art, literature, music, theatre and cinema all experienced analogous transitions from modernity to postmodernism.

The contrast between the eclecticism of the postmodern and the functionalist design of social engineers has been described by Jean-François Lyotard, a leading postmodernist, as the contrast between 'little stories' and 'grand narratives'.[21] The most extensive 'grand narrative' was Marxism, which purported to offer a unified explanation of human history and a prescriptive view of a just structure of society, linked by an assertion of historic inevitability. The fall of the Berlin Wall in 1989 has the same symbolic significance for economic systems as the demolition of the Pruitt–Igoe scheme for architecture. And the two events raise analogous questions. Did the Pruitt–Igoe scheme fail because the particular buildings were badly designed, or because any attempt at rationalist architectural design was bound to fail? Did Marxism fail because it was the wrong grand design, or because all grand designs for economic systems are misconceived?

For those who believe in 'the end of history', Marxism was defeated in competition with a superior 'grand narrative' – the American business model.[22] A combination of lightly regulated capitalism and liberal democracy is appropriate, not only for the United States in the late twentieth century, but for all countries and all times. The American business model is appropriate everywhere, and other styles of economic organization – even those of apparently successful European economies – are simply transitional measures towards it.

In an extraordinary reversal, the claims of historical inevitability and economic determinism, once made on the political left, have been taken over by the political right. Just as in Marxism, economic evolution is linked to technological evolution. The historical progress of Marxism was supposedly bound up with industrialization. The triumph of the American business model is supposedly bound up with the progress of information technology.[23]

In the first half of this book, I explored the assumptions which yield the intellectual basis of the American business model. In the second half, I shall examine each of these assumptions.

Economic Models, Little Stories

It is strange that economics and business should be the last bastions of modernity.[24] A book has an author, a building an architect, a constitution has its framers. We can try to divine the intentions of these creators, and believe that knowledge of such intentions might help us to understand their books, their buildings, their constitutions. That is why we study authors as well as texts, and resist the postmodernist claim that there is only the text. An economic system has no architect. There is nothing but the text to study.

As I described in Chapter 10, economists have mostly abandoned the attempt to build large models purportedly descriptive of complete economic systems. These efforts did not produce accurate predictions or many other insights.[25] Many economists do still want to be physicists. Hard though this is to believe, Becker's model of crime and punishment seems to be predicated on the assumption that such social behaviour is, like some natural science phenomena, a simple system capable of being described by a small number of variables and equations. Simple economic models of this kind may have value, but not in that way.

The task of large-scale modelling has more recently been taken up by business consultants, who offer quantitative descriptions of firms and markets, estimates of the profitability of nuclear power stations and the value of mobile phone licences. They believe that by incorporating more and more features of the world in their models, they improve the quality of their description. The power of spreadsheets today runs far ahead of the quality of the data or the capacity of the people who build these models to understand the worlds they describe.[26]

The error of principle – the reason these models will never be useful – is best exposed by Jorge Luis Borges' story of mapmakers who competed to build the best possible map. They eventually understood that the most accurate map simply replicated the world. The search for realism destroyed the purpose of the map.[27] A map is valuable precisely because it simplifies and omits. Economic models are maps for the market economy. A map can be false but never true. Our criterion for selecting among maps that are not false is usefulness, and a map can be too detailed or not detailed enough. We seek the simplest map adapted to our purpose, and it is a different map if we are walking or driving: not better or worse, but more fitted for its use. The London Underground map is a brilliant design for its purpose but useless to pedestrians. The 'little stories', or economic models, of this book are to be judged in the same way.[28]

I once debated the relationship between the social sciences with some anthropologists. We adjourned to the pub, and someone bought a round of drinks: the discussion naturally turned to the reasons why. For the economists, the explanation was obvious: the practice of buying rounds minimized transactions costs, reducing the number of exchanges between the patrons and the bar staff. The anthropologists saw it as an example of ritual gift exchange and described the many tribes that had developed similar customs. I proposed a test between the competing hypotheses: did you feel cheated or victorious if you bought more rounds than had been bought for you? Unfortunately, the economists and the anthropologists gave different answers to that question.

The attempt to test competing explanations, I now realize, was a mistaken application of a powerful methodology drawn from physical sciences. One could not establish the truth of one explanation at the expense of the other. Both the transactions-cost theory and the taxonomy of gift exchange contributed to a partial understanding of why people behave this way: neither could provide the whole story.

Social behaviour needs to be understood in many dimensions, and at many levels. The anthropologist Clifford Geertz, following Gilbert Ryle, has written of 'thick description'.[29] A wink is a contraction of the eye muscles but also a social signal. When the door-bell rings an electrical connection is completed which triggers a hammer in a metal box. A stranger seeks to gain admittance. A policeman arrives to tell parents of an accident to their child. All these can be accurate, but incomplete accounts of the same phenomenon. Thick description embraces them all.

The child prodigy Jedediah Barton, taken to see Shakespeare's *Richard III*, observed (correctly) that it contained 12,445 words.[30] As a postmodernist would recognize, he saw the same play as his parents, and yet a different one. Becker's description of family life as a means of deriving economies of scale is one account; the evolutionary biologist sees the family as a means of facilitating parental investment in offspring; and those who describe the family in terms of mutual love provide a further strand of explanation. There is no incompatibility and no need to choose between these elements of thick description. The economic imperialism which seeks to 'explain' all behaviour by reference to rational choice is absurd, but so is a purely anthropological account which denies or disregards the economic functions of social practices.

The Arrow–Debreu model is not a grand narrative, providing a 'true' description of the world, but a particularly elaborate and sophisticated little story, shedding light on the possibility of spontaneous order in complex economic systems. The very clarity and simplicity of the Arrow–Debreu model demonstrates its weaknesses. Indeed, its creators understood well that a primary purpose of their analysis was to spell out the elaborate and extensive assumptions needed to make that version of spontaneous order coherent.[31]

Economic research since Arrow and Debreu has drawn game theory, transactions costs and most recently behavioural economics into the mainstream of economic theory. In the Arrow–Debreu framework, interactions are anonymous and there are many buyers and sellers in every market. In game theory, the players are not anonymous and there are few of them. In the Arrow–Debreu framework, institutions do not exist, or are dealt with in a reductionist way. Institutional or transactions-cost economics recognizes that economic lives are lived in and through economic institutions. Behavioural economics contemplates alternative assumptions about motives and the nature of economic behaviour. I shall introduce game theory and institutional economics in the present chapter and take up behavioural economics in the chapter that follows.

Economic Theory after Arrow and Debreu

In 1944 John von Neumann and Oskar Morgenstern published *The Theory of Games and Economic Behavior*. This approach was, after an interval, to revolutionize economic theory. The analysis of competitive markets supposes anonymous interactions among many buyers and many sellers. The fragmentation and impersonality of these markets lead to incentive compatibility – there is no need to consider behaviour and responses of other market participants. If Part Three of this book was mostly concerned with these anonymous interactions, Part Four describes how the working of markets differs when these interactions are not anonymous. Game theory established mathematical tools for discussing strategic interrelationships in small groups and is essential for this analysis.[32]

Game theory has a popular appeal that fixed-point theorems will never achieve. This is partly the product of larger-than-life examples. The Prisoner's Dilemma, the most preposterous but the best known of all contributions to game theory, will appear in Chapter 20. Game theory's characters are also larger than life. Von Neumann, born in Hungary, was one of the geniuses of his age.[33] At 18 he was studying for three different degrees in different subjects at different universities in different countries. After making fundamental contributions to mathematics and quantum physics, he turned his attention briefly to economics, which he found 'a million miles away from an advanced science'.[34] Von Neumann became head of the US Atomic Energy Commission – and the inspiration for Dr Strangelove – before dying at the age of 53.

John Nash was author of the principal solution concept in game theory – the Nash equilibrium – but his productive career was ended by schizophrenia. His health partially restored, he was awarded the Nobel Prize in 1994.[35] Nash was played by Russell Crowe in an Oscar-winning film of his life, *A Beautiful Mind*.

Institutional (or transactions-cost) economics regards as its founder Ronald Coase[N], a British economist who spent most of his career at the University of Chicago. His claim to fame rests mainly on two articles, published almost twenty-five years apart. The first was concerned with the theory of the firm. In the perfectly competitive world of Part Three, firms played little or no role. There are many similar producers of every commodity. In Parts Two and Four of this book, there are frequent references to individual firms; in Part Three, almost none. Since common sense suggests that the firm is an important institution in the modern economy, this is a loud and clear warning of the limitations of the Arrow–Debreu framework. Coase's thesis was that the boundaries of firms – islands of organization in a sea of markets[36] – were determined by the balance between the costs of alternative systems. Transactions costs in markets must be set against the problems of incentive compatibility within organizations. Is it cheaper to hire someone and tell them what to do or to negotiate contracts with potential suppliers? This make or buy decision is a central issue for every business.

It was only in the 1970s that Coase's approach was developed much.

The economic historian Douglass North[N] described how the evolution of economic institutions, particularly property rights, had provided the basis of the historical development of the market economy.[37] Oliver Williamson argued that contracts between firms, and the internal structures of businesses themselves, were also determined by the costs of alternative institutional arrangements.[38] Twenty years later these ideas had developed into a comprehensive economic approach to the structure of economic organizations.[39]

Economics Evolving

Game theory and transactions-cost economics allowed economists to address issues excluded from the Arrow–Debreu framework. The generation of economists who followed gave particular attention to issues of risk and information. They asked 'How can co-ordination still be achieved if information is imperfect?' and 'Why do risk markets not function as the Arrow–Debreu model requires?'

Joe Stiglitz was a leading figure in that generation, and certainly the most prolific.[40] His work, and that of others, showed that dealing with risk and information required a much more complex truth about markets. In the 1990 Wicksell Lectures Stiglitz set out his revisionist stall:

For the past half century a simple paradigm has dominated the economics profession. . . . The most precise statement of that paradigm is provided by the model of Arrow and Debreu. It postulates large numbers of profit (or value) maximizing firms interacting with rational utility-maximizing consumers. . . . I want to argue in these lectures that the competitive paradigm not only did not provide much guidance on the vital question of the choice of economic systems but what 'advice' it did provide was often misguided. The conceptions of the market that underlay that analysis mischaracterized it: the standard analyses underestimated the strength – and weaknesses – of market economies.[41]

In 1995 Stiglitz joined the President's Council of Economic Advisers and in 1997 was appointed Chief Economist at the World Bank. Installed at the heart of the Washington consensus, Stiglitz did not change his views – nor refrain from expressing them. He found a sympathetic listener in the World Bank's president, James Wolfensohn, who had sought to broaden the institution's remit.

Stiglitz's outspoken views, however, went too far for Wall Street, and, more particularly, for a US Treasury basking in the warm glow of American triumphalism. It became clear that Wolfensohn's continued support for Stiglitz might be at the cost of his own job and in 1999 Stiglitz returned to research and teaching at Stanford University. In 2001, Stiglitz, along with George Akerlof and Michael Spence, was awarded the Nobel Prize for work on markets and imperfect information. That award was a formal recognition of how far modern economics had moved from the simplified theoretical framework of Arrow–Debreu and the simplified policy prescriptions of the Chicago School.

In the remaining chapters of this part of the book, I review successively various assumptions explicit or implicit in the Arrow–Debreu framework: what happens if individuals are not self-regarding utility maximizers? (Chapter 17); what happens if information about complex products is imperfect? (Chapter 18); what happens if our attitudes to risk are inconsistent and irrational? (Chapter 19); how do market economies achieve co-operative, rather than self-regarding, behaviour in households, teams and businesses? (Chapter 20); what brings about the co-ordination demanded by technological interdependencies, such as networks and standards? (Chapter 21); and how do market economies produce new knowledge? (Chapter 22). To list these questions seems to present a fundamental critique of the Arrow–Debreu model. The issues they raise – imperfect information, problems of technical co-ordination, the production of knowledge – are often described by economists as 'market failures'.[42] They would indeed represent failures of the market system if the Arrow–Debreu model were intended to explain the daily workings of markets – to tell us what is happening at the San Remo flower market, in the electricity trading system or in an airline reservation network.

But that was never the purpose. The Arrow–Debreu model is a framework for understanding more clearly the nature of competitive markets, not a description of a complex modern economy. I shall describe some of the many social, political and economic institutions which have developed to handle the problems listed above. These institutions demonstrate the success, not the failure, of the market system. The limited truth about markets which emerges from the perfectly competitive model provides a base for further exploration – no more, no less.

17

Rationality and Adaptation

People

Economic lives are lived by people. People like Heidi. Heidi's work is not necessary to support her family. She sometimes wonders if her family derives any financial benefit, after she has spent money on childcare, domestic help, driving to school, and TV dinners. But Heidi loves teaching, loves children, and knows that she would be bored if she spent every day at home.

Pedro's economic life as an illegal immigrant is the life of rational economic man. He hates his job, although he has sacrificed almost every other part of himself to it. His behaviour is mercenary. His principal aspiration is to have earned enough money to stop being a rational economic man and again become a normal human being. Raoul is tempted to follow Pedro, but values his family more than his material standard of living – or theirs.

Ivan is thrilled with his work. It is, by Russian standards, secure and well paid. For the first time in his life, his working environment is competently organized. He would happily do his job for less money. Olga's salary is ludicrous. She earns more from occasional pieces of translation than a month of teaching and scholarship. But it is the latter that gives her satisfaction, and Ivan earns enough to provide what they regard as an excellent standard of living.

A few minutes spent talking to Ravi shows that what he values most is his status as an official in a prestigious state institution. Sicelo's brother, Patrick, who works in a mine, conforms to the requirements of rational economic man – except that he maximizes his income not for himself but for his family. Despite conversations with his brother,

Sicelo himself finds it difficult to visualize what life would be like outside the village in which he has spent all his life. In any event, the family situation makes it impossible for him to take employment in the mines or in Durban.

These people are not freaks, or saints. They are often selfish. They are like you and me and, like you and me, they find it impossible to separate their economic lives from other aspects of their lives. Pedro and Patrick have achieved that separation. They are both unhappy individuals. Their lives are riven by the conflicts between social and economic values which arise when societies with very different standards of living are close together – as in Mexico's proximity to the United States, or the dual economy of South Africa.

Economists and Rationality

The Chicagoan emphasis on rationality is taken to extreme lengths.[1] But it is almost a badge of honour amongst mainstream economists to seek explanations in rational or self-regarding behaviour. Often, this is achieved by stretching the meaning of rationality. The approach is caricatured by Paul Samuelson[N]. When the governess of infants caught in a burning building re-enters it unobserved on a hopeless mission of rescue, casuists may argue 'she did it only to get the good feeling of doing it. Because otherwise she wouldn't have done it.' As Samuelson observes, this 'explanation' is 'not even wrong'.[2]

Rationality is generally used by economists in one or other of two senses: rationality as consistency, and rationality as self-regarding materialism.[3] Neither of these corresponds to the ordinary meaning of the word 'rational'. I may be consistent in offending my friends or eating more than is good for me, but few people would describe such behaviour as rational. Nor is rational behaviour necessarily materialistic and self-interested. We might not share Ravi's concern with his status at work, or follow Patrick in sending all our earnings back to our families, but these are not irrational things to do.

Most often, economists interpret rationality as self-regarding materialism. I am writing this after putting down an excellent book by William Easterly, a World Bank economist. Easterly is a careful

---

Box 17.1 Happiness and welfare

We don't learn much about happiness by being told that what we do must make us happy otherwise we wouldn't have done it. Research in at least three areas is increasing our real understanding of what makes people happy.

Statistical analysis relates descriptions of happiness (or other measures of satisfaction with life) either to characteristics of the society in which individuals live, or to characteristics of the individuals themselves. As explained in Chapter 3, there is some tendency for people in richer countries to say that they're happier, but it is not strong. And as societies become richer, the proportion of people who say they are happy does not rise much. There is strong evidence that within a country well-off people report themselves as happier than poor people. But other variables – such as marital and employment status – are also of great importance.*

Neurophysiological research has begun to identify activities within the brain which are associated with what people describe as happy experiences. The role of the chemical serotonin is central. A drug like Ecstasy produces an immediate rush of serotonin, while the effect of anti-depressants such as Prozac is to influence the uptake of serotonin by neurotransmitters. These relationships between behaviour and serotonin uptake are found in animals as well as humans.†

Experience sampling asks people to describe how they are feeling at instances of time over a longer interval. Generally the highest scores are recorded when they are successfully performing absorbing and challenging tasks. Work is usually more rewarding than passive leisure activities, such as watching television. These flow experiences seem to cause states of happiness independent of the intrinsic value of the activity – thus the curious mixture of pleasure and pain involved in mountaineering and other arduous sports.‡

*Easterlin (1974), R. H. Frank (1985), van de Stadt, Kapetyn and van de Geer (1985), Lane (1991), Clark and Oswald (2002).
†Davidson (2000), Breiter *et al.* (2001), Greenfield (2000).
‡Csikszentmihalyi (1992), Loewenstein (1999).

---

and sensitive observer of the economic problems of poor countries, and Chapter 23 is indebted to him. Yet Easterly begins by asking 'What is the basic principle of economics? As a wise elder once told me "People do what they get paid to do; what they don't get paid to do, they don't do." [4]

It is inconceivable that Easterly really believes this; the case studies which illustrate his book immediately contradict it. An Indian widow sacrifices her own health to secure an education for her children; Sudanese youths starve because their country is riven by a dispute over Islamic law; an Egyptian farmer sells a clover field to take a second wife.

Economists insist on rationality because they do not like the alternatives. [5] Self-regarding materialism is a better predictor of behaviour than altruism; [6] and Easterly's cynicism is the result of depressing experiences working with government officials in poor states. But the extremes of universal self-interestedness and universal altruism are not the only assumptions about behaviour which might be made. We know from our everyday lives – including our economic lives – that reality is somewhere in between.

Such a reality is necessarily complex, however. There are few ways to be rational, but many ways in which it is possible to be irrational. Self-regarding materialism is predictable; the actions of those who balance multiple objectives are more difficult to analyse, which is why economists adopt a concept of rationality that reduces to self-interest. It seems to offer an anchor in an ocean of otherwise unpredictable human behaviour. The assumption of rationality gives economics a rigour that distinguishes it from other social sciences. A further attraction for many economists is that conclusions can be drawn from wholly *a priori* reasoning. No empirical investigation is required. A joke about economists runs: 'If you ask an economist to study the behaviour of horses, s/he would sit at a desk and ask "What would I do if I were a horse?"' The analysis of economic behaviour requires us to look at actual choices of firms and households, not simply to impose assumptions on their behaviour. It is time to study horses.

Adaptation

Behaviour is a product of the environment in which people find themselves. What Easterly really means is that people respond to what he calls incentives.[7] Easterly provides an engaged, and engaging, description of a Lahore wedding, which vividly illustrates the paradoxes of Pakistan: creativity, intelligence and beauty, side by side with corruption, authoritarianism and poverty. Why are Pakistani scientists able to make atomic bombs but unable to organize a vaccination programme? Why are educated Pakistanis more productive in Silicon Valley than in Lahore? Why are World Bank bureaucrats more honest than Pakistani ones?

'People do what they get paid to do' is part of the answer, but it is a facile response. If human nature is everywhere self-interested, why is the Pakistani public service corrupt but the World Bank is not? Would James Wolfensohn, President of the World Bank, be corrupt if he were a Pakistani civil servant? A World Bank official is fired if he is corrupt, but a corrupt Pakistani civil servant is not. But this is a manifestation of the problem, not its explanation. That explanation is found in path-dependency and adaptation. Both corrupt and honest behaviour are self-reinforcing. A member of an organization with a reputation for its integrity will wish to expose dishonesty. A member of a corrupt organization will find it difficult to be honest. He cannot manage on his salary: he is not expected to.

The same people might be corrupt in a corrupt environment and honest in an honest one. But this is only part of the explanation: they are not the same people. We seek environments appropriate for us. A Pakistani nuclear scientist will get a better job in Pakistan than in the United States: for a Pakistani doctor or software engineer, the reverse is true. And that is why Pakistan can manufacture nuclear weapons but cannot organize a vaccination programme.

Pakistani economists who are committed to economic development in poor countries will prefer to work in the World Bank than the Pakistani civil service, which is why the World Bank employs many able Pakistanis. What would Mr Wolfensohn do in Pakistan? The question is absurd. Mr Wolfensohn is adapted by personality, training and experience to the job of being a senior banker in the United States. He is not and could never have been a Pakistani civil servant.

All these aspects of economic behaviour are adaptive. Adaptation means that the traits of behaviour we observe are those which are most likely to be replicated in the environment in which we find them.

Adaptive behaviour is very different in the monastery and on the trading floor. It is the behaviour that fits its environment. And both the monastery and the trading floor are adapted to their purposes, though some might query their purposes. Evolution favours what is good at replicating itself, rather than what is good. This fundamental distinction is essential to understanding any evolving system.

Workers of the World, Unite!

That distinction between adaptive behaviour and optimal behaviour was precisely the problem Jack Welch faced at General Electric. Organizations develop processes and routines and establish values of their own, and it is important that they should do so: this is how the experience and capabilities of the organization are passed to new members. But these values and processes may become ends in themselves rather than means to the organization's goals. The organization comes to measure the achievement of its members by their contribution to the internal cohesion of the organization rather than their contribution to its purposes. This is the nature of helpfulness, of superficial congeniality.

The same phenomenon was found in Mao's China, in Britain's electricity industry, in the later phases of Henry Ford's control of the Ford Motor Company. My own experience of Oxford University was an illuminating and instructive example.[8] The values prized within all these organizations were internally generated. Workers were praised for their diligence in regurgitating the contents of Mao's *Little Red Book*. Civil servants were promoted for the consensual skills which ensured that they spoke to ministers and the public 'with a single voice'. Managers were hired or fired for their devotion to Henry Ford's ideas. The rituals of Oxford University's committees, like those of the Chinese mandarinate or Ottoman empire, were pursued for their own sake, even by people who perfectly understood their futility.

In all these systems, organizational characteristics are self-reinforcing. In an organization which values helpfulness, people will tend to be promoted if they are helpful, so they learn to be helpful, and imitate the behaviour of the helpful. Moreover, those whose natural instincts are helpful will be attracted by the prospect of working in such an environment while others with different approaches and characters will go elsewhere. Helpfulness becomes ever more entrenched as a predominant value.

The common feature of these environments is that behaviour which is adaptive within the organization is dysfunctional for it. Never mind that Chinese industrial production is falling, that the AGR programme is billions over budget and years behind schedule, that General Motors is overtaking Ford and Oxford University is losing its status as an international university. It is not permissible even to say these things. This is the inability to face reality that Welch identified in General Electric's superficial congeniality.

Ultimately, if these structures last long enough, they resemble the organizations described in Kafka's *The Trial*. No one is in charge, and everyone is part of a system which they know is ineffective but are powerless to change. Václav Havel, the poet who became President of the post-Soviet Czech Republic, describes this as he writes of the greengrocer who displays in his window a sign demanding 'Workers of the World, Unite!'[9] Of course, he observes, the greengrocer is not impelled by desire that the workers of the world should unite. But who is? The answer is no one: everyone is trapped in a world in which it is adaptive, though universally understood to be pointless, to print, distribute and display these signs.

The phenomenon of self-regarding, self-perpetuating selection mechanisms is common in the public sector but can equally be found in private sector monopolies. The Western equivalent of the sign demanding that workers of the world unite is found in the meaningless sloganizing and mission statements of large corporations. These manifestations are sometimes the product of totalitarian corporate dictatorships; sometimes, as in Havel's example, the product of a self-policing culture in which no one dares to laugh; IBM's market dominance allowed it to maintain internal cultures which were not consistent with the external objectives of the organization.

For a time, but not for ever. Reality must be faced if there is an external layer of selection which reviews output rather than procedure. In General Electric, a new management culture applied different performance criteria to business units. Ford was ultimately obliged to react to competitive pressures. Organizations which face no competition, or have no mechanisms for responding to it, may continue in such behaviour for extended periods. The Chinese and Ottoman bureaucracies survived for centuries.

Mechanisms of Adaptation

Adaptive behaviour, therefore, is not necessarily efficient, or optimal, in any ordinary sense. In English, we use the word 'good' in both senses, and when we describe 'a good concentration camp guard', the ambiguity is obvious.[10] Similarly, a good decision or a good policy may be defined, not as one which leads to good outcomes, but one which meets the perceived need of the organization for consensus among varying interests.

What is adaptive may not be efficient: but the equation of adaptation with efficiency is one source of resistance to the use of evolutionary models in the social sciences. It was a century before the mathematics of Darwin's ideas were properly understood. In the meantime, confusion generated by the phrase 'survival of the fittest' led to an erroneous belief that evolution was a process of continuous improvement, that it carried moral authority, and justified assertions of racial superiority and eugenic policies.[11] The opprobrium which followed attached even to the much more careful theory of sociobiology, developed in the 1970s by scientists such as E. O. Wilson.[12]

We do not want to believe that the development of human institutions and thought is a random process, and it is not. While the Darwinian evolution of species is driven by chance – genetic mutations emerge accidentally – the evolution of social, political and cultural institutions is the result of many different selection mechanisms. These include learning, imitation and reward. Learning enables evolution to proceed much more rapidly. Genetic selection would, eventually, breed children who did not play in busy streets, but learning and imitation produce the same results more quickly. And a genetic predisposition to listen to parental advice is adaptive. Reward is an economic selection mechanism with no simple biological analogue. Companies whose competitive advantages match their market – whose characteristics are adaptive – grow in absolute and relative size. In this way, the competitive market economy selects for the distinctive capabilities of firms.

Chicago, Salem and Wall Street

In 1953 Milton Friedman published a collection of *Essays in Positive Economics*. The arguments Friedman presented there not only defined the approach of the Chicago School but influenced the development of economics much more widely.

Friedman claimed that rationality was not an assumption about motivation, but a prediction about behaviour.[13] Even if individuals were not self-interested, self-interested behaviour would drive out altruism. Firms might not seek to maximize profits, but the only firms to survive in competitive markets would be those which did maximize profits. Self-regarding, materialistic behaviour would be the norm because no other behaviour could persist in a market economy. This claim unites Friedman and anti-capitalist protesters. Yet both are wrong. This type of argument does not show that behaviour will be rational. It shows that it will be adaptive. And rational and adaptive behaviour may, but need not, be the same.

In December 1998 Henry Blodget, a journalist who had found a job as analyst at a small merchant bank, announced that shares in Amazon.com, the on-line book retailer, were worth at least $400. The price was then around $250. Jonathan Cohen, analyst at the respected Merrill Lynch, countered with the suggestion (subsequently shown to be correct) that $50 was a more realistic valuation. But within a month, Amazon shares had soared beyond $400. And Blodget soared with it: he succeeded to Cohen's job at Merrill Lynch. Blodget went on to promote a wide range of Internet stocks for his new employer, most of which turned out to be worthless. Whether Blodget believed these extravagant valuations, or whether he issued them to advance his career and bonus prospects, may never be resolved. In 2002, the New York State Attorney General Elliot Spitzer revealed internal memos written by Blodget, which displayed less enthusiasm than his public pronouncements. In one, he described a stock Merrill were recommending as a 'piece of shit'.[14] But enthusiasm by Internet analysts for Internet stocks, whatever its basis, was certainly adaptive. The person who occupied Blodget's post in 1999 was bound to be wildly optimistic about the prospects for Internet stocks. No one else could have continued to hold that position, as Cohen's experience showed. Whether the individual concerned was cynical or genuine in his beliefs is relevant to how angry we should feel and how legal action should be determined, but we do not need to know the answer to that question to explain what happened.

In Blodget we recognize a familiar historical figure. In Arthur Miller's play *The Crucible*, the part of Henry Blodget is played by Reverend Hale: 'on being called here to ascertain witchcraft he felt the pride of the specialist whose unique knowledge has at last been publicly called for.'[15] Both Hale and Blodget eventually understood that they had helped unleash madness beyond anyone's control. The behaviour of market participants in 1999–2000 was adaptive but irrational, just as it was adaptive but irrational to believe that Salem, Massachusetts was besieged by witches in 1691.

Adaptive behaviour, by definition, is self-sustaining and self-reinforcing. Honesty is adaptive in the World Bank. Superficial congeniality was adaptive in the heyday of strategic planning at General Electric. Corruption is adaptive in the Pakistani civil service. Bullishness is adaptive at Merrill Lynch.

Pursued by a Bear

An economist specializing in game theory is in the wilderness with a friend when they see a bear approaching. The theorist pulls out his laptop computer and starts to compute an optimal strategy. His friend cries out in alarm, 'Run, there is no time to waste.' The economist smiles complacently. 'Don't worry,' he says, 'the bear has to work it out too.'

The joke is not particularly funny, but it contains an important truth.[16] When economists adopted game theory, they assumed rational – self-regarding, materialistic – behaviour. In a Nash equilibrium, each player adopts the best strategy given the strategies of all other players.

Biologists also adopted game theory, but did not – could not – assume their subjects had access to laptops. They developed the concept of an evolutionarily stable strategy.[17] What behaviour by bears would allow them to survive and thrive, even in the face of incursion by other bears with different behaviour? That sounds like the same question, but it is not. It exemplifies the difference between adaptive and rational behaviour. The adaptive bear catches the rational economist. This distinction will, in Chapter 20, explain why adaptive co-operators do better than rational self-regarding maximizers.

I described in the last chapter how neoclassical economics was enhanced both by game theory and by transaction-cost economics. But neoclassical rationality assumptions were imposed on both. The transactions-cost solution to the wilderness dilemma is that the economist should optimize within constraints. He should do just the amount of calculation needed to find the best strategy in the light of his knowledge that every second devoted to calculation increases the chances of being caught by the bear.[18] Borrowing Herbert Simon's term (but for a very different concept) Oliver Williamson calls this optimization under constraints 'bounded rationality'.[19]

In this vein, transaction-cost economics often degenerates into a Panglossian view of the world: institutions which exist must be the solution to some constrained-optimization problem. Economists even have a word – recoverability – for deducing the maximization problem to which observed behaviour is the answer. But this version of bounded rationality confronts a fundamental problem. How could the economist know when to stop calculating when he cannot know the benefits of further calculation? If we knew enough to be boundedly rational, we would know enough to be completely rational. The best answer is an evolutionary one: but such an answer leads us to adaptive, instinctive responses – such as those of the bear. And that is our behaviour too. When a bear approaches – we turn and run.

Behavioural Economics

But this response is wrong. The instinct to flee from danger is powerful, and adaptive. It is wise to turn and run when faced with fire, flood, muggers and dangerous machinery. But not when you encounter a bear. (This is probably not what you expected to learn when you bought this book, but may be the most valuable information in it.) It is in the nature of adaptive responses that they work for us in general but may be inappropriate in particular cases. Many boundedly rational decisions are mistaken, some seriously so.

You have a ticket for a play which has cost £20. On arriving at the theatre, you find that you have lost the ticket. Would you buy a new ticket? You have decided to see a play for which tickets cost £20 and on your way to the theatre lose a £20 note. Do you still buy a ticket to the play? This is one of a set of pairs of questions posed in the 1970s by two Israeli psychologists, Dan Kahneman and Amos Tversky, who created the subject now called behavioural economics. Kahneman and Tversky found that practically all their subjects would still go to the play if they had lost £20, but less than half would still go if they had lost the £20 ticket.

Kahneman and Tversky did not simply challenge the standard economic assumption of rationality, but began to identify patterns of 'irrationality'. The ticket problem illustrates 'framing'. The choice we face is the same in both cases – to pay £20 and see the play, or go home and watch television. But the way in which problems are described influences our answer.[20]

These explorations beyond rationality begin to describe how we really think. We apply conventions and rules of thumb that generally serve us well. Some are probably genetic, some the product of learning, imitation and reward, some are universal, some culturally specific. We occasionally apply these rules in situations where they do not work for us – many so-called irrationalities are of this kind. People we deal with may attempt to exploit these irrationalities – some ways in which they do will emerge in the next two chapters.

We behave adaptively in our economic lives, and the institutions in which we act these lives are themselves adaptive. The remaining chapters of this part of the book illustrate various areas in which adaptive individual behaviour, and adaptive institutions, have coevolved. In the next chapter, I consider how households and firms have developed mechanisms to deal with the problems of imperfect information.

18

Information

In perfectly competitive markets there are many potential buyers and sellers of each commodity, such as apples. All apples are the same. Or perhaps all Granny Smith apples are the same. Or perhaps we can easily tell the quality of each Granny Smith apple and locate many producers of each grade. Even apples are not easy. Goods and services sold in modern market economies are often much more complex. What happens when we are not quite sure what it is we are buying?

The Wallet Auction

I have just pulled my wallet from my pocket. It is on the desk in front of me. How much will you offer for the money in it?[1] If you have read so far, you can probably guess something about my habits. But you do not really know how much I spend, or how often I visit the bank, or whether I prefer to pay with cash or plastic card. You might speculate that there is £50 in my wallet. But you would not be wise to offer that much. Your potential profit is the difference between what is in the wallet and what you pay. If you succeeded with a £30 bid, and your assessment that there is £50 in my wallet is right, you would gain a surplus of £20. But this won't happen. If there is more than £30 in my wallet, I will reject your proposal. If there is less than £30, I will sell it to you, but you will be worse off. The transaction doesn't make sense. The only offers I will accept are offers you should not make.

The problem is that I know what I am selling and you don't know exactly what you are buying. There is an information asymmetry between buyer and seller. And this is true of almost every transaction in a modern economy. The car manufacturer knows more about the car than the purchaser. The clothes retailer is better informed about current fashions and the quality of materials. The supermarket knows the provenance and age of its lettuces, and knows that you don't. The wallet example is striking because there is no motive for exchange except differences in information. There are no gains from trade through specialization or differences in capabilities.

Even when there are net gains from trade, transactions are clouded by differences in information. In the used-car market well-informed sellers face ignorant buyers. Suppose – as in a famous model of Akerlof[N] (1970) – there are two kinds of car – reliable cars and lemons. The seller knows which is which but it is difficult for the buyer to tell. The price of used cars will be discounted to reflect the incidence of lemons in the population. It will be an average of the values of good cars and of lemons. But that average is a good price for the owner of a lemon, and a disappointing price for the vendor of a reliable car. So owners of lemons will want to sell, and owners of reliable cars won't. As buyers discover this, that knowledge will push down the price of second-hand cars. But the problem is cumulative. The lower the price of used cars, the more reluctant owners of reliable cars will be to sell, and the more justifiably suspicious buyers will be. So second-hand car prices will be low, second-hand cars will be of poor quality and many second-hand cars will be bad buys even at these low prices. This is exactly what many people experience.

If information is imperfect, some people will regret their purchases. But there is a less obvious problem that is even more serious for the efficiency of competitive markets. Bad trades do happen, but many good trades don't. I need to sell my excellent and reliable car, but you will not pay what it is worth because you cannot be sufficiently confident of its quality. So the market will not be Pareto efficient. Allocations which would make both parties better off may not be achieved in competitive markets.

Sellers of cars try to overcome the lemons problem. They do not want you to think they are selling because the price is more than the car is worth. The small ads placed by private buyers often say 'Genuine reason for sale'. 'One owner' suggests a careful driver, or a serviceable car. The social context – the buyer's knowledge of the situation, or of the seller – makes the transaction possible. The most important mechanism for developing that context is reputation.

Reputation

Lord Halsbury was a distinguished nineteenth-century English jurist. His legal contemporaries valued his edition of the laws of England and Halsbury's reputation for scholarship and accuracy guaranteed extensive sales. Still, admirers of Halsbury today mostly know that he is dead. But it is worthwhile for the owners of the title *Halsbury's Laws of England* – the publishers, Butterworths – to maintain the accuracy of the work. The reputation of Halsbury has become the reputation of the book rather than the man. Butterworths know they have a valuable asset, and their customers know Butterworths will invest in maintaining its value. There will be a continuing need for an accurate record of the law.

Reputation is the principal means through which a market economy deals with consumer ignorance. When we are ill, we suffer not just pain but asymmetric information. Our confidence in the doctor deals with the asymmetric information and we hope that his prescriptions deal with the pain. Typically, there are several different layers of reputation in this transaction. We visit a doctor, relying on the reputation of doctors in general, and on the particular reputation of Dr Smith. If Dr Smith is away, we may consult another member of the practice. The person we consult enjoys some reputation simply through being a doctor. We expect that Dr Smith would not jeopardize his or her own reputation by associating with incompetent colleagues. We may also need to rely on the reputation of consultants whom Dr Smith recommends, the reputation of hospitals or the reputation of particular drugs.

Individuals and firms with established reputations – like Dr Smith and Butterworths – have incentives to maintain them. Every day, we rely on the reputations of doctors and accountants, supermarkets and newspapers, car manufacturers and banks. We rely on them because we do not wish to train for years to diagnose our own illnesses or understand the tax code. We do not want to visit factories to see that our food is prepared in clean conditions, or to go to Afghanistan to see the state of affairs for ourselves. We cannot ourselves judge the reliability of the cars we buy or the solvency of the banks to which we entrust our money.

It is simply wrong to think that a market economy does or could rely on the diligence of individual consumers to deal with these problems. Life is too short, and there are more interesting ways to spend it than studying the balance sheets of banks. We can never have enough information to assess the competence of our doctor because if we did we would not need to consult a doctor. Of course, individual experiences are the stuff of which the reputations of firms and practitioners are made. But these individual and commercial experiences take on life, and significance, only when they become part of shared social knowledge.

Reputation works best when reputations are contagious. Respected business people deal with other respected business people, and their continued reputation depends on behaving in this way. This is the most important mechanism for enforcing trust in business dealings. But it often breaks down. Institutions in the City of London which themselves had high standards of integrity, apparently felt that they could deal with Mohammed al-Fayed or Robert Maxwell without compromising their own integrity or diminishing their reputation with their other customers.[2] Doctors, believing it important to maintain public confidence in their profession, have been notoriously slow to act against incompetent colleagues.

Advertising

My uncle was a Scottish pharmacist of scrupulous integrity. When asked by a customer to recommend a brand of expensive skin cream, he struggled between his conscience and his desire to make a sale. 'Madam,' he said, 'the advertisements speak very well of it.'

Advertising is 'cheap talk'.[3] We expect advertisers to say that their products are good, and do not feel wiser when they do say this – to such an extent that they have mostly stopped. Copywriters have steadily drained all information from their work. Coca-Cola advertising a century ago told you that the beverage was healthful, refreshing, the preferred drink of ladies, available at any drug store. Today, the same company tells you only that 'Coke is it'. There are many advertisements where you cannot tell what is being advertised if you do not already know.

It is not only businesses which advertise. We dress to impress potential employers or potential partners. Commercial advertising – for clothing, cars or perfumes – sells goods which we in turn use to advertise ourselves. Many other species spend far more of their resources on advertisement than human beings. They devote effort to grooming, as we do, and, like us, they expend resources to show off beautiful bodies. The colours and petals of birds and flowers are impressive, but nature has many more extraordinary examples of advertisement. Male grouse engage in competitive displays (leks) of their charms to females, who note the best and return to mate with the winners.[4] Bower birds construct arbours many times their own size to impress and attract potential partners. Human beings sometimes behave in similar ways. In the 1970s economists, puzzled to explain the increasing prevalence of costly but contentless advertisement in the market economy, and biologists, puzzled to explain the ubiquity of costly but pointless display in nature, came up independently with similar answers.[5] Today a general theory of advertisement is common to economics and biology.

The information which these displays contain, and effectively the only information which they contain, is the information that the advertiser is able and willing to invest resources in impressing potential partners – mates, or customers. But this is important information for these potential partners, because it tells them that the advertiser is well endowed and willing to invest resources in a relationship. This is equally true of the relationship between the bower bird and his mate and the Coca-Cola company and its customers. The paradox – which is illustrated by extreme examples from nature such as the bower bird and the peacock's tail – is that wasteful communication is necessary to demonstrate its truth. Cheap talk is worthless precisely because it is cheap, which is why girls were traditionally taught to value an engagement ring above a man's promise that he will still love her in the morning.

Costly and wasteful advertisement demonstrates that the advertiser is also investing in the quality of the product and a continued relationship with customers, because otherwise the costly and wasteful advertisement would serve no purpose. And – as with peacocks and bower birds – advertisers are thrown into the competitive presentation of ever more extensive displays.

Brown Coal

Businesses also have to trade with imperfect information. Many senior executives of energy companies made the trip in a small plane from Melbourne to the Latrobe valley. Their destination became evident well before they saw the airport. A cloud of steam hangs over the area. The Latrobe valley contains one of the largest deposits of brown coal in the world, and its economy is entirely devoted to burning that coal. Huge mechanical diggers shovel this plentiful but poor quality fuel into power stations. Much of the electricity for south-east Australia is generated there. The cash-strapped government of Victoria decided to sell the three power stations in the Latrobe valley – Hazelwood, Loy Yang and Yallourn. They invited sealed bids in an auction. Three foreign companies, two of them British, one an American consortium, were successful – or so they thought. The auction raised far more than had been expected, and the sale of electricity assets allowed the government to retire most of the state debt.[6] Today, however, the winners of the auction are nursing their wounds. PowerGen, one of the British companies, has written off most of the value of its purchase, the American buyer is struggling, and the other British purchaser, National Power, is tight-lipped about the performance of its Australian venture. These companies discovered, expensively, the 'winner's curse'.

The effects of liberalizing the Australian energy market were unpredictable. The government's consultants painted a rosy picture of high prices and rising demand. But that was no more credible than the patter of a used-car salesman, and the serious contenders commissioned their own studies. Estimates of the future price of electricity from the Latrobe valley spanned a wide range. But the successful bidders expected prices at the top end of the range, and pitched their bids accordingly. That was why they were the successful bidders.[7] If prices had simply been in the middle of the range of estimates of informed buyers, the firms which won the auction would still have lost money handsomely. Even the average expectation of the bidders was likely to be optimistic: after all, the bidders had chosen to take part in the auction. Other firms had taken a look at the project, and, more pessimistic, had decided not to become involved.

The winner's curse was discovered when the US government auctioned offshore oil blocks.[8] Oil companies learned that their winning bids were for areas where their geologists had made more bullish assessments than similar geologists, with similar training, working for competitors. The blocks companies got were the ones where their advisers had screwed up.

Deciding which firm should operate Loy Yang power station, or drill for oil in the Gulf of Mexico, seems very like the problem of deciding who should have *Portrait of Dr Gachet*. In all cases, the issue is the allocation of a scarce resource between competing ends. But there is a key difference between a 'private value' auction – for *Dr Gachet* – and a 'common value' auction – for Loy Yang. In the private value auction of *Dr Gachet*, everyone has the same (accurate) information about the appearance and provenance of the painting. If different people make different bids it is because they have different preferences or because some are richer than others. These different bids are the result of different private values. In the common value auction of Loy Yang, all the bidders had similar financial resources. There were no differences in preferences: no subjective or aesthetic issues were involved. Bids differed only because different firms made different (and mostly inaccurate) assessments of the value of what it was that they were buying.[9] There are no differences in private values: only differences in estimates of the common value.

The three examples of this chapter so far – the wallet auction, the used-car market, the sale of Loy Yang power station – are all examples of how market institutions which work in a straightforward way when all parties have identical, and comprehensive, information, can operate in an entirely different manner when the information is imperfect. Oil companies have learnt about the winner's curse. They no longer bid what they think a block is worth.

Large companies understand that auctions are complex processes, and employ mathematical economists to devise their strategies. So governments hire their own mathematical economists to outsmart the bidders, as in the auctions of 3G mobile phone licences in Europe in 2000.

Mobile Phone Auctions

The UK government's mobile phone auction occurred at more or less the top of the bubble in 2000. Collectively, the five companies which received licences to operate third generation mobile services in the UK paid £23.5 billion. In the cold light of day, the businesses concerned wondered what they had done: there is no likelihood that the profits from providing these services will ever approach £23.5 billion. Given the costs of rolling out networks, it is not certain that the licences are worth anything at all. In July 2002, one of the 'successful' bidders in the German auction – which raised even more – abandoned its licence and wrote off its expenditure.[10] The auction was carefully designed to avoid the winner's curse, by ensuring that all bidders were well informed about the actions of the others. But if information is imperfect, adaptive behaviour can give rise to irrational outcomes, as it did with Henry Blodget's recommendations for Merrill Lynch.

Many layers of adaptive behaviour contributed to this overall irrationality. Telecoms stocks were owned by people who held exaggerated beliefs about their value. They had suffered a winner's curse in outbidding more-rational investors. Senior executives of telecoms companies were unreasonably optimistic about business prospects: like Henry Blodget, they would not have been in these positions otherwise. The advisers to the process hoped to be appointed as advisers in the successive auctions they knew were planned in other European countries. Given the fundamental irrationality of stock prices, many other kinds of irrational behaviour were adaptive. No company could have maintained its stock market value if it failed to obtain a licence.

Like Henry Blodget and Merrill Lynch, Sir Christopher Gent and Sir Iain Vallance (the CEO of Vodafone and Chairman of BT) made bad decisions, in the sense that these decisions were extremely costly to the people on whose behalf they acted, or claimed to act. But their decisions were adaptive: Blodget, Gent and Vallance would have found it difficult to hold their jobs if they had made different decisions (but also found it difficult to hold on to their jobs given the decisions they did make).[11]

Moving Office

Advertising and reputation are mechanisms that market economies have evolved to deal with the problems of imperfect information. They are signals that traders use to communicate. Sometimes the signals are prices themselves.

In England, the usual method of renting office space is to take a lease for a fixed period of up to twenty-five years. An occupier may move before that period ends, but the person moving out must find another tenant and remains liable for the rent originally agreed. The new rent is a matter for negotiation, and will be paid by the new occupier to the original tenant.

A few years ago, my business planned to move to larger premises. The property market in Central London at that time was depressed and so was the estate agent we consulted. He recommended that we should ask for a rent of £27 per square foot but was not optimistic about the prospects of an early letting. He was right. After two months, few people had inspected the property and there were no offers.

I went to see the agent and told him that we were unhappy. We were professional economists, and supply and demand were second nature to us. If no one wanted to rent our property at £27 per square foot, we should try something lower. How about £22 per square foot? The agent advised against, but we insisted. He remarketed the property at £22 per square foot. The agent was again right. A month later, almost no one had come to inspect the property and no offers had been made. He suggested we put the matter back in his practical and experienced hands. We reluctantly agreed. The asking price reverted to £27 per square foot. The following week, the agent rang me with an elated tone. A potential tenant was willing to pay £27 per square foot. There were snags: we would have to allow the new tenant six months rent-free occupation, and make a contribution to his fitting-out expenses. We quickly agreed.

I debated this experience with my colleagues. It seemed to defy the laws of supply and demand. But there was an entirely sensible explanation. Properties are complicated, and idiosyncratic. It is difficult to tell what a property is like from a description. All buildings are different. It is easy to waste time visiting properties that are obviously unsuitable the moment you step in the door. The price in the particulars isn't just there to equate supply and demand; it also gives information.

When our agent advertised the property at £27 per square foot, he said to potential tenants: 'This is similar to other properties for which I and my competitors ask a rent of £27 per square foot.' And when we insisted on a rent of £22 per square foot, we gave confusing signals to prospective tenants and their agents. We were saying 'Although this looks like a £27 per square foot property, it is a £22 per square foot property.' Those who heard that statement did not necessarily think 'This is a bargain': they might equally have thought 'There is something wrong with this property, which I shall discover when I spend substantial amounts of money having a surveyor inspect the building and a solicitor read the lease.'

The very economic theory we used to insist on the primacy of supply and demand suggests they were right to be suspicious. When we search for a property, we shall be lucky to find one which has similar characteristics to other properties but is cheaper: we are more likely to find one which is fully priced but ideally suited to our particular requirements. A good agent should be trying to achieve a full price for the seller. The efficient market hypothesis should apply to the property market, and in an efficient market there are few bargains to be had.

The practical wisdom of the estate agent incorporated considerable knowledge about his market. He would not have stayed in business otherwise. This does not mean he was able to explain why his market worked as it did, and he could not. But estate agents are adaptive people, and he was.

Prices of complex products convey information about products, and one of the functions of agents is to certify that information. When supply exceeds demand, as was true in that Central London office market in the early 1990s, prices are not immediately cut to match demand and supply, because this would generate confusing signals. The market adjusts, somewhat imperfectly, through side payments – rent-free periods and fitting-out expenses. The stickiness of prices creates periods of surplus and shortage.

Unemployment

In a perfectly competitive market wages and salaries should fall to equate supply and demand in each individual labour market. I have occasionally asked managers in large companies how they would react if a prospective employee offered to work for 10 per cent less than the person who was doing the job at the moment. If the caller got an interview, it would only be because of the eccentricity of the approach. We transmitted confusing signals to the market when we cut the price of our office space to £22 per square foot, and a worker who offers to undercut existing employees gives confusing signals to the market. The natural interpretation of the offer is 'I am desperate, there is something wrong with me'. The firm which accepts the offer is saying 'We are more concerned with our costs than with the calibre of our staff'. In a market in which quality is important but hard to judge, price competition is rarely effective or intense. And in the labour market, quality is important to both parties. The employer is concerned for the abilities and commitment of his staff, the worker wants a pleasant environment and congenial and capable colleagues.

Concepts of the 'going rate' are important to the decisions of employers and employees. Since prices have an informational function as well as a market-clearing function, there are good reasons for this, but a consequence is that in the labour market, as in the property market, prices will adjust only slowly to changing economic conditions. So there is unemployment in slumps, and labour shortage in booms.[12]

And so the Arrow–Debreu model can be no more than a partial explanation of how market economies solve co-ordination problems. In that world, price serves only to equate supply and demand and there are never any shortages or surpluses, because movements in prices eliminate them. But concepts of fair prices are not evidence of socialism, or relics of St Thomas Aquinas.[13] They are a necessary part of our economic lives. 'The going rate' is an essential tool for conveying information for the functioning of a market economy. Price instability is often economically damaging, and people who disregard 'the going rate', as we tried to do, may impede the operation of markets rather than lubricate them.

Imperfect Information Changes Everything

In perfectly competitive markets, products are homogeneous. But markets with imperfect information exist because products are differentiated. In perfectly competitive markets, exchange is anonymous. But in markets with imperfect information, the identity of the trader is a key element of the exchange. In perfectly competitive markets, price equates supply and demand. But in markets with imperfect information, price is a means for sellers to communicate with buyers, and because it serves this function it may fail to equate supply and demand. In perfectly competitive markets, all exchanges are efficient and only efficient exchanges occur. But in markets with imperfect information, exchanges occur which buyers regret and trades which would benefit both buyers and sellers may not happen.

Yet market economies have been resilient, even ingenious, in developing mechanisms for dealing with problems of imperfect information. To recognize the ubiquity of imperfect information is not to mount a critique of market economies, but rather a critique of the adequacy of the perfectly competitive model as a description of how market economies work. The truth about markets is much more complex.

19

Risk in Reality

Calculated, self-interested behaviour in perfectly competitive markets leads to the efficient market hypothesis and forms the basis of the modern financial theory of Chapter 12. That theory, at once sophisticated and practical, provides a set of tools which should enable us to manage and reduce risks in our private and business lives.

Yet reality is more complex.[1] We have seen how perfectly competitive markets may operate very differently when behaviour is adaptive, rather than rational, and when there are asymmetries of information. Markets in risk are particularly subject to imperfect information and vulnerable to 'irrational' behaviour. In fact, most trading in risk markets comes from one or both of these sources, while the same combination of factors ensures that many necessary-risk markets never come into being.

Our attitudes to uncertainty are born of a mixture of hopes and fears, grounded in instincts and social conditioning. Our reactions to risk are often intuitive. Some neurophysiologists argue we have a language instinct: small children manage the complex task of learning language quickly and easily.[2] The opposite seems true of probability theory: sophisticated adults find its simple mathematics hard. The most powerful argument for rationality in risk markets is that it is easy to devise strategies which make money from those who do not act rationally. That is precisely what happens.

Maurice Allais[N] is one of the few continental European economists to have won a Nobel Prize. His seminal attack on the economic theory of risk was published under the subheading 'Critique des postulats et axiomes de l'école américaine'.[3] Kahneman and Tversky pursued Allais's approach of observing subjects' choices between risky alternatives in laboratory situations.[4] All three discovered it was easy to persuade their subjects to make inconsistent choices, and these inconsistencies were not random. The subjects were more concerned to avoid small losses than to secure gains of similar amounts. They were ready to accept low probabilities of big losses but unwilling to accept high probabilities of small losses. They liked high probabilities of small gains but took less interest in lower probabilities of big gains. Above all, they were unreasonably confident about their own judgements; the feeling is familiar.[5]

Further evidence of inconsistency in behaviour towards risk comes from 'market anomalies' – securities market behaviour which violates the efficient market hypothesis. For example, US share prices tend to go up in January and down on Monday.[6] No insider knowledge is required to establish that Monday follows Sunday and January follows December. These market anomalies cast doubt on the claim that the price of risky assets incorporates all publicly available information. American shares fell by over 20 per cent on 19 October 1987. On 15 July 2002, they dropped by 5 per cent in the morning and rose 5 per cent in the afternoon. These movements could not possibly be explained by new information about company prospects.

The most important market anomaly is that the 'equity premium' – the historical difference between the return on stocks and shares and the return on risk-free assets – seems much too high. As financial economists have debated the 'equity premium paradox', estimates of the size of the premium have fallen.[7] Even so, an average return of 4–5 per cent over safe assets seems far more than is needed to compensate for extra risks. If equity returns were indeed so high, shares would almost certainly outperform bonds over all but the shortest periods of time. (This is of course what people selling shares advertise.)

Why do people play Britain's national lottery when only about half the takings are returned to players? The lottery offers a nicely judged combination of a very small number of very large prizes, together with a very large number of very small prizes. The jackpot provides the prospect that attracts attention, the proliferation of £10 prizes amplifies the punter's confusion about risk.[8]

Are Markets Efficient?

If the efficient market hypothesis is not necessarily true, that casts doubt on market efficiency in a wider sense. In 1999–2000, securities markets around the world were disrupted by noise traders – people who buy and sell stocks without knowledge or concern for fundamental values. Insurance markets did not minimize the unavoidable costs of an accident such as Piper Alpha. The resulting losses were focused on individuals who had no idea of the magnitude or nature of the risks they had taken.

Barings, one of the oldest and most respected banks in the City of London, failed in 1995 as a result of losses in derivatives markets by one of its traders in Singapore. Nick Leeson had not attended university and had no qualifications and little training. He made profits by the simple expedient of reporting his successful trades and stuffing his unsuccessful ones in a drawer.[9] Leeson's superiors did not understand the markets in which Leeson dealt but did understand that their bonuses were related to his reported profit. They had neither inclination nor capacity to question his activities. The fall of Barings symbolized the demise of gentlemanly, yet greedy, capitalism in the City of London.[10]

If Leeson's activities were naïve, those of Long Term Capital Management (LTCM) were sophisticated. Most investment funds simply buy portfolios of stocks and bonds. A hedge fund such as LTCM trades derivatives and arbitrages between similar securities in different markets. LTCM's partners included Robert Merton[N] and Myron Scholes[N], who won the Nobel Prize in 1997 for their contributions to financial economics. Merton and Scholes operated with experienced Wall Street traders.[11]

Sophisticated investors can use derivative markets to insure their portfolios. By buying a put option at 10 per cent below the current market price, maximum loss is limited to 10 per cent – the cost of the option is the insurance premium. After the Asian crisis and Russia's debt default in 1998, investors were particularly nervous. LTCM sold insurance against large price changes – in either direction. In market jargon, they traded swaps and equity volatility. The $4 billion of assets which LTCM managed may seem a lot of money, but not in the context of all the share and bond markets of the world. With this capital base, LTCM held derivative contracts worth around $125 billion. The value of the underlying securities on which these derivative contracts were based was much larger. LTCM did not have enough capital to provide the insurance which markets sought. Its actions could transfer risks but not eliminate them – the risk of a general stock market collapse can only be shuffled round the market in a game of pass the parcel.[12] LTCM was betting that the price of the insurance the fund was selling would fall sufficiently quickly for it to be able to buy it back at a profit. The price didn't, the fund couldn't, and LTCM was pushed to the edge of bankruptcy. LTCM's positions were so large that the Federal Reserve Board, concerned by the consequences of collapse, orchestrated a rescue.

Participants in Piper Alpha – the underwriters – were ignorant fools who did not know the risks they took. Participants in LTCM – the managers and investors – were clever fools whose sophistication had blinded them to the risks they took. In both cases recirculation and repackaging of risks turned a limited problem into a systemic one. A single failure jeopardized the entire Lloyd's insurance market (in one case) and American securities market (in the other). Far from spreading risks and reducing their costs, markets in risk concentrated them and made them threatening, even fatal, to the solvency of participants.

Asymmetric Information and Adverse Selection

The risk that Lochnagel will not come in first in the five o'clock at Ascot; the risk that the Monetary Policy Committee will unexpectedly lower interest rates; the risk that a gas explosion will destroy an oil rig in the North Sea: these risks are the currency of specialist risk markets in modern market economies.

They are not, however, the principal risks which people face in everyday life. These are the risks of divorce and the breakdown of relationships, the loss of job and a career, the possibility of chronic illness. Unwanted pregnancy, or single parenthood cannot be insured against. There is a limited market for insurance against redundancy and unemployment. The premiums are high and cover is limited to the payment of outstanding loans. Yet people who cannot buy protection against these threatening events do have insurance against comparatively trivial risks. Insurance against a broken windscreen, insurance against bags going missing when their owners are on holiday, insurance against a video recorder being stolen, or a washing machine breaking down. We can and do insure things that don't matter much, but can't and don't insure things that do.

Why is it not possible to insure against divorce? Statistics on marriage and divorce are readily available to enable an insurer to set a fair premium. But few recently married couples would buy divorce insurance. Most newly-weds think that their relationship is less likely to break down than the gloomy statistics suggest, otherwise they would not have married in the first place. The insurance company, which looks only at statistics, takes a different view, and the premium seems high.

Soon, however, information asymmetry is reversed. Perhaps the relationship develops well, perhaps it does not. Happily married couples will not be interested in divorce insurance; those whose marriages are rocky will. Couples visiting their insurance broker will be as representative of the whole population as couples visiting the marriage guidance counsellor. This is the problem of adverse selection: the people who want the policy are bad risks. A 'fair' premium based on the average incidence of divorce would be unprofitable for the insurance company.

Asymmetric information issues pervade risk markets. The insurer would sensibly raise the premium to match the characteristics of those who want policies. But this makes divorce insurance attractive only to those whose marriages are truly on the rocks. The cautious insurer must raise the premium still further. A divorce insurance market would be like the market for lemons. As in the wallet auction, there is no price at which a seller would wish to sell and at which a buyer would wish to buy. So no market can exist: and there are no markets in divorce insurance.

Divorce is extreme: the gap in knowledge between the potential insurer and the insured is insurmountable. To offer marriage and divorce insurance an insurance company would have to make intolerable intrusion into personal affairs. For similar reasons, there is no effective insurance against unemployment or redundancy. The prospective insured is better informed about the risk than the insurer.

Markets for medical and life insurance work better. Individuals do not know much about their susceptibility to disease or their life expectancy. Inexpensive and non-invasive tests of height, weight and blood pressure can give the insurer equivalent knowledge about the prospective policy holder's state of health. Even so, adverse selection is a problem. Medical insurance is cheaper when bought by an employer for a group of workers. This is not primarily because of the employer's greater bargaining power. The insurer insists that the employer provide cover for all employees, and so reduces or eliminates the adverse-selection issue. Private individuals seeking medical insurance are likely to be sick more than the average, or to be hypochondriacs.

Markets for life and medical insurance are possible because medical knowledge is still rudimentary. But some biological and environmental factors which cause disease and mortality can already be identified – genetic defects cause Huntington's chorea, smoking predisposes to lung cancer.

This is the tip of a large iceberg. The problem it raises for insurance markets cannot be solved by limiting the use of genetic information by insurers. That would only aggravate the issue of adverse selection. The only solution to the potential information asymmetry is to stop such information being collected at all – which would be impossible even if it were desirable. In fifty years' time, private medical and life insurance may be as difficult to obtain as divorce and unemployment insurance today, and for the same reasons.

Moral Hazard

Most risks in our environment depend on the actions we take. If we have financial protection against risk, we expose ourselves to more risks. This is the problem of moral hazard.[13] People do not allow their houses to burn down just because they have fire insurance. Young women do not set out to become pregnant because there are social benefits for single mothers. But their behaviour is adaptive. Social habits and economic institutions evolve together. With no fire insurance, there would be fewer chip pans and open fires. When single mothers were very harshly treated, there were fewer of them.[14] As always with adaptation, cause and effect work in both directions.

The patchy evidence we have suggests that the risk of violent or accidental death in England has remained more or less constant since the thirteenth century. 'The axe of the drinking companion and the neighbour's open well were regulated, to be replaced by unruly horses and unbridged streams; when these were brought under control it was the turn of unfenced industrial machinery and unsignalled locomotives: today we battle with the drinking driver.'[15] Given the changes in the economic and natural environment, and in legislation and regulation over the period, this constancy is extraordinary. The metaphor of the risk thermostat is powerful. We have a certain tolerance for risk and adjust our behaviour to the risks in the environment. We walk more gingerly on a mountain path than on a pavement. Fewer children are killed in road accidents in Britain today than eighty years ago. Roads have become more dangerous, but precautions by children and their parents have more than offset the dangers of heavy traffic.[16]

Moral hazard makes it dangerous to insure risks which are under the control of the insured. In 1982 Congress deregulated America's mortgage banks – Savings and Loans Associations.[17] But it maintained a system of insurance for their depositors. The combination proved irresistible to fools and crooks.[18] The government met losses while the Savings and Loans, and their executives, kept the gains. When those insured can influence the risks covered, they must be supervised.

Social Insurance of Personal Risks

When people can opt out, adverse selection is a problem. If what they're doing can't easily be watched, moral hazard is a problem. The combination of adverse selection and moral hazard means that risks are best managed by groups which have other common bonds, typically families, communities, workplaces and nations. The management of everyday risk is best and principally undertaken through social institutions. Purely economic agencies such as insurance companies and securities markets play only a minor role.

Risk sharing in social groups is effective because there are many different advantages to participation in these groups, and also because solidarity and sense of obligation come into play. The traditional marriage vow – for richer, for poorer, for better, for worse – could hardly be more explicit in identifying risk sharing as characteristic of the relationship. Only in the twentieth century did marriage become a put option, in which either party could exit the contract at a pre-arranged price. Social risk sharing, however, extends beyond family groupings. The notion that uncertainties of illness and accident should be shared in communities goes back for millennia. As illustrated in George Eliot's novel *Middlemarch*, before railways and the National Health Service arrived, well-to-do local people recognized an obligation to maintain hospitals and doctors tailored their fees to the means of their patients. Communities can be effective providers of medical insurance. Employers can be efficient providers of unemployment insurance. They are far less vulnerable to problems of moral hazard than either private insurers or the state: who could be better placed to judge an employee's commitment to work? And the issue of adverse selection simply does not arise.

For most of the twentieth century, large businesses did provide such insurance. Not as a formal contract, but as a mutual expectation. An employee of a bank or similar institution could assume that, in the absence of misconduct, there would always be a job. The consequence was that the employer took much of the risk of changes in technology or in demand. The employee paid a price: pay scales related to seniority, and pensions which deferred remuneration, emphasized the long-term nature of the contract. In the last two decades of the century, many of these implicit contracts were broken.[19] The benefits were an immediate gain in earnings per share; the long-run effect is that the government is now the only credible provider of unemployment insurance.

The term 'social insurance' originated in Germany in the late nineteenth century.[20] It describes the formalization of risk sharing at work and in communities within a modern state. Government took over the insurance functions of voluntary organizations – mutual societies and trades unions. Government is well placed to reduce adverse selection, because it can compel participation, but is less effective at reducing moral hazard than the social pressures of a local community. Formal social insurance schemes address the moral hazard problem by limiting the generosity of the benefits they provide and the time period for which the benefits are paid, and attaching conditions – such as a test of genuineness of the search for work – to their benefits.

Business Risk

Some economic risks are inescapable: the risk that crops will fail, uncertainty about the growth in demand for mobile phones. Other risks are the products of the market economy itself. Intrinsic uncertainty about the size of the harvest is compounded by market volatility. No one knows how quickly the demand for mobile phones will grow, but the individual firm, and its employees and shareholders, confronts the additional uncertainty of which business will do well in the marketplace.

Business risks bring problems of asymmetric information and moral hazard. Investors should always have the tale of the wallet auction in their minds. There are people who know more about this venture and have more influence over its outcome than I do; why are they offering a share of its potential profits to me? Why should I buy when they want to sell?[21] Many people would be better off today if they had asked that question five years ago.

The good reason for relinquishing a share of a potentially profitable investment is that the risk is too large for one individual or institution. Antonio could handle the loss of one ship, but not of three. Marine insurance would have enabled him to diversify the risk of storm at sea, but the risks associated with his own business judgement remained. Christopher Columbus could not finance a venture to find a shorter route to the spice islands of the Indies, but Queen Isabella of Castile, substantially richer, could. Sicelo's economic life is precarious because one crop failure can exhaust his assets and reserves.

Yet a business partner in Antonio's venture would sensibly be nervous of information asymmetry and moral hazard. Even if Antonio is completely honest, and truthfully reveals all he knows, he may be more inclined to offer participations when he is nervous about the prospects for his trade than when he is optimistic.[22] Antonio will certainly take more risks if he does not bear the whole consequences of failure. This is not entirely a bad thing; optimism and risk sharing enable many more new businesses to be started, and contribute to the pluralism of a market economy.

Information asymmetries extend more widely. Those who invest with Antonio will not be a random sample of the population. Investors will be those who know Antonio, or believe they do. Investors, like those telecom shareholders, will be those who are more than averagely optimistic about the prospects for Antonio's trade. In all investment booms – from the South Sea Bubble to the dot.com mania – money is raised cheaply from people who expect very high returns but do not in the end receive them. Investment banks have become skilled in managing the issue process so as best to appeal to 'irrationalities' in the minds of potential investors – the attraction of 'prospects', their aversion to even small losses.

In Chapter 13 I described how the stock market had developed, not as a primary means of raising capital for new businesses, but as a market for the sale and resale of secondary participations. The most publicized British Internet business – the appropriately named lastminute.com – was floated on the London Stock Exchange in March 2000. It had been founded eighteen months earlier, and had earned total revenues of less than £1 million. The sale of shares raised £70 million from investors and notionally valued the whole company (including the stakes of its founders) at £400 million.[23] Of the £70 million around £7 million went to advisers associated with the sale. The balance was for unspecified 'general corporate purposes'. It was a ridiculous amount of money for a small start-up business, and a year later most of it was still in the bank. The punters who subscribed lost most of their investment. The price of the shares fell to a level which reflected the actual value of the company – essentially, what was left of its £70 million.[24]

Stock markets are not, and never really have been, important sources of capital for industry. They do allow the risks of business to be spread and diversified, but the volatility of stock markets creates its own, larger risks. Most traders are speculative: someone who believes or has been told that Cisco is a better bet than IBM deals with someone who has concluded that IBM is a better bet than Cisco. The talking heads encourage investors to make these judgements.

Is Speculation Useful?

In 'The Methodology of Positive Economics', Milton Friedman presents the example of speculative trading to illustrate the thesis that rationality is imposed by competitive market processes. He claims that market speculation is necessarily stabilizing. Speculators make money only if they buy cheap and sell dear; only speculators who make money will stay in the market for long. So prices will fluctuate less in a market with active speculation than without.[25]

Yet speculation in the US stock market bubble was obviously destabilizing, driving prices to fantastic levels from which they subsequently collapsed. If all traders were perfectly rational (consistent, self-interested, profit maximizing, well informed) there would be no room for speculation, profitable or unprofitable. To give Friedman's argument a chance of being true, there needs to be a little bit of irrationality – noise trading – but not too much. Noise traders lose money to clever speculators. But if noise traders predominate, speculators who base their trading on fundamental values risk oblivion as noise traders sell paper to each other at ever higher prices. This is what happened in 1999. In the previous year LTCM simply did not have enough money to support its – correct – judgement of market irrationality.

Odds on the different horses in a race reflect an average of assessments of their prospects. Similarly, the price of a share reflects the average of investors' views of the value of the company. This information may or may not be helpful in guiding decisions about where new capital should be invested. Banks considering lending, and firms contemplating borrowing or reinvestment, are both likely to be better informed than the stock market about business prospects. The informational function of the market is provided at large cost, and portfolio trading is – necessarily – on average unprofitable for the individuals who undertake it.

The paradox of Piper Alpha was that what had once been primarily an insurance market had become primarily a securities market. The participants were not deriving gains from trade by passing risks to those who could manage them most cheaply. They were exchanging risks on the basis of different opinions about their true nature. The outcome was that risks landed with those who did not know what they were doing and could not afford to bear them.

An omniscient observer, who could penetrate all information asymmetries, might establish the true value of investments. There is no reason at all to think that this price is the one at which such investments actually sell in the marketplace. Most transactions in securities markets are not about sharing or spreading risks; they are like transactions in the betting shop. The people who engage in them believe they are deploying their superior knowledge, but this can never be true of more than a small minority of players.

The Truth about Markets for Risk

Most financial market analysis is still based on the efficient market hypothesis, and more money will probably be lost by defying it than believing it. But that belief should be tempered with scepticism. Rational individuals were overwhelmed by noise traders in 1999–2000. Rational behaviour in financial markets is not necessarily adaptive – it wasn't for LTCM. And what about the flotation of lastminute.com? 'When the allocation of capital is the by-product of the activities of a casino, the job is likely to be ill done.' Keynes wrote this in the aftermath of the bubble of 1929 but his words are equally relevant to the bubble of 2000.

The outcomes of LTCM, Barings and Piper Alpha were perhaps adaptive, in the sense that people who mismanaged risk went out of business (although not for long: John Meriwether, the creator of LTCM, was back in business fifteen months later soliciting money for his Relative Value Opportunity Fund).[26] But the outcomes were not efficient in either the technical or the ordinary sense of market efficiency.

The concept of an efficient market in risk, which manages for us the uncertainty inherent in modern economic life, is an attractive one. It is aesthetically attractive, because the theory of such markets is intellectually challenging yet soluble; and practically attractive, because economic security is one of the principal concerns of every household.

Most of what happens in risk markets – betting, insurance and securities markets – is not efficient in this sense. It is designed to exploit the 'irrationalities' of our everyday behaviour towards risk – practical rules that are adaptive in everyday life, but are not adaptive when we consult our financial adviser or our bookmaker.[27] At the same time, the risks that really concern us – the risks associated with our jobs, our relationships, our health – are not dealt with by risk markets. For these risks, we rely on the help of our friends, our social institutions and the state.

20

Co-operation

The Stag Hunt

'If a deer was to be taken, every one saw that, in order to succeed, he must abide faithfully by his post: but if a hare happened to come within the reach of any one of them, it is not to be doubted that he pursued it without scruple, and having seized his prey, cared very little, if by so doing he caused his companions to miss theirs.'[1]

The author of this passage, Rousseau, recognized that self-interested individuals would not necessarily co-operate even though such co-operation would make everyone better off. There is an economic need for social institutions to enforce co-operative behaviour. Rousseau developed Hobbes's metaphor of the social contract – it makes sense for us all to agree to give coercive power to the state. So government is an adaptive institution: societies with the power to enforce co-operation will catch more deer than societies without. But we do not necessarily need a state to solve the problem of the stag hunt. Market economies also rely on teams – groups which work together regularly. Reciprocity within groups encourages co-operation. We co-operate because we expect similar favours in future.

Yet modern economies require, and obtain, more co-operation than can be explained either by coercion or by reciprocity. We help other people even when we do not expect that they will have an opportunity to help us in future. If a stranger asks the way, we usually tell them. And we expect that strangers will do the same for us. We display generalized as well as particular reciprocity. This behaviour is not rational, if rationality means self-regarding materialism. But it is adaptive – societies in which people help strangers are not only nicer but more prosperous.

To the Lighthouse

The Eddystone Reef lies fifteen miles south of Plymouth at the entrance to the English Channel. A granite mass, its summit is only three feet above the water at high tide. Hundreds of ships are known to have been wrecked on it. Many which simply never returned to port probably foundered there. Other ships were driven on to the English or French coasts by captains too anxious to avoid the Eddystone.

The solution has been known for thousands of years – the lighthouse at Alexandria was one of the seven wonders of the ancient world.[2] A distinctive light on the reef enables sailors to steer clear of it. Implementation is more difficult: lighting desolate rocks is not easy. The first Eddystone light was not built until 1698, and it lasted only five years before the lighthouse and its builder were swept away in a storm. No trace of either was ever found.

These technical difficulties emphasize the economic problem. Who will pay for a lighthouse?[3] The current Eddystone lighthouse – the fourth – cost £59,000 when it was built in 1882, equivalent to £2 million[4] at current prices. This cost is small relative to potential loss of life, ships and cargoes. But it is a substantial sum for any individual ship owner. The benefits of the Eddystone lighthouse are widely distributed and their incidence is difficult to identify or predict; it is a public good, and public goods will not be produced by self-regarding individuals in competitive markets. The builder of the first Eddystone light was not self-regarding. Mr Winstanley, who perished in the subsequent storm, was an eccentric but public-spirited gentleman who also constructed Winstanley's Waterworks to amuse visitors to Hyde Park. He undertook the project after two of his ships had been wrecked on the Eddystone Reef.[5]

If the Eddystone light did not exist, a major oil company might build it. Exxon, BP and Shell each have large traffic in the English Channel, and the consequences for them of a major accident would be serious. But Exxon might reasonably ask why it should do it rather than BP and vice versa. That suggests a role for associations of like-minded people. Clubs work best when the number of beneficiaries is not large or diverse and there is a community of interest between them. But when there are many disparate members, there is a temptation to free-ride. No one feels their individual contribution is essential to the project's viability. Social pressure to participate is less intense.

If voluntary co-operation does not work, or work well enough, government can impose it. Public goods may be financed from general taxation. Or the right to impose charges may be transferred to the agency which provides the service: British lighthouses are financed today by levies on port users.[6]

The Market in Public Goods

Social institutions, mainly government, provide a range of public goods – the police, street cleaning, national defence, a framework of rules and laws, and mechanisms for enforcing the state's laws and the private contracts of its citizens. As with lighthouses, what is provided for one is provided for all; no one who refuses to contribute can be excluded. Once built, the lighthouse shines equally brightly for all seafarers.

For a broader category of goods, it is possible but undesirable to exclude those who refuse to contribute. Perhaps it is more costly to set up mechanisms of exclusion than to allow universal access – broadcasting, public parks. Perhaps exclusion is undesirable because everyone benefits from general provision – education, refuse collection. Perhaps exclusion would violate norms about the kind of society we want – medical treatment, rural transport. These goods must be provided in productive economies, and also paid for. That requires a mechanism for deciding the level of provision and the distribution of the costs. There is variety in preferences for public goods, just as there is variety in preference for private goods. Some people want more defence expenditure, some less. There are different views about the ways in which defence forces should be used. But no economic system can accommodate this variety of views; whatever is provided is provided for all. There is only one army. The street is equally clean, or equally dirty, for everyone who uses it.

Incentive compatibility – how to obtain the information needed to calculate the costs and benefits of projects – is a fundamental problem for the provision of public goods.[7] Democratic governments – and undemocratic but benign governments – decide what to fund, and what not to fund, by reference to the demands of citizens, although the demands may be influenced, not just by calculations of overall costs and benefits, but also by the costs and benefits to the individuals concerned.

Most interest groups – from environmentalists to abortion campaigners – believe, rightly or wrongly, that what they want is in the public interest. But other lobbyists simply use political processes to seek economic benefit for themselves. Naturally, people who are doing the latter say they are doing the former. The most vociferous advocates of the construction of lighthouses hope to obtain contracts for the construction of lighthouses. Most Scottish lighthouses were built by the austere Stevenson family,[8] better known through Robert Louis Stevenson, who did not build lighthouses and instead created the romantic adventures of *Kidnapped* and *Treasure Island*. The Stevensons built lighthouses because they believed in the value of lighthouses, and they believed in the value of lighthouses because they built lighthouses. Adaptation means that characteristics match the environment.

So the level of provision of public goods is rarely decided dispassionately. Well-off people might naturally want higher levels of provision of public goods than poorer people. They can afford more parks, just as they can afford more champagne. Their votes, however, are usually cast for lower taxes and lower levels of public provision. They assess, generally correctly, that their share of the cost will be greater than their share of the benefits. The exceptions are services, like protection of property by the police, whose benefit goes disproportionately to the better-off.

When self-interested lobbying becomes dominant, voting is based on economic interest. Coalitions are formed in which I will support benefits to you if you will support benefits for me. Measures are adopted which give largesse to small groups – farmers or defence manufacturers – for whom it is worthwhile to invest in lobbying, at the expense of small costs to a wide public. This view of politics as a marketplace is the theory of public choice, pioneered by James Buchanan.[N9]

Public choice theory gives some insight into modern American politics. A key function of the Congressman is to secure benefits for his constituents and those who have contributed to his campaign. Public choice is also relevant to kleptocracies such as Zaire, whose government is simply a vehicle for the economic interests of those who control it. The European states in which the market economy developed fit neither of these models. Louis XIV, who built Versailles and proclaimed 'L'état c'est moi', was both self-regarding and materialistic: but he was still far from an economist's model of rationality. Louis, his courtiers, and the peasants who paid for it all, were acting out traditional roles in an adaptive manner. Their world cannot be explained in individualistic terms.

The French court's failure to respond sufficiently to a changing environment led Louis XVI to the guillotine in 1793. In Europe, government as social contract – a disinterested agency meeting its citizens' needs – was superimposed on structures of traditional authority. The place and time is important. Disinterested government is a key element in the coevolution of social and economic institutions, and although European governments today often fall below the standards of disinterested government, everyone uses that language. All but the most brazen of lobbyists claim that the public will benefit from the policies they seek. Once again, altruism and self-interest both provide inadequate accounts of adaptive political and economic behaviour.

Teams

We are usually more productive when we work in co-operative teams. Many species – most primates, many birds, ants – live and work in groups. But humans are amongst the most social of species. This sociability is fundamental to our economic organization.

Team working serves two purposes. Through team working, we can make use of the division of labour and exploit gains from specialization and differences in capabilities. An orchestra needs a violinist, a flautist, a conductor. An orchestra of thirty people sounds a lot better than thirty one-man bands, and can play a much wider range of music, because the gains from specialization are very large.

These benefits of specialization and capabilities were the subject of Part Two of this book, and they can be derived from anonymous interactions in the perfectly competitive markets of Part Three. It is enough that there be a violinist and a flautist. They don't have to know each other, like each other, talk to each other, and, with modern technology, their separate contributions could even be recorded separately and pieced together. But the best orchestras, like the best teams in all areas of life, are more than the sum of their parts. The performers on a budget compact disc may be an unknown or scratch orchestra: a group of competent studio musicians who met that morning to play that score. The best recordings are made by standing orchestras: groups of people who work together frequently, develop each other's strengths and compensate for each other's weaknesses.

Rousseau's hunt would also have gained by working together, by sharing information and pooling risks. Public goods require co-operative behaviour. Yet, as Rousseau explained, teams of hunters composed of self-regarding materialists would encounter problems. Everyone would do better if huntsmen focused exclusively on catching deer, but each individual member will be tempted into diversions to catch hares. If everyone does this, the hunt will catch no deer.

Today, Rousseau's problem is generally framed as the Prisoner's Dilemma. The story of the Prisoner's Dilemma has always seemed to me unnecessarily complex to illustrate its point but, since it is one of the finest of little stories, I reproduce it here. Two prisoners are arrested and put in separate cells. The sheriff admits he has no real evidence but presents the following alternatives. If one confesses, he or she will go free, and the other can expect a ten-year gaol sentence. If both confess, each will be convicted, but can expect a lighter sentence – seven years perhaps. If neither confesses, the likely outcome is a one-year sentence for each on a trumped-up charge. Prisoner One is uncertain what his partner in crime will do. He notes that, if she confesses, he will get seven years by confessing and ten by remaining silent. He also sees that if she does not confess, he will go free if he confesses and serve a year in gaol by remaining silent. Whatever his conjecture about her actions, he does better to confess. So he confesses. The same analysis applies to her, and she confesses. Both go to gaol for seven years.[10]

People often miss the force of the Prisoner's Dilemma when it is first explained to them. They think that self-regarding people will want to co-operate when they see the benefits of co-operation: the Prisoner's Dilemma arises only because the prisoners do not understand the consequences of their actions. But the paradox is much deeper. The self-interested benefits of co-operation are not enough to persuade self-interested people to achieve them. Even after the Prisoner's Dilemma has been explained, and both parties understand that they will go to gaol for seven years as a result, the self-regarding action is to confess. Indeed, there is some evidence that people who understand the problem posed by the Prisoner's Dilemma are *more* likely to confess than people who don't.[11]

The Prisoner's Dilemma explains why lighthouses will not be built. Replace 'don't confess' by 'contribute' and 'confess' by 'don't contribute': the inevitable outcome is that no one contributes. Replace 'don't confess' by 'watch for deer' and 'confess' by 'pursue hares', and Rousseau's hunt will catch no deer. Replace 'don't confess' by 'co-operate fully' and 'confess' by 'hold back', and people in organizations will never work effectively together, and joint ventures will never work.

These pathological outcomes do happen. The eight isolated pillars that stand on the Calton Hill, just above where I went to school, are popularly known as 'Edinburgh's Disgrace'. The burghers of that rich Georgian city agreed to erect an imitation of the Parthenon to celebrate victory over Napoleon. But the process of collecting subscriptions fell victim to the Prisoner's Dilemma.[12] There are teams that catch no deer because their members are chasing hares, organizations whose goals are defeated because mutual suspicion is the dominant internal value.[13]

Managing the Prisoner's Dilemma

But there are also many lighthouses, successful teams and productive organizations. Adaptive societies protect themselves from the

Prisoner's Dilemma in many ways. Two obvious mechanisms are to change the game or to repeat it. The easiest way to change the game is to employ an enforcer to punish anyone who confesses. If the punishment is worse than a year's gaol, the best course of action changes immediately: both players should keep quiet. The punishment need never be applied: the prospect of it has the desired effect.

There are many candidates for the role of enforcer. In primitive societies, the leader of the tribe, a religious deity, or the combined authority of both, might assume the role of enforcer. Today we use the civil and criminal law. Albert Tucker, who invented the story of the Prisoner's Dilemma, probably used that example precisely because criminals cannot invoke the courts to enforce nefarious agreements. But criminals often have their own enforcers. We talk of 'honour among thieves': those outside the law create their own social institutions to handle Prisoner's Dilemmas.

But there is also honour among the honest. The social and economic lives of hunters were linked, and shirking in the forest implied penalties around the campfire. Yet community enforcement has its own Prisoner's Dilemma. It is in the best interests of the group that everyone should penalize shirkers, but not necessarily in the interest of one individual. So we must not only penalize shirkers, but people who fail to penalize shirkers. There is a common economic interest in the enforcement of social norms. Contagious reputation – which is valuable in dealing with information asymmetry – also helps secure co-operation.

The best strategy for a Prisoner's Dilemma changes if the game is repeated. The American political scientist Robert Axelrod organized tournaments between strategies for repeated Prisoner's Dilemmas.[14] One simple strategy – tit for tat – proved very successful. Tit for tat begins with co-operation, but defects – once – every time the other player defects. Tit for tat exemplifies common features of good strategies for the Prisoner's Dilemma. It is nice – it trusts people until proved wrong; it is responsive – it doesn't ignore what others do; but it is forgiving – it allows occasional mistakes.

We know that already. Tit for tat is part of our instincts and our learned behaviour. Britain's reaction to the invasion of the Falkland Islands, or America's response to the destruction of the World Trade

Center, was not based on any calculation of costs and benefits. Tit for tat, like fleeing from danger, is an adaptive response. Behaviour, attitudes and beliefs have developed in ways that are not necessarily self-interested but are to our economic benefit.

Co-operation is Adaptive

That issue has wide ramifications. In the fifty years or so since the Prisoner's Dilemma problem was first formulated, economists have struggled to explain why there is so much more co-operative behaviour in the world than the pursuit of self-interest would imply. There is a serious literature on why we tip waiters and taxi drivers in places we shall never visit again.[15] We conform to a social norm. That norm is part learned, part instinctive and part enforced by the expectations of others. Only those economists who insist that human behaviour is always self-regarding, whatever the evidence to the contrary, see any issue to be resolved.

For most people – and organizations – tit for tat is an instinctive response. Western societies encourage such behaviour. We teach children to stand up for themselves, but we also teach them not to bear grudges. Our inclination is often to administer several tits for a tat but this feeling tends to pass: we tell ourselves that it is not worth it. We are still not making a rational calculation; we just find the emotional price of continued animosity too high.

In Chapter 18, I described how biologists and economists, working simultaneously on advertisement in nature and advertisement on billboards, had found common answers. This is also true of altruism and co-operation. Despite the image of 'nature, red in tooth and claw', there is much altruistic behaviour in nature. Not only does the co-operative activity of ants go far beyond anything found in human societies, but birds and animals cry out to warn others of impending danger even at the cost of increasing their own exposure to that danger. Biologists do not consider rational explanations. Like bears, the ants and birds have not calculated solutions to games involving reiterated Prisoner's Dilemmas. Their behaviour is adaptive, not rational.[16]

These biological models show that self-interest is not the necessary outcome of competitive evolution, a view as inaccurately attributed to Charles Darwin as its economic equivalent is to Adam Smith. Because the level of natural selection is the gene, maternal – and paternal – investment in nurturing offspring is adaptive, even if it is not rational. We live in families because we have strong instincts to do so, and evolution explains why we have such instincts. This is a much more persuasive and more satisfying account of family life than the account of marriage as economic institution proposed by Gary Becker (see Chapter 16).

However, we also make sacrifices for people outside our immediate family group. When there are large gains to be made from co-operative behaviour, an instinct to form and enforce co-operative groups is advantageous, not just for the group, but for each individual member. It is also advantageous – in cold-blooded evolutionary terms – to be naturally co-operative, to sweat, blush and avoid the eyes of our colleagues when we make promises we do not intend to keep. These characteristics make it possible for colleagues to trust us.

These arguments are subtle. When biologists understood that evolution did not necessarily imply self-regarding behaviour, some developed theories of group selection. Natural selection would favour traits that benefited the group even if they disadvantaged the individual. But these biological arguments are mistaken.[17] In the evolution of species, the fitness of an individual has a much larger influence on reproduction than the fitness of the group to which the individual belongs. This sets a limit to co-operation in the natural environment.

But competition in business and economics mostly does take place at the level of the group. The prosperity of Heidi and Hermann, and of Sven and Ingrid, owes more to the groups to which they belong than to their own personal characteristics. An individual who can tell lies with a straight face can do well in economic life, but only so long as such people are in a minority. When there are gains from team working, groups of self-regarding materialistic individuals will not prosper. Co-operative value systems are key to the development of successful businesses. We co-operate 'irrationally' because co-operation is an adaptive instinct and an acquired value.

Fire and Blood

When fire breaks out in country districts, neighbours rally round to help, as they have done since humans first learned to control fire. As urban communities grew, this worked less well. A more transient population meant less solidarity, and the density of building made fire more dangerous. The Great Fire of London burned for four days and destroyed 13,000 houses before it was extinguished.[18] The more complex street plans of towns also required more professional fire fighters. Early fire brigades were established by insurance companies, which would arrive to minimize the damage to their policyholder's property. In the nineteenth century the fire brigade developed into a universal service provided by local government and financed from taxes. The benefits of lighthouse provision are particularly difficult to attribute to the individuals who receive them. How can anyone know which particular ships would have come to grief on the Eddystone if the light had not been there? Fire prevention is a private good. Most of the benefits of the fire service accrue to the people whose fires are extinguished, and businesses which are victims of major fires meet part of the costs of the fire brigades. But fire prevention is also a public good, like the lighthouse. We hope that the fire in our neighbour's house will be promptly extinguished – even if he is overdue with his insurance premium.

But the fire service is a public good in a wider sense as well. If a pipe bursts, we turn with trepidation to Yellow Pages, uncertain about who will arrive, or when. If we suspect fire, we dial the emergency services, with reasonable confidence of prompt intervention from disciplined, trained officers. The organization of the fire service is an expression of social solidarity in misfortune – the same solidarity behind shared responsibility for medical or financial misfortune. Fire fighting is urgent, and requires constant improvisation. We expect fire fighters to slide down greasy poles, not wait while they negotiate fees. Fire fighters need to be trusted, and to have their instructions obeyed. The effectiveness of a fire service depends on public attitudes towards it.

The only rich country in which the collection of blood is a commercial activity is the United States. There, blood donation is a means for poor people and students to enhance their incomes. In Europe, blood is obtained more or less entirely from volunteer donors, and appeals to social solidarity usually produce sufficient supplies. In 1970 a survey by the sociologist Richard Titmuss claimed that the European system produced higher quality blood more cheaply.[19] Poor people were more likely to supply infected or contaminated blood, and the commercial transaction created information asymmetry: the prospective donor might conceal his or her medical history.

Although the USA was the first rich state to experience a widespread HIV problem, the spread of the disease by contaminated blood was quickly halted as competitive blood collection agencies began to test and treat their supplies. In centralized France the blood collecting agency and the civil servants and ministers responsible concealed mounting evidence of problems; drawing attention to the dangers of HIV was not 'helpful'. Many French recipients of blood, particularly haemophiliacs, contracted AIDS as a result.[20]

The provision of public goods benefits from both solidarity and competition, and these are not always easy to reconcile. It is not beyond imagination to contemplate a world of competitive fire-fighting services, in which some companies won the respect of the public while others, which did not, received fewer calls and encountered less willingness to make way for their vehicles. No market economy, however, organizes its fire services that way. Competitive suppliers of blood do exist, and the results are not clearly worse, or clearly better, than state-organized voluntary supplies. The complex truth about markets implies complex policy choices.

There are many public and semi-public goods in modern economies, such as blood, fire services and lighthouses. For all of them, the social context of the transaction is vital: it determines the quality of output, the quantity of output, and may influence whether they are provided at all. But economic systems don't just depend on co-operation in the provision of public goods. They need mechanisms which restrain individualistic behaviour. The development of long-term relationships and the linking of social relationships with commercial ones sustain team working. Our predisposition is not simply to be self-regarding material-ists. It is to be nice, to retaliate when we are let down, but not to bear grudges for too long. There are good adaptive reasons for this behaviour. We are more prosperous as a result, both individually and collectively.

21

Co-ordination

Co-ordination without a co-ordinator is the extraordinary genius of market economies. The Arrow–Debreu model offered a possible account of how prices achieve co-ordinated assignment, production and exchange even when decisions about all these things were decentralized, but the assumptions of the model exclude many difficult issues of co-ordination. This chapter is concerned with three different groups of co-ordination problems – those which arise from compatibility standards, networks and pollution. Each of these involves an externality, which is a technological relationship between the production or consumption of one firm or household and the production or consumption of another firm or household. If there are externalities, there may be no perfectly competitive equilibrium and the fundamental theorems of welfare economics do not hold.

Standards

In Britain, Japan and Australia, vehicles are driven on the left-hand side of the road. In France, Germany and the United States, they are driven on the right. It does not matter which side of the road people use, so long as it is the same one, and, once a decision has been made, large investment in that standard follows – the arrangement of the steering and pedals of cars, the positioning of street furniture, the design of intersections. Sweden – which drove on the left until 1967 but now drives on the right – is the only major country to have made a recent change.[1]

Driving on one side of the road, or the other, is an unusually clear example of a co-ordination problem. The two options are – initially – equally good, and there are no intellectual or ideological commitments or commercial interests which support one view or the other.

The resolution of co-ordination problems is often path-dependent. Britain, Ireland and Sweden were not invaded by Napoleon, who imposed across his empire the French custom of driving on the right. The design of motorway junctions today is determined by Napoleon's victory in the Battle of Austerlitz and defeat at the Battle of Waterloo. The qwerty keyboard layout is another example of a path-dependent solution to a co-ordination problem. Standards, like keyboard layouts, are everywhere. Currency is a standard. So is language: we need to use the same money, the same words, as the people around us.

Television sets need to be compatible with television broadcasts. PAL is used in most of the world but different standards are found in France and the United States. The wheels of railway wagons have to be the same distance apart as the rails, and both are separated by 4' 8½'' more or less everywhere. Traders want the credit card network with the most members, and cardholders want cards with the most traders. So Visa has become dominant.

Standards often emerge through a process of competition. Early railways were built to different gauges. But there is an instability in standard setting: once a standard, not necessarily the best, gains a decisive lead, everyone has an incentive to follow. Installed base, not technical quality, is what matters: there is no intrinsic superiority in having rails 4' 8½'' apart. English is the dominant world language because it is spoken by the largest number of educated people, not because Shakespeare was a greater writer than Goethe, or because English is easy to learn.

Some standards are imposed. The Académie Française has for centuries defined what is French, and governments regulate television broadcasts. The advantages of compatibility allow bad standards – like qwerty – to survive. But a new bad standard cannot be introduced, and very bad standards are displaced: early word-processing systems disappeared because new ones were so superior that it was worth investing time and money in upgrading. Many standards are constructed by industry agreements. DVD player protocols were determined by a group of hardware and software producers. It is rare for standards to be set and controlled by private companies. We see a major exception to this rule, however, almost every day: the logo of the Microsoft Corporation appears on almost all our computer screens.

It is difficult to maintain private ownership of a standard, because the attempt to maintain control limits the rate of adoption. Being first to secure widespread adoption is key in standards battles. Sony's first video cassette recorders were designed for broadcasters and other professionals. Sony believed that its reputation and market position among experts would give the company a powerful springboard for the consumer market, and that success in this strategy would enable it to impose its own proprietary technology, Betamax, and dominate the entire market. Sony was wrong on both counts. JVC, a subsidiary of the huge Matsushita Corporation, developed a different system, VHS, which was licensed freely. Soon there were many more VHS machines than Betamax recorders in homes. Moreover Sony, and most other firms in the industry, misjudged how people would use their recorders. They thought they would buy camcorders to make home movies. But consumers did not use video recorders to show pictures of weddings and family holidays, or even to watch *Coronation Street* late in the evening, but to play pre-recorded movies, and for this Sony's Betamax was inferior. Since more people had VHS recorders, many more tapes were available in VHS, and so still more new purchasers preferred VHS to Betamax.[2]

Ultimately, Sony abandoned Betamax. Apple also failed with its proprietary operating system: the price of exclusivity was low market share. Indeed, the only historical example of a private standard comparable to Microsoft's is the dominance of nineteenth-century rail-braking systems by Westinghouse. The company tried to reproduce its success by imposing a proprietary standard for railroad signalling, and failed.[3]

Sometimes standards simply fail to emerge. If we need a replacement windscreen-wiper blade, what we need is specific not only to the manufacturer but to model and year. The governments of most countries of the world agreed, through the International Telecommunications Union, to a common standard for mobile phones (GSM). GSM phones can be used world-wide – except in the United States, whose systems are not fully compatible with each other, far less with GSM.

As a result, mobile phone use developed more rapidly in Europe than in the USA.

There is nothing in the organization of a market economy that guarantees a good, or any, solution to standards issues. But the truth about these markets is that they usually work, often through regulation or government-sponsored agreement; sometimes through spontaneous order emerging in the marketplace; occasionally through the success of the products of one particular firm.

Networks

A few years ago it was still possible to holiday in the troubled but beautiful province of Kashmir. I flew to Delhi, caught a smaller plane to Srinigar, and travelled on by jeep and boat. As a porter carried my bags up a dusty track to my destination, I encountered a friend from London. What a small world, we said. But there was really no coincidence. If I had arrived at some random point on Earth, and had met an acquaintance, that would have been extraordinary. There are six billion people in the world, and no one can know more than a tiny fraction of them. But my arrival in Kashmir was not at all random. Travel agents in London deal with a small number of representatives in India, who deal with a few providers in Kashmir. If my friend and I had expressed similar requests, it was not surprising we should end up at the same place. We were in closely connected networks.

Network externalities are a new buzzword in business economics. Connectedness is vital, and it is best to be connected to the largest network.[4] Telephones are the archetypal network externality. There is no point in being the only person with a telephone, and the more people have them the more valuable an individual phone becomes. Such network externalities seem to give huge advantages to early, large players. But these markets can go badly wrong. Either we have competing and incompatible networks, or one company, with the largest network, establishes an unassailable monopoly. There are around 2 billion telephones in the world, and the company which has the highest proportion of this population signed up will attract most new subscribers.

There is one problem with this analysis: it is not how the telephone industry is organized. The world telephone system consists of many operators, large and small. Most provide service in a particular geographical area, and connect each other's calls through negotiated access agreements. The same phenomenon of interacting local networks is found in other network industries, such as the banking system, gas and electricity distribution, and airlines. There are many operators, large and small, and they organize interchange and access. These arrangements are not universal but are nevertheless general enough to allow a network to function. The phenomenon I discovered in Kashmir explains why. In a famous sociological experiment, participants were instructed to contact a named but unknown recipient by identifying someone they knew who would be 'closer' to that person. The experiment tested, and largely confirmed, the hypothesis of 'six degrees of separation' – a small number of links is enough to connect anyone to anyone else.[5]

Our 'small world' experiences show that overlapping clusters produce a very high degree of connectedness from a modest number of direct links. Social organization solves the apparent technical and economic problem. The widespread evolution of networks in market economies is another instance of the power of spontaneous order in social and economic organization. This spontaneous interconnectedness between competing providers is true of the most famous new network of all – the Internet. The Internet is a universal network which evolved with little regulation and outside the control of any single organization. CERN, a European physics research institute which developed the key protocols for the World Wide Web, chose to put these protocols in the public domain. Almost everyone required local telephone companies for Internet access, but regulation in the USA, Britain and several other countries stopped telephone companies using that power to establish a monopoly of Internet connections. Despite the wild optimism of investors, companies such as AOL, Yahoo, Netscape and Microsoft all failed to establish network monopolies. The potential problems of capturing network externalities effectively in a market economy don't seem to be serious in practice.

Pollution

Many externalities in modern economies arise from pollution – of air, land and water. Indeed, the term 'pollution' is now widely used to cover many types of externality. Noisy lawnmowers are said to emit noise pollution, offensively sited billboards represent visual pollution. Not all externalities are bad, however; my beautiful garden is an asset to you as well as me. Pollution can be handled by rules, by agreement between the parties, or by the creation of artificial markets in externalities. Rules against pollution are familiar enough: no litter, no busking, no horns to be sounded after half past eleven.

Rules against externalities work well when the objective is clear and enforcement straightforward. But this is rarely the case. No air pollution is a desirable goal, but it would mean shutting down all transport, all electricity generation and most industrial processes. What we want is a little air pollution but not too much. So we come up with formulas like 'best available technology not entailing excessive cost',[6] which is a statement of the problem not an answer.

'The polluter pays'[7] sounds like a simple and attractive rule, but it quickly unravels. It seems appropriate that people should pay for the pollution they cause, but the attempt to handle environmental problems through legal processes has not worked well. The problem is by now a familiar one: the definition of rights and rules is not obvious, but the result of a social decision. An electricity generator is not negligent in emitting carbons and sulphur dioxide until we formulate a specific rule that says it is.

Attempts to define the rules retrospectively create worse problems. How long and indirect can the chain of consequences be? Were the emissions caused by the electricity-generating company, or by whoever sold the polluting fuel, or financed the power station, or used the electricity – or by all of these? An American attempt to pursue this route – through the 'Superfund' – has simply ensured that funds intended to benefit victims of pollution have ended up in the hands of lawyers, and have increased business uncertainty by holding individuals and companies liable for events long in the past for which they justifiably feel no responsibility.[8]

In any event, pollution is in the eye of the pollutee. You may be offended by my dress, my taste in music or by what I read, but it would be preposterous to suggest I should compensate you for these things. Yet we do have rules against indecent exposure and display, against holding noisy parties late into the night, and to restrict the circulation of violent and pornographic material. To make the principle of 'the polluter pays' work, we have to define the default position: exactly what a world without pollution would be like.

These default positions are the product of social norms, and they change over time. It was once acceptable to deposit excrement in the street, and, until recently, quite normal to allow industrial waste to accumulate in the environs of a plant. In a few decades Heidi and Hermann may find electricity pylons across tracts of beautiful countryside equally extraordinary.

Externalities may be dealt with by bargaining between the parties. This works best where the externalities are big but the numbers affected are small, as when I own land near your proposed factory extension or you are playing your radio too loudly. Such bargaining usually takes place 'under the shadow of the law' and the default position matters here also.[9] I will bargain more confidently if I have a right, rather than a desire, to object to your factory extension, or if a notice says 'no radios to be played'. Markets in externalities are new. They work best for an externality like sulphur or carbon dioxide emissions with many sources. Tradable permits allow those who can reduce emissions relatively cheaply to benefit by selling rights to those for whom the costs are greater. The advantages of the competitive market – incentive compatibility and low information requirements – allow reductions in pollution to be achieved at lower cost.

Market economies solve co-ordination problems through a combination of spontaneous order and social institutions. Nothing guarantees that solutions will be reached, or that those that are reached are efficient. But coevolution has usually produced answers.

22

The Knowledge Economy

Big Knowledge

It is a cliché that we live today in a knowledge economy.[1] At first sight, it seems that market economies should have a problem with knowledge. Once created, knowledge can be transferred relatively cheaply to other people at little cost. If the people who create new knowledge can't protect it, they can't sell it. And if they can protect it, they will restrict its distribution. Either way, the market economy won't produce and disseminate the knowledge it needs. Yet this doesn't really seem to happen. A remarkable feature of modern market economies is the speed with which they do create knowledge – important and unimportant. We complain about information overload, not underload. So how is new knowledge created? And how is it paid for?

Albert Einstein, a clerk in the Patent Office at Zurich, devised the general theory of relativity in his spare time. This led to the university appointment which had previously eluded him, and thereafter Einstein worked in universities. Einstein was honoured wherever he went, but he never became a rich man, not even by the standards of a competent investment banker. Nor did he enjoy the perquisites – the personal staff, the waiting jet – which ease the life of the modern chief executive.[2] Charles Babbage built the first 'analytical engine', or mechanical calculator, in the nineteenth century. But Babbage's machine was designed to do arithmetic. What turned a calculator into a computer was the insight that a machine that can do very long strings of calculations can do almost anything – write letters, check spelling, remember addresses and turn on the central heating. This was first realized by Alan Turing, at the time a fellow of King's College, Cambridge. At the outbreak of the Second World War Turing joined the code-breakers at Bletchley Park. This group – an astonishing concentration of intellectual fire-power – built the first operational computer.[3] Turing spent eight years working for the British government. He returned to King's College and then took a Royal Society professorship at Manchester University.[4] Francis Crick and James Watson, postdoctoral research workers at Cambridge University, discovered the structure of DNA in 1953. Both became fêted scientists,[5] but neither became what the City would describe as seriously rich. The Nobel Prize – the highest accolade in science, and usually an award of financial as well as honorific signifi-cance to those who receive it – is currently about $1 million and is often shared between two or three scientists.[6]

Relativity, computing and DNA are probably the most important contributions to twentieth-century knowledge, and also discoveries of great commercial importance. The economic implications of comput-ing are all around us. Relativity not only led to nuclear power but, by redefining modern physics, influenced devices from spaceships to computers. Genetics and biotechnology will transform medicine and nutrition in the next few decades.

Relativity, computing and the double helix are ideas: antibiotics, television and improved seed varieties are products. Slovenly practice in Alexander Fleming's laboratory at St Mary's Hospital, Paddington, in 1928 led to the discovery that certain moulds would kill bacteria. Although the practical significance of this discovery seems obvious, it was over a decade before research by Howard Florey and Ernst Chain at Oxford University, sponsored by the Rockefeller Foundation, pro-duced a drug fit for patients. Antibiotics virtually eliminated infectious disease as a cause of death in otherwise healthy adults in rich countries, and formed the basis of the modern pharmaceutical industry.[7]

The most important economic event in Palanpur in the last fifty years was the 'green revolution' – the introduction of semi-dwarf wheat. These new varieties were bred in Mexico in laboratories funded (again) by the Rockefeller Foundation.[8]

Sometimes all the bits of science and engineering needed for a new product come together: who puts them together first is pure chance, and often several people do so simultaneously. So it was with television, and it was Philo T. Farnsworth who put them together first in the

United States, or so the courts decided when they upheld his patents. Farnsworth spent years in litigation with the Radio Corporation of America (whose chief executive said 'we don't pay royalties, we receive them'), and ultimately won credit for the invention but little financial return: he was almost ruined by legal costs and sold out to RCA for a modest sum.[9]

The most important twentieth-century innovation from a private sector company was the transistor, discovered by William Shockley at Bell Laboratories in 1947. Silicon Valley is founded not on silicon, but on transistors. Yet this is a peculiar story. Bell Laboratories had a stunning record of technological innovation: but its owners, AT&T, had a virtual monopoly of US telephony, and regulatory restrictions effectively prevented the company deriving any competitive advantage from discoveries at Bell. Development of the transistor proved rewarding for Sony, and for Shockley and the business he established – Fairchild Semiconductor – but not for AT&T.[10] After the break up of AT&T, Bell Laboratories enjoyed rather modest success as an independent company, Lucent Technologies.[11]

Who Paid for Big Knowledge?

My sample of major twentieth-century innovations is small, and controversial. But computing, DNA, antibiotics, green revolution crops and television undoubtedly helped transform our economic lives. How did these innovations come about? Financial incentives played only a small part, and the financial rewards for the discoverers were not very great. Einstein wanted to get a better job. For the rest, the principal motives appear to be the excitement of the process of discovery, and the social rewards offered to a renowned scientist.

The system matters more than the heroic individual. Einstein, Turing and Watson were geniuses. Philo Farnsworth, no genius, was an energetic entrepreneur. But relativity, computers, DNA and television were all discoveries about to happen. If these particular individuals had not found them, others would have made these discoveries instead. Neither commercial sponsorship, nor the prospect of large financial rewards, played any major role.

Yet the role of government in promoting innovation is also unimpressive. The Soviet state was active in promoting scientific research but the results were poor. Russia and the USSR won eleven science Nobel Prizes in the twentieth century, compared with thirteen each for Switzerland and the Netherlands. Although Soviet medicine achieved high standards, no important new drugs were discovered. The evolution of electronics and computers – even for military purposes – lagged so far behind the West that the USA regarded export bans on computers as a weapon in the cold war.

The most extreme blight on Soviet science was Lysenkoism. An undistinguished biologist gained the ear of Stalin because his theory – that there was no genetic basis to evolution and that any desired development was possible in an appropriate environment – fitted the modernist rationalism of socialist philosophy. 'If you want to obtain a certain result, you will obtain it.' The application of Lysenko's principles contributed to the Soviet famines of the 1930s and, in a horrific application of the principle of the single voice, his opponents were hounded, imprisoned and shot.[12]

Only Einstein was employed by a government institution at the time of his discovery, yet the Swiss government employed Einstein as a clerk in the Patent Office, not to work out relativity. Private charitable foundations have been a major source of funding for innovations. The record of the Rockefeller Foundation alone – in both penicillin and the green revolution – is remarkable. With the contributions to knowledge – good and bad – from the University of Chicago, the economic effects of Rockefeller's philanthropy may outrank the creation of Standard Oil.

Philanthropy is the vehicle of pluralism in support of research. Three of the six innovations described above – antibiotics, computing and DNA – occurred in Britain. Chauvinism in selection perhaps: but any pride I feel as a British writer relates to the past, not the present. The institutions in which the research occurred – St Mary's Hospital, Oxford and Cambridge Universities and their colleges – were not government agencies when that relevant work took place, but depend on state funding now. The growth of government finance and control of universities in Europe has been directly paralleled by their decline as centres of research. Europe accounted for 75 per cent of Nobel

Prizes in science before 1939; the USA has taken over 75 per cent of Nobel Prizes in science since 1969.[13] New big knowledge is most likely to be discovered in the pluralist higher education system of the United States.[14]

Small Knowledge

Not all knowledge achieves the exquisite abstraction of the theory of relativity, the concept of a computer or the nature of life. Some is the product of diligent record-keeping, like the times of television programmes, the level of share prices or where to find Bristol Gardens. No one will produce this knowledge in any hope of the fame achieved by Albert Einstein, Alan Turing or Jim Watson. Such knowledge is produced and disseminated through the products designed around them: magazines, financial information systems, maps and street atlases.

In the 1929 stock market crash, share price information was distributed not through Bloomberg television, but on 'the tape'. Clerks on the exchange floor would type in data and a machine would print it out across the country. The speed of flow of information was limited by this primitive technology and when prices plummeted on large trading volumes, the tape ran increasingly late. It was a frightening experience for speculators gathered round machines in brokers' offices. They might already have gone bust ten minutes ago.

News agencies such as Reuters reported events 'down the wire' in a similar way. But these products could be delivered far more efficiently with modern electronics. Financial information could be made immediately available to screens on traders' desks. This transformed securities markets and it transformed Reuters, where imaginative managers were quick to see the potential of this new activity. The Reuters financial information service soon dwarfed the original news-gathering business. When the company was floated on the London Stock Exchange its value exceeded that of the newspapers which owned it.[15] But today Reuters has competitors, like Bloomberg. Both services provide continuously updated information about securities prices, bond yields and exchange rates. They attempt to make their services attractive by adding gossip, sports information and interviews with market celebrities – the talking heads. Although the core information provided is the same, such differentiation enables competitive providers to enter the market profitably.

Television schedules are indispensable for viewers. But the broadcaster also wants us to have that information: we are less likely to watch a programme if we don't know it's on. There are competing objectives. The company is torn between a commercial desire to maximize the value of such information, and an anxiety to disseminate it as widely as possible. Until 1990, British broadcasters balanced these interests by themselves publishing weekly magazines, *Radio Times* and *TV Times*. These magazines contained listings of the broadcaster's own programmes, though not those of their rivals, along with glossy features describing television celebrities and copious advertising. The only way to obtain comprehensive information about programmes was to buy the two. Both were extremely profitable. A change in the law required broadcasters to allow other newspapers and magazines to carry their listings.[16] Newspapers now provided advance schedules, and competitive listings magazines appeared. *Radio* and *TV Times* continue, though less profitably, and with details of programmes on all channels, not just their own. Again, a competitive market supports differentiated versions of the same information.

The first maps were products of art and scholarship. The world grew (more of it was known) and shrank (access to it was easier). Map production became a business and mapmakers competed in the clarity and accuracy of their mapping. A mapmaker's reputation was crucial: a map would not be known to be defective until the purchaser had used it, and got lost. The movement of large armies required careful logistics that demanded accurate mapping. So governments commissioned maps. The British government's maps agency is called the Ordnance Survey, in recognition of its military origins, and other rich states maintain similar databases. But the needs of the army for maps no longer seem so pressing (though they still exist), so governments expected mapmakers to find commercial outlets for their data and skills, while commercial businesses have developed products to meet other demands for maps. The army's requirements are not the same as those of someone invited to dinner in Maida Vale. This insight led

Phyllis Pearsall, rain-soaked in her attempt to find Bristol Gardens, to compile the first street atlas of London. Mrs Pearsall walked London, recording junctions, house numbers and recent construction. Today there are many street atlases of London, and (fewer) street atlases of most towns.[17]

In March 2001 the Automobile Association (AA) paid £20 million to settle a legal dispute with the Ordnance Survey. The AA is not allowed to copy other maps, but the law does not protect the knowledge that the M1 runs from London to Leeds. There is a large grey area in between, and the AA seemed to have moved too far across. 'We spent a day together looking at various different sheets containing lots of different examples. There are some publishers who put deliberate mistakes in their maps,' said a spokesman for the Ordnance Survey.[18]

Precious Knowledge

The AA had fallen foul of intellectual property legislation – they had infringed the Ordnance Survey's copyright. Such rules have a long history. Patents allowed people who invented new gadgets or processes – like John Kay's spinning frame – to enjoy exclusive rights to build and use them for a limited period. Copyright allowed writers and engravers to prevent other people copying their works without permission. This protection continued until the death of the author, and beyond. And trademarks provide an easy means by which the Coca-Cola company or Marks and Spencer can stop other people calling their products Coca-Cola or their shops Marks and Spencer.

The legal structure today is far more complex. The information that *Coronation Street* is on at eight o'clock in the evening is not copyright, but a list of the evening's television programmes is. The knowledge that the M1 goes from London to Leeds is not copyright, but a drawing of it is. The idea of relativity is not protected, nor is Einstein's explanation of it, but the article in which it was published cannot legally be copied. Turing did not patent the idea of a computer, but with a good modern lawyer he might have been able to; the US Courts now recognize patents for business methods, so that one-click ordering is exclusive to Amazon. Ricardo's concept of economic rent is now called Economic Value Added, a registered trademark of an American consulting firm.[19] Today there is a confused structure in which the degree of legal protection for new knowledge bears no relation at all to its originality or economic value.

The patents on John Kay's spinning frame were appropriated by an entrepreneur, Richard Arkwright, who became one of the richest men in England. Arkwright's approach of using intellectual property rights to establish monopolies in related businesses has become a central strategy in many industries. Two immensely precious pieces of knowledge were described in Chapter 9 because of the important role they played in the development of industrial structures. These are not relativity, or the structure of human life: they are the chemical formulation of anti-ulcerant drugs and the software code for Microsoft's operating system, MS-DOS.

US copyright law allows Microsoft exclusivity in the software code of MS-DOS but denies Apple exclusivity in the concept of the graphical user interface: this gave the Seattle company sole rights to Windows. US intellectual-property law creates this monopoly, but, following court decisions in 2001 and 2002, US anti-trust law controls it only weakly.[20] This interaction between intellectual-property rules and anti-trust rules has made Microsoft one of the world's most valuable companies and Bill Gates one of the world's richest men.

Copyright and patents can be invented around. After James Black discovered Tagamet for Smith Kline, a smaller British pharmaceutical company, Glaxo, refocused its related research and created another anti-ulcerant, Zantac. Zantac has similar pharmacological properties but fewer side effects. Zantac became the world's best-selling drug: the profits of the company earned from it (over \$10 billion) made it one of the world's leading pharmaceutical businesses (and helped fund the Wellcome Trust's genomic research). Zantac and Tagamet do not cure the underlying condition but reduce its adverse effects. Patients need extended treatment, possibly for life (blockbuster drugs typically relieve but do not cure common chronic illnesses such as depression or hypertension). As Glaxo launched Zantac, two Australian physicians, Robin Warren and Barry Marshall, discovered that many ulcers were caused by a bacterium, *Helicobacter pylori*, which could be eliminated by an intensive programme of antibiotics. Chemical substances are patentable; treatment protocols are not. Warren and Marshall's rewards for their discovery have been limited to academic kudos and the gratitude of patients.[21]

But not only corporations benefit from intellectual property. Manitoban soldiers in the First World War brought with them a bear cub, named Winnie after the state capital, Winnipeg. Winnie was presented to London Zoo and became a favourite character with young visitors, including Christopher Robin, son of A. A. Milne. Milne amused his son with stories involving the bear and between 1926 and 1928 published them in three slim and engagingly illustrated volumes. Winnie the Pooh has delighted children ever since. In 1929 Milne established a trust to receive royalties from the books and merchandising. The beneficiaries included not only Christopher Robin but institutions of which Milne was fond, such as the Garrick Club and Westminster School. Winnie the Pooh has made the club and the school among the best-endowed institutions of their kind. In 1999 the Disney Corporation bought television and movie rights to the Pooh books and products for approximately £200 million.[22]

The market economy's production of knowledge is not efficient. There are many slightly differentiated products of marginal value – in maps, in software, in pharmacology. Intellectual property law today is a morass which sometimes fosters innovation but often stifles it. Contributions to fundamental knowledge – such as those of Einstein, Turing, and Crick and Watson – are of incalculably large economic and commercial significance, but there is no mechanism, and probably could be no mechanism, for connecting value to reward, nor would it necessarily lead to a faster advance of knowledge if there were.[23] But along with the disciplined pluralism of today's rich states has come a pace of innovation that is both extraordinary and unstoppable.[24]

Part Five

HOW IT ALL WORKS OUT

23

Poor States Stay Poor

The Tryst with Destiny

'Long years ago, we made a tryst with destiny.' On 14 August 1947, Jawaharlal Nehru accepted Indian independence from Louis Mountbatten, the country's last British viceroy.[1] The birth of modern India was accompanied by high hopes and immense goodwill, largely the creation of Mahatma Gandhi, the remarkable leader of Indian nationalism. Gandhi had believed that only the integrity of his movement would ensure the success of its campaign and a basis for subsequent good government. As a result, Nehru and his colleagues and officials were men of exceptional calibre. The architect of economic planning in India was P. C. Mahalanobis, a polymath of formidable intellect and analytic capability.[2] If planning would ever transform a poor state into a rich one, it would be in India.

The same optimism that supported India provoked new interest in development economics. The hope was that other newly independent poor countries could quickly raise their living standards. Walt Rostow described the history of economic development in terms of stages of economic growth – take-off from an industrial society, drive to maturity once take-off had been achieved.[3] Could similar take-offs be achieved in poor countries?

Development economics might have taken Chapter 4 – how rich states became rich – as its starting-point. It did not. Little attention was paid to economic history, and perhaps for good reasons. All innovations and scientific knowledge since the Industrial Revolution were available immediately to poor countries in the modern world, and their growth path could be accelerated through this contact with already developed economies. Technology would be imported, but not institutions. The political framework of modern development would be very different. Government had played a limited role in the evolution of rich states and processes of central co-ordination almost no role at all. It was assumed that productivity growth had occurred in spite of the uncoordinated development of the market, not because of it, and that its chaotic progress had led to hardship and to gross inequalities of income and wealth. Planning of development in countries such as post-war India could not only accelerate growth but achieve fairness in its distribution. Many people thought this had happened in the Soviet Union. It was not until the 1980s that the magnitude of Russian economic failure became widely apparent.[4]

So development economics looked to economic theory rather than to economic history. An influential model of economic growth was developed by Roy Harrod, an aristocratic Oxford don. His framework was developed and expressed more mathematically in the United States, first by Evsey Domar and then by Bob Solow[N]. This is representative of the transition in economics – from prose to mathematics, from amateurism to professionalism, and from Britain to the United States – that was described in Chapter 14. Harrod, Domar and Solow were concerned with the relationship between savings, investment and output growth.[5] Since technology was universal, the level of output was determined by the stock of capital and so by the level of savings, the rate of growth by the rate of advance of technology. Poor countries might be trapped by low savings into low output levels, but if they could escape that trap through foreign aid and forced domestic savings, their growth potential was equal to that of productive economies.

Arthur Lewis[N] – the only black economist to win a Nobel Prize[6] – described the economies of poor countries in terms of two sectors. An industrialized sector, an enclave with the economic laws and rules of rich states, might coexist with a traditional society. An industrial sector of sufficient size would continuously attract labour and eventually take over the whole economy. Lewis's approach re-emphasized a role for external help and internal co-ordination in achieving critical mass for the modern economy.[7]

A generation of development economists and policy-makers in poor countries and international agencies believed that central direction and rapid capital accumulation could not only help unproductive economies achieve take-off, but achieve far more rapid take-off than had been achieved in already rich states. Virtually all poor countries followed India in introducing planning systems, and state ownership. International agencies such as the World Bank would fill the funding gap – the transition to a higher level of savings.

It was not to be. India had sophisticated planning and substantial aid.[8] But from 1950 to 1990 Indian GDP per head grew by an average of 2 per cent per year, and the gap between India and rich states widened. Yet other poor states did worse. India was a beneficiary of those green revolution crops, which contributed far more to rural living standards than the Delhi planners. Latin American economic growth was lower than that of India, and most countries in sub-Saharan Africa are today poorer than at independence. Only in Asia have once poor countries narrowed the gap in productivity and living standards. Productive economies have continued to grow richer, and their growth has been stable. In rich states, productivity rarely falls: even New Zealand has seen its economy grow slightly in absolute terms since 1984.[9]

Shoes

What went wrong? The growth models above contain no institutions – firms, industries or governments. If there is capital, labour and technology, output follows. But imagine introducing in Sicelo's village the capital, technology and methods of organization which are used on Sven's farm in Sweden. They wouldn't work (literally). The difference in capital per head is only a small part of the story. Without changes in the organization of land holding, without a reorganization of social relationships, without an educational revolution and without the infrastructure – from roads to repairmen – needed for different methods of production, imported capital could never be usefully employed. Although this hypothetical experiment is absurd, it is not so far from what has happened with large-scale projects in poor states. Output is a function not just of capital and labour but of institutions, in industrial sectors as in the traditional economy.

In one widely cited early work of development economics, P. N. Rosenstein–Rodan[10] illustrated the need for a 'big push' – an organized, co-ordinated approach to take-off – with the example of a shoe factory. If a poor country were to begin industrialization by establishing a shoe factory, where would it find demand for its products? Its workers would not want to spend all their income on shoes. Lewis's industrial sector would need to develop many activities at once. Development required the simultaneous establishment of a shoe factory, a clothing factory, a bicycle factory. Shoe workers could use their income to buy clothes and bicycles and bicycle workers would buy shoes. A planning agency could co-ordinate this simultaneous development.

Fifty years later anti-capitalist journalist and author Naomi Klein visited a shoe factory in the Philippines.[11] She did not find it a pleasant experience, and no sensitive person from a rich state would. Most employees at the factory were young women, daughters of peasant families. They worked long hours under tight discipline for very low wages, living in small dormitories shared by four or six people. They had been lured by bright lights, depressed by lack of opportunities in their remote villages, encouraged to send money back to support their families. These workers did not buy all the shoes they made. They did not buy any of them. Rosenstein–Rodan's problem had been solved by exporting the factory's entire output. The shoes were branded by Nike, and bought for kids in rich states at a price which represented a month's wages for a Filipino assembly worker.

In Tanzania, the World Bank financed the Morogoro shoe factory. It was built with modern equipment and shoe-making technology to satisfy all Tanzania's demand for shoes and have capacity for exports to Europe.[12] The Morogoro shoe factory was not a success. Its equipment regularly failed because of lack of maintenance and shortages of spare parts. Workers and managers stole from the plant. The Morogoro plant was designed like a modern Western shoe factory, with aluminium walls and no ventilation system, inappropriate for the Tanzanian climate. The Morogoro shoe factory never operated at more than 5 per cent of capacity, and never exported a single shoe. It closed in 1990.

Naomi Klein did not need to go to the Philippines to see the unpleasantness of early stage industrialization. She could have read accounts of conditions in English factories during the Industrial Revolution, or Korean economic development in the 1950s. What she saw in the Philippines was Rostow's 'take-off' as it had been in England and Korea. It would be wonderful – and very profitable – if the technology, capital and equipment used productively in rich states could be transferred to poor countries which have not simultaneously evolved a matching set of social, cultural and political institutions. The Morogoro shoe factory is a memorial to how difficult that is.

Morogoro is a sad case. As is Tanzania itself. Julius Nyerere stands out among the corrupt and vainglorious politicians of modern Africa for his decency and integrity. A socialist who believed in planned development, he devoted himself to the welfare of his people in twenty-one years as President. The state he ruled united Tanganyika – a beautiful area of East Africa, transferred from German to British control after the First World War – and the spice island of Zanzibar.

Tanzania received extensive aid, as public agencies and private donors supported a hopeful development in a depressing environment. Western advisers filled the hotels of Dar es Salaam – Nyerere could never have found people of the quality who had managed India's central planning from the country's internal resources. Yet Tanzanian GDP per head is lower today than when Nyerere became President.[13] After his retirement, Nyerere faded from view, conceding, with the honesty and modesty that had characterized his life, that he and his policies had failed.[14]

India's development is also littered with failed projects. The high hopes of Indian planners were frustrated by endemic corruption at lower levels of politics and bureaucracy; corruption spread upwards as the Gandhi dynasty extended its power. But India's saving grace was its commitment to democracy. As the failures of Indian economic planning became evident in the 1980s, the battery of state controls was progressively dismantled.[15]

India remains desperately poor. Technology has improved life expectancy and reduced infant mortality as much as it has contributed to economic development.[16] So population growth has meant that growth has not raised living standards by much. As with China, the poor economic performance of the mother country contrasts with the achievements of people of Indian origin outside India.[17] Institutions matter, and output is not simply a product of capital, labour and technology.

Government as Theft

I am writing this in the hills overlooking Cap Martin, between Monaco and the Italian frontier. The family of the late President Mobutu of Zaire still owns four villas in its most exclusive quarter. The part of Central Africa bounded by the Congo River is rich in mineral resources – copper, cobalt, zinc, tin, nickel, uranium and diamonds – but these riches have harmed the country, not helped it. The Congo has been a magnet for thieves – the curse of Kurtz.[18] The area was first looted by King Leopold II of Belgium, who also spent his profits on the Côte d'Azur.[19] One of Mobutu's villas is on an avenue named after Leopold's wife.[20]

The Congo became a regular Belgian colony. While Britain and France sought an orderly process of decolonization, the Belgians just packed up and (mostly) went home. The state quickly collapsed into four zones. Most mineral resources were in the province of Katanga, ostensibly ruled by Moise Tshombe, a Western puppet. Patrice Lumumba, the first Prime Minister, was murdered, with the connivance of Western security agencies. Dag Hammarskjöld, the Swedish Secretary-General of the United Nations, died in a mysterious plane crash on a peace-keeping mission.[21]

Joseph Mobutu, an army commander, proclaimed himself head of state in 1965 and maintained that claim until his death thirty-two years later, establishing and keeping control through terrorism and bribery. His principal associates were known as *grosses légumes* (fat vegetables). In the 1970s Western banks lent heavily to the ostensible government of Zaire (Mobutu's name for his country, and its currency, of steadily declining value). There was aggressive competition to give Mobutu money. Walter Wriston (the Citibank CEO who was later to write *The Twilight of Sovereignty*) memorably remarked that 'the country does not go bankrupt',[22] and Citibank was a large lender. Zaire ran up debts it could never repay while its leaders became immensely rich. As private lenders withdrew, the World Bank filled the gap.[23] Much of the borrowed money never reached Zaire but was channelled directly into foreign bank accounts by Mobutu and the *grosses légumes*.

Before Mobutu's death in 1997, copper and cobalt production had collapsed. Even the power lines and equipment had been stolen. In the words of an American ambassador: 'Mobutu has not only killed the golden goose, he's eaten the carcass and made fat from the feathers.'[24] The diamond trade was mostly under the control of bandits. Mobutu himself, surrounded by his presidential guard, occupied a boat on the Congo River, the only place where he could feel safe.

The history of Western involvement in the Congo has been entirely disgraceful. Western countries destabilized its politics, supported terrorizing governments and armed oppositions, and gave criminals the trappings of statesmen. The motives were cynical, but the policies futile. The Congo is an anarchy, mineral production has collapsed and large amounts of money have been handed to thieves by international agencies and commercial banks. It is hardly credible that the World Bank continued to lend to the Mobutu regime for over twenty years. The Congo's external debt today is around $15 billion, a purely notional figure because it can never be repaid. Its existence is an obstacle to economic development, but such economic development is not likely. The process described in Lewis's two-sector model has operated in reverse. Depreciation of capital in the modern sector has led to relapse to a traditional economy based on subsistence agriculture.

The Congo may have been extreme, but the general experience of sub-Saharan Africa since 1960 makes grim reading. Natural resource endowments may actually damage economic development because these resources distort the structure of economic institutions. Nigeria – rich in oil – has been ruled by a succession of dictators whose grand larcenies have institutionalized corruption throughout Nigerian life.[25]

In the nineteenth century, economic institutions in Australia and the western United States were distorted by gold discoveries. The oil wealth of Saudi Arabia makes balanced economic development impossible.[26] Some rich states – Norway and Iceland – have managed bountiful resource endowments well. Others – like Switzerland and Japan – may have benefited from their absence.

Tom Friedman, the herald of globalization, notes a still greater paradox. Sub-Saharan Africa is the place to find societies characterized by unrestrained greed and weak government: 'come to Africa – it's a freshman Republican's paradise. Yes sir, nobody in Liberia pays taxes. There's no gun control in Angola. There's no welfare as we know it in Burundi and no big government to interfere in the market in Rwanda. But a lot of their people sure wish there were.'[27]

The 'governments' of these countries are corrupt businesses, more akin to the mafia than to public services of Britain, Germany or the United States. The term 'failed states' describes situations – as in Afghanistan or Somalia – where no group of warlords is sufficiently dominant to be described as a government. Rich states function through a variety of established social conventions and political institutions, which were not successfully transplanted to Africa during short periods of colonial occupation.[28]

Dependencia

Colonial regimes in countries of settlement put in place the building-blocks of successful market economies. This did not happen in countries which experienced only colonial occupation. Perhaps this occupation not only failed to promote economic development, but actually hindered it.

For more than one Latin American theorist of the process of growth, 'The now developed countries were never underdeveloped, though they may have been undeveloped.'[29] The suggestion is that undevelopment is a state of nature, but underdevelopment an imposed status. The poverty of poor countries (victims of the international economic system) is the corollary of the prosperity of rich countries – dependencia. To escape from this servitude, their growth path must be fundamentally different from the history of today's rich states. Although the model is very different from the Harrod–Domar–Solow growth theories, that implication is the same. Such arguments have obvious attractions for economists and politicians in poor states. They also appeal to people in rich states who feel guilty about their own prosperity. We tell children not to leave food while others starve. The children point out that the food they leave is not available to the starving – a response which gets to the heart of the matter. There is no fixed pool of food, and neither by clearing my plate nor by eating less do I make food available to people thousands of miles away.

The most coherent models of victimhood were developed by the Economic Commission for Latin America, established in 1947. The Commission's articulate spokesman was the Argentine, Raoul Prebisch. Hans Singer developed a similar argument in England at about the same time, and their description of dependency has become known as the Prebisch–Singer thesis.[30]

The central claim is that industrializing Europe imposed on 'peripheral economies' – like Argentina and New Zealand – an obligation to specialize in primary goods such as agricultural products and natural resources. Since technological advance was in and around manufacturing production, this led to a widening gap in incomes between the centre and the periphery. Peripheral economies could only achieve growth by withdrawing from the international trading system and developing their own manufacturing sectors. The policies which follow are not very different from those which were pursued without success in India, and they were equally unsuccessful in Latin America.

There are elements of truth in dependency theory. Resource-rich economies may find themselves at a disadvantage – the curse of Kurtz.[31] The headquarters of a corporation creates spillovers – management training, research and development facilities, need for supporting services – which are not needed for branch offices, and many countries have protected their fledgling industrial sectors from competition in the early stages of economic development. The most striking exception, Britain, was also the first developing nation.

There has, however, been rapid technological advance in agriculture, in oil production and in mining, just as in manufacturing, and some peripheral economies have prospered: Australia and Canada – and the United States. The different economic experiences of Australia and Argentina do not originate in differences in relationships between these peripheral economies and Europe but in the economic, social and political institutions of the peripheral economies themselves.

Dependency theory is a poor explanation of Latin America's disappointing economic performance, and it has faded from view. The Brazilian economist Fernando Cardoso was an associate of Prebisch and a leading proponent of the dependency thesis.[32] When he became Finance Minister in 1993 and President the following year, he followed policies of an impeccably conventional nature. Cardoso suffered the humiliation of being forced to announce a currency devaluation from a public lavatory to which mobbing crowds had forced his retreat. But his tenure of office can be rated a moderate success. Cardoso had learnt some of the truth about markets.

Poor but Happy

India's planners, Nyerere's advisers and the Economic Commission for Latin America wanted poor states to be like rich states. Nyerere may have had different objectives, although it was never very clear what they were. Mobutu, with no concern for his people, sought – and achieved – the trappings of extreme wealth for himself. The common assumption is that the values of the modern economic system are universal.

Yet some communities, with little or no exposure to that modern economic system, are very happy. Visitors to Ladakh, an inaccessible province in the Himalayan foothills, repeatedly observe the cheerful demeanour of its people.[33] Only in the 1930s did the West discover that the central plains of New Guinea were densely populated by tribes which had developed their own agriculture, politics and culture in an environment cut off from external influences for thousands of years. The lives of these people seemed full and satisfying. But their autonomy was destroyed for ever by the arrival of visitors in aeroplanes and helicopters carrying transistor radios.[34] Once material goods become available, people want them, and some will make great sacrifices of personal well-being to obtain them, perhaps for themselves, perhaps for the benefit of their families – that is why the Mexican Pedro is in Los Angeles and Sicelo's brother Patrick works in the South African goldfields.[35]

The relationship between expectations and achievement is central to happiness, and that is why the juxtaposition of different economic lives in South Africa and on the Mexican border creates such social tensions and personal distress. The anthropologist Colin Turnbull contrasted the well-adjusted forest people, the Itun, with the Ik hill tribe: the Ik, facing environmental deterioration and a reduced standard of living, had retreated into a selfish materialism that might disturb even Gary Becker.[36]

Individuals may be attracted to industrial jobs and unfamiliar places by illusions about other lifestyles, and misjudgements about their own prospects. Perhaps economic development requires that people make such mistakes – or are forced into a modern sector because they have no choice. The first farmers may have had lower standards of living than nomads.[37] Working conditions in Britain's Industrial Revolution were horrific, and some people argue that standards of living declined.[38] The growth of agriculture and the industrialization of Britain ultimately raised material standards of living for everyone, and by large amounts, but these effects were not immediate.

It is easy to romanticize life in what we consider primitive societies. Agriculture in peasant communities is rarely the healthy outdoor life enjoyed by Sven: it normally involves long days of backbreaking toil. The myth of Shangri-la is an enduring image in Western thought, and few descriptions survive critical scrutiny. It remains true, however, that our economic lives are not our only lives and happiness comes from the range of our experiences, not the quantity of material goods found in our homes.

Eastern Europe

The gap between expectation and achievement was wide in Eastern Europe, and these countries achieve particularly low scores for self-reported happiness.[39] The collapse of Soviet influence in Eastern Europe in the late 1980s, followed by the disintegration of the Soviet Union itself, created many and varied new states. The architecture of the capital cities of Slovenia, Hungary and the Czech Republic demonstrates the strength of their European heritage. Tiny Baltic countries like Estonia and Latvia look naturally to Scandinavia, failed states like Romania and Moldova sit on the edge of Europe, and Tajikistan and Uzbekistan enjoy an uneasy relationship with other Asian Islamic republics.

Experience since the Communist collapse has varied widely. The most successful economies were always geographically and culturally close to established rich states of Western Europe. If the Czech Republic had been independent after the Second World War, it would probably be today a rich European state. Poland – whose modern territory includes much of German Prussia – Hungary, for long joined in empire with Austria – and Slovenia, an enclave of 2 million people on Italy's eastern border, are today the most promising Eastern European economies. Russia itself is the largest new state. Experience here is not encouraging. Mikhail Gorbachev's attempts to reform the Soviet system failed: it proved impossible to introduce economic pluralism without undermining political centralism, and all structures of economic and political authority depended on that centralization.

The combination of pluralism in economic matters with centralism in political affairs was more successfully achieved in China. China inherited from Mao a dysfunctional economic system, and perhaps this was almost an advantage. The economy of the Soviet Union did, after a fashion, work. In China, change could only be for the better: in Russia, change did not have to be for the better and was not. From 1990 to 2000 Chinese economic growth averaged 10 per cent per year, while Russia's GDP fell by half.

The assets of the Soviet state were rapidly transferred to the private sector – too rapidly. Much former state property fell into the hands of criminals. Anatoly Chubais, leader of the Russian economic reform process, reportedly said: 'They are stealing absolutely everything and it is impossible to stop them. But let them steal and take their property. They will then become owners and decent administrators of this property.'[40] This did not happen, however. The new Russian oligarchs were more concerned to transform the assets they controlled into negotiable currency than to develop them. Having secured economic power, they used it to extend political influence. The lack of legitimacy of the new distribution of income and wealth, and the corruption of Russian politics, aggravated inherent political and economic instability. The experience of Argentina should have acted as a warning; the mechanisms and consequences of Russia's allocation of state assets mirrored Argentina's allocation of empty land, and the adverse results may be as enduring.

Foreign investors had initially seen Russia as an opportunity for the profitable transfer of capital and technology. But these hopes were shaken by large-scale defaults on Russian debt, increasing disillusionment over Russian willingness to protect the interests of investors in Russian businesses, and the steady decline of the Russian economy. The fall in output in Russia's 'capitalist' phase is almost without precedent among large countries in peacetime. Once again, the application of capital and technology failed in the absence of an appropriate economic, political and social infrastructure.

24

Who Gets What?

People

Heidi ($2,500) is a school teacher in Switzerland, Sven ($1,700) a farm worker in Sweden, Ivan ($900) a telecommunications engineer in Moscow, and Ravi ($320) an accountant with the State Bank of India. The figures in brackets are their monthly earnings. Although a dollar buys more in India than in Switzerland – purchasing power parities differ from official exchange rates – their earnings correctly rank their material standards of living. Heidi is best off, followed by Sven, Ivan and Ravi. Why?

There are productivity theories and bargaining theories of income distribution. In productivity theories, earnings reflect the value of an individual's contribution: if people don't earn very much, that is because what they do or make isn't worth very much. In bargaining theories, earnings reflect the distribution of power in society: if people don't earn very much, that is because they do not have control over political institutions and the means of production.

Productivity theories appeal to the rich. Their good fortune is the result of their own abilities. If they take out a lot, it is because they have put more in. Bargaining theories appeal to the poor. They can blame their status on the unfair organization of society. If they receive only little, it is because others have taken out more. Productivity theories appeal to the political right. Inequality is the inevitable, even fair, result of differences in abilities. People dissatisfied with their economic lives should put in more personal effort. Bargaining theories appeal to the political left. Inequality is the result of social and political injustice. People dissatisfied with their economic lives should seek political power through collective action.

The right won the cold war and the left lost, so productivity theories have the upper hand today. The profits of Goldman Sachs and Coca-Cola are the fruits of victory. The rewards of investment bankers and American CEOs may seem outlandish, but the market tells us they are worth it. After declining for decades, income inequality within rich states has again increased in the last twenty years.

But can these theories explain the different economic lives of Heidi and Ivan, Ravi and Sven? Whose output is more valuable, Heidi's or Ravi's? I don't know how to answer that question and am certain that the people who hired Heidi and Ravi, or sign their pay cheques, have not thought about it. But it is even less plausible that Heidi earns so much because she is a tough negotiator, or that Swiss teachers are a uniquely influential political group. Most people do not know their personal productivity, nor are they often able to bargain over wages. Productivity theories and bargaining theories are both inadequate descriptions of how rewards are determined in market economies. However, a synthesis helps towards the answer.

The Product of Teams

Rousseau's hunters did better by co-operating to catch a deer than by individually chasing hares. But when they did kill a deer, who got what? Each member must receive at least as much meat as they could get catching hares, otherwise the team would fade into the forest, but even after they have had that much, there is venison to spare. This surplus is the economic rent attributable to the team: by analogy with the rents to Saudi oil described in Chapter 11, it is the difference between the revenues of the hunt and the minimum needed to keep them together.

How is that meat to be distributed? The simplest solution would be for the hunt to divide the catch equally between the members. One team member might be better than others at catching hares. She might suggest that only the surplus, the economic rent, should be divided

Box 24.1 Economic rent

A country like Saudi Arabia derives substantial economic rent from its oil supplies because the market price is so far above the cost of Saudi production.

Economic rent is a central economic concept. But the phrase is unfortunate. In everyday language, rent is what we pay for land and buildings. To use the term 'economic rent' when we talk of oil is puzzling, and the usage becomes even stranger when applied to Coca-Cola, Madonna and the Harvard Business School. The explanation is historical. When David Ricardo (the nineteenth-century economist behind the principle of comparative advantage) introduced the concept the economy was mainly agricultural.

Ricardo's model explained how the rent of land was determined. The land of England could be ordered from best to worst, from the fertile fenlands of Lincolnshire to the acid moors of Dartmoor. The price of corn would determine the margin of cultivation – a graphic term to describe land at the frontier, which was barely worth bringing into production. However low grain prices were, it would be worth planting in Lincolnshire; however high, it would not be sensible to sow corn on Dartmoor. But the margin of cultivation would move back and forward between these extremes. The swings in grain prices that had been experienced during the Napoleonic wars made the issue very real in 1817. Land outside the margin of cultivation earns no rent. It is not worth cultivating, and, like Dartmoor, usually not cultivated. The rent of productive land is equal to and determined by its competitive advantage over land at the margin of cultivation.

Ricardo's framework is powerful and general and can be applied to the rewards earned by any scarce factor – not just Saudi oil or Lincolnshire land, but the competitive advantage of businesses and the talents of individuals. The receipt and allocation of economic rent is a central determinant of the distribution of income in modern economies. But there are few economic rents in perfectly competitive markets, because the assumption of many buyers and sellers of every commodity ensures that there are few scarce factors.

equally, and if she would otherwise leave the team, it might be best for all to agree. Or a member might be a particularly skilful hunter. If he has the opportunity to defect to another team, the hunt would be wise to offer him a larger share – it would be Pareto efficient, and members might agree that it was fair. These factors reinforce each other.

Even if team members have similar skills and alternative opportunities, they may have different roles. The conductor isn't necessarily the most talented member of the orchestra or the most important: simply the person who fulfils the co-ordinating function. Great conductors can, and do, impose their style – as can bad conductors – but the quality of the sound depends principally on the score and the musicians. Even if all hunters are equally skilful, a team may need a leader, just as an orchestra needs a conductor. As with which side of the road we drive on, it is often more important that there should be a decision than what the decision should be. Should we hunt to the north or south tomorrow?

Leadership roles are universal in human society. The leader may be the best hunter, but this is not a necessary, or even a sensible, way to choose. Weber[1] explained how leadership roles may be filled by tradition – the incumbent King, or CEO, breeds or chooses a successor. This is how Louis XVI succeeded Louis XV on the throne of France and Jeff Immelt succeeded Jack Welch in the top spot at General Electric.[2] The leader may achieve that position by personal charisma, or be chosen by a rational process, such as democratic election or selection by a search committee of the board. All these mechanisms – dynasty, anointment, meritocratic search, election and charisma – are found in economic life.

Leaders almost always seek a larger share, and are usually in a position to get it. The maximum the leader can extract, if membership is voluntary, is the whole of the economic rent: otherwise members defect in pursuit of hares. But if team members cannot opt out, the leader may try to eat the whole animal. Citizens of countries cannot easily opt out, and the shareholders of companies can opt out only by finding someone to take their place. The last kings of France tried to eat more and more of the animal, as did Mobutu, and some American executives.[3] The only limit to this rapacity is that the leadership is overthrown, as happened to Louis XVI and some executives.

The allocation of rewards by teams reflects a complex balance of factors. How much do members contribute to the work of the team? What alternatives are available to them? Political factors, and norms and traditions, matter too. Both productivity and bargaining play a role in arriving at the final outcome.

Economic Rents

The surplus from team working – the difference between the value of the deer caught by the team and of the hares which could be captured by its members working individually – is the economic rent created by the team. The concept of economic rent was introduced in Box 24.1 as the difference between the cost and selling price of Saudi oil, or the operating costs and yield of fertile land. The 'margin of cultivation' describes the marginal oil, or marginal land, for which (unlike Saudi oil or fertile land) receipts only just cover costs. But the concept of economic rent is quite general. It is the difference between the value of a resource or collection of resources and the value which these resources could generate in other uses.

The economic rent created by the Coca-Cola Corporation is the difference between the revenues of the company and the revenues which would be derived if the company were broken up and its capital, its plants and its workers were employed elsewhere. A rough and ready measure is the difference between Coca-Cola's profits and what could be earned if its capital were put in the bank. Madonna's economic rent is the difference between the profits from her stage appearances and sales of albums and what she would earn in her next best job. (I shall not speculate on what that job might be.) The economic rent created by Harvard Business School is the difference between the value created by that institution and the value which would be created if its faculty and students were dispersed elsewhere. The concept is clear enough, but measurement is impossible.

Ricardo's framework is equally applicable to soft drinks, pop stars and universities. The least successful firm in the soft-drink business will earn just enough to satisfy its shareholders and employees. It is at the industrial 'margin of cultivation'. Coca-Cola has a competitive advantage over that firm, and earns economic rent equal to its competitive advantage. In Madonna's world, there are many aspiring stars. Most never get a recording contract – they are, in Ricardo's language, outside the margin of cultivation. Her economic rent is the difference between her earnings and those of someone who is just talented enough to attract the attention of an agent or record company. This is probably no more than the person concerned could earn in an everyday job, as hairdresser or shop assistant.

The possibility of large Madonna-type rents gives us a further insight into what happened in the Colombe d'Or. Popular music, and painting, are activities in which the distribution of rewards is particularly uneven. The rewards to those who are outstandingly talented are outlandishly high.[4] Eventually, Braque no longer needed to exchange his paintings for food, and sold them at high prices. The prospect of the high returns earned by top sportsmen, pop stars, actors and lawyers prompts many to enter these activities, few of whom succeed. The small possibility of Madonna-like success ensures a crowd of hopefuls at studio doors. It makes sense – and is often necessary – for them to share some of their potential rewards with sponsors.[5]

Patrons of young artists hope that a few successes will compensate for the many pictures which will never have any real commercial value. The painter values the certain return now. His attitude to risk has a convexity property: he prefers the average of the rewards of stardom and the likelihood of penury to taking a chance on one or other. No doubt most of the pictures Paul Roux accepted in lieu of payment for board and lodging turned out to be worthless. The collection at the Colombe d'Or demonstrates that despite these mistakes he still benefited himself as much as he benefited the artistic community he supported.

Madonna earns rent as an individual, and Coca-Cola earns rent as a corporation. At Harvard, we see both. The faculty earn individual rents, like Madonna, from their star talents. The institution – like Coca-Cola – creates its own economic rent. It adds value through team working – the division of labour allows professors to teach their speciality rather than the whole of management, and the reputation of the institution makes the whole more valuable than the sum of the parts.

Bargaining to a Perfectly Competitive Equilibrium

All economic rents result from scarce factors. Coca-Cola has a distinctive brand; Madonna has a unique talent; the Harvard Business School has a distinguished faculty and an enviable reputation. In a perfectly competitive market there are many buyers and sellers and none is large enough, or distinctive enough, to have significant influence over price. No scarce factors: no distinctive brands, unique talents, distinguished faculty or enviable reputations. There are few economic rents in a perfectly competitive market.

In a perfectly competitive market Coca-Cola cannot earn economic rents, because it must compete not only with other manufacturers of colas but with other producers of Coca-Cola. In a perfectly competitive market Madonna cannot command high fees, because clones can provide identical services. In a perfectly competitive market Harvard must compete with other institutions indistinguishable from it. In a perfectly competitive market, all university professors are the same. In a perfectly competitive market there will be no surplus from the successful stag hunt: competing teams of hunters will crowd the forest until only sufficient deer can be caught to make deer hunting on a par with chasing hares. The margin of cultivation is always at the front door.

Game theory's framework of individuals bargaining over rents offers a quite different account of spontaneous order. Imagine a large group of people trying to decide on an allocation of scarce resources between competing ends. They have different skills and capabilities and there are many different uses to which these skills and capabilities could be put. No one will agree to a proposed allocation unless there is some benefit for them. Individuals must gain from trade. And so must states. And groups of individuals – such as firms – are free to form groups and trade among themselves and with other groups. No group should agree to a proposed allocation if they could do better by opting out and forming a mini-economy of their own.

A group which could do better by staying out of a planned allocation is called a blocking coalition. If there are enough individuals and firms of each kind – if there is enough pluralism in the economy – there is one and only one allocation which cannot be blocked. It is exactly the allocation which would emerge from the Arrow–Debreu model of competitive equilibrium.[6] Bargaining theory and the Arrow–Debreu model gave identical results. With no economic rents, there is nothing left to bargain over. If there are no scarce factors in an economy, bargaining and productivity theories converge. This is an intriguing result, but it probably does not reveal much of the truth about markets. In modern economies, many factors are scarce and there are many sources of rents. The acquisition and defence of rents, and bargaining and dispute over their distribution, are the main influences on income distribution in practice.

Rent Seeking

Economic rents are returns to scarcities – the exceptional talents of individuals, the distinctive capabilities of corporations. But not all individuals have scarce talents, not all corporations have distinctive capabilities. If scarcity does not exist naturally, perhaps it can be invented, and rents garnered anyway. The grant of monopolies has been a source of patronage and revenue for governments for thousands of years, and continues today in poor countries and corrupt states.[7] In post-Communist Russia, the Orthodox Church won an alcohol monopoly. Tax-free status entered the Russian language as *ofshorraya zona*.

The costs of monopoly to the public are usually greater than the profits of monopolists. Monopoly closes down disciplined pluralism and stifles innovation in products and technology. The monopoly often goes to the best lobbyist, not the best competitor, so gains from trade due to specialization and differences in capabilities are likely to be lost.

Under disinterested government, it is difficult to earn rents by buying monopolies or tax concessions. Rent seeking is most common in rich states when there are genuine public interest reasons for restricting entry – such as protection from untrained doctors, unsafe aircraft and dishonest financial advisers. But all entry restrictions, whatever their rationale, can create rents, and those who have entered each as a powerful lobby for tightening entry restrictions still further. Milton

Friedman, following Gellhorn, provides an extended list of the skills needed – such as knowledge of barber history and barber law – to be allowed to cut hair in some American states.[8] When supervising bodies are more vigorous in monitoring the standards of prospective entrants than of established practitioners, that is a warning that regulation is directed more towards increasing rents than maintaining standards.

Many economic resources are scarce, and mechanisms are needed to regulate access. Mineral resources are limited, and broadcast spectrum is scarce. Unless indiscriminate development is allowed, construction sites will be limited and permission to develop them valuable. These restrictions often create large rents, and firms will spend correspondingly large sums to get them. A government that creates or assigns these resources can impose heavy taxes, or large upfront fees, for their use – as with specific taxes on oil and mineral deposits, or the allocation of spectrum for mobile phone companies. These fees and taxes yield revenue and discourage rent seeking.

Rent seeking impedes the functioning of a market economy – the pursuit of gains from trade through specialization and differences in capabilities. It limits innovation through disciplined pluralism. It corrodes the integrity of the political process. These adverse political and economic effects often reinforce each other.

Rents and Competitive Advantages

Firms derive rents from their competitive advantages. Coca-Cola earns rents because it is well inside 'the margin of cultivation' – its returns are much better than those of an ordinary soft-drinks business. The competitive advantage is not the secret recipe for the fizzy water. In 1985 the company replaced the classic formula with a flavour which users preferred in blind tasting. The result was disastrous. Consumers identify with the brand for other reasons. Coke is indeed it.

Chapter 6 described other corporate competitive advantages, past and current: the brands and reputation of Marlboro and McDonald's; the structure of relationships established by Benetton and Marks and Spencer; the depth of management capabilities at General Electric; Microsoft's ownership of the Windows interface; the quality of production-line engineering achieved by BMW and Mercedes and the associated brands. Shareholders take the lion's share of business rents. Firms with competitive advantages earn returns in excess of the cost of capital, and the market capitalization of these companies is much greater than the value of the plant, machinery and inventories which they use in the business.[9] But successful companies share rents with workers and customers. This enhances the rent itself. Companies with competitive advantages are good companies to do business with, good companies to work for.

In the 1980s corporations were urged to direct economic rents exclusively to shareholders. The threat of hostile takeover focused managers on the pursuit of 'shareholder value'. Imaginative financiers put together packages which made it possible to attack even the largest of companies. ICI, Britain's leading company for decades, dismembered itself in response to such a threat. The pressure sometimes went up to, or beyond, the bounds of legality. The battle for Distillers, the whisky firm, ended with some participants in prison. Michael Milken, who put together some extraordinary deals for shady figures in the United States, was jailed and the firm for which he worked, Drexel Burnham Lambert, went into liquidation.[10]

Managers of large corporations had previously felt insulated from the stock market. In 1980 General Motors dismissed contemptuously an enquiry from its largest shareholder, the Californian public employees retirement scheme, about its succession planning.[11] The effects of the shareholder-value movement spread from the United States to Britain, and on to continental Europe, even though unwanted takeover there remains virtually impossible.

As this trend developed, executives in large corporations no longer compared themselves with those who had risen to the top of other professions or large organizations – top lawyers or doctors, civil servants, managers of nationalized industries. The comparison was with dealmakers and financiers, and they revised both the amounts they were paid and the ways in which they were paid. Although their salaries rose, the real growth in pay came from bonuses and stock options (call options on the company's shares). This gave a strong incentive to ensure that share prices continued to rise, and some professional managers became extremely rich men. Steve Ross of Time

Warner and Michael Eisner of Disney received over a billion dollars for their services.[12]

Companies could satisfy the stock market, and add value to executive share options, only by reporting earnings growth faster than the growth of their business – increasing the rents from scarcity and competitive advantage. But how was this to be achieved in markets which were becoming more competitive, not less, as a result of globalization? The talking heads struggled to answer this question. Perhaps rents would come from consolidation into firms with stronger competitive advantages. The analogy of Microsoft was widely used: but Chapter 21 showed how unusual in business is the control of a proprietary standard by a single firm. The history of past technological revolution, such as railways, electricity and automobiles, is that most benefits go, through competition, to consumers.

The alternative was to squeeze more from existing sources of competitive advantage. Marks and Spencer's competitive advantage lay in the company's legendary reputation with customers and its relationships with suppliers and employees. Yet the business was mature: it was unrealistic to think that sales or profits could grow much faster than GDP. However, this was not enough to sustain shareholder value. Throughout the 1990s the company achieved rapid earnings growth by raising prices, reducing costs and putting pressure on suppliers, and in 1998 it achieved higher margins on sales than at any time in the company's history.[13] But suddenly the contagious mechanism of reputation, which had so long worked in the company's favour, turned into reverse. Sales fell, profits collapsed. The magic of Marks and Spencer had gone, probably for ever: the attempt to squeeze more rents from an established competitive advantage undermined the competitive advantage itself. Marks and Spencer was not alone. Businesses, from banks to Railtrack, tested the loyalty of customers and employees in pursuit of shareholder value. The last resort of businesses whose returns did not meet market expectations, or the needs of option holders, was to make the numbers up. In Chapter 28 I shall come back to the collapse of Enron, Andersen and WorldCom.

The Very Rich

Forbes magazine produces an annual list of the richest Americans.[14] Three names are always close to the top: Bill Gates, Warren Buffett and Robson Walton.

Bill Gates is too well known to need description but the Waltons and Buffett are famous only in the United States. Robson Walton is son of Sam Walton, founder of Wal-Mart. The company, still based in Bentonville, Arkansas, where Sam grew up, is the world's largest retailer and, with a million workers, the world's largest private-sector employer. Despite its size – it is three times larger than any other retailer – it has only modest operations outside the United States and is not well represented in the most populous and frequently visited areas of America, such as the north-east seaboard and California.[15]

Warren Buffett is the most successful investor in history. Buffett and his partner, Charlie Munger, run Berkshire Hathaway, an investment company. Berkshire Hathaway owns a number of businesses – such as America's largest reinsurer, GEICO – and has major stakes in other companies, including Coca-Cola. This portfolio, which today is worth around $40 billion, has grown entirely through Buffett's continued success in choosing investments.[16] Buffett still lives in the bungalow in Omaha, Nebraska, he bought in 1957. He has never been a Wall Street figure – although he was for a time chairman of Salomon Brothers, after illegal activities by the bank's traders jeopardized the value of his investment. His favourite drink is Cherry Coke (he switched from Pepsi after becoming Coca-Cola's principal shareholder). The annual meeting of Berkshire Hathaway, at which Buffett delivers a lengthy and engaging homily, attracts a huge audience to Omaha: many small shareholders have become rich by following Buffett.[17] Buffett, now 72, harbours no dynastic ambitions. On his death, the Buffett Foundation will become the world's largest charity.

Both Buffett and Walton are modern American heroes and with reason. Sam Walton's habits were even more modest than Buffett's and he drove a utility pick-up until his death.[18] Both became extraordinarily rich through their own remarkable abilities, and conducted uncomplicated lives and businesses with transparency and integrity.

The economic rents of Wal-Mart come from its competitive advantage over other US general retailers – Sears Roebuck, for decades America's largest store chain, and Kmart, which went into administration in 2001. Walton was quick to see the potential of out-of-town shopping and positioned Wal-Mart stores outside small towns across America. Wal-Mart also pioneered the effective use of information technology to match stock to consumer needs. The sheer scale of the Wal-Mart business means that a margin of 2 per cent on its sales yields $7 billion of profit, and the Walton family, as legatees of Sam, enjoy a substantial share.

Microsoft, although ubiquitous, is a much smaller company. Wal-Mart employs twenty-four times as many people and its sales are ten times greater. Gates is as rich as Walton because Microsoft enjoys a near monopoly while Wal-Mart is in a competitive market. Microsoft's rents are much larger relative to its sales.

One of the richest men – perhaps the richest – outside the United States is the Sultan of Brunei, a tiny state on the western coast of Borneo, whose offshore oil reserves produce around 70 million barrels of oil per year – more, per head of population, than Saudi Arabia. The Sultan's brother, Prince Jefri, became internationally famous for extravagance. The royal family is reported to own 350 Rolls-Royce cars. Jefri allegedly kept forty prostitutes on standby at London's Dorchester Hotel, and having been for many years the principal customer of Asprey's, London's most expensive shop, he finally bought the store itself. The effect of Jefri's expenditure and incompetence was to reduce the family fortune from $110 billion to a more manageable $40 billion.[19]

The riches of Walton, Gates and the Sultan are all based on economic rents – derived from, respectively, the competitive advantage of Wal-Mart, the dominance of Windows, and the oil reserves of Brunei. The individuals concerned are entitled to a large share of these rents. The Sultan, through tradition and heredity; Gates, through his role in the foundation of the company; Robson Walton, through a combination of the two.

It is clear who pays what the Sultan, Gates and Walton spend: the users of Brunei's oil, the customers of Wal-Mart and Microsoft. Motorists, Wal-Mart shoppers and Windows-users pay willingly. Even if they resent the wealth of these men, they value the product: there are mutual gains from trade. But who contributes to the resources of the Buffett Foundation? Buffett's investment strategy has always been based on identifying sustainable economic rents. 'As a child the clanging of the trolley car would put a thought in Warren's mind. All of that traffic with no place to go but right by the Russells' house, he would say – if only there were a way to make some money off it.'[20] Buffett's investment coups – in American Express, the *Washington Post*, Gannett (US local newspapers), Gillette and Coca-Cola – all involve businesses with strong competitive advantages, yielding sustainable economic rents.

Buffett simply understood more of the truth about markets than the talking heads of Bloomberg television. Yet the rents created by Wal-Mart, Microsoft and Brunei oil did not exist before Walton opened his stores, Gates founded Microsoft, and the Sultan invited oil companies to drill. American Express, the *Washington Post* and Coca-Cola would all have been powerful rent-generating businesses if they had never heard of Warren Buffett. Buffett's gains were made at the expense of less successful investors – advisers and their clients with less understanding of the truth about markets. Buffett's contempt for Wall Street is legendary. In December 1986 he wrote, under the heading 'How to Tame the Casino Society', that 'if a graduating MBA asks me how to get rich in a hurry, I hold my nose with one hand and point to Wall Street with the other'.[21]

Who Gets What?

Productivity and bargaining theories of income distribution are synthesized in the theory of economic rent. Many rents are the product of scarce talents in individuals or competitive advantages in firms; some reflect arbitrage gains of securities houses or the rent-seeking activities of successful lobbyists. The creation of rents is the result of a combination of productivity and bargaining.

Where rents are the product of the scarce talents of individuals – Madonna – then it is obvious who benefits from the rents. But most rents in modern economies are the product of teams, or can only be effectively exploited through teams. The distribution of rents within teams is the result of a combination of individual productivity and internal bargaining.

The most important influence on our incomes is the teams we belong to. Many teams and kinds of team are relevant to world income distribution. These teams include the residents of the Canton of Zurich, the Organization of Petroleum Exporting Countries, the shareholders and employees of Wal-Mart stores, the family of the late Sam Walton, the citizens of Brunei, and its ruling family, the executive directors of the Disney Corporation.

Some teams are highly exclusive. If someone is not born a Walton or in the household of the Sultan of Brunei, marriage to an existing member is the only way to join the family. Wal-Mart, on the other hand, recruits employees and shareholders actively. If people want to join, it will very likely take them. The Canton of Zurich is less exclusive than the Waltons but more so than Wal-Mart. It will admit citizens of another Swiss canton, but only selectively and reluctantly those born elsewhere. The more exclusive the club, the more valuable is membership.

Heidi and Sven have high material standards of living because they are members of many different teams, and the organization of these teams has evolved over centuries in a highly sophisticated manner, not only to exploit fully the division of labour to the greatest possible extent, but also to manage information, pool risks, achieve co-operation and co-ordination, and generate knowledge, and to do so within an extensive and elaborately developed set of conventions and rules. Sicelo is a member of almost no economic teams, barely deriving benefit even from the division of labour. Ravi and Ivan are members of fewer teams, and some of these are ineffective: because of poor internal organization, or because they are not directed to relevant social and economic objectives.

25

Places

Küssnacht

Heidi benefits from a division of labour which Adam Smith could never have imagined as he wandered round the pin factory. Smith had been paid by students to whom he delivered lectures and acted as private tutor to the Duke of Buccleuch, but the modern division of labour in education would have astonished him. Heidi takes her own children to a carer while she teaches larger groups of other people's children. This division of labour makes mass education possible. Sicelo's children can learn only the little their mother knows.

Heidi sees two hundred children each week and is paid by the Canton of Zurich. She teaches: Gary Becker would say she develops their human capital. That will yield direct benefits for them – they earn more because they are better educated – and it will benefit their future employers – banks, manufacturing businesses, the Canton itself. Their education and skills will enhance the social, political and economic infrastructure which makes life pleasant, and possible, for Heidi – safe streets, stable institutions.

Heidi is contributing to innumerable products and very large numbers of people help to make Heidi's economic life possible. Her car alone required thousands of workers. Heidi does not know who they are, and no one need know who they are. This is the power of spontaneous order. The pin factory would have been unaware of all those who contributed to its much simpler product. But Nissan probably can identify most of those who made Heidi's Micra. The modern division of labour makes very complex products possible, but it also reduces the anonymity of exchange of the perfectly competitive market.

Heidi benefits from this very detailed division of labour, in which differing capabilities and specialization are exploited fully. Sicelo is part of a small, largely isolated community, producing mostly for its own use. This is the most important reason why Heidi is so rich and Sicelo so poor.

Heidi also shares various economic rents. Her Swiss nationality is important. The division of labour from which she benefits so much is supported by an elaborate and extensive economic infrastructure. Heidi benefits every day from the competitive advantages of national and international brands and the skills and reputation of local traders. She enjoys the advantages of co-operative structures which operate at every level of Swiss society, and from the co-ordination which gives her access to the world's most efficient rail system, an electricity grid, a network of cash machines: a comprehensive list of elements of this Swiss economic infrastructure would occupy the remaining pages of this book. Her economic life is conditioned by the elaborate structure of rules and conventions, mostly tacit, which govern Swiss society and create large and enduring rents.

Heidi also benefits from rents created by Swiss corporations. They are derived from competitive advantages of international businesses like Nestlé and Novartis, from the world-wide reputation of Swiss banks for prudence and discretion, and the specialist skills of those small chemical and engineering businesses scattered along the lake shore and in the lower valleys. Their exports are the dynamic of the Swiss economy.

Heidi and Hermann benefit directly from these rents through their modest portfolio of shares. Hermann also shares some of the rents of his Swiss bank. The bank prefers to employ Swiss nationals, and as a result Hermann earns a very comfortable living without the pressures of the financial services industry in London or Manhattan. Because of the competitive achievements of the business for which he works, Hermann is probably paid more than someone of his abilities, education and experience would secure anywhere else in the world. This is not to downplay his skills and achievements. Hermann is good at his job, and his organization is successful because everyone is good at their jobs. The team is more than the sum of its parts and the team rewards are distributed among the parts.

However, the pool of talent on which internationally successful Swiss businesses can draw is limited. Although large enough to support these businesses, their very success has created pressures. The division of labour itself limits the resources available to the international sectors of the Swiss economy. Not everyone can work in a bank, or an engineering firm: these businesses, and the people who work in them, require architects and accountants, shop workers and car mechanics, town planners and schoolteachers. Their earnings are set by reference to the earnings of people who work in the internationally competitive sector of the economy. That is both fair and necessary if there are to be car mechanics as well as engineering workers, and it is why Heidi is one of the best paid schoolteachers in the world.

Ravi has friends in Mumbai who are as well qualified to teach as Heidi, and earn a fraction of her salary, but they do not speak German, and would mostly prefer to live in their familiar environment. Swiss schools prefer staff who are knowledgeable about Swiss culture and society. It is unlikely that an Indian teacher would be allowed to work in Switzerland. Jamaican nurses relieve nursing shortages in Britain and keep down the pay of British nurses, while creating scarcities in Jamaica and raising wages there, but nursing skills are unusually transferable. These barriers to mobility protect the economic rents of Swiss nationals, and limit the potential for equalization of earnings internationally.

Heidi's material standard of living is the product of three interrelated groups of factors. She benefits from a very extensive and well-co-ordinated division of labour, domestically and internationally. She is part of a complex set of social, political and economic institutions which have evolved to manage the problems of information, risk sharing, co-operation and co-ordination in rich states, and directly and indirectly she shares in numerous economic rents from Swiss institutions and Swiss corporations.

Kivik

Sven and Ingrid are agricultural workers, like most of the population of the world, today and throughout history. But few have imagined farming as it is for Sven and Ingrid.

Most agricultural workers engage in arduous physical labour. The energy expended on a Swedish farm comes almost entirely from machinery. Most agricultural workers worry about weather and diseases. So do Sven and Ingrid: but their finances are largely insulated from the productivity of their crops and they are able to control animal and pest diseases. Although well educated – both have a spattering of foreign languages – Sven and Ingrid are not intellectuals. They do not read much; their recreations are sport and television. They enjoy almost everything that romantics have admired in rural life – a job outdoors, contact with nature, freedom and flexibility to manage their day without close supervision – with very few of its disadvantages. They have a regular salary, extensive social benefits, a wide range of opportunities and new experiences; they do not work particularly hard.

Sven and Ingrid are well off for much the same reasons that Heidi and Hermann are well off. They benefit from the same finely demarcated and well-organized division of labour as Heidi and Hermann. There are many differences between the social and economic infrastructures of Switzerland and Sweden, but both are sophisticated, developed market economies. The rents that Switzerland earns from Novartis and Nestlé, from speciality chemicals and engineering, Sweden obtains – not quite – from Abba and Volvo, and from other branches of precision engineering.

Yet Sven's economic position is more vulnerable than Heidi's. It is not economic to grow wheat in Sweden on a large scale. The profitability of the farm depends on the Swedish government and the Common Agricultural Policy. This farm support is under pressure.[1] And while some others could do Heidi's job, there are many millions who, with modest training, could do Sven's. In some rich countries, work like Sven's is undertaken by migrant workers on low wages. There are many potential migrants in the candidate states of the

European Union. The union which represents Sven understands well that the willingness of other Swedes to share rents with Sven may be eroding and that the Swedish and West European clubs to which he belongs may become less exclusive.

Moscow

Ivan and Olga are discussing, as they often do, the extraordinary political events through which they have both lived: the initial excitement of perestroika in the 1980s, when change became possible; the collapse of the Soviet Union and Soviet system which followed; the mixture of corruption and chaos, opportunity and innovation, which they see around them today, at once exhilarating in its potential and depressing in its outcomes.

Why did the planning systems of the Soviet Union fail so comprehensively? Disciplined pluralism proved far more innovative than central direction. The considerable talents of Russian scientists and engineers – like Ivan – achieved very little. They were most effective in developing the country's military capabilities. Defence objectives were relatively clear, and there were few limits on the resources devoted to them. This was the basis of the Soviet Union's one great achievement – the defeat of Nazi Germany in a European war. The development of military technologies was impressive, though not comparable to that of the United States. Russia put the first man in space, but in other spheres the record was poor. Standards of Russian medicine were often high, but advances in medical protocols and in pharmacology were imitative. Soviet consumer goods were laughably bad. When Heinz drove his Trabant across the border in October 1989, the failure of Communism was most clearly demonstrated in the shop windows of the Kurfürstendamm. The inefficient, chaotic processes of competitive markets manufactured cars in the quality of Mercedes and the quantities of Volkswagen, while the East produced Trabants. The disorganized experimentation of the American computer industry created the personal computer – a competitive weapon so fearsome that the US defence establishment tried to stop the Russians getting hold of it. The task forces of the USSR, like the task forces of IBM, produced nothing.[2]

But Soviet planning was not just insufficiently innovative. It was also inefficient. It managed the division of labour and the associated problems of information and co-ordination far worse than market economies. The Soviet regime had opted out of the international division of labour, but the resources and size of the Soviet economic bloc could have yielded large gains from specialization and differences in capabilities, if incentive-compatibility problems had not prevented effective exploitation. Central authorities lacked the information needed to develop the distinctive capabilities of their citizens and businesses. Citizens and businesses themselves lacked incentives to exploit and extend these capabilities. The mechanics of co-ordination were less effective under central direction than in the spontaneous order of market economies.

No economy has ever been so vulnerable to rent seeking as the collapsed Soviet Union. Russia is rich in natural resources. Its centralized economy had established many monopolies of production, communication and transportation. Western firms, anxious to do the business which had been opened to them, required political and economic connections. Never have so many rents been on offer in such a short space of time. The beneficiaries of the process were the politically well connected, managers of established Russian businesses, and criminal gangs. Public choice – the self-amplifying cycle of political corruption and economic rent seeking described by Buchanan's model (pp. 240–1) – found its fullest expression. As oligarchs bought politicians, they could demand further favours.[3]

Few rents in Russia are derived from scarce talents or the competitive advantages of firms. Talents are plentiful: organizations that can exploit them effectively are scarce. Some Russian firms have competitive advantages – relative to each other – but none has competitive advantages in the global market. International businesses bring their own competitive advantages to Russia, but rents from their Russian operations are future hopes not present realities.

Ivan and Olga do not share the rents of Russia's rent-seeking society. By working for an American company, Ivan experiences American business as it really is, not the caricature of it that has been imposed on the former state sector. Still, AT&T is a successful world-wide business with competitive advantages, but is not profitable in Russia.

It pays Ivan more than it need but far less than it would pay a similarly qualified worker in the United States. That is the price Ivan pays for living in an ineffectively co-ordinated environment which has developed very few of the social, political and economic conventions and institutions which underpin a market economy.

Mumbai

Ravi is, as often, discussing politics with his friends. They focus on the frustrations of young, well-educated Indians over the inability of their country to realize its potential. British influence on the structure of Indian institutions remains both wide-ranging and superficial. Ravi's accountancy qualification is modelled on its British equivalents. The atmosphere of the bank in which he works would be familiar to someone who had worked (not very recently) in a London bank. The framework for the endless debates of Ravi and his friends is still provided by the mild and benign socialism which captured the intellectual life of Britain for a large part of the twentieth century (its government for a much shorter time, but one which covered the period of Indian independence).

Yet there is also so much that is Indian about their economic lives and social environment; the open good humour which has led so many visitors to India to fall in love with the country. The debates of Ravi and his friends are intense but also full of laughter, which is one reason they are so frequent. They will go on arguing late into the night. It has never occurred to them that these debates may be part of the problem rather than part of the solution. India is spontaneous, but while Switzerland and Sweden display spontaneous order – everyone falls into allotted roles with a minimum of conscious direction – India seems to exemplify spontaneous disorder. The theorems of Arrow and Debreu, and the mathematics of complexity, show how disorganized systems might yield ordered outcomes, but they do not demonstrate that they will. In India disorder seems to remain.

The best reasons for believing that economic systems will drift towards order is that selection functions through disciplined pluralism. India has elements of pluralism – its mixture of civilizations is one of its joys – but its pluralism is often undisciplined, and in many respects Indian society is not pluralist at all.

In a village like Palanpur, the economic roles of individuals are largely determined by caste, religion and gender. This traditional organization establishes the division of labour – that is its economic function. But it does so in a way that does not allow differences in capabilities to emerge, far less be exploited, and it cannot easily handle change. Ravi could not hold the job he does had he not been born into a well-off – by Indian standards – middle-class household in Mumbai. Only exceptional talents and good fortune would permit Indians from humble backgrounds to achieve as much. Nandini will bring up their sons to similar aspirations: only gradually is it understood that daughters might fulfil these roles.

The State Bank of India is not a pluralist institution in origin or intention. Its objective – often pursued with skill and integrity – is to promote the economic development of the country as seen through the eyes of the Indian government, and the directors and managers of the State Bank. Today, India has an increasingly competitive banking system. Not very competitive – it is in the nature of bankers, from Walter Wriston down, to hold conventional views and to follow the instincts of the herd. The bubble touched even the Bombay Stock Exchange. But some of Ravi's circle are successful entrepreneurs. Two of his friends are employed in hi-tech businesses in California.

Supporting institutions for the market economy can be found in embryonic form in Mumbai. Traders have competitive advantages, brands and reputations. India is full of nepotistic networks of co-operation, many of them devoted to rent seeking, many still engaged in petty deceit and corruption. Ravi and his friends are honest but take pride in knowing the ropes, and, occasionally, pulling them to get things done. Increasingly, they understand that the successful co-ordination of economic systems is not the result of either government direction or personal contact, but systems of organization.

KwaZulu Natal

All this is very distant from Sicelo's life in KwaZulu Natal. Sicelo ekes out a living from subsistence agriculture, as his parents and grandparents did before him, and as he expects his children to do. For Sicelo, the division of labour does not extend much beyond some villagers focusing on crops and others on animals: most, including Sicelo, do both.

Sicelo is in distant contact with the international economy through his brother Patrick. There are large rents from goldmines which mostly went to those who discovered and developed the mines. These enterprises did not see any economic or political need to share these rents, and did not do so. Even from a narrowly self-interested perspective, this may not have been a wise decision. Yet the experiences of the Congo, Nigeria and Saudi Arabia demonstrate that rich resources are a mixed blessing for a poor country.

The institutions of a modern market economy, imported to South Africa by Western European settlers, were set beside a traditional economy based on subsistence agriculture. The settlers attempted to preserve the two systems separately, to draw on the subsistence sector for unskilled labour, and yet to protect the living standards of low-skilled white workers. This impossible balancing act ultimately led to apartheid: morally repulsive, and in the end politically and economically unsustainable. But none of this affects or affected Sicelo much. Even now, he derives no benefit from the economic rents which come from South Africa's resources: in any event, these rents are not so large that a fair share would make much difference. Sicelo is marginal to the international economy and the international economy is marginal to him. Sicelo derives little benefit from either rents or the international division of labour, and his standard of living is based on simple agriculture on unpromising land. In common with much of the population of sub-Saharan Africa, he has one of the lowest material standards of living in the world. There is occasional joy in Sicelo's world – wedding feasts are extended celebrations for the whole village – but life is hard.

Part Six

POLITICAL ECONOMY

26

The American Business Model

When Alexander Youngson addressed students in the David Hume Tower, he did so as Professor of Political Economy. The course he taught is now called economics. The adjective 'political' is considered unprofessional. No one teaches courses in political physics and we would be rightly suspicious of a course in political biology. The central theme of this book, however, is that economic systems are embedded in a social and political context; so there is no escaping political economy.

At the start of the twenty-first century, the American business model (ABM) plays the role in political economy that socialism enjoyed for so long. All political positions, even hostile ones, are defined by their relationship to it. Globalization and privatization have displaced capital and class as the terms of discourse. The label 'market forces' immediately evokes hostile or supportive reactions. The term 'Washington consensus' is for some a statement of inescapable realities of economic life; it is demonized in many poor states as an attack on democracy and living standards. The right has determined the terms of political debate.

The philosophy of the ABM, as articulated by Milton Friedman, is of government as referee:

It is important to distinguish the day-to-day activities of people from the general customary and legal framework within which these take place. The day-to-day activities are like the actions of the participants in a game when they are playing it; the framework, like the rules of the game they play. . . . These then are the basic roles of government in a free society: to provide a means whereby we can modify the rules, to mediate differences among us on the meaning of the rules, and to enforce compliance with the rules on the part of those few who would otherwise not play the game.[1]

The claims of the American business model are of four kinds:

self-interest rules Self-regarding materialism governs our economic lives.

market fundamentalism Markets should operate freely, and attempts to regulate them by social or political action are almost always undesirable.

the minimal state The economic role of government should not extend much beyond the enforcement of contracts and private-property rights. Government should not itself provide goods and services, or own productive assets.

low taxation While taxation is necessary to finance these basic functions of the minimal state, tax rates should be as low as possible and the tax system should not seek to bring about redistribution of income and wealth.

Amongst those sympathetic to the ABM, there are two views of how market fundamentalism is to be reconciled with the minimal state. Some proponents believe an anti-trust policy is needed to preserve competitive markets. For others, even that degree of government intervention is inappropriate.[2]

Support for the American Business Model

Some European readers of this book have suggested that my characterization of the American business model is a straw man. Proponents of the ABM are suggesting a direction, not identifying a goal. A few days with the *Wall Street Journal* would dispel this illusion. The constituencies which support the ABM include academics – the Chicago School has outposts at the University of Rochester and a retirement home at the Hoover Institution in sunny California. There is a strong acceptance among business journalists – the relentless ABM tone of the *Wall Street Journal* is also found in *Business Week*; *Forbes* magazine is more strident, and its offshoot *Forbes ASAP* borders on the hysterical.

Think tanks and organizations whip up support. The American Enterprise Institute is generally scholarly and thoughtful, the Cato Institute less restrained. The success of these organizations has led to the foundation of counterparts in Europe – the Institute of Economic Affairs is Britain's equivalent of the American Enterprise Institute.

The expression of business opinion today is more subtle than the braying of Henry Ford or the ramblings of Lord Nuffield: less personalized, more discreet, using professional communicators. The Business Round Table is a low-key but powerful lobby of chief executives. A European equivalent was established in 1983. New Zealand's Round Table was influential in that country's neo-liberal experiment.

The phrase 'Washington consensus' came into use in the 1990s. It is associated with policies advocated by the International Monetary Fund (IMF), and to a lesser extent the World Bank and US Treasury, for poor states and transition economies in Eastern Europe. John Williamson, who coined the term, is bemused. 'How is it that a term intended to describe a technocratic policy agenda that survived the demise of Reaganomics came to be used to describe an ideology embracing the most extreme version of Reaganomics?' Williamson's original prescriptions were relatively modest. 'The practices being challenged in 1989 had been much more statist than was by then regarded as advisable. . . . This need for liberalization did not necessarily imply a swing to the opposite extreme of market fundamentalism and a minimalist role for government, but such boring possibilities were repressed in the ideological debates of the 1990s.'[3]

The three Washington agencies include many talented and independent individuals who are allowed considerable freedom; there is no single voice. But the IMF promoted a consistent set of policies through the 1990s: privatization, the opening of financial markets, free capital movements, combined with restrictive monetary and fiscal policies.[4] In the coded language of international agencies, 'structural reform' means a move towards ABM principles.[5] Yet there is an inherent contradiction in the promotion of the minimal state by a public agency. By the end of the decade, the IMF was under unprecedented criticism, both from the left, who resented its policies, and from the right, for whom its very existence was an affront to market fundamentalism.[6]

'Globalization' is an even more ambiguous term than 'Washington consensus'. Sometimes the word describes facts about the modern world – the improvements in communications which make the world more connected. Sometimes globalization is a policy programme – moderate, market-friendly measures like those of Williamson's version of the Washington consensus, or full-blown ABM principles of market fundamentalism and the minimal state. Often 'globalization' is a euphemism for Americanization, the ubiquity of McDonald's hamburgers and Goldman Sachs. The term has today acquired too many meanings, and too much emotional force, to be useful.

Defending the ABM

The strongest support for the ABM is found in the international financial, business and consulting community. This support is largely unreflective. For Wriston, the principles of the ABM are unavoidable because global business will migrate to the jurisdictions closest to them. For Tom Friedman, globalization is inevitable as the dawn.[7] Like religious or political fundamentalists, market fundamentalists regard the precepts of the ABM as self-evident and inevitable.

No economic commentary on Japan omits a reference to the need for structural reform.[8] Descriptions of New Zealand's reforms written by or for outsiders would lead the reader to conclude that the experiment had been a great success.[9] International agencies are obliged to confront statistics, but conclude that if the magic has not worked, it is because the subjects did not believe in it enough.[10]

The *Wall Street Journal*, commenting on the French elections of 2002, argued that France is well placed to tackle its economic problems – high taxation and excessive state intervention – because of its economic performance – 'a stable currency and a dynamic enterprise sector. Its transportation infrastructure and mixed public–private health system puts Britain's to shame.'[11] A French observer might reasonably suggest this gets things the wrong way round. If outcomes are dynamic and put other countries to shame, what is the problem with policy?

This conflation of measures and outcomes reaches extreme form in the measurement of national 'competitiveness'. There are, amusingly, two competitive surveys of competitiveness. One is published by the World Economic Forum (organizers of the Davos conference), the other by IMD, a Swiss business school.[12] These rankings receive extensive media attention and are representative of the opinions of business people and sympathetic economists, on which they are based. IMD's 'principles of international competitiveness' are a mixture of facts – 'prosperity of a country reflects its past economic performance' – and opinions about policy – 'state intervention in business activities should be minimized'. The major European economies all have scores which lag behind their actual economic performance. When France, Italy and Japan rank behind Estonia in competitiveness, what does competitiveness mean? What it means is that international agencies have more influence over the policies of Estonia than in France, Italy or Japan. Competitiveness is consonance with the policies of the ABM, and the United States regularly tops the rankings.[13]

Economic policies should be ranked by reference to relative economic performance. This requires us to distinguish performance from policies. GDP per head, or per hour of work, is the obvious starting-point. Economic stability – perhaps measured by inflation and unemployment – is clearly relevant; so are the quality of the environment and public infrastructure. Taking these criteria together, Norway and Switzerland are probably the world's most successful economies.[14]

It doesn't really matter what the answer is: the key point is that it is not immediately obvious that the world's best-performing economy is the United States of America. A search for societies characterized by overriding self-interest, market fundamentalism, the minimal state and low taxation, would not begin in Norway or end in Switzerland. Economic history demonstrates decisively the superiority of market economies over centrally planned regimes. It fails to demonstrate the superiority of any particular model of a market economy. The embedded markets of Norway and Switzerland are particularly idiosyncratic.

The US economy demands attention because of its sheer size. American GDP is twenty times that of Norway and Switzerland together. The USA has not only a disproportionate share of the world's economists but an even more disproportionate share of its best economists.

The United States is also the mainspring of innovation for the planet. But innovation is not the only source of competitive advantage (Chapter 6), and Swiss strengths in speciality chemicals and precision engineering have given the country productivity levels and living standards comparable with those of the USA. The failure of US businesses to maintain competitive or comparative advantages across a range of manufactured goods explains why the US share of manufacturing in GDP is well below the European average.[15]

The variety of national competitive advantages based on differences in capabilities and specialization defines the international division of labour and creates gains from trade – the USA produces software, Germany exports luxury cars. Even if there were a best model of an economic system, it would not necessarily be appropriate for everyone to adopt it. But there are no such universals.[16]

It is probably true that the USA was the best-performing major economy in the 1990s, although a final verdict must wait for the full consequences of the bursting of the bubble. But the 1990s followed a period of relatively slow US productivity growth.[17] As was emphasized in Chapter 3, differences in economic performance among rich states have been small and transitory relative to differences in performance between rich and poor states.

The ABM, Economic Theory and Economic Efficiency

The ABM case is often founded on arguments of general principle. This is not a book about moral philosophy, or the ethics of markets, but moral issues are fundamental for many people. Some supporters of the ABM see government action in economic matters as an attack on liberty, an improper use of the coercive power of the state. Freedom of contract requires a minimal state; market fundamentalism and low taxation are immediate corollaries. Although people who believe this mostly also believe that the ABM is economically efficient, presumably they would still favour it if it were not. If it could be shown that some regulation of markets would make everyone, or very many people, better off, they would still judge it wrong for government to implement it.

Others find the premise of self-interested motivation morally repugnant. Even if it is true, it ought not to be true, and social institutions should restrain greed rather than accommodate it. The accountability of democracy is preferable to the anonymity of markets. If market fundamentalism, the minimal state and low taxation are necessary for economic efficiency, material sacrifices must be made to secure a just society. But people who hold this view tend also to believe that such sacrifices would not be large.[18]

This clash of moral values cannot be resolved by economics: perhaps it cannot be resolved at all. The issue for this book is narrower: it is the relationship between political structures and economic outcomes. The claim that the ABM is the only route to material prosperity has given it its political power and intellectual influence.

In Chapters 15 and 16, I described how the Arrow–Debreu model and the fundamental theorems of welfare economics could be combined with the political philosophies of Nozick and Rawls to provide a theory of political economy. This is the intellectual foundation of the ABM. Adding Nozick's conservative political philosophy to the mix yields its final proposition – low and non-progressive taxation.

A Rawlsian approach leads to redistributive market liberalism. This version of political economy broadly accepts the first three elements of the ABM – self-interest, market fundamentalism and the minimal state – but rejects the fourth – the impermissibility of redistribution. It is both proper and necessary for government to use taxes and benefits to secure a just distribution of income. Free markets are combined with high levels of state provision of social benefits and public services. Redistributive market liberals, less sceptical of the value of state intervention than supporters of the ABM, generally support a vigorous competition policy. Let us start with the assumption common to the Arrow–Debreu model and the ABM – self-regarding materialism is the principal influence on economic behaviour.

Is Greed Good?

Even the most enthusiastic supporters of the ABM acknowledge that it has a public relations problem. Yergin and Stanislaw acknowledge regretfully that 'few people would die with the words "free markets" on their lips' (p. 398). It is not difficult to explain why people will die with 'Stalin', 'Heil Hitler' or 'Jihad' on their lips, but will not give the same accolade to free markets. Stalin, Hitler and bin Laden recruited followers by demonizing other people. The American business model demonizes itself. We dislike the ABM most of all for its unattractive account of our behaviour and our characters.

Some practitioners revel in this unflattering self-description. Al Dunlap, author of *Mean Business*, writes: 'If you want a friend, get a dog. I'm not taking any chances, I've got two.'[19] John Gutfreund, chairman of Salomon Brothers, one of the most aggressive investment banks in the 1980s, said successful traders must wake up each morning 'ready to bite the ass off a bear'.[20]

In the most extreme versions of the ABM, it is a mistake to deplore materialism and regard selfishness as a vice. Greed is good: nice guys finish last. The rambling but strident philosophy of Ayn Rand, Alan Greenspan's former mentor, proclaims the virtues of selfishness under the title of 'objectivism'.[21] The logical conclusion of extreme individualism is that concern for others is an emotion which can properly be called on only to the extent that we feel it spontaneously. Private charity is the only proper mechanism of redistribution, and any further claim by the community would infringe our autonomy.

In an alternative view, ethical issues which puzzled great thinkers from Aristotle to the present day disappear in a haze of confusion and goodwill. Modern advocates of 'corporate social responsibility' and well-meaning business people claim that if only self-interest is interpreted sufficiently widely, there can be no conflict between self-interest and the public good,[22] as when Charles Wilson asserted that 'what was good for our country was good for General Motors, and vice versa'.[23] History interpreted his remark as malign, but it was simply naïve.

A more plausible argument is that there is simply a dichotomy between economic life and public morality. The values appropriate to business are just different from those appropriate to our private lives. As Goethe observed at the beginning of the Industrial Revolution, 'everything which is properly business we must keep carefully separate from life'.[24] Goethe's position mirrors Milton Friedman's: 'the social responsibility of business is to maximise its profits.'[25]

This position is acceptable to many business people because it puts few restrictions on their behaviour. The corollary is the general contempt amongst intellectuals for business and those who engage in it. A wasp has been named after Gutfreund, *Eruga gutfreundis*: 'she stings and paralyses the insect, and then lays her egg on its back. The hatched larva feeds off its host's blood for about six months before devouring the money spider.'[26] The dichotomy between economic values and ordinary values achieves sophisticated expression from philosophers like Michael Walzer, who identifies 'spheres of justice':[27] criteria for distinguishing the proper boundaries of the market.

Greed as Motive

But the primary objection to the description of human behaviour in the ABM is not that it is immoral, but that it is incorrect. Greed is a human characteristic, but not, for most people, a dominant one. The minority for whom it is an overriding motive are not people we admire. Nor do we think of them as successful: they do not 'leave their footsteps in the sands of time'. When we read that Hetty Green, possibly the richest woman in history, dressed in second-hand clothes to secure admission to a charity hospital for her injured son,[28] we feel sadness and even sympathy that she made such a mess of things. Our sense of what constitutes a good life is very similar to that which Aristotle described more than two millennia ago. Most of us still find Thurow's assertion that those who do not achieve great wealth are 'by definition, second rate' bizarre.

Politics is attractive to people obsessed by financial reward – such as Mobutu, although even Mobutu was more interested in money as a means to power rather than an end in itself.[29] Productive economies have adopted systematic, and usually successful, policies to exclude

THE TRUTH ABOUT MARKETS

such people from public life. Those who enter politics in Europe or the United States today may have other personality disorders, but not that one. Modern business is not appealing to the truly greedy, such as Nicholas van Hoogstraten, the disgraced property trader who said 'the only purpose of great wealth like mine is to separate oneself from the riff raff' shortly before he was sent to prison.[30] Building successful businesses requires considerable abilities and hard work. Successful business people – from Andrew Carnegie, in the nineteenth century, the ruthless steel tycoon who wrote that 'a man who dies rich dies disgraced', to Bill Gates in the twentieth century – regard building a successful business as a primary, not an intermediate, goal. That is what they tell us and we should not disbelieve them.[31] When Carnegie and Gates declared their intention to crush competitors, they were not trying to persuade us to like or admire them.

Even in financial services, self-interest is not an overriding motivation. Donald Trump is perhaps the most aggressive and high-living American trader of the last two decades. Yet Trump's autobiography begins with 'I don't do it for the money.' He goes on: 'I've got enough, much more money than I'll ever need. I do it to do it. Deals are my art form.'[32]

What of Warren Buffett? His motives are complex. Buffett's biographer reports: ' "It's not that I want money," Warren replied. "It's the fun of making money and watching it grow." '[33] This, presumably, is why Buffett still lives in that Omaha bungalow and enjoys nothing more than a Nebraskan steak washed down with Cherry Coke.

The aspiration of the bond traders at Salamon Brothers described by Michael Lewis was to be regarded by their peers as a Big Swinging Dick. He reports that 'what really stung the traders . . . was not their absolute level of pay but their pay in relation to the other bond traders'.[34]

This is not to deny that self-interested materialism is an important feature of economic life. Economic systems based on appeals to work for the common good will fail. But self-interest is necessarily hedged in by the complex institutions of modern economic, social and political life – formal regulation and implicit rules, mechanisms of reputation and co-ordination, instincts and structures of co-operation, feelings of solidarity. Without that, the answer to Arrow and Hahn's question –

'What will an economy motivated by individual greed . . . look like?' – is indeed the common-sense one they cite: there will be chaos. Modern societies did not develop ethical norms which limit and deplore self-regarding materialism out of a perverse desire to restrain entrepreneurial spirits.

Economic motivations are complex, multi-faceted and not necessarily consistent. The study of human behaviour is an empirical subject. It cannot rely solely on introspection and *a priori* assumptions. Still less should it rely on introspection and *a priori* assumptions that do not correspond to experience. The best starting-point is to expect that behaviour will be adaptive – that people will behave in the way they are normally expected to in the circumstances in which they find themselves. This expectation will sometimes be false. Economies would not develop otherwise.

Property Rights

The ABM emphasizes the central importance of property as an institution, so central that its defence is the principal function of the state. The Arrow–Debreu framework generally takes a distribution of property rights as its starting-point. This assumes that the nature of property rights is obvious. But property rights are socially constructed, and can be defined in many ways and allocated among individuals, households and firms in many ways.

Milton Friedman, unlike many of his less sophisticated followers, understands this. 'What constitutes property and what rights the ownership of property confers are complex social creations rather than self-evident propositions.' But, he goes on, 'in many cases, the existence of a well specified and generally accepted definition of property is far more important than just what the definition is.'[35] But Friedman produces no evidence for this conjecture, and experience of economic history and geography demonstrates the opposite. The development of agriculture, of employment and of limited liability companies is an evolution from one group of definitions of property rights to another. The legitimacy of property rights determined the different economic experiences of Argentina and Australia. We continue to argue over the scope of intellectual property and the nature of media regulation in a pluralist society. It is not easy to see how the current coevolution of technology and institutions in the Internet and genome will play itself out. But no one could think that the outcome of these debates doesn't matter.

'Let them steal,' said Anatoly Chubais, mirroring Friedman.[36] Russia's economic disaster is an enduring reproach to those who claim that the only requirement of a market economy is a system of private-property rights. The quality of economic institutions – which is too simple to characterize as property rights – is the most important difference between rich and poor states.

The possibility of many different property-rights regimes, with differing effects on economic efficiency, imposes severe limits on the efficiency claims of the Arrow–Debreu model. The fundamental theorems of welfare economies can be true only with respect to a particular structure of property rights. It is then no longer possible to claim that any particular competitive equilibrium is Pareto efficient. A different property-rights regime could – and very probably would – make everyone better off.

The Truth about Markets

Misunderstandings about motivation and simplifications of property rights are not the only problems. Markets function effectively only if they are embedded in social institutions which are poorly – if at all – accounted for within the ABM.

(i) Information in complex modern economies is necessarily incomplete and imperfect. Competitive markets fail when there are major differences of information between buyers and sellers. Transactions usually take place within a social context. We prefer to deal with people we know, or we rely on trusted suppliers or trusted brands. This social context develops, and is necessary, to deal with these differences (asymmetries) of information (Chapter 18).

(ii) Markets for risk do not work as described in the efficient market model of Chapter 12. Most of the important risks we face are not handled through the market, but in households, among communities and by government. Securities markets are better described as arenas for sophisticated professional gambling than as institutions which minimize the costs of risk bearing and allocate capital efficiently among different lines of business (Chapter 19).

(iii) Most economic activity cannot be organized by negotiations between large numbers of potential buyers and potential sellers in impersonal markets. We need to work in organizations and in teams, and to co-operate in small groups. Self-interested individuals would often fail to co-operate with each other, even when it was in their mutual best interests to do so. Corporate cultures, ethical values and the blending of working and social lives are all necessary for effective co-operation (Chapter 20).

(iv) It is often true that co-ordination is more effectively achieved through mechanisms of spontaneous order than central direction. But spontaneous order does not emerge immediately and infallibly. Many co-ordination mechanisms are the product of government interventions, social institutions and agreements between firms (Chapter 21).

(v) Knowledge and information are key products in complex modern economies. They cannot be produced in competitive markets in which there are many buyers and sellers of each commodity. Non-materialist motivations – the thrill of discovery and the satisfactions of philanthropy – have been more important stimuli to major innovation than profit seeking (Chapter 22).

The ABM is deficient for its naïve approach to issues of human motivation, its simplistic analysis of structures of property rights, its inability to maintain efficiency in the face of imperfect information, its misleading account of markets in risk, its glossing over of problems of co-operation and co-ordination, and its failure to describe the generation of the new knowledge on which its very success depends.

The Distribution of Income and Wealth

There is a final problem for the ABM – the legitimacy of the distribution of income and wealth which results from it. The fourth premise of the ABM denies that this distribution is a proper concern of government in a market economy. If differences in income and wealth are the result of differences in productivity, and these are in turn the consequence of differences in effort, talent and skill, redistribution of income and wealth is potentially inefficient. If rewards to differences in efforts, talents and skills are suppressed then talents and skills will not be fully exploited. This is not a conclusive argument against redistribution, but redistribution may involve a high price in economic efficiency.

Yet, as Chapter 24 demonstrated, it is hard to believe that differences in income and wealth are completely, or even mainly, explained by differences in effort, talent and skills. Why does Heidi earn so much more than Ravi, Sven more than Ivan? Why is Sicelo so poor? Bill Gates made an important contribution to the personal computer industry, but his wealth would allow him an annuity of $5 billion per year for the rest of his life. Are his effort, talent and skills really so exceptional? Do they justify an income many thousands times greater than that of, for example, Alan Turing? Would Gates have put in much less effort if the prospective reward had been, for example, only $1 billion per year?

If GDP would fall by $5 billion if Gates stayed at home, then we are all better off by paying him $5 billion to come to work. But it is not very likely that this is true. We certainly don't know that it's true. Even if it were true, we might still be able to cut a deal, in which he agreed to come to work for, perhaps, only $1 billion per year. Most of Gates's reward is economic rent. I suspect he likes his job more than people who struggle to work each morning to earn much smaller sums.

What of the people on the trading floor behind the talking heads on Bloomberg television? They are valuable to their employers, which is why they receive multi-million dollar bonuses. But trading profits are mostly arbitrage gains, whose impact on GDP is small. GDP might be higher if securities markets were less active and less liquid. Corporate executives are paid a lot, not because of their productivity – which is impossible to measure – but because of their bargaining power. They take a slice of the rents they control. The complexity of the way in which market rewards are determined makes it impossible to argue such rewards are necessarily just or efficient. Thoughtful conservatives like Friedman and Nozick do not make that claim; they assert instead that interference with the process that gives rise to them would be unjust, because it would involve illegitimate state coercion.[37]

Some people might agree with this argument, but many would not. That disagreement is itself a problem. If the distribution of income and wealth in the market economy does not meet widely shared notions of legitimacy, that distribution will be expensively disputed. The direct and indirect costs of litigation and crime may be a serious burden on the market economy. In Argentina, and modern Russia, problems of legitimacy have led to structures of politics which have blocked effective economic development.

The ABM and the American Economy

If the ABM is not a plausible description of how market economies function, why is the American economy so successful? The answer should by now be obvious: the ABM does not describe the American economy. We do not look to Norway or Switzerland for societies populated by the exclusively self-interested: but nor do we look to the United States. We point instead to countries such as Nigeria or Haiti, in which there is an insufficient basis of trust for market institutions to develop. Or to Colin Turnbull's description of the Ik mountain people, whose social institutions had been shattered by adversity, and callous materialism had led to a spiral of economic decline.[38]

The ability to form supportive groups which enhanced the lives of individuals and households but did not involve the processes of government has always been a distinguishing feature of American society. Tocqueville once more: 'the most democratic society on earth is found to be the one where men in our day have most perfected the art of pursuing the object of their common desires in common and have applied this new science to the most effect.'[39] The market economies of rich states depend on such institutions. The most important today is the corporation. Corporate man, the epitome of the American submergence of the individual in the company, was once the butt of jokes. But corporate men, and corporate women, are the social individuals who make the economic lives of Americans rich and fulfilling.

27

Beyond the American Business Model

Capitalism should be Replaced by Something Nicer

Will Hutton's *The State We're In* was an unexpected bestseller in Britain in 1995. In it, Hutton captured the moment when the tide turned against the Thatcher reforms. In the following year Viviane Forrester's *L'Horreur economique* spent several weeks at the top of the French bestseller list. Hutton is a well-informed economic journalist. Forrester, although a scion of the formidable Louis-Dreyfus business family, is a novelist and literary critic, and neither her c.v. nor her writing reveals any qualifications to write on business issues.[1]

After the Seattle riots of 1999, the stream of anti-globalization books grew, among them Naomi Klein's *No Logo*, Noreena Hertz's *The Silent Takeover* and George Monbiot's *Captive State*. Marxist jargon was dusted down for Michael Hardt and Antonio Negri's *Empire*. What is significant is not just that these books find a large market in Europe. These are almost the only books about business and economics to sell well in Europe.[2] They express the anger and frustration of educated Europeans. In academic or artistic circles, among religious leaders, for people successful in any sphere of life outside business itself, the market, the market economy and market forces are terms of abuse.

On May Day 2001 demonstrators gathered in London to denounce the American business model. Among the mob which had thrown stones at every opportunity from the storming of the Bastille in 1789 to the siege of Genoa in 2001 were also sandal-wearing, bicycling protesters who wished the world were a better place. One carried a placard: 'Capitalism should be replaced by something nicer.'

The slogan captures the incoherence of modern anti-capitalism. It is clear what the demonstrators are against, but not clear what they are for. The puzzlement in Ms Hertz's voice is evident as she deplores a 'world in which consumerism is equated with economic policy, where corporations spew their jargon on the airwaves, and stifle nations with their imperial rule'. She acknowledges 'business is now in many ways better placed than any other institution to act as the primary agent of justice in much of the developing world'. Her answer (whatever that means) is to reclaim the state.[3] Even Hardt and Negri no longer seek the restructuring of society but demand free immigration, a right to a social income, and the reappropriation (whatever that is) of the means of production.

This bewilderment extends to European parties of the left. Their socialist origins are discarded, yet the loss of ideology makes them more, not less, electable, especially as European voters react against what they see as the excesses of the American business model. As the twenty-first century opened, the left was in power in Britain, France and Germany. In Britain and Germany (less so in France), former socialist parties espouse market forces, but the conversion is superficial and unenthusiastic. Blair's 'third way' decayed in platitude and derision. But the new centre-left project can succeed only if it locates a coherent political economy appropriate for a new century.

The collapse of socialism has also created dilemmas for the European centre-right. The British Conservative Party entered the 1990s with two distinct traditions. One, liberal individualist, espoused the American business model; the other, conservative traditionalist, emphasized the continuity of institutions. Both had been united through the century by socialism, a common enemy – a cement smashed with the Berlin Wall. In Thatcher's government the individualists triumphed, for the first time, over the traditionalists, but the triumph was not permanent. Despite the Thatcher victories, a European political party committed to the American business model is normally unelectable. The intellectual roots of modern European politics seem to have withered away.

Social Democracy

The political economy of Europe since the Second World War has been dominated by social democracy. This has failed; most obviously in Britain, where the radical optimism of the post-war period turned to disillusionment. By the time of the weak Labour administration of 1974–9, dissatisfaction with nationalized industries, public services and the welfare state was widespread. Britain was often described as ungovernable.[4] The Thatcher government elected in 1979 scrapped much of the apparatus of social democracy. It launched a successful attack on trade unions, dismantled habits and institutions of collective dialogue between government, employers and labour, and privatized most state industries. When Labour returned to power in 1997, the party described itself as 'New Labour' to distance itself from its social democratic past.

Sweden was long regarded as the exemplar of social democracy, but the model lost lustre. The Social Democratic Party had seemed since 1946 to be the permanent government of Sweden, but lost power in 1976 and again in 1991. After a long period in which Sweden's combination of strong GDP growth and exceptional social cohesion was widely admired, the recent economic performance of the Swedish economy has been one of the most disappointing in Europe.[5]

The zenith of social democracy was from the end of the Second World War to the 1960s. Britain and even the United States had fought the war with planned economies; the Soviet Union had demonstrated impressive capacity to mobilize resources. Most European states, with the important exception of Germany, built a partnership between business, trade unions and government around a centralized national plan. These plans eschewed the detail of Communist direction but set ambitious targets.[6] The greatest success of economic planning had been the pursuit of the single goal of an Allied victory. But modern economies require myriad small decisions. Should laundry detergents be liquids or concentrated powders? What size of turbine should be installed in power stations? Should we grow more carnations, or more roses? These decisions cannot be made through democratic political choices: the mechanisms of democracy are too slow and cumbersome, the individuals who participate in them lack information and expertise.

Social democrats once genuinely believed that these problems could be solved. At the foundation of Britain's National Health Service, Aneurin Bevan declared that 'the sound of a bedpan falling in Tredegar hospital would reverberate around the Palace of Westminster'.[7] In the 1960s the development of information technology seemed to some people to offer the answers: in national economies and individual businesses, democratic principles would be implemented by modern computers.[8] Some modern social democrats still cling to the illusion that participation is the objective, technology the means. For Tony Giddens, 'the only route to the establishing of authority is via democracy. The new individualism doesn't inevitably corrode authority, but demands it to be recast on an active or participatory basis.' What does this mean in practice? 'More direct contact with citizens, and citizens with government, through "experiments with democracy" – local direct democracy, electronic referenda, citizens' juries . . . One model is the approach used in Sweden twenty years ago, when the government drew the public directly into the formulation of energy policy. The government, unions, parties and education agencies set up day-long courses in energy. Anyone who took such a course could make formal recommendations to the government. Seventy thousand people participated in an exercise that decisively shaped policy.'[9]

Representative Versus Participative Democracy

Giddens reopens an old debate: that between participative democracy, in which each decision is an aggregation of the wishes of individuals, and representative democracy, which vests authority in political leaders but ensures that the right to exercise that authority is routinely contested. The issues were framed by Burke two centuries ago, in his address to the electors of Bristol:[10] Burke asserted that he acted, not as their delegate, but as their representative.

Giddens is not alone in making the claim that modern technology makes participative democracy possible and modern individualism makes it necessary. But a complex modern economy could not conceivably be directed by participative democracy. The problem of information is fundamental. Computers manage data, but it is not storage or calculation that is at issue. We need qualitative as well as quantitative information, much of which is simply unknowable. All this runs up against issues of incentive compatibility. The information we offer – as customers or voters, managers or employees – depends on the purposes for which we expect it to be used.

A one-day course in energy policy was not long, but long enough to exclude 99 per cent of the Swedish population. Voting in a national election takes a few minutes, every four or five years: turnout in many European states exceeds 80 per cent, but in Britain it is closer to two-thirds, in the United States a little over half. More frequent elections over smaller issues experience much lower participation. 'The trouble with socialism is that it takes too many evenings.'[11] Most people are more interested in families and leisure than in political activity. Representative institutions – political meetings or public inquiries – are attended by individuals who are not representative. If they were genuinely representative, they would be at home, watching television.

So the governing bodies of health and education institutions are dominated by people who work in health and education – people who have interest and incentive to devote time – and by people who have strong opinions, which may or may not be widely shared, about health and education. Local government is served by local business people, who hope for contracts and contacts. Public inquiries into major projects are attended by construction companies and professional protesters. The transactions costs of participative democracy are too high, so its decisions are neither adaptive nor representative. The ways in which technology changes this – government websites, emails to the President and electronic voting, are essentially superficial. And – as was seen in Chapter 7 – there is nothing to stop participants voting for inconsistent proposals.

Representative democracy tackles these problems by ceding authority to make decisions, ideally to an honest person, like Burke, who makes tough choices. The representative secures re-election, or fails to do so, on the basis of voters' assessment of integrity and competence. Representative democracy is itself a mechanism of disciplined pluralism. Government is intrinsically a monopoly, and representative democracy establishes competition for that monopoly; it is a powerful selection mechanism.

There are no defined criteria of success. We are not required to answer the politician who asks 'What must I do to secure re-election?': defining the job is itself part of the job.[12] And there is no appeal: perhaps it was unfair that the British electorate celebrated victory in the Second World War by ejecting Winston Churchill from office.[13] Representative democracy is a mechanism which has itself been selected for. Attempts within rich states to subvert it have sooner or later failed, although the most extensive subversion – in Germany from 1933 to 1945 – was protracted and horrific in human and material cost.

A complex modern economy cannot be managed through participative democracy. Modern democracies do not have mass involvement in decision-making; they use pluralist and disciplined processes to establish the legitimate authority of those who do make decisions. Social democratic control of economic policy is feasible only if centralization reduces the number of decisions and establishes powerful levers of central control. This is the reality of the most successful social democracy – France.

Social Democracy in France

The mutual distaste of the French and the Americans for each other's economic systems borders on the comic. Before the modern anti-American polemics of Viviane Forrester, there was Michel Albert's *Capitalisme contre capitalisme* and Charles Servan-Schreiber's *Le Défi américain*. The *New York Times* – through Thomas Friedman and its European correspondent, Roger Cohen – runs a litany of anti-French sentiment. The *Wall Street Journal* is not far behind.[14]

But both France and the United States are rich countries. The United States grew more rapidly than France in the 1990s after four decades in which the opposite was true. GDP per head in the USA is about 20 per cent higher than in France, but French working hours are 20 per cent shorter than in the USA, so that hourly output is much the same in the two countries. From a statistical perspective, the difference between the two countries is that the French take lunch, and five weeks' holiday.[15]

The reasons why social democracy has been successful in France and unsuccessful in Britain would occupy a book in their own right, and this is not it.[16] France's social democracy is not participative, and its government barely contested. Whoever is elected, economic management and control of public services remain in the hands of a homogeneous cadre. In the post-war era senior politicians (regardless of party), civil servants and the top management of most large French businesses have been drawn from a single élite class, selected through a rigorously meritocratic process, trained in France's *grandes écoles*. This political class administers the most centralized of large Western states.[17]

In Britain, politicians, civil servants, business leaders and public service managers have different background, training and experience. They view each other with at best wary respect and, more frequently, active contempt. Britain's apolitical civil service, and its distinction between policy and implementation, are not reproduced in France: a minister in Paris operates with a cabinet of sympathetic public officials.

French officials are strongly output-oriented, but British officials, politically neutered, are more concerned with appropriate process. In Britain, orderly decision-making is prized above the beneficial outcome of decisions themselves which – as with electricity – may not ever be measured or reported. There is no more powerful symbolism than the Eurostar journey from Paris to London: trains speed along dedicated high-speed tracks from the Gare du Nord to the tunnel, emerging to amble gently through the Kent countryside before arriving at the station the English defiantly call Waterloo. The French government, recognizing an obvious national interest, eliminated opposition to the line with a mixture of inducements and steamrollering. The chaotic, participative British process, crafted to partially satisfy a range of self-interested objectors and self-imposed constraints, drags on ten years after the tunnel has been completed.[18]

Electricity demonstrates the same contrast. Both countries made (mistaken) centralized decisions to pursue large nuclear programmes. France delivered reactors (based on American PWR technology)[19] efficiently while the British programme, itself a compromise between conflicting commercial and political interests, dragged on for twenty-five ineffective years.

This goal orientation has made the French the dominant nationality in the development of the European Union, even though much of the workload is shouldered by the British and Germans. As Eurostar exemplifies, French public services are technically excellent, though not customer-friendly, and French people are proud of them. In Britain, public dissatisfaction is widespread and there is destructive tension between centre and periphery. These forces destroyed Britain's nationalized industries and undermine its health and education systems. France is social democracy's best shot, and it is not a bad one.

The Problems of Social Democracy

There is growing discontent in France with the rule of the enarchs.[20] The populist Jean-Marie Le Pen knocked the Socialist Prime Minister, Lionel Jospin, out of the first round of presidential elections in 2002, and the re-elected Jacques Chirac looked outside the conventional élite for Jospin's successor. France displays some of the 'ungovernability' that characterized 1970s Britain: a product of the desire to maintain consensus, regardless of consequences. When commitment to consensus is absolute, there are no bounds to the demands which can be made.[21] But there is no prospect of a Thatcherite revolution in France. And centralization allows large-scale mistakes, as with blood supply or the commercial failures of Crédit Lyonnais and Vivendi.[22]

Ironically, the most conspicuous failure of British social democracy was the legacy of modern social democracy's most eloquent spokesman, Tony Crosland.[23] The introduction of comprehensive education was a well-intentioned attempt to break down class divisions in British society, but the experiment failed in that objective and reduced educational standards. What was wrong was not the experiment itself, but the usual characteristics of centrally planned initiatives – the scale, the absence of a substantive attempt to monitor consequences, and the slowness to recognize failure.[24]

In a representative democracy, politicians are still under pressure to make decisions which satisfy their constituents. Functionaries in a democracy are under pressure to make decisions which please their superiors. Neither of these pressures necessarily relates to the allocation of scarce resources between competing ends, not on the big issues of resource allocation, such as planning ahead for electricity generation, nor the small ones, such as the best way to dispense laundry detergent. Politicians do not have the knowledge or information to make such decisions and the systems they head can never supply it to them.

If we require a single centralized energy strategy for the next fifty years, then the best decisions are likely to be made by enarchs, followed, not closely, by Lord Plowden and his committees. But the enarchs got it wrong and Lord Plowden got it more seriously wrong: it would be better if no such decisions were made. Energy policy is not just about big-picture questions: the size of the turbines matters as much as the fuel that turns them. No one knows the answer to these questions, large or small, and solutions can only be reached by trial and error – processes of disciplined pluralism.

Business people are not inherently better at making economic decisions than politicians or civil servants. They are as often ignorant, opinionated and surrounded by sycophants as their political counterparts, but in a market economy they make decisions in an environment that quickly demonstrates to them – and to others – the wisdom or otherwise of their choices. In social democracy, this objective discipline is replaced by the requirements of popularity with those to whom the decision-makers report – voters, politicians or more-senior bureaucrats.

Legitimate Authority in the Market Economy

'In a society where tradition and custom are losing their hold, the only route to the establishing of authority is via democracy.'[25] If the only proper source of authority is democracy, it is easy to see why the activities of companies which operate in rich states and have greater resources than many poor states may cause concern. But authority in a modern rich state is a matter of perception and consent. Authority – including the authority of the state – can be exercised to the extent that it is seen as legitimate, but only to that extent. That is why the young Alan Greenspan's claim that 'the basis of regulation is armed force. At the bottom of the endless pile of paperwork . . . lies a gun' is absurd.[26] If you need a gun to enforce regulation in a democratic state, you will fail.

The coercive power of the democratic state is limited, and the democratic state has no monopoly of coercion. Stalin's foolish question 'How many divisions does the Pope have?'[27] is the converse of Greenspan's error. Outside the economic sphere, we find no great difficulty in acknowledging as legitimate the authority of spiritual, religious and intellectual leaders, an authority which is not acquired through democratic election. The basis of their power may be tradition and custom, or more often earned respect. Somewhat paradoxically, anti-capitalist demonstrators assert the legitimacy of their own unelected NGOs as they dispute the legitimacy of corporate power.

There are many sources of authority in modern society, and success in the marketplace is one. The management of Sainsbury's enjoys a legitimacy in organizing the supply of our groceries which arises from the effectiveness with which they have done this in the past. In the 1990s this argument was taken to fanciful extremes. 'Microsoft should have argued that we have a monopoly because customers want us to have one.'[28] For the *Wall Street Journal* the verdict of the market overrode that of the courts, and expressed the will of the people with more authority than the democratically appointed officials of the Department of Justice. 'Markets are voting machines, they function by taking referenda.'[29]

It is frustrating to mediate an argument polarized between two untenable positions. On the one hand, the purpose of corporations is to do good under democratic direction. On the other, their sole function is to maximize shareholder value. Neither proposition offers a viable basis for a corporate economy. When Friedman asserts that 'the social responsibility of business is to maximize its profits',[30] he immediately raises the question which concerns protesters: Why should such corporations be allowed to exercise power and authority in a democratic society? The pragmatic answer, that corporations are necessary to deliver goods and services we all want, defeats Friedman's argument. If we concede authority to corporations because they deliver the goods and services we want, that defines their social responsibility.

BEYOND THE AMERICAN BUSINESS MODEL

Corporations may aim to make profits, and there is nothing wrong with that, but their aims and their responsibilities are not the same. Heidi's primary aim may be the welfare of her family, but her responsibility is to her students. It is on that basis alone that she is allowed in the classroom, and she encounters no particular difficulty in reconciling these obligations.

The legitimacy of capitalist organizations is not self-evident: it needs justification. The more competitive the environment, the easier that justification. We cede authority more willingly when we have a choice of whom we cede authority to. This is a fundamental precept of democracy; and we recognize authority more willingly when those who exercise it have earned our respect through competitive success – in either the ballot or the marketplace.

Legitimacy which is earned in the market is confined to the market. Business has no proper authority in matters which are properly the subject of democratic process – the desirability of lower taxes or the importance of protecting the rainforest – which is why its political lobbying is improper and the demands for corporate social responsibility misconceived. Corporate power is legitimate so long as it is constrained by competition, limited in extent and exercised in circumstances in which no one enjoys too much of it: trammelled by the forces of disciplined pluralism.

The Social Market in Germany

Germany and Russia have experienced the complex relationship between political and economic power more traumatically than other states. When the process of reconstruction in Germany began after 1945, the disaster of German totalitarianism ruled out centralized, élite structures such as those of France. German political economists were determined to map a different, more pluralist route. The social market economy was both a political and an economic project. Its intellectual architects were the ordo-liberals, or Freiburg School, led by Armand Müller-Armach.[31] The key concept is *vollständige Konkurrenz*, which seems to translate naturally into English as 'perfect competition', the ideal of the Arrow–Debreu model. But German scholars[32] insist that its German meaning is wider: it implies resistance to any form of concentrated economic power, in cartels, corporations or the state. Along with *vollständige Konkurrenz* goes an assumption that risks will be managed through public institutions and private businesses.[33] 'Ordo-liberal' seems almost an oxymoron to an English ear: perhaps the appropriate translation is 'disciplined pluralist'.

In 1948 the ordo-liberal, Ludwig Erhard, was appointed director of economic affairs in the American and British occupation zones. His economic reform programme removed price controls and instituted a new currency. This provoked a Russian blockade of Berlin which was defeated by a massive Allied airlift. The creation of a West German state followed in which Erhard became first Economics Minister and then Chancellor.

The divergent experiences of Friedrich and Heinz (which were described in Chapter 2) began. Erhard is today indelibly associated both with the economic miracle that was West Germany and the term 'social market economy'.

Redistributive Market Liberalism

Today the phrase 'social market' has two distinct meanings, as was recently described by Adair Turner. He acknowledges that 'simplistic market fundamentalism can be as dangerous to sensible market liberalism as was Marxism. Capitalism can have a human face, but governments and political processes need to ensure that it does.' Turner goes on: 'Two different approaches can be pursued – the classical liberal model in which wider objectives are achieved through the constraints of tax and regulation within which individuals pursue their own self-interest, or the communitarian or stakeholder which seeks to humanize capitalism by asking of individuals and corporations that they take upon themselves a wider set of responsibilities.'[34]

Turner favours the first of these approaches, following an eloquent British tradition established by James Meade[N] and Britain's leading economic journalist, Samuel Brittan.[35] Within 'the constraints of tax and regulation', the pursuit of self-interest is allowed, even encouraged. For Brittan, 'in matters such as buying and selling, or deciding what and how to produce, we will do others more good if we behave as if we are following our self-interest rather than by pursuing more altruistic purposes.'[36] Under the particular influence of James Meade, I classified myself for many years as a redistributive market liberal, along with many other professional economists. Brittan has argued that there is a professional consensus around this position.[37]

Redistributive market liberalism (RML) makes a sharp distinction between our economic lives and our social roles as citizens and neighbours. At work, in business, through our commercial dealings, we may – even must – pursue our self-interest. We then vote for high taxes so that the proceeds of our successful pursuit of that self-interest can be redistributed. However, for most people it is difficult to be a beast in the boardroom and a concerned citizen at the ballot box. People who have successfully pursued commercial self-interest usually support tax and benefit policies which further advance that self-interest. Rich individuals who engage in philanthropy do so in reflection of a 'wider set of responsibilities' rather than self-interest within 'the constraints of tax and regulation'.

For capitalism with a human face to be tenable, the face must be one not two. In Brecht's parable of *The Good Woman of Setzuan*, the kindly prostitute Shen Te establishes a business with good intentions, but dresses as a cousin when hard-nosed decisions are required. As with Jekyll and Hyde, the inhuman face takes over.

A mild version of RML proposes that government should simply be concerned with equality of opportunity, not equality of outcome. Inequalities in access to education and other barriers to mobility are primary sources of injustice in almost any political philosophy. But could a government ever claim to have met the needs of its citizens by ensuring equality of opportunity in the market economy? Could we ever frame fair rules and institutions without knowledge or concern for their outcomes? Could we set just rules for competition policy and copyright without considering that we were giving Bill Gates $50 billion, or taking it away? Could we set policies for university admissions independent of the structure of graduate earnings? Could we determine an access regime for telecommunications by reference to general principle rather than effect on market structure, call charges or share prices? Because markets are embedded in a social framework, the distinction between process and outcome – Friedman's distinction between the rules and the play of the game – becomes untenable.

The fundamental objections to redistributive market liberalism are those which were used against the American business model in the last chapter. They are the mistaken assumptions about motivation and behaviour, the failure to acknowledge the socially constructed nature of property rights, the inability of market institutions to deal with risk, the problems of securing necessary co-operation among self-interested individuals and the difficulties of handling asymmetries of information within a complex modern economy. For all these reasons we cannot simply wind up the mechanism of the market economy and let it run. For all these reasons market economies function only by virtue of being embedded in a social context. The real objective is not to 'humanize capitalism' by 'asking of individuals and corporations that they take upon themselves a wider set of responsibilities'. Rather, it is to understand that capitalism works in practice only because it is humanized. Capitalism does indeed need to be replaced by something nicer, but perhaps that something nicer is capitalism itself. I turn now to the political economy of the embedded market.

28

The Embedded Market

The assumptions of the American business model (ABM) are false, but that does not imply their opposite is true. There are people who think economic behaviour is mostly altruistic, political mechanisms of allocation are always preferable to the anarchy of the market, government should control and preferably own all productive assets, and highly progressive taxation should be imposed to bring about an egalitarian distribution of income and wealth. Such people are, however, in a minority, and I doubt if many of them will have read this far.

The economic world is complex. Self-interest is an important motivation, but not an exclusive motivation. Our other concerns influence work and business lives as well as personal lives. We need the approbation of our friends, the trust of our colleagues, the satisfaction of performing activities that are worthwhile in themselves and give others pleasure. These motives are not materialistic, but that does not mean they are not economic. They are an essential part of the mechanisms through which successful business operates. Without them business and economic systems would be impoverished – in material as well as other terms.

Markets work, but not always and not perfectly. Pluralist market structures promote innovation, and competitive markets meet many consumer needs, but there is no general reason to believe that market outcomes are efficient. Social and economic institutions manage the transmission of information in market economies. These institutions depend on culture and values, laws and history. In the perfectly competitive model, and the simplicities of the ABM, it is obvious what the rules of a market economy should be and easy to enforce them, and the description of products and the definition of their properties are also obvious and easy.

However, market economies have been successful relative to other societies precisely because the rules that govern them are not obvious to frame and easy to implement, and rich states have evolved complex governance structures embedded in other modern social and political institutions. That allows the development of sophisticated products which consumers are confident to buy and use without needing to understand them. Market economies handle well co-ordination problems associated with logistics – co-ordination between manufacturers and component suppliers, reliable deliveries, overall balances between supply and demand. They do less well when even temporary imbalances are intolerable – as in electricity supply, when the lights go out. Mercury Energy did restore supplies to Auckland, but only after seven weeks. Markets, however, do not necessarily succeed at all, or succeed in producing good outcomes, when other forms of co-ordination are required, as for networks and standards, and markets for risk and capital, dominated by speculative traders, are prone to bubbles and overshooting. These fluctuations in securities markets destabilize markets for goods and services, and divert resources from productive activities to the pursuit of small arbitrage gains.

The very concept of a market for labour is offensive to many people, and with cause: workers are citizens as well as suppliers of labour, and enjoy rights that are not held by apples, pears, software – or corporations. Laws that prohibit slavery and regulate the organized sex industry are hardly controversial. They restrict freedom of contract on the grounds that even voluntary transactions may degrade society and deprive individuals of dignity. The issue is not whether the labour 'market' should be subject to social and legal regulation, but the nature and extent of such regulation. That is a matter for moral judgement, social values and empirical evidence.

Many services cannot be provided in competitive markets: public goods like lighthouses, environmental protection, police and defence, and the framework of rules within which the modern market economy operates. There are natural monopolies, in water and electricity distribution, road and rail networks, air traffic control. Other services, such as education and health, could be provided by competitive markets but are not, for reasons that most people find compelling. It is desirable to find pluralist structures for these industries, but acceptable market solutions will not emerge spontaneously. In addition, the distribution of income and wealth and the process by which that distribution is established must, like the structure of market institutions itself, enjoy legitimacy if the market economy is to survive and evolve. Many failures of the market economy follow from this: Russia, obviously; also Argentina and New Zealand.

The embedded market describes the successful market systems of Western Europe – and the reality of the United States. It does not function within a minimal state: productive economies have the largest, most powerful and most influential governments the world has ever seen. Throughout most of history, and in poor countries today, government rarely impinge on the everyday lives of ordinary people, like Sicelo or the villagers of Palanpur.

In rich states, we are always conscious of the influence of government. We pay its taxes on every transaction we make, and most of us also receive social benefits. Regulation governs everything we do, from the way we drive to the butter we spread on our bread. We look to government to provide a wide range of goods and services, from education to rubbish collection. The market economy relies on intermediate institutions greater than individuals, smaller than governments. The most important of these are corporations, but there are many others.

Because markets are embedded in social institutions, it is not only, or mainly, by voting that we influence the development of the market economy. Economic policy is not a list of things the government should do. We make economic policy as consumers, employers, entrepreneurs and shareholders. We influence economic policy when we conform to, or resist, the norms and values of the market economy. Economic policy is as much about social attitudes and customary behaviour as about law and regulation.

The job of government under the ABM is to define and enforce the rules of the market economy. The economic role of a social democratic government is to determine through the democratic process how society wishes scarce resources to be allocated between competing ends, and to direct the activities of businesses and households in order to bring that allocation about.

Neither of these models describes the function of government accurately. The complex institutions of the market economy developed largely without central direction and are constantly evolving. Government is an agent in that evolution, not a bystander, but government cannot control the process and should not seek to. The political economy of the embedded market is best understood by examining policy areas which illustrate these subtleties. Inevitably, the story begins in Germany.

After School

German vocational training, universally admired, underpins the competitive advantages of German manufacturing business. Young workers undergo apprenticeships which involve a combination of formal general education, training specific to the proposed career, and personal supervision and advice on the job from an experienced worker. Apprenticeships are available not only to craft trainees such as engineers and plumbers but also for hotel workers and shop assistants.

There is no legal obligation on individuals to take such training or on firms to provide it, but the credentials obtained are valued, able students wish to have them, and as a result employers wish to hire both apprentices and qualified workers. The largest German firms, such as Siemens and Daimler Chrysler, organize training nationally, but training is mostly administered locally. Chambers of Commerce co-ordinate the efforts of business and the contribution of provincial governments. Large firms, responsible for a high proportion of industry-specific training, probably make a disproportionate contribution, to the benefit of smaller businesses and the economy as a whole. If we ask 'Why do firms do this?' the answer is 'They just do': participation is a norm of the German business community and local business organizations reinforce social pressures.[1]

Attempts in Britain to replicate the system,[2] by agreement between government and national business organizations, were a fiasco. In the early 1990s around 800 National Vocational Qualifications (NVQs) were established, across a wide range of industries. Most successful schemes were a simple rebadging of existing, well-established qualifications. Almost half of all NVQs have yet to receive their first candidate.[3]

German training works because, and only because, the system is embedded in other German institutions. Economic policies based on abstract blueprints and imposed by government are rarely effective. This is not to say that there is no role for government, or that only institutions which develop spontaneously can be effective. Policy results from the interaction of norms and values and is part of a subtle relationship between private and social institutions, and the powers and resources of the state.

This complex approach to economic policy making is uncomfortable for both social democrats and supporters of the ABM/RML position. It denies the social democratic premise that the only legitimate source of economic authority is democratic election. Who gives employers the right to determine the content of vocational qualifications? By what authority do Chambers of Commerce impose obligations on their members? However, it is fundamental to the success of market economies that power is dispersed in this pluralist way. A supporter of the ABM would be suspicious of the imposition of training obligations on employers, and insistent that any such obligation must be framed in a clear and transparent way. But this immediately encounters problems of incentive compatibility. How is training to be defined? How are rules to be framed which distinguish between the development of career skills and the delivery of inspirational messages from the company's chief executive?

Formal training obligations are less effective than Germany's informal norms. In Britain, the rise of the ABM relieved companies of a former sense of duty to train employees for their role in the industry and community.[4] It required a demonstrable business benefit. The attempt to replace these training obligations by corporatist agreement between government and national business leaders failed because expert committees responding to political imperatives did not establish qualifications that were valued by workers or their employers.

If Germany leads the world in vocational training, the United States leads it in higher education. The leading US universities are private institutions (Berkeley, part of the University of California system, is the most prominent exception). The US government supports research and organizes and guarantees systems of student finance, but there is no central direction of universities and no systematic policy for higher education of the kind which is universal in Europe.

Overall comparisons of the quality of higher education are difficult, but at élite level the answer is entirely clear. The United States is completely dominant in research and postgraduate education. The ten leading research centres in the world in virtually all mainstream subjects are found in American institutions. The eclipse of other universities, particularly those of Britain and Germany, occurred in the twentieth century: the impact on the distribution of Nobel Prizes was described in Chapter 22. The broader economic implications are hard to assess, but advanced commercial research facilities are clustered around major institutions of higher education. Silicon Valley is not built on reserves of silicon, but close to Stanford University.

Leading American universities receive substantial government research funding, but from pluralist sources. They charge fees, which are largely rebated to those who cannot afford them. Large endowments are raised from alumni and corporate donors. In effect, top US universities are funded by informal taxation of businesses and individuals who benefit from their activities. The taxation is, in a sense, voluntary, but anyone who has seen the activities of US alumni fundraisers knows the strength of social pressures to conform. The amounts raised are larger and more equitably levied than could be true under any likely scheme of graduate taxation or corporate taxation on knowledge- and science-based industries. The mechanisms of social regulation that support American universities are very different from those that support German vocational training, reflecting different but equally effective cultures.

The ABM has nothing to say about higher education. Materialistic, self-regarding individuals would produce only innovations they could themselves sell. They would not contribute to an advancing body of scholarship or engage in the fundamental research on which modern economic development has relied. Fortunately, the United States is not like the ABM.

Social democracy has much to say about higher education – there is no subject on which educated people have stronger views than education – but it would be better for all if it ceased to say it. The proliferation of opinions and controls, inside and outside higher education institutions, has made their effective management impossible. Higher education, like vocational education, flourishes in an embedded market in which government participates but does not control, financial incentives exist but do not dominate, structures are pluralist and evolving rather than directed, and social norms secure compliance with a system of which the community feels justly proud.

After the Ball

Two companies came to symbolize the triumph and failure of the American 1990s – Enron, the Houston-based energy business, and WorldCom, a telecoms operator with headquarters in Clinton, Mississippi. Both companies had grown rapidly through acquisition and for a time enjoyed iconic status with investment bankers and many investors.[5] The collapse of these businesses in late 2001 and summer 2002 provoked widespread allegations of fraud and corruption[6] and was an important factor in the final deflation of the bubble.[7]

Most people who have neither knowledge of nor interest in accounting imagine that the profits of a company are a matter of fact, like its bank balance or the number of employees. It is, however, a matter of complex judgement to assess the annual profitability of even a simple organization. Controversies at Enron and WorldCom concerned two major issues. Large businesses often have many subsidiary companies, and consolidated accounts must incorporate them all. Some of these activities may have outside shareholders, partners and investors: to what extent should these be included? Companies can depreciate the cost of new investment over several years, rather than deducting it from profit straight away. But what part of operating costs are associated with this new investment? The Securities and Exchange Commission and Federal Accounting Standards Board prescribed appropriate rules. Enron and WorldCom pushed to the limits of these rules and their auditors agreed an expansive interpretation. Other blue-chip auditors and companies did the same. Respected corporations established special-purpose entities, as Enron did; other corporations capitalized operating expenditures, as WorldCom did. But

Enron and WorldCom were flattering the profits of businesses which were inherently unprofitable, and ran out of cash, as inherently unprofitable businesses do.

US government and corporate leaders were quick to denounce fraud and demand stiff punishment, like tribes who throw the weakest of their party to the wolves in the hope of preserving their own lives. Senior executives of Enron and WorldCom took large bonuses from poorly performing companies, made transactions with no commercial rationale but which allowed flexibility in reporting present and future profits,[8] exploited flaws in the details of accounting standards and lobbied against attempts to remedy these flaws. At Enron and WorldCom these activities differed only in degree, not in kind, from the actions of other major US corporations.

US accounting standards had attempted to establish prescriptive rules. UK accounting standards require that accounts present a true and fair view, and allow latitude for the professional judgement of accountants. This exaggerates the operational difference: US accountants retain considerable discretion, and UK accountants are also under commercial pressure to exercise judgement in favour of their clients. However, the difference in regulatory strategy is clear. It is the difference between the regulatory approach of the ABM – Adair Turner's 'classical liberal model in which wider objectives are achieved through the constraints of tax and regulation within which individuals pursue their own self-interest' – and that of the embedded market, which functions 'by asking of individuals and corporations that they take upon themselves a wider set of responsibilities'. There is the same difference in occupational health and safety. The USA prescribes detailed regulation and the UK imposes a general duty to provide a safe working environment.[9]

In regulating corporate America, the prescriptive approach – which allowed players freedom within rules – failed. The rules did not so much exclude the unacceptable as define the limits of the permissible. In complex, democratic societies, rules are implementable only if they define behaviour which most people would adopt in any event. That is why the approach of allowing maximum freedom within a framework of rules is bound to fail – and did.

Government and Governance

Disinterested government is a prerequisite for a successful market economy. Those who run the state must distinguish carefully between their own money and that of the government. It never occurred to most rulers in history to make such a separation. Even in advanced economies, relics survive. Hyde Park is a glorious open space which occupies 630 acres of the centre of London. It is the property of the Queen, and that is why it is not covered in houses. Today the public pays the cost of upkeep in return for access. It is an arrangement which works well in practice, but is, nevertheless, odd.

Such a structure breaks down in the hands of a Mobutu. The villas on Cap Martin are not open to the public, even in the unlikely event that the impoverished Congolese were able to visit. The austerity of government in rich states is at times ridiculous – the dingy offices, the packets of tea labelled by their owners – but the line being drawn needs constant and vigorous defence.

Direct payments to politicians and officials are rare in productive economies, but payments by corporations and wealthy individuals to parties and political campaigns are part of everyday life, in all but the most rigorous of rich states (the Scandinavian ones).[10] David Lloyd George – British Prime Minister from 1916 to 1922 – established a political fund which allowed parvenus to buy peerages and, although formally illegal, the practice effectively continues. American political action committees launder corporate contributions to congressional campaigns. The organization of African politics on tribal lines produces governments whose objectives are to distribute the spoils of office to the relatives and kinsfolk of those elected. This debilitating practice was true of US politics in Tammany days.

Modern political tribalism is more often based on shared views, or on personal friendships. Margaret Thatcher would ask 'Is he one of us?' President Warren Harding's proclivity for the advice and company of his own drinking companions was notorious.[11] The human tendency to identify with groups is so strong that – as with football supporters – intense political loyalties develop with no objective basis. In the closely contested US presidential election of 2000, the decisions of judges and public officials were generally predictable on the evidence of previously expressed political affiliations.[12] Corruption can be restrained only by a combination of externally imposed rules and internally sustained values. It is always adaptive for corrupt individuals to migrate towards corrupt structures.

With the rise of the modern corporate economy in the twentieth century – the emergence of corporations such as ICI, General Motors and General Electric – came the rise of the professional manager. These individuals saw themselves, and were seen by others, as comparable in status to leaders of other professions – top solicitors, accountants or surgeons, judges and senior civil servants. They were paid accordingly. Performance bonuses were unknown, as insulting and inappropriate as a bonus to a distinguished judge or a tip to a helpful accountant.

This ethos began to break down in the 1980s. The rise of the ABM allowed the claim that greed was good. The continual rise in the stock market generated very large earnings in the financial services sector, and managers who engaged with financial institutions naturally compared their own salaries with Wall Street bonuses. Top American executives took larger and larger sums of money out of the corporate till – the early example of Steve Ross of Time Warner was described in Chapter 24. So long as share prices were rising, few objections were raised. It became normal for American chief executives to receive tens, even hundreds, of millions of dollars in bonuses and share options.

Only as the stock market crashed in the new century did the extent to which senior managers at companies like Enron and WorldCom had run them for their own enrichment and aggrandisement become widely apparently. The failure of these businesses also took with it an army of advisers – such as the accounting firm Andersen – for whom it had been adaptive to collude.

Within the ABM framework, preventing political or corporate corruption is a matter of institutional design. The public choice model of politics assumes that public officials will be self-regarding, and structures its minimal state around that assumption. The principal-agent model of the corporation attempts to align the incentives of managers with those of shareholders. But the difference between corrupt and honest public administration, between corrupt and honest business, is not the result of differences in rules. Laws against corruption are often more draconian in corrupt states than in disinterested ones; extensive rules more often the symptom of a problem than its solution. The attempt to structure elaborate incentive schemes to align the interests of managers and shareholders did not eliminate fraud: it provoked it.

Incentive compatibility and adaptive behaviour explain why this is so. The integrity of an institution is not the product of its governance structure, but of the values of those who work within it. Many different value systems will be supported by adaptive, self-reinforcing behaviour. If institutions are designed on the assumption that individuals are self-interested, self-interested behaviour will be adaptive within them. If the premise is that people are not to be trusted, that expectation will be fulfilled.

Self-interested behaviour by managers of large companies is corrosive of the integrity of companies, just as self-interested behaviour by government officials is corrosive of the integrity of government. The central premise of the ABM – that economic life is or could be successfully organized around the instrumental behaviour of self-regarding materialists, constrained only by externally imposed rules – is mistaken, and the mistake threatens both the viability and legitimacy of market systems. In both politics and business, the rise of the ABM created the very problem of controlling self-interest it purported to solve.

Individualism and Communitarianism

The dominant strand of thought in modern political philosophy is an individualistic one, identified in this book with Rawls and Nozick. The most extensive critique of that political philosophy is provided by a group loosely labelled 'communitarians': Alasdair MacIntyre, Michael Sandel, Charles Taylor and Michael Walzer. The philosophy of Joseph Raz, and the political theory of John Gray, are also often associated with this group. I say 'loosely labelled' because none shows much enthusiasm for the term 'communitarian', there are substantial disagreements between them, and the term 'communitarian' has been appropriated in more-popular discourse by another political economist, Amitai Etzioni.[13]

The common element in the communitarian attack is a rejection of the individualistic notion that humans have preferences, moral sense or concepts of justice that are derived from outside the society in which they live. 'One cannot be a self on one's own.'[14] 'It is not only the familiar products of their experience that people value, but the experience itself, the process through which the products were produced. And (the dig at Rawls is obvious here) they will have some difficulty understanding why the hypothetical experience of abstract men and women should take precedence over their own history.'[15] Just as there is an affinity between individualistic political philosophy and the economics of the Arrow–Debreu model and ABM, there is an affinity between the communitarian critique of that philosophy and the embedded market critique of the associated economics. In the communitarian perspective personal morality is formed in society, and conceptions of the good society are not just aggregations of the views of individuals. Social bonds have value in themselves. They are not just pursued instrumentally for their advantage to individuals. Communitarian philosophers are sceptical of claims of universal principles of rights and constitutions – there is no end of history.

In the embedded market, no individual or household preferences are formed in isolation from knowledge of what is available and what is desired by others. Happiness is determined, as it is for Ivan and Ravi, by the relationship between experiences and aspirations. We cannot make statements about economic efficiency based simply on the aggregation of individual preferences. Social ties are not simply the means of advancing our economic self-interest, but are central to our economic lives. The appropriate economic institutions are specific to the context in which they are implemented.

Both Rawls and Nozick write in the tradition of Hobbes and Rousseau, which uses the metaphor of the state as social contract. The ABM employs the same metaphor of the corporation as creation of private contract. Citizens came together to agree the rules under which a sovereign would advance their interests; shareholders came together to agree the terms on which Jack Welch would manage their wealth on their behalf. Political theorists know they are using a metaphor: in business the metaphor is so powerful that people often talk as if it were literally true.

Most communitarians are deeply hostile to the market economy, which they see as inescapably linked to individualism and instrumental rationality. Walzer's definition of 'spheres of justice' hopes to limit the encroachment of market values. John Gray fulminates against markets as destructive of community and tradition.[16] Alasdair MacIntyre's scorn was noted in Chapter 10.[17]

More Fish

It is time to go fishing again, in the company of Alasdair MacIntyre.[18] MacIntyre envisages two crews, one organized on strictly self-regarding, materialist, rationalist lines:

> organized and understood as a purely technical and economic means to a productive end, whose aim is only or overridingly to satisfy as profitably as possible some market's demand for fish. . . . when the level of reward is sufficiently high, then the individual whose motivations and values are of this kind will have from her or his own point of view the best of reasons for leaving this particular view.

The second crew comes from one of the close-knit fishing communities which MacIntyre admires, and in which fishing constitutes what he calls a practice. In it we find

> a crew whose members may well have initially joined for the sake of their wage or other share of the catch, but who have acquired from the rest of the crew an understanding of and devotion to excellence in fishing . . . the interdependence of the members of a fishing crew in respect of skills, the achievement of goods and the acquisition of virtues will extend to an inter-dependence of the families of crew members and perhaps beyond them to the whole society of a fishing village.

MacIntyre does not ask the commercial question: Which crew would catch more fish? Why should he? He regards it as self-evident that the first crew would be more successful: this is why he sees modern economic life as destructive. However, the answer is far from self-evident: large-scale instrumental organization in the fishing industry failed. A Harvard Business School case study describes the Prelude Corporation, once the largest lobster-producer in North America. Its objectives were defined by its President: 'the fishing industry by now is just like the automobile industry was sixty years ago: a hundred companies are going to come and go, but we'll be the General Motors. . . . The technology and money required to fish offshore are so great that the little guy can't make out.' The Prelude Corporation went bankrupt soon after the Harvard Business School case was written.[19] It did so for reasons which emerge clearly from MacIntyre's account: fish are not made, but hunted. Incentive compatibility is a key problem in fishing. The catch depends on the flair, skills and initiative of people who cannot be effectively supervised. The product of people who have genuine mutual commitment, who 'have acquired from the rest of the crew an understanding of and devotion to fishing', exceeds that achieved when the 'only aim is overridingly to satisfy as profitably as possible some market's desire for fish.'

Obliquity and Instrumentality

MacIntyre's fishing expedition reveals a deep truth about markets. We live in a complex world which we only imperfectly understand. Our success in it depends crucially on our relationships with other people. In this environment, what has evolved will often outperform what has been designed, and purely instrumental motivation will often fail in its objectives. This gives rise to the paradox of obliquity revealed by the relative success of MacIntyre's crews: the crew which values the practice of fishing is more financially successful than the crew which is organized in pursuit of financial goals.

In his autobiography, John Stuart Mill, the greatest exponent of utilitarianism, recognized the paradox that self-interested behaviour does not necessarily promote self-interest. 'I never, indeed, wavered in the conviction that happiness is the test of all rules of conduct, and the end of life. But I now thought that this end was only to be attained by not making it the direct end.'[20] We understand this well from everyday life. We distinguish hedonism, the repetition of pleasurable actions, from happiness, which is the product of the whole relationship between our activities and our environment. From Herbert Simon we understand that we do not know enough to maximize our utility: we only know, from our own experience and that of generations before us, that generally recognized components of a good life – material well-being, economic and physical security, the respect of colleagues and friends, stable personal relationships – help make us happy.

We cannot be rational, calculating, maximizing agents, because we do not have, and could never have, sufficient knowledge of the world. The quality of our experiences is largely determined by our interactions with others in a complex world. We pity hedonists, as we pity people who are entirely selfish, not just for their moral shallowness but for the poverty of their experiences. Hetty Green (see Chapter 26), immensely rich and unfathomably mean, is not only someone we dislike, but someone we do not wish to emulate.

This obliquity is equally true of the corporations which play so large a part in our economic lives. Whether or not they should maximize shareholder value, they cannot: the people who run them do not have, and never can have, the information to make these calculations. We know that the ICI executives who invested in its pharmaceutical business made a decision which benefited shareholders, but in 1960 they could not have formed any realistic view of the value of Zeneca when it was floated in 1993. Consultants and investment banks build models which purport to make these calculations, but the apparent rationality is spurious. ICI was no more maximizing shareholder value than its employees were maximizing their utility. Like individuals in search of a fulfilling life, the company was pursuing broad strategic goals – strengthening its capabilities in research and development, building new businesses in areas related to the company's established strengths. The strategy was manifestly successful, in the obvious sense that it created a large and profitable business. Whether it maximized shareholder value, relative to other strategies that ICI might have adopted at the same time, it is impossible to tell, either in advance or with hindsight.

The purely instrumental motivations of the ABM are ultimately self-defeating. It is not true that profit is the purpose of a market economy, and the production of goods and services is a means to it: the purpose is the production of goods and services, profit the means. The happiest people are not those who single-mindedly pursue happiness: the most profitable companies are not the most profit-oriented.[21] Successful individuals, and successful companies, adapt their behaviour and their capabilities to the environment which they face. The consequences of adaptation resemble the *outcome* of a process of maximization, but are not the *product* of a process of maximization. The motion of the planets follows a system of differential equations despite the inability of the planets to compute the solutions. The song and flight of birds displays a beauty and efficiency of design which was not part of the intention of the birds, or of any other agency. We do better to flee the bear than to calculate an optimal strategy, and to follow the advice of park rangers is better still. Sometimes we understand best when we do not try too hard to understand.

29

The Framework of Economic Policy

Incentive Compatibility

Socialism failed because it substituted centralized direction for disciplined pluralism and because it could not handle issues of incentive compatibility. Government agencies and large businesses face exactly these problems. Indeed, the ways in which capitalist economies fail are often similar to the ways in which socialist economies fail.

Competitive markets minimize problems of incentive compatibility because they are economical with information. Russian planners had to investigate the capabilities of each factory and production unit. In a competitive market, buyers do not have to do very much of this investigation, because competition allows them to make comparisons and switch suppliers. Suppliers of capital and buyers of risk can diversify their portfolios and assess the performance of the business, rather than its internal operations.

Russian planners also needed to ascertain consumer preferences. Firms in a market economy undertake market research, but they learn principally from the choices consumers make. These answers are reliable and definitive (unlike the results of market research). The market economy is a discovery process which both reveals information and reduces the need for it. We gain some advantage from the activism involved in choosing the shortest supermarket queue, but only some, and we shall not lose out, much, if we leave it to other people.

Whenever competitive mechanisms are not available, or not used, there are potential problems of incentive compatibility. The common response is to set targets, and reward or punish by reference to the targets. This is the system that worked so badly in the Soviet Union. It worked badly for two main reasons. One was that the centre did not have sufficient local information to set the targets effectively. The other was that the targets could only imperfectly reflect the centre's real objectives. These problems arise whenever target setting is tried, in public sector activities such as health and education, in the regulation of utilities or in encouraging executives to maximize shareholder value. The same fundamental difficulty arises in each case. If the target setters had enough information to set targets appropriately, they, not the people on the ground, would be the effective managers of the business. So managers aim to meet the targets, not the objectives of the targets. 'Plan bargaining', strategic negotiations between the various parties, and the proliferation of more and inconsistent targets cause cynicism and demoralization. We read of the – literally – thousands of pages of contracts between the various parties to the privatization of the London Underground. This structure will not work. If it would work, the Soviet Union would have worked.

The contractualization approach has been applied not just between the public and private sectors but within the public sector itself. Unlucky New Zealand has taken this farthest, to the extent of writing 'contracts' between civil servants and their ministers.[1] In Britain, the establishment of executive agencies served a similar function,[2] as has the more recent specification of targets for many branches and agencies of government.

These mechanisms produce appearances of market disciplines without substance. Real contracts – the contracts described in Chapters 5 and 6 of this book – are voluntary, mutually beneficial agreements between autonomous agents. And it is only possible to make such contracts in competitive markets where there are credible alternatives for both buyers and sellers. The New Zealand Finance Minister has no possible supplier of services other than the New Zealand Treasury, nor does the New Zealand Treasury have any buyer other than the Finance Minister. The relationship is so fundamentally symbiotic that the contract is a sham.

These arrangements often attempt to shed responsibility but not authority. They enjoy their best chance of success when there is a genuine readiness to delegate power – as when authority to set interest rates is given to a central bank. They are least likely to work when there is no real intention of devolving authority. Sometimes this degenerates into farce, as when the Home Secretary holds the (very far from autonomous) Director of the Prison Service responsible for prison escapes. After all, the policy of the government is that no one should escape from prison.[3] The Treasury sets the Department of Social Security a target for reducing poverty while itself retaining control of the level of benefits received by poor people.[4]

The alternative is to try to align the interests of the various players. Outside the American business model, this is not hard. People who work in health and education, on railways or in water companies, have selfish and material concerns like everyone else, but they also, for the most part, want to provide these services effectively and efficiently. Corporate managers were once concerned to promote the interests of shareholders, and of their business – and generally still are, though some, having been told that greed was the driving force of the market economy, believed it and discovered that very little would be done to stop them helping themselves to the company's money. The objective is not to design institutions that are robust to self-interest, but to stimulate elements of behaviour that are not purely self-interested. These are divergent objectives: in structures designed around self-interest, self-interested behaviour becomes adaptive.

This is not a matter of simply appealing to people to do a good job. There are too many lazy academics, arrogant doctors and deceitful businessmen for trust alone to be sufficient. Autonomous bodies tend to define their own values and purposes. These may – as with MacIntyre's fishing crew – match their objectives but may equally – as with Havel's bureaucracy – be self-generated and self-sustaining. Autonomy is only possible in conjunction with the processes of audit and selection, and these function most effectively in conditions of disciplined pluralism.

Disciplined Pluralism

Market economies are not about harnessing greed, and the elevation of greed as their dominant value undermined them. Market economies succeeded because they established disciplined pluralism and put in place mechanisms which solved, or at least reduced, problems of incentive compatibility. The twin pillars of disciplined pluralism and incentive compatibility should support economic policy.

Disciplined pluralism is contrary to the natural instincts of most political or business leaders. For politicians to support it requires them to struggle with their own inner natures.[5] When governments make economic policies, their constant inclination is to suppress pluralism – to find the big idea – and to override discipline: to favour new ventures that the market will not accept or old industries which the market has already rejected. Frequently, they succumb. This is why the record of government economic intervention, even in rich states, is generally poor.

Personal computers happened because pluralism encouraged experiment, and discipline closed many experiments which failed. The AGR programme went badly wrong because there was no pluralism – the government attempted to 'hit the jackpot' – and no discipline: the programme was not terminated, or even seriously reviewed, although its costs and timetable were out of control.

Centralized structures cannot cope easily with the normal fact of economic life, that it is very difficult to determine what the right thing to do is and the best recourse is to try many things on a small scale and see which few work. Pluralism necessarily conflicts with uniformity. But if government structures genuinely allow pluralism and decentralized authority, variability in the quality of what is provided is inevitable. It is tempting to argue that everyone should receive 'the best', but the consequence is that 'the best' will not be very good. If everyone to whom power is delegated makes the same decision there is no pluralism and no real delegation.

Disciplined pluralism in public services requires that there be careful audit – of outcome, not of contribution to process. Disciplined pluralism requires that there be real accountability for these outcomes, of a kind which is only possible when agents have the autonomy which makes then genuinely responsible. The corollary of autonomy is research-assessment exercises, school league tables, hospital performance measures and rigorous accounting standards and corporate-governance rules. Performance can be compared because other people are trying to achieve the same goals. These are all things that did not happen when the British electricity industry spoke with Lord Plowden's 'single voice'.

'Discipline' is perhaps not quite the right word: it is the recognition of error, not its punishment, that matters. Centralized structures find this hard. The democratic will, or the heroic leader – politicians or chief executive – can rarely conceive of making a mistake, and still more rarely wish to be told of a mistake. Apparent failures must be failures of implementation, for which those engaged in implementation are responsible. The result is a culture of blame in which it is difficult – and personally costly – to admit mistakes, and therefore few mistakes are admitted to: hence there is no process of retreating from mistakes or abandoning mistakes. Khrushchev's maize, the Great Leap Forward, and the AGR programme all went forward within such a culture. The simplest means of not being blamed for a mistake is not to make a decision. This is a common recourse. Organizations in decay are often simultaneously authoritarian and indecisive.

It seems similarly paradoxical that large organizations, public or private, fail to provide discipline when their superficial problem is not too little accountability but too much. However, such accountability is often directed to the suppression of pluralism and the avoidance of blame. Accountability takes the form 'Why are you doing that?' 'Have you consulted x?' 'Is this consistent with policy?' The criteria of evaluation relate to legitimacy of process not quality of outcome. The objective should not be to introduce measures which bear superficial resemblance to the management systems of private sector businesses into the public sector, but to understand sufficiently well how market disciplines work to make it possible to introduce within the public sector systems which have analogous effects.

Government involvement in economic matters, therefore, should never be about 'foresight' – the single voice that was quite sure we hit the jackpot with the AGR programme. It is unlikely that anyone has such foresight. Since exploring new opportunities for goods and services is precisely what market mechanisms are particularly good at, the probability that government and its agencies will identify neglected avenues is extremely low. Much of the poor record of government economic intervention is of this kind.

The British government insisted in 1967–8 that the indigenous motor industry merge into a single entity (in defiance of pluralism), and then bailed British Leyland out when it went bust in 1974 (in defiance of discipline). It then appointed a businessman, Lord Ryder, to come up with the right answer (in defiance of pluralism), and subsidized his extravagant investment plans (in defiance of discipline). Matters started to get better only when the government made clear in 1980 that it would not provide further funding (reimposition of discipline). There followed the break-up of Leyland, the intervention of Honda, and the establishment in the following decade of new car plants on greenfield sites (return to pluralism).[6]

The privatization of Britain's electricity industry in 1990 ended further nuclear construction by forcing disclosure of its costs. After privatization, the industry built small-scale plant, using conventional technologies, mostly to time and to budget, and discovered that the existing power stations could be run with only half the people who had been employed before.[7] This wasn't because the private managers of the new electricity businesses were abler than the bureaucrats who ran the industry before. They were often the same people and, when they weren't, they were often worse. The new managers quarrelled among themselves and engaged in foolish diversification. Many companies fell into the hands of foreign parents with more money than understanding of what they were doing. But authority was distributed and mistakes had consequences for the individuals concerned. Disciplined pluralism had replaced centralized control.

However, the contrast between disciplined pluralism and undisciplined centralism is not a simple distinction between the private and the public sector. The personal computer revolution happened and probably could only have happened because IBM did not control the evolution of the computer market, but it was close to having such control and Microsoft is close to having such control today. There are many industries – brewing, retail banking and insurance are examples – in which group-think, the single voice that comes with the dominance of a single firm, or a group of like-minded firms, closes down pluralism.

There are failures of discipline, too. The late 1990s were characterized by a proliferation of hopeless business ventures, excessive physical investment and over-ambitious acquisitions. Telecommunications, the media and information technology were the focus but the effects spread into other industries, such as energy and financial services. The behaviour of the institutional investors, investment banks and corporate executives responsible for these excesses was, at best, unprofessional and incompetent. It is impossible to have lived through that period and believe that the securities markets allocate capital efficiently. However, there is more pluralism and more discipline in market economies. IBM was successfully encircled by its competitors. The stock market boom, and the pyramids of paper it created, ultimately collapsed. These mechanisms of correction were slow, but ultimately effective, and those involved bore some of the costs.

Privatization

Privatization may be a means of introducing pluralism or discipline, or both. The word was coined in Britain, and the first flotation of a government-owned utility was the sale of 51 per cent of British Telecom in 1984. The policy has spread around the world, most of all to poor states and former centrally planned economies.

Many poor states believed economic development would be achieved through state ownership and extensive regulation. Justification was found in Marxist doctrines, and in those early theories of economic development described in Chapter 23 which emphasized the scope for growth through planning. These interventions diminished or destroyed disciplined pluralism. The competitive advantages of businesses depended, not on success in market competition, but on political skills: rent seeking became dominant in economic behaviour. The outcome was often worse, because few of these countries had disinterested governments. Ownership and regulation of business became a mechanism for siphoning resources for the benefit of those who controlled the apparatus of the state.

In these environments, there is no point in theorizing about the role and structure of economic policy.[8] Where government economic policy is only accidentally benign even in intention, the less there is of it the better. The dismantling of regulation and state business activities in poor countries will not, of itself, lead to economic development or economic growth. It is nevertheless a prerequisite.[9]

Privatization in Eastern Europe was a necessary consequence of the breakdown of the centrally planned state. Yet while state economic activity in Zaire was worse than nothing, in Russia it was better than nothing. Soviet state enterprises did meet some of their citizens' needs for food, clothing, housing and transport. The 'privatized' businesses which emerged from them frequently did not; their purpose was not to provide goods and services but to create value for their shareholders, and that is what they did.

Governments in all productive economies, except the United States, took the 'commanding heights' of the economy into state owner-ship.[10] It was never clear what precisely constitutes the commanding heights but similar instincts seem to have prevailed in most countries. Utilities – gas, electricity, water, telecommunications – are almost always commanding heights. Some industries – such as airlines – are thought to have special importance, and governments everywhere are obsessed with steel,[11] perhaps because of its role in the original industrial revolution.

Pluralist market structures produce better outcomes than monopol-istic ones. There is not much evidence that privately owned firms are more efficient than public if competition is not possible, or not achieved.[12] Popular discussion frequently conflates the introduction of competition with change in ownership. Market entry, privatization and new technology arrived more or less simultaneously in telecom-munications. There have been spectacular gains in efficiency and growth of new services but it is impossible to disentangle these different components. In businesses like water supply, or the management of rail networks, where competition is not possible there is little evidence of gains from privatization.

Pluralism implies that goods and services which can be supplied in competitive markets should be. Where monopoly is inevitable – as in the distribution of electricity and water – the loss of pluralism should be minimized. The existence of a monopoly in one area of a business should not be used as a basis for extending monopoly. Electricity distribution is a natural monopoly but electricity generation is not. Whether or not the monopolies that remain after all possible competi-tive businesses have been established are publicly or privately owned is not very important, and, since they will necessarily be closely regulated, may not make a great deal of difference. The objective should be managerial autonomy combined with audit and accountability.

The Cost of Markets

Running a market economy is expensive. It needs accountants and police, bankers and checkout assistants, insurance agents and lawyers, all engaged in defining and enforcing the rules of the market economy or recording its processes. These activities could be dispensed with in a society in which goods and services are produced for own use. In non-market societies very few people are engaged in them. Sicelo does not need an accountant and there is no lawyer in Palanpur.

The distinction between those who make things and those who monitor those who make things, between bean growers and bean counters, is described as the distinction between transformational and transactional employment. One estimate is that almost half of US GDP is devoted to transactional rather than transformational activities, a figure that had risen from one quarter a century earlier.[13] The reform process in New Zealand increased the proportion of workers engaged in transactional activities from one in three to one in two.[14]

It is, in a sense, a tribute to the productivity of the market economy that it can bear costs of this magnitude and yet provide high standards of living. The cost of counting beans is repaid many times by the extra beans which result from careful counting. We often affect to despise bean counters like accountants and lawyers. It is easy to win applause by proposing that money spent on hospital managers should be used to hire extra doctors and nurses. But people engaged in transactional activities can greatly raise the productivity of transformational activities and, for the economy as a whole, this is what has happened. Many hospital administrators are, indeed, useless, but better management could and does produce better medicine. Under the Soviet national accounting system, which classified only transformational activities as productive, there was not much transformational activity to count.

Transactions expenditures are necessary, but since it is transformation that meets needs for goods and services, market economies become more efficient by reducing transactions. The costs of dispute are large, and avoidable. Rich people and corporations litigate and, to avoid litigation, they write detailed contracts. Rich people dispute property rights in court. Poor people dispute them in the streets. The costs of law enforcement, the wasted resources associated with crime and its consequences, are also costs of the market economy. These costs are large. Two per cent of adult male Americans of working age are in gaol and many others are employed to put them there and keep them there.[15]

Social pressures and social consensus are cheaper and often more effective ways of avoiding and settling disputes. In all societies, the expectations of parties to an agreement are fulfilled less from fear of legal action than through a common interest in going on doing business together. Or people fulfil agreements simply because it is the right thing to do. All civil societies rely on this: their citizens respect property rights and other rules of the market from recognition of their legitimacy, not from fear of prison. This is how Japan and Nordic countries run market economies with lower levels of transactions costs than the United States.

A market economy needs financial services and products such as mortgages, and shares in corporations are among the central institutional innovations of productive economies. The average daily value of foreign exchange trading, however, is $1,500 billion. This is three hundred times the volume of cross-border trading in goods and services: for every $1 that is traded because someone with euros wants to buy goods priced in dollars, $300 is traded because someone thinks the euro will rise against the dollar and someone else thinks it will fall; and, since the sum of all speculative gains and losses in foreign exchange is zero, the majority of trades are unsuccessful, after the transactions costs of the market are accounted and paid for. Most of these costs are an unnecessary burden on the market economy but, since the gambling instinct among individuals and corporations remains strong, it is not easy to see how they can be reduced.

Keynes advocated a small tax on all financial transactions to discourage speculation and this idea is today associated with James Tobin[N].[16] The major objection to such a tax is not one of principle, but the practical difficulty of making it work in an electronic world. Business would take place in jurisdictions – including cyberspace[17] – in which the tax could not be imposed.

The most important restraint on financial speculation has always been lack of respect for those who engage in it. From Aristotle through Shakespeare and Trollope to Tom Wolfe and Michael Lewis, disdain for the middleman has been a recurrent theme.[18] In the 1980s and 1990s these sanctions declined, and with the rise of the American business model has come a growth in the size of the financial services sector and in the quality of the talent which it attracts. Many of these resources could be more usefully, if less profitably, employed elsewhere.

30

A Primer in Economic Policy

Chapters 26 and 27 rejected two unhelpful grand narratives: the fundamentalist belief that there is a market solution to any question about the nature of society; and the socialist contention that democratic opinions are a sufficient basis for the complex resource allocation of a modern economy.

Keynes once wished that economists would be treated as plumbers, or dentists: technicians with specific skills, not co-venturers on an ideological crusade. This chapter is written in the spirit of economics as dentistry. I shall focus on a small number of policy issues and relate them to the analysis of specific chapters of this book. My purpose is to exemplify rather than to offer wide-ranging prescriptions. Indeed, a principal objective is to demonstrate that, with the failure of grand narrative, there are no wide-ranging prescriptions. There are some general principles – the recurrent difficulties of incentive compatibility, and the overriding necessity for disciplined pluralism – but the premise is that economic understanding, like plumbing and dentistry, is a piecemeal process of acquired knowledge, driven by little stories.

Perfect Competition or Disciplined Pluralism?
(Chapters 11–15)

Market economies did not succeed because business people were cleverer than politicians. They succeeded because disciplined pluralism is more innovative and more responsive to customer needs than centralized decision-making.

Most rich states have policies to maintain competition. But competition policies are often predicated on the assumption that the world should be aligned with the perfectly competitive market model of Part Two. If the world does not conform to the model the fault lies with the model, not the world. Part Three demonstrated why market economies are not perfectly competitive, and could not be efficient if they were. Disciplined pluralism implies that rivals pursue differentiated strategies and the more successful of them earn rents. Competition policy should not seek to eliminate these rents: if it tries, it will diminish pluralism. The purposes of competition policy are to promote pluralism and make discipline effective.

In the last two decades, economists have gained influence on competition policy in both America and in Europe. Competition policy must be framed in legal terms, but the law is an expression of economic ideas and economic concepts. The economic approach to competition policy has invited economic engineering – a belief that the courts can make cost-benefit analyses of alternative industry structures.

Computer firms, however, were unsuccessful in predicting the future of their industry. Neither Bill Gates nor Lord Plowden can make these forecasts; still less can a district judge or a case-handler at the European Commission. Competition policy should reflect the presumption that disciplined pluralism is the mainstay of a market economy. It is no more possible or desirable to review that principle on a case-by-case basis than to review the presumption against burglary on a case-by-case basis. A court which tries a burglar does not consider arguments for and against respecting private property, only whether the burglary took place. We have a speed limit, rather than an offence of driving at an inappropriate speed, because the latter rule cannot be enforced and gives honest citizens little guidance.

Pluralism requires that there be several businesses in each strategic group – the firms which see each other as rivals.[1] The perceptions of companies themselves define the competitive battleground. A merger between Tesco and Sainsbury would be a disaster for British retailing, because the rivalry between these two underpins the vitality of the British retailing sector. The reality of disciplined pluralism is only marginally affected by calculations of how far a customer might have to drive to reach a competitor's store.[2]

When James Black became disenchanted with ICI, he took his

research to SmithKline. His alternatives would be more limited today. A British scientist who needs the resources of a large company can work only for Glaxo SmithKline or AstraZeneca. Even in a global world, we need pluralism nationally. After British financial markets were liberalized in the 1980s American investment banks brought professionalism to the City of London, and raised standards generally, but today all the leading investment banks in London are American or American-owned, and pluralism has again been diminished.

Forces that work for pluralism today, therefore, can work against it tomorrow. It seems paradoxical that the very success of Standard Oil, or Microsoft, forces us to act against these companies to maintain both discipline and pluralism. But that is how it must be. The case for the market economy is not that the democratic decisions of the market are better than the democratic decisions of the electorate – 'Microsoft has a monopoly because we want it to have one.' The pluralist processes of competition within the market economy reveal information and promote innovation more effectively than any centralized organization, public or private. The battle to maintain pluralism never ends.

General Equilibrium and DIY Economics (Chapter 14)

Every government is confronted by rent-seeking lobbyists. Farmers ask for agricultural support, manufacturing industries seek protection from international competition, workers in declining industries seek subsidies for their products. Business asks for policies to support 'competitiveness'.

DIY economics flourishes here. At first sight, every economic activity promotes jobs, and either adds to exports or substitutes for imports: every subsidy increases competitiveness. And, as was explained in Chapter 14, the people who present these arguments know, from their own experience, the truth of what they say: they often genuinely believe that their self-interested arguments promote a wider good. But the lobbyists do not know, from their own experience, the general equilibrium context – the 'adding up' constraints for the economy as a whole – within which they operate. Their misleading, partial perspective often leads them to argue for policies which are not in their own interests, far less those of the public at large.

The taxi fare between Central London and Heathrow Airport is too high – a cab earns substantially more between the city and the airport than in the same time in city streets. A queue of taxis waits – sometimes for several hours – in a perimeter holding area to obtain one profitable journey. From the perspective of the individual taxi driver, the high fare is necessary to make his wait worthwhile, and this case is made forcibly to Transport for London, which fixes taxi rates. Taxi drivers are an organized lobby group for higher fares, but it is not worthwhile for passengers, few of whom spend a large proportion of their income on taxis, to campaign in opposition. Taxi drivers do not see that the high fare causes the waiting time, only that the waiting time requires the high fare: just as pharmaceutical companies do not see that the high cost of developing drugs is as much the result as the rationale of the large profits from successful development. Why should they? What they know is their own business, and they do not see the equilibrium of the market.

There are good reasons for regulating taxi fares from Heathrow. People who get into someone else's car are vulnerable, and have claims to protection. It is not only the individual cab driver's reputation which suffers if the first person a visitor to England encounters is dishonest. But the implications of regulatory policy are complex and cannot easily be generalized from the experience of an individual taxi driver, and this is true of this simplest of market interventions.

The case against price controls, tariffs, subsidies and tax breaks is not that the market always gets it right. The direct consequences of these policies are always to benefit the rent-seeking group, and the indirect consequences are impossible to determine. There should be a strong presumption against arguments which are based on generalized economic benefit – growth, employment, efficiency, 'competitiveness' – from measures that are specific to an industry. There is generally no way of demonstrating the claimed benefits, other than through DIY economics: and only by establishing a general principle is it possible to deflect the queue of lobbyists who today stretch round Capitol Hill.

The case for regulating taxi fares rests on valid arguments of limited application, just as there are arguments for subsidizing agriculture, or for protecting domestic media and culture, which relate to specific, largely non-economic, aspects of the nature of society. These issues can be debated, but arguments for such intervention cannot be rebutted by generalized claims about the merits of free markets.

Where such arguments have force, the policies which follow should be related directly to these specific issues. Instead, European agricultural policies are a nightmare. Valid specific arguments for the environmental benefits of agriculture have become confused with assertions of generalized economic benefits based on DIY economics, and then used as a basis for central direction of the farming industry which demonstrates all the incentive-compatibility problems – the proliferation of inconsistent targets and the endless strategic negotiation – described in Chapter 8.

Rationality and Adaptation (Chapter 17)

We behave adaptively in our economic lives. Adaptive behaviour will reproduce itself in the environment in which it is found. We co-operate much more than rational, self-interested individuals would because it is adaptive for us to do so (Chapter 20), but it is also adaptive for us to follow the rules of dysfunctional cultures whose outcomes do not benefit us or the organizations themselves. Adaptive behaviour is determined by social and business values we impose on each other – the phenomenon of contagious reputation (Chapter 18) is a good example – and the prevailing values of a market economy are key to its success. This is an important part of the explanation of why Norway and Switzerland are rich states and Kenya and Indonesia are not.

It is difficult to overstate the damage done by those who have claimed that self-regarding materialism is the dominant value of a successful market economy. They have set back the cause of economic development in the East and undermined the legitimacy and performance of the market economies of the West. There is no substantive difference between the pyramid schemes that crippled the Albanian economy in the mid-1990s and the stock market bubbles in America and Europe in 1999–2000. We shall only gradually learn how much the competitive advantages of businesses in rich states have been eroded in the pursuit of unsustainable reported growth in earnings: banks which have lost the loyalty of their employees; pharmaceutical companies whose pipelines are increasingly thin; media companies which have alienated their creative talent; insurance companies which no longer have the confidence of their customers.

The selection mechanisms of competitive markets deal, not necessarily quickly, with inappropriate but internally adaptive cultures in business organizations. Because adaptive behaviours are self-reinforcing, these cultures are difficult to alter, as chief executives seeking to impose change on their organizations complain: the extreme case is the government minister who, powerless to change personnel, has no influence on the organization of which he or she is nominally the head. For many effective businesses, this is a good thing: chief executives come and go, taking their foolish visions and missions and legions of strategy consultants with them.

Adaptive bureaucracies impose an appearance of rationality on decision-making. The AGR programme was carefully analysed: but the numbers these analyses contained were nonsense and, except in a formal sense, irrelevant to the decisions that were made. Dot.com valuations of 1999 and mobile phone bids of 2000 were justified by elaborate spreadsheets. These exercises gave the appearance of rationality to adaptive processes, but often made decisions worse by concealing the reality of decision-making and blurring responsibility for it.

Because behaviour is adaptive, not rational, we support social institutions that interfere with our freedom of choice. Odysseus had himself tied to the mast to resist siren voices. That is why there are subsidies to pensions and compulsory contributions; taxes on things we know we ought not to indulge in, like alcohol, tobacco and gambling; and subsidies to things we think we should engage in, like libraries, concerts and adult education. Social norms and legislation define the nature of adaptive behaviour in economic life; and we favour norms and legislation which change economic behaviour, including our own. Odysseus would not have been impressed by the argument that the behaviour he fears, being irrational, will not happen, and nor are we.

Information (Chapter 18)

As I write this, I am sitting in an aeroplane, drinking coffee from a styrene cup. 'Contents hot' is printed on the side. I do not find this information helpful, and am not expected to. Its purpose is to help protect the airline against absurd legal claims.[3] A pot of jam accompanies my breakfast. It is not jam, but 'extra jam', which means that its fruit content is above 45 per cent. I know that, but the passengers on either side of me do not: the revelation causes them amusement but no interest. The jam also contains E330 and E334. This means that these ingredients have been tested and found safe by a European Union scientific committee, but, in a bizarre misinterpretation, many people have come to interpret it as an indication that the jam contains harmful chemicals.

Asymmetric information is endemic in modern market economies. It is easy to conclude that the remedy for asymmetric information is to tell consumers more, either by regulation ('extra jam' and E330) or by recognizing disclosure of risks (the dangers of hot coffee) as a legal defence. Yet, as these examples illustrate, such measures are almost useless. The normal market mechanism for dealing with asymmetric information is reputation. When we place a deposit with a bank, or visit a doctor, we rely on the reputation of the bank and the doctor to assure the security of our deposit and the wisdom of the advice. No regulation can ensure that banks will not go broke or that doctors will make correct diagnoses, and regulation directed to information disclosure – rules that compel banks to display their balance sheets, or require doctors to explain fully risks and prognoses – does not work well either. The bank's balance sheet is out of date, incomprehensible and in any case conveys little relevant information. We don't want to hear long extracts from medical textbooks when we visit our doctor: we want to trust his or her professional competence.

Self-regulation has one advantage over statutory regulation. Self-regulating entities – companies, groups of professionals – have the information to do it, and a government agency does not. It has one disadvantage, too. Self-regulating entities do not have much incentive to take regulation seriously, and government does. Yet again, the problems of information and incentives interact. Regulation can get the best of both worlds by giving insiders the incentive to undertake policing which only they have the information to perform. Self-regulation is stimulated by external supervision; autonomy, audit and accountability once more, in an adaptive environment.

In Britain, the Financial Services Authority has achieved this in some areas of retail financial services. Commission-hungry salesmen pushed products towards bemused and trusting customers regardless of, and typically in ignorance of, their needs. The key to changing this situation was not product regulation, nor insistence on information disclosure, nor rules about training and competence. The 'naming and shaming' of individual firms led to concern for reputation and forced them to take their own compliance procedures seriously.[4]

Contrast this with failures of self-regulation in law and in medicine. The weakness of the General Medical Council, and the comprehensive failure of the Law Society and Solicitors' Complaints Commission,[5] to monitor the competence of members they regulate, follow from the absence of external supervision. These supervisory bodies believe that the best means of maintaining the reputation of their professions is to engage in mutual self-congratulation rather than to expose incompetent practitioners, and in the environment in which they operate they may well be right to believe that. Reputation is a powerful mechanism, but only external supervision can ensure that reputations are only earned when deserved.[6]

Risk in Reality (Chapter 19)

Market economies manage uncertainty expensively but badly. Private markets fail to provide effective protection against the principal risks of life – accidents, redundancy and unemployment, and relationship breakdown. Moral hazard and adverse selection are widespread; we are bad at assessing risks and calculating probabilities. The major risks of life cannot be handled by markets.[7] The policy choices we have are between letting risks lie where they fall or trying to manage them through social institutions.

If risks lie where they fall, costs to unlucky victims may be very high.

Some US households are crippled by large medical bills; many more are paralysed by fear of them; yet others manage with no or inadequate treatment in a country where the highest standards of medical care in the world are available to some. When life seems a lottery, losers become detached from society. With greater inequalities of income and wealth in the USA go high levels of street crime, a prison population many times the European average, and the growth of gated communities.[8]

Nor is it always clear where risks do fall. If there is no social provision for misfortune, the only recourse for victims is to blame their misfortune on someone else. The possibility of such recourse may bear little relationship to the reasonableness of the claim, and none to the severity of the misfortune. Legal processes are costly to all parties and often ineffectual in compensating real distress. It is profoundly shocking that almost none of the billions of dollars spent pursuing and settling asbestos claims relieves the suffering of mesothelioma victims.[9] At the same time the risk of being sued has become an additional hazard of modern life. Hence playgrounds are so risk-free, or at least so liability-free, that any normal child would be too bored to use one.[10]

When private markets and the tort system fail, and they mostly do fail, the major risks of daily life are better managed by social insurance. Social insurance differs from private insurance in that there is no actual matching of payments to expected costs. These systems developed in Europe to manage medical risks, loss of income through sickness and unemployment, and the consequences of family breakdown.

Social insurance expresses social solidarity. Membership cannot be optional, because that leads to free riding, moral hazard and adverse selection. The sustainability of social insurance depends on general acceptance of its legitimacy, but the essentially communitarian concept is undermined by attempts to shoehorn it into a framework of individualistic politics. The political left has adopted a rhetoric of rights, in a mistaken belief that this would give claims to social solidarity greater weight in a world increasingly influenced by self-regarding materialism. But the fanciful nature of Rawls's 'veil of ignorance' demonstrates the difficulty of giving a persuasive account of the origin of welfare rights. The assertion of rights requires a collateral, and missing, willingness to accept obligations. The communitarian perspective eschews the language of rights, restores the concept of desert, and emphasizes exclusion rather than low income as such as the primary target of policy.[11]

Solidaristic institutions need not, and should not, only be agencies of the state. Large companies are the most efficient providers of unemployment and work-accident insurance for their employees. Companies and fellow workers can distinguish the malingering from the unfortunate, with a flexibility that no rule-bound bureaucracy can achieve. Yet the expectation that an ordinarily competent employee of a major private company or a public authority could expect job security – at a price, and in all but exceptional circumstances – has been shattered as companies have asserted they cannot afford to provide jobs for life any more. In the market revolution this assertion was quickly followed by the discovery that the state could not afford to bear such costs either.

The risks of economic fluctuations, of illness, accident, unemployment, and broken homes and marriages, are inescapable. Society has no choice but to afford them. But its institutions can increase or reduce the costs: partially collectivizing them reduces the cost by spreading them, but invites moral hazard. Sharing risks within communities achieves the best balance between these conflicting forces.

Co-ordination (Chapter 21)

Standards and networks in a market economy require co-ordination. Government can impose co-ordination, or it can be established by private agreement between firms, or it can emerge from the spontaneous operation of market forces. These mechanisms are not incompatible, or mutually exclusive. Standards are often the product of a combination of these forces. Governments have imposed broadcasting standards and required interconnection to telecoms networks; agreements between hardware producers established standards for compact and video discs; banks and airlines created networks to provide compatible payment systems and interlining facilities; VHS, Windows and Visa became dominant in market-based competition.

In the United States, there are competing networks of bank cash machines (ATMs) and usually a charge for using the machines of another bank. In France, an agreement brokered by the Banque de France ensures that all cards can be used in all machines. The American structure puts pressure on providers to be cost efficient and makes it competitively attractive to install machines – the largest provider is now the software company EDS. However, customers like universal acceptance and free use. The evolution of Britain's system was, in 2000, poised between these two outcomes, but pressure from public opinion, expressed forcibly in newspapers,[12] tipped the balance to the French system.

But collective solutions often seek to reconcile too many conflicting interests and to gold-plate their standards. British Satellite Broadcasting and ITV Digital, two consortia of broadcasters, failed in competition with Rupert Murdoch's Sky. Protracted negotiations between banks and retailers to establish a common system for electronic funds transfer led nowhere.[13] Debit cards became widespread only when attempts to find a co-ordinated solution were abandoned and replaced by individual negotiation.[14] Taurus, the London Stock Exchange's planned electronic settlement system, was finally abandoned after the costs of protecting every participant had spiralled out of control. A successor system, Crest, came into operation only because the Bank of England imposed it. Proprietary standards are rarely successful, because an open standard can achieve a larger installed base. This is how VHS defeated Betamax and Windows defeated Apple.

There is no single best way to bring co-ordination about, nor any general reason to suppose that any of these processes will reach the best outcome. VHS and Windows are probably not the best standards for the job they do, but they are good enough. Who knows how the world airline industry should be organized? In a pluralist market economy, the best possible structure may not be reached but a manifestly inadequate structure will usually fail. The differing solutions on ATMs illustrate how the solutions to problems of technology and economics are often the product of the political and social environment in which they function.

Rules and Property Rights (Chapter 5)

The term 'property rights' invites us to believe that it is easy to define what they are and to require observance of them, but the rules of a market economy are extensive, and largely implicit. The rules are determined and enforced more by social convention than legal process. Government is only one agent in the simultaneous evolution of technology, market institutions and the social and political context.

Once, consumers relied mainly on the retailer's reputation when they bought goods and services. The growth of product branding and national advertising meant that they could rely on the quality of packaged goods made in large manufacturing plants. The rise of chain stores restored power to the retailer, but consumers now relied on the retailer's brand and the scientific skills of its head office rather than their personal knowledge of individual shopkeepers. These developments were driven by changing technology and the increasing complexity of products. These factors in turn determined the success and failure in the marketplace of different businesses. The support of evolving law protected trademarks and prohibited misleading advertising. Other innovations in the rules of a market economy, such as the development of limited liability, require more deliberate legal and regulatory structures.

New policies are required to establish a legal framework for new activities – such as the Internet and the genome – and to modify old rules to meet modern technologies. Good rules cannot be made by general principle: solutions are usually specific to technology and a market. The legal framework of both genome and Internet has mistakenly been allowed to depend on judicial interpretation of legislation directed to quite different purposes. Government must often be the pro-active rulemaker, not a referee.

The American business model emphasizes freedom of contract, and responsiveness in contract design has been a strength of the market economy. The flexibility of the common law systems of the English-speaking world has been a source of competitive advantage for financial services and for the legal business itself. But genuine freedom of contract is prohibitively expensive. We don't negotiate contract terms when we buy most goods and services, because we would never get out of the shop, or on the train.

Market fundamentalists might ask why we need a company law. After all, shareholders and managers are free to make any agreements with each other they like. This is not a realistic proposal, because negotiation is costly and litigation over the interpretation of idiosyncratic contracts is overwhelmingly costly.[15] That is why there are so many standard forms and procedures even in common law countries. The many types of business organization that used to exist have more or less been reduced to one limited company as partnerships and mutual organizations have disappeared. One is probably too few (it usually is).

Pay, Taxes and Benefits (Chapter 24)

What people earn is the most important factor in their economic lives. Even the smallest business needs a pay policy. Government is the largest employer in all productive economies, and the dominant employer in many sectors, from education to waste collection. So government pay policy for its own employees has an economy-wide impact. The sharing of income within households and families is the most important mechanism of redistribution. Charity and philanthropy also play a role, but are now minor relative to formal tax and benefit systems. Social policies reallocate income not only among households, but within families and across lifetimes.

If either productivity theories or bargaining theories were true to the exclusion of the other, policy for income distribution would be relatively easy. Productivity theory allows little scope to influence the distribution of income. Productivity is fixed by technology and the market: any interference with the implied distribution involves losses greater than the amounts redistributed. Bargaining theory implies that earnings are politically determined, both within organizations and in the nation as a whole. There is more or less unlimited scope to implement a democratic conception of fairness in rewards. Both theories, however, have elements of truth without being the complete truth. Anyone who has ever had to determine pay in the real world recognizes the conflicting pressures of politics and the market, of fairness and efficiency. The very fact that pay needs to be determined demonstrates that the market does not tell the whole story: if it did, we should not need to have a remuneration committee or tell a human resources director to fix a pay scale. But justice in the distribution of income must be tempered by hard realism, as the Good Woman of Setzuan learned.

Almost all rich states have set a minimum wage. A legal minimum forces a change in the distribution of rents within organizations. It raises the costs of activities, such as cleaning, supermarket checkouts, services, and fast food, which use casual unskilled labour. This will increase their price and reduce demand for them. The balance between more pay and fewer jobs is an empirical question, and there is no way in which the consequences can be estimated without detailed quantitative research. But social norms about decent wages are a flexible and responsive mechanism that no statutory regime can ever replicate.[16]

The Future of Poor States

The disparities of income and wealth in the world today are an affront to any reflective person. Money and economic growth do not necessarily buy happiness, but money and economic growth could certainly buy more happiness for Sicelo and his family.

However, we who live in rich states are not rich because those who live in poor states are poor. It is simply not true that the market economy and the world trading system are structured in ways in which the rich gain at the expense of the poor. If the nineteen rich states of Chapter 3 traded only with each other, and had no economic dealings with the rest of the world, their standard of living would not fall by much. Most of their trade is already among themselves.[17] The most important consequence would be a rise in energy costs. Rich states are rich because of the high productivity which results from their effective exploitation of the division of labour and their own modern technology, skills and capabilities.

In such a divided world, the standard of living of poor countries would also fall, perhaps by relatively more. The small number of poor countries which are resource-rich – like the Congo and Saudi Arabia – would lose. But, as described in Chapter 23, these resources so distort the structure of their economies that the long-run benefit is uncertain. More serious would be the loss of equipment – from oil production facilities to telecommunications switching equipment – which could not be manufactured at all without access to Western technology.

Nor are poor countries poor because of a 'funding gap' which it is within the capacity of rich states to bridge. The effectiveness of aid given in the past, not particularly generously, was low. It is easy to make an emotional case for debt relief, but the issues are complicated. Campaigners invite us to imagine that the inhabitants of poor countries spend much of their day working to pay off the debts which we imposed on them. The reality is that most of the money lent to highly indebted governments has gone and can never be recovered. The practical consequence of indebtedness is that it limits the capacity to borrow more. Since much of what was previously borrowed was stolen or wasted, this may be a good rather than a bad outcome.[18]

The difference between rich and poor states is the result of differences in the quality of their economic institutions. After four disappointing decades, development agencies have recognized this and used their authority to demand reforms. But the prescriptions have often been facile. What was offered to Russia was not American institutions, but the nostrums of the American business model. The institutions of the market – secure property rights, minimal government economic intervention, light regulation – were supposed to be simple and universal. If these prescriptions were implemented, growth would follow.

The truth about markets, however, is far more complex. Rich states are the product of – literally – centuries of coevolution of civil society, politics and economic institutions, a coevolution which we only partially understand, and cannot transplant. In the only successful examples of transplantation – the Western offshoots – entire populations, and their institutions, were settled in almost empty countries. The appeal of the American business model today, as of Marxism yesterday, is the suggestion that the history of economic institutions, the structure of current society and the path of future development have a simple economic explanation and an inevitable outcome. This is as misleading a view of political economy as the Marxist one.

There is no grand narrative, only little stories. But the need for grand narrative is so firmly ingrained in human thinking that the fruitless search for it will never end. This book is dedicated to those for whom a partial understanding of complex reality is better than the reassurance of false universal explanations.

Epilogue

Across the bay, Mobutu's villas are shuttered. Disputes between his family and creditors are still before the French courts. On Bloomberg television, the figures are all in red: the decline of world stock markets borders on panic. The talking heads in the top left screen are a lawyer, an accountant and a Congresswoman. They follow a rambling discourse by President Bush on the need for high standards in public life. The trio are discussing the need for tighter regulation in front of a sign that says 'Corporate Greed'.

Jean-Marie Messier – the water company chief turned media mogul, who proclaimed the end of the French exception from his glitzy Manhattan apartment – has just been ousted. Staid technocrats are beginning the process of unwinding his company's debts, and selling Universal Studios. Joe Stiglitz has published an attack on the Washington consensus.[1] Two criticisms cause particular resentment: the suggestion that IMF managers are self-regarding, and the assertion that their economics is third-rate.

Today even Bloomberg television disapproves of greed: this does leave one wondering what other motive people have for watching it. And the suggestion that self-interest influences the behaviour of international officials is a vile slander.[2] It is such a short time since William Easterly wrote that 'what people don't get paid for, they don't do'.

We misheard, it seems, when we thought we had been told the pursuit of self-interest was the mainspring of the market economy and only the very wealthy leave their footsteps in the sands of time. Was it really a surprise that such an era ended in wild speculation, corruption and fraud? The apologist's script is already being rewritten to claim that the exposure of fraud demonstrates, not the weakness of the market economy, but its strength.[3] Every success of capitalism was, for Marxists, further evidence of its inherent contradictions. Every failure of capitalism is, for supporters of the American business model, further evidence of its inevitable triumph.

The certainties and simplicities of the 1990s are falling away. The market economy is a remarkable institution, but in the decade after the fall of the Berlin Wall the most vigorous advocates of the market economy proved to be its worst enemies. They understood neither the genius of markets, nor their limits. The version of them they presented, inaccurate and repulsive, was intellectually flawed and failed when applied in practice. In this, too, it resembled Marxism. The peculiar ill-fortune of Russia was to be the subject of both experiments. On both sides of the demolished wall there will now be a time of sober reappraisal. But the losers from the follies of markets will not just be failed oligarchs, fraudulent chief executives and financiers. They will include many ordinary people who suffered in 1990s Russia as their grandparents had suffered years earlier; workers in America who lost jobs as businesses were expensively acquired, or slimmed down in the pursuit of shareholder value; savers who believed those confident reassurances that the New Economy would provide for their pensions. Markets will continue to display their genius, test their limits and display their follies.

Menton
July 2002

Appendix: Nobel Prizes in Economics

The Nobel Prize in Economics was established in 1968 by the Bank of Sweden. Like the other Nobel Prizes (for Physics, Chemistry, Medicine, Literature and Peace), it is awarded by the Swedish Academy of Sciences on the recommendation of a specialist sub-committee after wide consultation.

The Nobel Prize in Economics has always been controversial. Many people (including many economists) feel that economics is not, or not often, characterized by definitive and seminal advances in knowledge of the kind recognized by the science prizes. Even if that is true, the Nobel Prize list is a good indication of what a well-informed group judge to be the most important developments in modern economics and the most important contributors to these developments.

I suspect that the entire group would have made only a handful of appearances on Bloomberg television in total. There are few prizes in macroeconomics – Milton Friedman (1976), James Tobin (1981), Robert Lucas (1995) and arguably Franco Modigliani (1985) and Robert Mundell (1999). Macroeconomics – the study of inflation, interest rates and aggregate employment – is a much less important part of academic work in economics than most people might suppose. But there have also just been fewer good new ideas in macroeconomic theory in the last fifty years than in other branches of economics.

About two-thirds of Nobel Prizes in Economics have gone to the United States, this despite an attempt by the organizers to lean over backwards to favour non-Americans – it is hard to argue that the average achievement of the non-Americans is as high. However the proportion of awards in economics going to the United States is no higher than in the sciences.

Several awards (Heckman (2000), McFadden (2000), Haavelmo (1989), Klein (1980) and arguably Frisch (1969) and Tinbergen (1969)) have been made in econometrics. Econometrics is not, as many people believe, the application of mathematics to economics. Most economic theory is now developed mathematically – indeed, there is an inappropriate premium for expressing ideas in this way, and the mathematics used is often trivial. Econometrics is the application of statistical techniques to economic data-sets. The development of these methods has partly compensated for the inability of economists to engage in controlled experiments, and the sophistication of statistical techniques in econometrics now runs far ahead of its development in other subjects – such as medical statistics – where similar problems arise. The state and contribution of econometrics requires another book, however, and I am not the person to write it.

The majority of prizes have been given for microeconomic theory – the issue is the functioning of individual markets for goods and services, the concerns of this book. There is wide agreement that the future development of macroeconomics will be from a microeconomic base, although that has now been said for many years without major practical consequence.

Around the Second World War, the work of Hicks and Samuelson, described in Chapter 14, established formal economic analysis based on rational choice, and this has been the dominant methodology – for Becker the only methodology – of modern economics. It proved an initially rich vein which today seems to be approaching exhaustion. At the start of the twenty-first century, it perhaps begins to be possible to see where future discoveries might lie – where the next generations of Nobel Prizes might be earned.

Behavioural economics implies more concern for observation, less for *a priori* assumption, and the same will be true as transactions-cost economics frees itself from the rational choice framework. But more observation does not lead to less mathematics: on the contrary, it opens the way for the more difficult analysis of complex dynamic systems to take the place of the routine application of maximization and duality which have been the professional economist's stock-in-trade for half a century. This pincer movement of softer observation and harder mathematics is already taking hold in financial economics, and the events of the bubble and its aftermath will give strength to that. From financial economics, these methods are likely to spread to the mainstream of economics itself.

E. O. Wilson's aspiration to consilience – the absorption of the social sciences into the mainstream of scientific knowledge through their integration with biology – may be a bridge too far, but it is almost certain that this is a direction of research in the coming century. As we understand better the evolutionary and neurophysiological bases of psychology, it is inevitable that the insights obtained will change the way we think about the behaviour of individuals and organizations. It is possible that in a few decades we may have the knowledge to undertake the control of behaviour and events which today's politicians and business leaders assert but do not enjoy. This is an exciting, but also frightening, future for those who study economics and business and continue to seek the truth about markets.

Economic Science: Laureates and Prizes

Name:	Country:	Year:	Subject:
George A. Akerlof	USA	2001	Asymmetric information
Maurice Allais	France	1988	The theory of markets and efficient utilization of resources
Kenneth J. Arrow	USA	1972	General equilibrium theory
Gary S. Becker	USA	1992	'For having extended the domain of microeconomic analysis to a wide range of human behaviour and interaction, including non-market behaviour.'
James M. Buchanan Jr.	USA	1986	Public choice
Ronald H. Coase	UK	1991	Theory of the firm, property rights and transactions costs
Gerard Debreu	USA	1983	General equilibrium
Robert W. Fogel	USA	1993	Quantitative economic history
Milton Friedman	USA	1976	Macroeconomics
Ragnar Frisch	Norway	1969	Economic dynamics
Trygve Haavelmo	Norway	1989	Econometrics
John C. Harsanyi	USA	1994	Game theory
Friedrich von Hayek	UK	1974	Economic systems
James J. Heckman	USA	2000	Econometrics
John R. Hicks	UK	1972	General equilibrium theory
Leonid Vitaliyevich Kantorovich	USSR	1975	Optimization modelling
Lawrence R. Klein	USA	1980	Econometrics
Tjalling C. Koopmans	USA	1975	Optimization modelling
Simon Kuznets	USA	1971	Empirical studies of economic growth
Wassily Leontief	USA	1973	Input-output analysis
Arthur Lewis	UK	1979	Development economics
Robert E. Lucas Jr.	USA	1995	Real business-cycle theory

Daniel L. McFadden	USA	2000	Econometrics
Harry H. Markowitz	USA	1990	Finance theory
James E. Meade	UK	1977	Trade theory
Robert C. Merton	USA	1997	Finance theory
Merton H. Miller	USA	1990	Finance theory
James A. Mirrlees	UK	1996	Asymmetric information
Franco Modigliani	USA	1985	Macroeconomics and finance theory
Robert A. Mundell	Canada	1999	Exchange rates and currency areas
Gunnar Myrdal	Sweden	1974	Economic systems
John F. Nash Jr.	USA	1994	Game theory
Douglass C. North	USA	1993	Application of economic theory to economic history
Bertil Ohlin	Sweden	1977	Trade theory
Paul A. Samuelson	USA	1970	'For the scientific work through which he has developed static and dynamic economic theory and actively contributed to raising the level of analysis in economic science.'
Myron S. Scholes	USA	1997	Finance theory
Theodore W. Schultz	USA	1979	Development economics
Reinhard Selten	Germany	1994	Game theory
Amartya Sen	India	1998	Welfare economics
William F. Sharpe	USA	1990	Finance theory
Herbert A. Simon	USA	1978	Decision-making
Robert M. Solow	USA	1987	Theory of economic growth
A. Michael Spence	USA	2001	Asymmetric information
George J. Stigler	USA	1982	Industrial structures, functioning of markets and causes and effects of public regulation
Joseph E. Stiglitz	USA	2001	Asymmetric information
Richard Stone	UK	1984	National income accounting
Jan Tinbergen	Netherlands	1969	Economic dynamics
James Tobin	USA	1981	Finance theory and macroeconomics
William Vickrey	USA	1996	Asymmetric information

Notes

Chapter 1. Welcome to the World of Bloomberg Television

1. The monthly reports of the National Association of Purchasing Managers are widely followed as a 'leading indicator' of inflation.

2. In Britain, tighter control of state spending had begun with the economic crisis of 1976: the oil shock of 1974 was a trigger for changes in economic policies around the world.

3. Fukuyama (1989, 1992).

4. Wriston (1992), N. Klein (1999).

5. Yergin and Stanislaw (1998), p. 13.

6. T. Friedman (1999), p. 298.

7. The term 'new economy' appears to date from an article in *Business Week* in December 1996 by its economics editor, Michael Mardel, entitled 'The Triumph of the New Economy'. From then, *Business Week* was to be one of its principal cheerleaders; see 'The New Economy, What It Really Means', November 1997.

8. See chapter 1 of Princeton economist Bob Shiller's book *Irrational Exuberance* (2000) for a history of this phrase – and of the related stock market valuations.

9. Woodward (2000), pp. 180–81.

10. See, for example, Kevin Kelly (1998), or *Wired*, the magazine of the 'new economy'.

11. Portraits of Meeker and Blodget, and of Abby Joseph Cohen, the leading 'talking head' of the 1990s boom, can be found in Cassidy (2002). After the collapse in 2000, disgruntled investors sought to reclaim losses from the investment banks involved. Blodget left Merrill Lynch with a substantial payout in 2001. The following year, Merrill paid $100 million in a settlement with New York Attorney General Elliot Spitzer.

12. The NASDAQ composite index was at 1200 in March 1997. It reached

its all-time high of 5048 three years later. In 2002 it had fallen back to its 1997 level.

13. Thurow (1999), p. 15. This quote, and many similar, is found in T. Frank (2001), the most brilliant dissection so far of the fads and fashions of the American 1990s.

14. Three extraordinary essays by Greenspan can be found in Rand (1967). This was not Greenspan's only lapse of judgement before his elevation to the chairmanship of the Federal Reserve Board: in 1985 he wrote an influential letter commending Charles Keating, who as CEO of the Lincoln Savings and Loan institution was later charged with major fraud. Keating's conviction on these charges was ultimately quashed on the grounds that the jury might have had knowledge of his previous conviction for fraud.

15. 'The Great CEO Pay Heist: Tables' in Executive Compensation Advisory Services, *Fortune*, 25 June 2001, provides details on the total pay of many US CEOs.

16. The USA, Britain, France, Germany, Japan, Canada and Italy. In 1998 this became the G8 with the inclusion of Russia.

17. *Financial Times*, 22 June 1997.

18. The German Neue Markt index far outpaced Wall Street: the Nemax Kurz index, below 500 in March 1997, rose to over 8500 in March 2000. In 2002 it was below 1000. The British Techmark 100 index reached 5700 in 2000 and fell back to 1000 by 2002.

19. Freedland's book (1998), and an economic counterpart, Leadbeater's (2000), influenced the admiration on the part of New Labour politicians for things American which reached a peak during the bubble; see, for example, Andrew Marr, *Observer*, 14 November 1999, and Leanda de Lisle, *Guardian*, 3 November 1999. *Bring Home the Revolution* was also reported to be the favourite book of Mohammed Al Fayed, proprietor of Harrods: 'when the book (which Tony Blair cannily had on display at Chequers the day Johnnie went to interview him) came out, Mr Fayed rang up and asked to have 100 copies biked round'; Matthew Norman, *Guardian*, 29 November 1999.

20. The phrase was first used in 1989 by John Williamson of the (Washington-based) Institute for International Economics. See J. WILLIAMSON[W] (2000*a*) for a history.

21. The IMF is principally concerned with stabilizing the international monetary system. Its role emerges during major financial crises (such as the Asian crisis of 1997), where it makes loans to governments conditional on approving the associated economic policies. The World Bank provides finance for specific development projects – roads, dams, etc.

22. The World Economic Forum was founded in 1970 when an entrepre-neurial Swiss academic, Klaus Schwab, invited a group of European chief executives to a meeting in Davos in January 1971. Today, funded by major corporations, it attracts a wide range of leading politicians and business people to its inaccessible location and has become a major networking opportunity for these groups.

23. There are several websites dedicated to JOKES[W] about economists.

24. J. A. Kay (1996), chapter 2.

25. As in *Bloomberg on Bloomberg*, by Michael Bloomberg (with invaluable help from Matthew Walker) (2001).

26. Bloomberg spent $69 million, equivalent to $92 per vote obtained.

Chapter 2. People

1. A fine discussion of many of these issues is Olson (1996): this section draws significantly on his arguments.

2. This led to the 1997 Asian crisis; see Chapters 4 and 23 below.

3. Hoffman (2000) estimates capital per head in 1994 at $54,000 for the USA and $13,000 for Mexico.

4. Between 1950 and 1960 the West German economy grew at over 8 per cent per year and unemployment fell from 11 per cent to 1 per cent.

Chapter 3. Figures

1. Small countries with population below 2 million are excluded.

2. The other EU countries are Luxemburg, which is too small, and Greece, Portugal and Spain, which are too poor. Ten further countries joined the EU in 2004. None of these would have qualified as rich countries for the purpose of Table 3.1.

3. Quah (1996).

4. Measured height and weight follow the normal distribution – a specific statistical distribution – which is often fitted to the distribution of examination marks. Television watching is log normal. The observation of these standard statistical properties in data generated by processes with random elements forms the basis of econometrics.

5. World Development Indicators, World Bank (2001), table 2.8.

6. Schultz (1998), Milanov (1999), Melchior, Telle and Wüg (2000) begin the process of assessing the inequality of household incomes across the world.

For a survey of these issues and those of Box 3.1, see Gottschalk and Smeeding (1997).

7. The way in which the product of a team is divided between its members is a central issue, to which I return in Chapter 24. For the moment, however, it is enough to say that some division of the team's output happens.

8. Lanjouw and Stern (1998).

9. Even with productivity at twenty times Indian levels, Swedish wheat is not really economic: without the support of the European Union's Common Agricultural Policy, it is unlikely that wheat would be grown in Kivik at all (see Chapter 25).

10. The Komi Republic is about 1,000 miles north-east of Moscow and there is good skiing around its capital, Syktyvkar. In 1994–5 oil leaks from the Kharyaga–Usinsk pipeline produced a spill three times the size of the *Exxon Valdez*.

11. Nathan Rothschild died on 28 July 1836, probably from either staphylococcus or streptococcus septicaemia, which came either from an abscess on his back or from the surgeons' knives used to treat it. This story is told in David Landes (1998), pp. xvii–xviii.

12. Heston and Summers (1991), World Bank (1993). For Penn World Tables, see PENN[W].

13. Landes (1998) has an extended discussion of this. See also Sachs (2000). Sachs, a forceful proselytizer for the American business model, needs to reconcile the universality of his prescription with manifestly large differences in productivity and living standards. Hence the emphasis on climate. In Sachs's model poor countries are poor because they are too hot for capitalism.

14. Fukuyama (1992), pp. 49–50.

15. Kornai (1992), p. 179; World Bank (2001), table 3.13.

16. Inglehart *et al.* (1998), table V128.

17. Ibid.

18. See Lane (1991), Oswald (1997) and the World Database of HAPPINESS[W].

19. United Nations Development Programme (2002).

20. Steckel (1995), p. 1914.

21. Transparency International (2001), Corruption Perception Index, p. 234.

22. World Bank (2001), table 2.8.

23. IMF World Economic Outlook 2000: INFLATION[W].

24. UNDP Human Development Index 1998; some poor states, however, such as Malawi and the Indian state of Kerala, have very high literacy rates.

25. Inglehart *et al.* (1998), table V264.

26. IMD (2002), Freedom House (2002).

27. Maddison (1993), table A-2 of 2000 edn.
28. Freedom House (2002), p. 11.
29. Inglehart and Baker (2000), pp. 19–55.
30. Inglehart *et al.* (1998), tables V70, V77.

Chapter 4. How Rich States Became Rich

1. On the subject matter of this chapter see Diamond (1997), Landes (1998) and Baumol (2002) for contrasting but integrative perspectives from science, history and economics.
2. Stringer and Gamble (1993), Diamond (1997), pp. 40–41, Tattersall (1995).
3. Tudge (1998).
4. Flannery (1973), B. D. Smith (1995), Grigg (1992).
5. See, for example, Aristotle (1984 edn.), *Politics* 1258^a39–1258^b7.
6. As described in for example, Dickens (1977).
7. 'Among the loveliest inventions of the human mind,' said Goethe (*Wilhelm Meister's Apprenticeship and Travels*, 1796, trans. T. Carlyle, 1824).
8. Weber (1930), Tawney (1926), Merton (1936), Samuelsson (1961).
9. This discussion rests heavily on Maddison (2001).
10. Brad de Long, HISTORICAL GDP[W].
11. Maddison (2001).
12. I shall follow a convention of ignoring short sea crossings.
13. The EU candidate-states (apart from the two small islands of Malta and Cyprus) are at best poor intermediate; several are simply poor. The gap is much larger than at the accession of Greece and Portugal.
14. GDP per head in Canada and Australia is more than four times that of the West Indies or South Africa; Kenya is far poorer than any of these.
15. De Soto (2000) provides an intriguing discussion of these issues, and the discussion here reflects his approach.
16. North (1990) stresses the significance of the North West Ordinance of 1787 in establishing a secure structure of property rights in the USA. There is some force in this. English property law still rests on the fiction that land rights derive from the Crown, a fiction difficult to maintain in the post-revolutionary United States, and the North West Ordinance was adopted to provide a basis for modern property law. But the attempt to substitute the Federal Government for the Crown as the source of land rights largely failed in the face of a different local reality. See de Soto (2000).

17. Gold was discovered in California in 1848, when San Francisco had a population of 800. In 1849 alone, 80,000 people migrated to California (the '49ers). The lag in communication with Washington and the scale of the influx relative to the existing infrastructure made government control of developments impossible. See Rohrbough (1997).

18. O. Marshall (2000).

19. Shumway (1991), Bethell (1993).

20. There may have been worse prime ministers in rich states than Muldoon, but not many. Even after his electoral defeat, he cost the country a large part of its foreign exchange reserves by insisting on maintaining the exchange rate, until he was removed from office.

21. MERCURY[W].

22. There is an extensive literature on the New Zealand reforms. Almost all of it is congratulatory in tone: the congratulation relates to the fact that the reforms have happened. See, for example, Evans *et al.* (1996), a careful survey of the programme but which then derives lessons from the 'success' of the reforms without substantive discussion of effects. Douglas, Richardson and Robson (2002) is similar. It is presumably self-evident that the results will be beneficial, and therefore there is no need to enquire into the consequences. This is a feature of much commentary on the American business model. Dalziel and Lattimore (1999) give factual background and Hazledine (1998) provides an informed critical assessment of what happened in New Zealand.

23. J. A. Kay, *Financial Times* (30 August 2000).

24. Pomeranz (2000) describes the issue and the range of views taken on it. The discussion in Landes (1998) is close in spirit to the arguments here.

25. These quotations from Louise Le Comte and Evanske Huc, respectively, are found in Landes (1998), p. 342.

26. Kornicki (1998), Buzo (1999), Jeffries (2001).

27. Mitsui, Mitsubishi, Dai Ichi Kangyo, Sumitomo and Sanwa.

28. See Economist Intelligence Unit (2002), Buzo (1999), Jeffries (2001).

29. There is extensive discussion of the Asian 'miracle'. The World Bank's (1993) presentation attracted responses from Krugman (1994), Young (1995), Little (1996).

Chapter 5. Transactions and Rules

1. Ofcom is the agency regulating telecommunications.

2. Condominiums are the normal legal arrangement in the United States and strata title in Australia. In 2003 a new institution, commonhold, was introduced in Britain. Administrative law countries (most European economies) have different, and often simpler, processes.

3. Nor to the common 'battle of forms' when each party sends to the other its own assertion of the contract.

4. Bertram (1865), Roughley (1951), FISH[W].

5. Vegemite is a malt extract spread.

6. Durham (1991) describes a variety of accounts of genetic and cultural coevolution.

7. The average length of a job in Britain is twenty years for men aged 31–50, and fourteen years for women aged 31–50: Burgess and Rees (1996).

8. The economics of enclosure has an extensive literature, recently developed by McCloskey (1989, 1991).

9. A story told influentially by Chandler (1963). See also Hannah (1976).

10. Lessig, Slaughter and Zittrain (1999), Sulston and Ferry (2002).

11. Wolff (1998) is an entertaining discussion of these issues.

12. Napster allowed users – estimated at 50 million – to share compressed audio files; Merriden (2001).

13. The Wellcome Trust is a powerful illustration of the role of foundations in basic research discussed in Chapter 22. Much of its resources are derived from Glaxo's profits on Zantac. Its pluralist interventions have had a transforming effect on British science.

14. See Davies (2001) for an account of the problem of gene sequencing.

15. The living thing was a genetically modified bacterium: the case was *Diamond* v. *Chakravarty*.

16. There is an extensive literature which uses property rights in an extremely broad sense, e.g. Demsetz (1964), Furbotn and Pejovich (1972). Barzel (1997) says that 'the insurer is thus one of the owners of the building: he or she owns the fire occurrence attribute of the building' (p. 61). North (1990) defines property rights as 'the rights individuals appropriate over their own labour and the goods and services which they possess'. This definition – narrow by economists' standards – is still much wider than property as it would be defined by legal theorists.

Chapter 6. Production and Exchange

1. His work on the concerns of this book (Youngson 1959) is disappointingly judicious and inconclusive.

2. Youngson (1966).

3. This derives from Robbins (1935): 'Economics is a science which studies human behaviour as a relationship between ends and scarce means which have alternative uses', p. 16.

4. Saint-Paul is now full of tourists, although the nearby Fondation Maeght is one of the world's most beautiful galleries. There are many more attractive and less visited hill villages around Nice – Peillon, for example, is magical.

5. Buchet (1993).

6. According to legend, the Manhattes tribe sold Manhattan Island to Dutch settlers for $24 in 1626. Warren Buffett, following calculations by David Dennis, has claimed that the money invested at 6 per cent interest would today be sufficient to buy the Island back. Since it is not clear that the Manhattes tribe owned the island, the issue of who got the better deal will reverberate for ever.

7. The Saint-Paul is a better restaurant in Saint-Paul itself. Twenty miles away is Mougins, the gastronomic centre of this area of France.

8. 'One man draws out the wire, another straightens it, a third cuts it, a fourth points it, a fifth guides it at the top for receiving the head': A. Smith (1976), p. 14.

9. 'What a blessing it was that the idea of cooperation . . . came and prevailed to take the place of this chaotic condition in which the virtuous academic Know-Nothings about business were doing what they construed to be God's service in eating each other up': John D. Rockefeller to W. O. Inglis, quoted in Chernow (1998), p. 4.

10. Neale and Goyder (1980) describe the evolution of US anti-trust law.

11. The 1948 Act established a Monopolies Commission. The scope of legislation was extended to cover cartels (in 1956) and mergers (in 1965).

12. The allied powers broke up the traditional Japanese *zaibatsu* and some large German concentrations, notably that around IG Farben, which had been closely associated with the Nazi regime.

13. By rejecting the proposed takeover of Honeywell, another large US corporation. The US Department of Justice had already agreed to the merger.

14. Ford, General Motors and Chrysler produced half of world car output in the 1950s: before Chrysler's acquisition by Mercedes this figure had fallen to a third.

15. The Atlanta pharmacist was John Pemberton, whose business was bought by Asa Griggs Chandler, who developed the business with wide distribution and aggressive advertising. Chandler ran Coca-Cola for twenty-five years before becoming Mayor of Atlanta in 1916.

16. For an elaboration of the relationship between competitive advantage and firm capabilities, see J. A. Kay (1993).

17. This example was used in Ricardo's *Principles of Political Economy* (1817).

18. Own estimates from world trade statistics.

19. Own estimates from Swiss trade statistics.

20. Porter (1990) has repopularized the emphasis on industrial 'clusters' noted by Alfred Marshall a century before.

Chapter 7. Assignment

1. This account of the history of *Portrait of Dr Gachet* is based heavily on Saltzman (1999).

2. Gachet (1994).

3. Van Gogh's brother, Theo, was an art dealer who died soon after the painter, and it was his sister who effectively commercialized his work: *Dr Gachet* was first sold in 1897 for 225 francs.

4. In July 2002 Rubens's *The Massacre of the Innocents* was sold in London for £49.5 million. This is a larger sum in sterling, but not dollars.

5. The art historian Louis Anfray has alleged that the Musée d'Orsay version is a copy by another artist; Landais (1999).

6. 'Éditions 1999' (1999).

7. Owen, 'Business of Sport: World Cup 2002: Cries of Foul Right up to the Final Whistle', *Financial Times* (28 May 2002).

8. The distinction between exit and voice is due to Hirschman (1970).

9. Karl Marx (1875), p. 12.

10. Kornai (1992), chapter 7.

11. 'Any observed statistical regularity will tend to collapse once pressure is placed upon it for control purposes': Goodhart (1984), p. 96.

12. Buchan (1997) provides an entertaining history of the evolution of monies. Del Mar (1895) is exhaustive.

13. Radford (1945).

14. The initial 'voting paradox' is due to the French Enlightenment mathematician and philosopher Condorcet (1785); Black (1958). Arrow's theorem was first demonstrated in Arrow (1951a). See Sen (1970) for a survey.

15. Lynch and Kahn (2000), pp. 21–34.

16. This might alternatively be interpreted as a manifestation of a more fundamental problem: that individuals themselves may not have consistent preferences over social issues.

17. Vickrey (1961, 1962).

18. For auction design, see Bulow and Klemperer (2002), AUCTIONS[W].

19. See the repeated attacks by one art critic on what he describes as a 'Serota clique' dominating British art: Sewell (1994).

Chapter 8. Central Planning

1. The two-week trip was dogged by incident and surrounded by controversy but increased Khrushchev's popularity at home and (especially) abroad; Jasny (1965), Talbott (1971).

2. Hosking (1992), pp. 358–9.

3. The Great Leap Forward is described in scholarly detail by MacFarquhar (1993) and literary skill by Chang (1992). See also Karnow (1973), Teiwes (1999).

4. Josephson (1995) describes some of the many grandiose schemes planned during the history of the Soviet Union.

5. Church (1996).

6. Halberstam (1987) provides an immensely readable account of the decline of Ford and the role of its proprietor in that decline.

7. In 1952 Morris merged with Austin, its principal domestic rival, to form the British Motor Corporation and in 1967 the government promoted a further merger in which the smaller but supposedly better-managed Leyland became the dominant partner. However, the business faced liquidation in 1974 and was nationalized. After nationalization, the government commissioned the Ryder Plan, which proposed huge investment in the failed business. Efficiency gains only came after the election of the Thatcher government in 1979: the Conservatives made clear that they would not provide further funds and were indifferent to the fate of the company. Under Michael Edwardes the company began to tackle its twin problems of poor management and abysmal labour relations. Still, the volume car business – the Morris legacy – continued to lose market share. In 1988 it was sold to British Aerospace, and in 1994 to BMW.

8. Harold Wilson – who became Prime Minister in 1964 at the (then) young age of 46, was the author of this phrase.

9. Henney (1988), p. 17.

10. These figures include capitalized interest up to the date of effective operation; own calculations based on data from CEGB and Nuclear Electric reports. The best account of this disaster is Burn (1978). Some more recent analysis is in Green (1995).

11. Department of Energy (1976), pp. 15–16; quoted by Henderson (1977), p. 192.

12. This story is told in Hannah (1982), although since Hannah's history was authorized by the Electricity Council, some reading between the lines is required.

13. 'One thing that you might think would count, but which in fact is given no attention whatever, is whether or not your advice has been any good': an anonymous civil servant, in Henderson (1977). 'It is much more important for a paper to be competent than for it to be right or enlightening': Sir Samuel Brittan, quoted by Henderson (1977).

Chapter 9. Pluralism

1. In 1981, the year Welch became CEO at GE, his predecessor, Reg Jones, was voted the best CEO in America by a poll of other chief executives, and by a considerable margin; Goold and Campbell (1987), p. 273.

2. Quotes from Havermesh (1986), pp. 181, 202.

3. Welch (2001), p. 104.

4. These quotes come from S. M. Cohen (1982).

5. Mintzberg (1994) describes the rise and fall of strategic planning in companies in parallel with the rise and fall of planning in national economies.

6. Welch (2001), p. 104.

7. Sizewell B was one of the very few nuclear plants subsequently built by an American company.

8. Welch (2001), p. 97.

9. The Commission concluded that 'the combination of the leading aircraft engine maker with the leading avionics manufacturer would create a dominant position in various relevant markets'. The US Department of Justice had earlier approved the merger. See Patterson and Shapiro (2001) for a discussion of this divergence.

10. ICI received heavy fines from the European Commission in 1986 for price fixing in polyethylene and in 2001 for price fixing in sodium glucomate.

11. This was in part a reaction to the dominance of Harry McGowan in the interwar period.

12. Pettigrew (1985).

13. Glaxo in 1972 had seen itself as having no successful independent future; Monopolies Commission (1972).

14. For some history of the British pharmaceutical industry, see Lynn (1991), pp. 163–6, 193–207.

15. Flatow (1992), chapter 11.

16. The Rank Organization was itself established as a hobby by a member of the Rank milling family.

17. The history of Xerox Parc is told by Hiltzik (2000).

18. Xerox 'was cursed by the Chester Carlson vision . . . all you have to do is give us the right technology and the world would come to us': Paul Strussman, former Xerox chief technology officer, in Hiltzik (2000).

19. The history of the development of personal computers is told by Ceruzzi (1998). There is a bookshelf of hagiography of Gates and Microsoft: see, for example, Ichbiah and Knepper (1991) and, of course, Gates's own self-congratulation in Gates (1995, 1999).

20. Cannan (1927).

21. The rise and fall of Boo.com is told in Cellan-Jones (2001). One of Boo's founders had the effrontery to write a book on it: Malmsten, Portanger and Drazin (2002).

22. As, for example, in Leadbeater (2000).

23. Cassidy (2002) is the best account of the American dot.com boom.

Chapter 10. Spontaneous Order

1. For surveys of the Scottish Enlightenment thinkers, see Berry (1997), Broadie (1997).

2. Paley (1802), Hume (1779).

3. A. Ferguson (1767), p. 187.

4. Which became the title of a book by Richard Dawkins (1991 edn.).

5. Dawkins (1989) proposed the idea of 'memes' as a social analogue to genes. Blackmore (1999) is the most extensive development of the notion. As Dawkins says in his introduction to that book 'any theory deserves to be given its best shot'. But its best shot is not persuasive enough.

6. In the nineteenth century the battle between Lamarckian evolution and Darwinian evolution was won by Darwin: characteristics acquired during life cannot be genetically transmitted. But – as with French – they can be transmitted in other ways.

7. Arrow and Hahn (1971), p. vii.

8. Kornai (1992) is a source of evidence on repeated co-ordination failures in planned economies.

9. In 1990, US steel capacity was 60 per cent of Soviet capacity; calculations from OECD data.

10. Wal-Mart, founded by Sam Walton in 1962, is now the world's largest retailer.

11. Yergin and Stanislaw (1998) begin their book with an admiring description of the Izmailovo outdoor market. In the United States, however, the massive organization of Wal-Mart does the job.

12. Price discontinuities resulting from supply shortages routinely generate consumer protests in market economies.

13. Lynch and Kahn (2000), pp. 21-34.

14. See e.g. Bunday (1996).

15. Heilbroner (1955), p. 214.

16. Weaver (1948), p. 536. See also Johnson (2001), pp. 46-9.

17. Gladwell (2000) provides a popular discussion of 'tipping points', the characteristics of systems with this property.

18. For an introduction to chaos theory, see Gleick (1988); for economic and other social applications see Kiel and Elliott (1996).

19. The modern emphasis on path-dependency in economics originates from Arthur (1989).

20. The qwerty problem was described by P. A. David (1985), who shares with Arthur the credit for defining this approach. For (unpersuasive) responses from American business model supporters, see Liebowitz and Margolis (1990).

21. For an introduction to the issues and personalities, see Waldrop (1994).

22. Darwin (1859).

23. Due in particular to the empirical work of Wilson (1971), who will reappear in other contexts, and the theoretical insights of Hamilton (1964).

24. For discussions of the relationships between social insects and human social processes, see Ormerod (1998), Kirman (1993).

25. MacIntyre (1981), p. 75.

26. Simon (1969).

27. Kauffman (1995, 2000).

28. Waldrop (1994), however, treats Arthur as a principal founder, and other economists – such as Arrow – have played an active role in the work of the Santa Fe Institute.

Chapter 11. Competitive Markets

1. See for example Office of Fair Trading (2001).

2. The inclination to view resource reserves and resource availability in physical rather than economic terms is deep rooted. The Club of Rome report (Meadows *et al.*, 1972) which predicted that the world would by now have run out of several major resources – gold, silver, mercury, zinc – is only one example of a large literature that goes back many centuries. We are dependent on oil because (for the moment) oil is plentiful just as we were once even more dependent on coal (which was then plentiful and, at a price, still is) and, earlier still, on wood (which was then plentiful). This does not mean that no resource shortages can ever arise, but it is unlikely they will arise in the way many environmentalists think.

3. About 30 per cent of world oil production comes from the Middle East, another 20 per cent from rich states (principally the USA, UK, Canada and Norway).

4. R. E. Williams (1997), Suzuki (1997).

5. Brunekreeft (1997) describes the structure of the UK electricity generation system.

6. Klopfenstein (1989), chapter 2.

7. Levy (1989).

8. The industry was privatized in 1990. In England and Wales there were two generating companies and twelve regional distribution businesses. The nuclear power stations remained in public ownership: the AGRs (see Chapter 8) were sold in 1996.

9. Brunekreeft (1997).

10. The National Grid continues to operate a control room which assures continuity of supply while bids and offers determine the associated financial statements. Analogous arrangements are found in all other electricity markets.

11. Prices were raised in 1974 to levels which equate to $20 per barrel (in 2002 prices).

12. The most famous Dutch flower market, at Aalsmeer, operates quite differently, with a clock and an auction mechanism. This 'Dutch auction' is a different process to the 'English auction' procedure used for *Dr Gachet*.

13. On the London Stock Market, brokers were until 1986 required to be agency brokers, i.e. they earned commissions but did not themselves take positions in stocks. Once this restriction was abolished, the distinction between agency brokers and brokers acting on their own account disappeared.

Brokers perceived themselves to require capital for own-account trading and mostly sold to banks.

14. Covent Garden and Billingsgate have moved to new, less central locations – as has the greatest produce market of all, Les Halles in Paris, which relocated to Rungis in the suburbs. Smithfield remains, anachronistically, on the edge of the City of London, and during the night refrigerated lorries trundle between empty office blocks to deliver meat carcasses.

15. Most individual markets have their own price-reporting systems. 'Real-time price feeds', i.e. up-to-date pricing information, are available from market services such as Reuters and Bloomberg. Delayed price quotes (even a 15- or 20-minute delay is thought to destroy the value of information to professional traders) are readily available on the Internet for many markets.

16. The Hunts began buying silver in 1973 and aggressive accumulation in 1979. It is claimed that at the peak of the market (the price of silver rose from $2 per ounce in 1973 to $54 in 1980) they controlled half the deliverable (i.e. not in jewellery and heirlooms) supply. In early 1980 the price collapsed. The two Hunt brothers became bankrupt and were eventually convicted of market manipulation.

17. The International Tin Council collapsed on 24 October 1985. See 'ITC Pulls the Plug on Supporting the Tin Market', *Metals Week: Tin Section* (1985), p. 1; Rodger, 'Dented Image in the Can Market', *Financial Times*, 28 October 1985, p. 11; Crabtree, Duffy and Pearce (1987).

18. A forward market is a derivatives market: how these work is described in the next chapter.

19. Kanfer (1993), Carstens (2001), Gregory (1962).

20. Stephens (1996), pp. 250–51.

21. Soros is a major philanthropist, particularly in Eastern Europe, and has written books sceptical about the American business model: Soros (1998, 2000).

22. Tsurumi (2001).

23. Wholesale electricity prices fell substantially in 2001.

Chapter 12. Markets in Risk

1. There is an extensive literature on the problems of the Lloyd's insurance market. Raphael (1994) is a readable description of the main events. The cascade of claims (the LMX spiral) was investigated by a Committee of Inquiry chaired by Sir David Walker (Walker and Coleridge, 1992). The £16

billion figure emerged in Walker's evidence in a Canadian court (Hong Kong Bank of China *et al.*, Anne Hendive *et al.*, Ontario Court of Justice, 1994).

2. Bernstein (1996) is a brilliant study of the history of risk analysis and risk markets.

3. Albert (1990), chapter 5; translated as *Capitalism vs Capitalism: How America's Obsessions with Individual Achievement and Short-Term Profit has led to the Brink of Collapse*, somewhat prematurely published in 1993.

4. *The Economist*, 15 June 2000.

5. Haigh (1999) describes this and other market-making processes.

6. This sounds paradoxical. If Lochnagel wins the five o'clock race at Ascot, isn't it obvious that those who backed Lochnagel won and others lost? In a sense, yes. And yet it might have been that the odds on Lochnagel were shorter than the horse's form deserved, so that if you had (hypothetically) made 100 similar bets you would have lost. When you buy a lottery ticket, you make a mistake – you almost certainly should not bet at such poor odds. But if the winning ticket is yours, chance redeems your mistake. When people succeed in risky situations, the outcome is a mixture of their good judgement and their good luck, and it is impossible to disentangle the elements of the two. This is of central importance to considering successful businesses and successful business people. To what extent were Henry Ford, William Morris and Bill Gates people who had the good judgement to choose the right number, or lucky people whose number came up?

7. Kendall (1953).

8. See Financial Services Authority Occasional Papers 6 and 9, K. R. James (2000), Rhodes (2000) and WM Company (2002). In a well-publicized court case in 2001, Merrill Lynch settled for an estimated £70 million a claim by Unilever for negligent management of their pension fund.

9. Black and Scholes (1973).

10. Jensen (1978).

Chapter 13. Markets in Money

1. 'This was a venture, sir, that Jacob serv'd for . . . was this inserted to make interest good?' *The Merchant of Venice*, Act I, scene iii, line 85.

2. 'Ancient Egypt was doubly fortunate, and doubtless owed to this its fabled wealth, in that it possessed two activities, namely pyramid building as well as the search for the precious metals, the fruits of which, since they could not serve the needs of man by being consumed, did not stale with abundance': Keynes (1936), p. 131.

3. Euroland (or the Eurozone) is a common description of the twelve EU members (Austria, Belgium, Finland, France, Germany, Greece, Ireland, Italy, Luxemburg, Portugal, Spain, the Netherlands) which trade in euros.

4. Rowley (1994), Widdig (2001).

5. As reported in *Gone with the Wind* and supported by Ball (1991). The dot.com version is awaited.

6. Dimson, Marsh and Staunton (2002).

7. N. Ferguson (2001).

8. Geared split-level investment trusts, many of which collapsed in 2002 (as they had done in previous stock market crashes), were examples of the same phenomenon.

9. Seventy per cent of US companies listed in 1999 had never paid a dividend (Fama and French 2001).

10. Chartism is generally not mentioned in corporate finance courses at major business schools. See for example Brealey and Myers (1981–99). A description of chartist techniques can be found in Malkiel (1996), which is a readable, accessible and reliable introduction to the issues of this chapter. There is, however, the possibility that infinitely more sophisticated mathematical techniques might genuinely identify patterns; see Bass (1999). Evidence of this would, of course, refute the efficient market hypothesis: see Chapter 19.

11. Insider trading is the use of information gained through a relationship with the firm, e.g. as director or adviser. It is now illegal in Britain, the USA and many other countries.

12. See e.g. estimates of rates of return to higher education in Harkness and Machin (1999).

13. These 'intangible assets' are the capitalized value of rents arising from competitive advantages. This is why 'Tobin's q' – the ratio of the market value of a company to its tangible assets – can appropriately exceed one.

14. Putnam (2000).

15. 'Americans of all ages, all conditions, all minds, constantly unite', Tocqueville (2000 edn.), p. 489.

Chapter 14. General Equilibrium

1. Note that this is true of any co-ordinated system, whether the co-ordination is designed or not.

2. Henderson (1986).

3. Brittan (1996), pp. 276–7.

4. As in the repeated suggestion that practical businessmen should sit on the Monetary Policy Committee which fixes interest rates.

5. Thus she writes: 'My father's background as a grocer is sometimes cited as the basis for my economic philosophy. So it was – and is.' But, to be fair, she continues: 'My father was both a practical man and a man of theory. He liked to connect the progress of our corner shop with the great complex romance of international trade which recruited people all over the world to ensure that a family in Grantham could have on its table rice from India, coffee from Kenya, sugar from the West Indies and spices from five continents'; Thatcher (1993), p. 11.

6. *England's Treasure by Foreign Trade* is a work of the 1620s by Thomas Mun. As is typical of DIY economics, it is hard to pin down precisely what mercantilists thought: hence Viner's description of it as 'essentially a folk doctrine' (*International Encyclopedia of Social Sciences*, 1968).

7. The workers who threatened Kay actually preceded the Luddites, followers of the (possibly mythical) Ned Ludd in the early nineteenth century. A picture of Kay fleeing is found at LUDDITE[W].

8. Marshall described his methodology of economics as follows: '(1) Use mathematics as a shorthand language, rather than as an engine of inquiry. (2) Keep to them till you have done. (3) Translate into English. (4) Then illustrate by examples that are important to real life. (5) Burn the mathematics. (6) If you can't succeed in 4, burn 3. This last I did often': A. Marshall (1925), p. 427.

9. Keynes was not only the leading figure in economics before the Second World War but mentor to a group of outstanding students and lecturers. After the Second World War, the economics of Cambridge, England seemed to atrophy, as the Keynesian legacy was vigorously protected against new developments in the subject. In England, Oxford enjoyed a meteoric rise under Hicks[N] and Mirrlees[N] but declined from the 1980s and leadership in UK economics moved to the LSE. Although four Nobel Laureates (Meade[N], Mirrlees[N], Sen[N], Stone[N]) ended their careers in Cambridge, none were at Cambridge when they did the relevant work.

10. The works described are Hicks (1939), Samuelson (1947), Arrow and Debreu (1954), Debreu (1957). Overviews are found in Koopmans (1957) and a definitive textbook is Arrow and Hahn (1971).

11. The original fixed-point theorem is due to Brouwer; the version commonly employed by economists is by Kakutani (1941).

12. Although the general idea of convexity has always been known, the mathematics of convex sets was fully developed only in the twentieth century: Hardy, Littlewood and Polya (1934), and applied to economics even later.

13. Langlois, Roggman and Musselman (1994), Etcoff (1994), Perrett, May and Yoshikawa (1994).

14. This discussion concerns the stability as well as the position of equilibrium. Convexity is relevant to both.

15. Lyapunov's theorem shows how many small non-convexities can be consistent with overall convexity if the numbers of firms, industries, etc. are sufficiently large; Aumann (1964).

Chapter 15. Efficiency

1. Bowlby (1991), Desmond and Moore (1991).

2. Pearce (1992) attempts to resolve this muddle, but continues to assert universal commensurability; this follows almost inescapably from the rationality postulates described in Chapters 16 and 17.

3. Buchholz (1999), p. 199, Posner (1998).

4. Dworkin (1977), chapter 4, Waldron (1984), pp. 153–67.

5. Berlin (2000).

6. For a summary of the standard economic approach to the value-of-life issues, see Jones-Lee (1976); for a well-balanced background to why this approach is untenable, see Douglas and Wildavsky (1982).

7. This is often called a Pareto optimum.

8. Perfect – 'first degree' – price discrimination tailors the price for each good sold precisely to its user so that all consumer surplus is extracted.

9. Arrow (1951b), pp. 507–32.

Chapter 16. Neoclassical Economics and After

1. For example, for James Tobin[N] the invisible hand is 'one of the great ideas of history and one of the most influential' (Tobin 1992, p. 117).

2. This curious list contains, reasonably enough, several works by Joseph himself, some economic classics, Jacobs's (1961) fine work on cities, but no major modern work in economics. Denham (2001), pp. 136–7.

3. Yergin and Stanislaw (1998), p. 398. More or less the same sentence is found at the beginning of the book, p. 24.

4. Leacock (1936). These are not Stephen Leacock's own views.

5. A. Smith (1759), pp. 184–5. For a discussion of the role of the 'invisible hand' metaphor in Smith's work, see Rothschild (2001), chapter 5. Shakespeare's original 'invisible hand' is as follows:

> Come seeling night
> Scarf up the tender eye of pitiful day
> And with thy bloody and invisible hand
> Cancel and tear to pieces that great bond
> Which keeps me pale.
>
> (*Macbeth*, Act III, scene ii)

6. This is why Keith Joseph's reading list for civil servants in the Department of Trade and Industry was ludicrous. The politician as intellectual manqué is often an embarrassing figure – cf. Al Gore in the 1990s – and this was certainly true of Joseph.

7. 'Austrian economics' is often today used simply as a description of right-wing and libertarian sentiment, sometimes combined with resistance to the application of mathematical technique. These features make the label attractive to many DIY economists; see, for example, the reading lists on economics offered on the Amazon.com website. A discussion of the various meanings of 'Austrian economics', with a judicious summary ('economists and other intellectuals in Austria today are cognizant of – and proud of – the earlier Austrian school . . . but see themselves today simply as a part of the general community of professional economists', p. 149) is found in Kirzner's essay in Eatwell, Milgate and Newman (1988).

8. Although Thorstein Veblen, whose trenchant criticism of the consumption of the rich (Veblen, 1899) is still readable today, was a faculty member, his personal habits were as uncongenial as his views and he was asked to leave.

9. There is a – possibly intentional – trap in this quotation. At a quick reading, it seems to describe self-interested behaviour. On a more careful reading, it does not: it is not the behaviour which is relentless and unflinching, but the economist who studies it. This difficulty in distinguishing consistent behaviour from self-interested behaviour recurs repeatedly: see below.

10. Although the Chicago influence in New Zealand is widely cited (Easton, 1994), the reality is less clear. 'There is a view in New Zealand that the reforms were driven by Chicago. It is certainly true that Friedman's *Free to Choose* was read widely in New Zealand. . . . But to the best of my knowledge none of those most closely involved in the reform process ever studied at Chicago. In fact the most common academic background . . . was probably the University of Canterbury'; Brash (1996).

11. Becker (1973, 1974, 1981).

12. Becker (1993).

13. The key feature of this account is that it contains no ethics or norms, or more precisely that what we describe as ethics or norms are adopted as

the result of self-interested calculation, i.e. honesty may be the best policy, but will be abandoned if it ceases to be the best policy. Honesty is not a trait of character. 'someone is honest only if honesty, or the appearance of honesty, pays more than dishonesty'. Telser (1980), pp. 27–44; see also Becker (1968).

14. Hamermesh and Soss (1974), Blinder (1974).

15. It follows that only unpredicted – and unpredictable – shocks create cyclical fluctuations in economics. Moreover, the closely related 'Lucas critique' excludes most empirical testing of these models, because the information generated (including the results of the test itself) should already be incorporated in behaviour and prices.

16. Knight (1921), Alchian (1950).

17. See Lazear (2000).

18. The post-autistic movement was launched by French students in 2000 with a petition on the Internet and a long article in *Le Monde*. The movement prompted a response from the Education Minister, Jack Lang, who commissioned a (fairly sympathetic) report from the respected French economist Jean-Paul Fitoussi. POST-AUTISTIC[W].

19. For modernism and postmodernism in architecture, see Jencks (1986).

20. Jacobs (1961) developed these arguments with great literary skill; Certeau (1984) adopts a similar approach on a wider canvas.

21. Lyotard (1992).

22. The conservative (in a European sense) philosopher Michael Oakeshott saw this at an early stage: 'This is perhaps, the main significance of Hayek's *Road to Serfdom* – not the cogency of his doctrine, but the fact that it is a doctrine. A plan to resist all planning may be better than its opposite, but it belongs to the same style of politics'; Oakeshott (1962), p. 26.

23. As in for example Kelly (1998).

24. It is less surprising that those involved in business and economics should not be receptive to postmodernism. Among the postmodernists, comment on business and economic issues rarely rises above tired Marxist clichés – see for example the turgid works of Jameson (1992). The scientific pretensions of postmodernism were deliciously parodied by Sokal, who succeeded in publishing a crude parody in the journal *Cultural Studies* (Sokal and Bricmont, 1998). None of this precludes the possibility that there are postmodernist truths about business and economics.

25. See OECD (1993) for a sceptical, informed review of the performance of economic forecasters.

26. As noted by the National Audit Office (2001) in its comments on the elaborate spreadsheet models built to justify public–private partnerships.

27. Borges (1946).

28. For discussions of economic models in similar vein by major contemporary economists, see Akerlof (1984), Krugman (1995).

29. Geertz (1973), chapter 1.

30. Boyle (2000), p. xi.

31. 'In attempting to answer the question "could it be true?" we learn a great deal about why it might not be true'; Arrow and Hahn (1971), p. vii.

32. Dixit and Nalebuff (1991) is an accessible introduction. Binmore (1994, 1998) relates game theory to some of the wider issues of this book.

33. Macrae (1992).

34. Quoted Strathern (2001), p. 300.

35. Nasar (1998).

36. 'I was once in the habit of telling pupils that firms might be envisaged as islands of planned coordination in a sea of markets': Richardson (1972), p. 883. Richardson goes on to say: 'This now seems to be a highly misleading account.'

37. North and Thomas (1973), North (1990).

38. Williamson (1975).

39. Milgrom and Roberts (1992).

40. Stiglitz (1994) is a good introduction to his research.

41. Ibid., p. 5.

42. The term 'market failure' was popularized by Bator (1958). For the interpretation of market failure as violation of Arrow–Debreu assumptions, see Ledyard (1988).

Chapter 17. Rationality and Adaptation

1. See Ch. 16, n. 13.

2. Samuelson (1993), p. 143.

3. Amartya Sen[N] has done much to clarify these issues: see Sen (1987), pp. 12–22, Sen (1988).

4. Easterly (2001), p. xii.

5. The argument and the answer to it are well described by Gintis (2000): 'the most common informal argument is reminiscent of Louis XIV's "*après-moi le déluge*" defense of the monarchy: drop the assumptions and we lose the ability to predict altogether. The models developed recently . . . show that we have little to fear from the flood.'

6. Though cf. Stigler: 'let me predict the outcome of the systematic and comprehensive testing of behaviour in situations where self interest and

ethical values with wide verbal allegiance are in conflict. Much of the time, most of the time, in fact, the self interest will win': Stigler (1981), p. 176. Note that Stigler predicts the result: he does not report results, and in fact, as Sen (1987) notes, there are few such tests. Correct predictions – demand curves slope downwards – can be derived in many ways – see Becker (1962).

7. Easterly's quotation is immediately followed by another: 'People respond to incentives; all the rest is commentary' (Easterly 2000, p. xii).

8. J. Kay (2000), OXFORD[W].

9. Havel (1985), pp. 27–8.

10. MacIntyre (1981), pp. 57–9.

11. Francis Galton was not only a major figure in the development of scientific genetics but a sponsor of the eugenics movement.

12. Wilson (1975). Wilson was subject to a variety of tirades and famously had a pitcher of water poured over him at the American Association for the Advancement (*sic*) of Science.

13. 'The relevant question to ask about the assumptions of a theory is not whether they are descriptively realistic, for they never are, but whether they are sufficiently good approximations for the purpose in hand. And this question can be answered only by seeing whether the theory works, which means whether it yields sufficiently accurate predictions': M. Friedman (1953).

14. The 'piece of shit' was 24/7 Media.

15. Miller (2000).

16. In another – also instructive – version of the joke, the game theorist runs. The friend says 'You can't run faster than the bear.' The economist responds 'I only need to run faster than you.' JOKES[W].

17. Maynard Smith (1982), Taylor and Joncker (1978).

18. Williamson (1985).

19. Gigerenzer *et al.* (1999) report that Simon 'once remarked with a mixture of humour and anger that he had considered suing authors who misuse his concept of bounded rationality to construct ever more complicated and unrealistic models of human decision making' (p. 12).

20. Kahneman and Tversky (2000).

Chapter 18. Information

1. The wallet problem is due to Stiglitz, who would occasionally attempt to auction his wallet to a class.

2. Bower (1995, 2001).

3. 'Cheap talk' is a threat or promise which is not credible because it pays to make the promise or threat but not to carry it out.

4. Cronin (1991), pp. 222–6 describes this and other similar biological phenomena.

5. For the biological explanations, see Zahavi (1975); the economics of signalling was pioneered by Spence (1973) and the specific application to advertising by P. Nelson (1974).

6. AUSTRALIA[W].

7. Thaler (1991) discusses this (and other economic paradoxes).

8. Capen, Clapp and Campbell (1971).

9. Bulow and Klemperer (2002), Borgers and Dustmann (2002); KLEMPERER[W].

10. The Sonera/Telefonica consortium.

11. At the date of writing, Vallance and Blodget have gone.

12. The first extensive argument that information issues were an explanation of cyclical unemployment was given by Leijonhufvud (1968), who suggested that it was the correct interpretation of the thesis of Keynes's General Theory.

13. 'Matthew Parris . . . has reminded us that most people do not escape the market system. . . . Parris writes of an aunt of his who believes that there is such a thing as a fair price or wage that can be determined by contemplation rather than the state of the market. . . . I have made a few soundings of my own among business journalists, who might be expected to have a higher degree of sophistication': Brittan (1996), p. 49.

Chapter 19. Risk in Reality

1. For a review of the current status of this theory see Starmer (2000).

2. Pinker (1994).

3. Allais (1953).

4. Kahneman and Tversky (2000) is a collection of their work.

5. Adam Smith observed that 'Such in reality is the absurd confidence which almost all men have in their own good fortune, that whenever there is the least probability of success, too great a share of it (investment) is apt to go to them [mining projects] of its own accord': Smith (1976), book IV, chapter 7, part 1. See Shiller (2000), pp. 142–6, for a demonstration that only the methods of empirical research have changed.

6. Shleifer (1999) and Siegel (1998) survey market anomalies. The January effect is discussed by Siegel (p. 254), the 1987 crash by Shiller (2000), pp. 88–95.

7. The equity premium paradox was first described by Mehra and Prescott

(1985) and elaborated by Benartzi and Thaler (1995); see Dimson, Marsh and Staunton (2002) for evidence on it.

8. Haigh (1999), pp. 13–35 gives a careful discussion of the structure of the lottery and its implications.

9. Leeson was subsequently sentenced to six years' imprisonment.

10. On Barings, see Hunt and Heinrich (1996), Fay (1996), Bank of England (1995), Leeson (1996) and Augar (2000).

11. The story of LTCM is told by Lowenstein (2000).

12. This is the undiversifiable risk for which the equity risk premium is the reward in the capital asset pricing model.

13. Arrow[N] (1971) is a seminal discussion of moral hazard and adverse selection.

14. 'Total Period Fertility Rate, 1924–1998', *Social Trends*, 30 (ONS, 2000), p. 41.

15. Hair (1971).

16. Adams (1995), pp. 12–13.

17. Barth (1991), White (1991), Calavita, Pontell and Tillman (1997).

18. Including Charles Keating; see Chapter 1, n. 14.

19. Shleifer and Summers (1988). 'When asked how GE had managed to increase its earnings by fourteen percent per year, vice-president Frank Doyle replied, "We did a lot of violence to the expectations of the American workforce"': Hay and Moore (1998), quoted Hutton (2002).

20. For a history of social insurance see Dilnot, Kay and Morris (1984), chapter 1.

21. 'Part of selling bonds for Salomon was persuading yourself that a bad idea for Salomon was a good idea for a customer': M. Lewis (1989), p. 162.

22. And yet new issues – IPOs – are more frequent when stock markets are high (Ritter, 1991). This is another case where adaptation provides a more compelling account of behaviour than rationality.

23. Cellan-Jones (2001) describes the flotation; data is drawn from the prospectus for the issue.

24. Much of this has now been spent on acquisitions.

25. 'People who argue that speculation is generally destabilising seldom realise that this is largely equivalent to saying that speculators lose money, since speculation can be destabilising only if speculators on the average sell when the currency is low in price and buy when it is high': M. Friedman (1953), p. 175.

26. Lowenstein (2000), p. 236.

27. For an introduction to these issues of behavioural finance see Shleifer (1999); for a practical guide see Belsky and Gilovich (2000), Shefrin (2000).

Chapter 20. Co-operation

1. Rousseau (1913), p. 111.

2. The Pharos of Alexandria, built around 280 BC, was a marvel for the combination of its scale of construction and the technological sophistication of its reflective mirrors. (See Forster 1982; Fraser 1984.)

3. Socrastus – named on the Pharos and identified as its architect by Pliny – was probably in fact the public-spirited courtier who paid for it (Fraser, 1984, p. 19).

4. Bathurst (1999).

5. Winstanley is described by Bathurst (1999), p. 59, as 'an English eccentric of the finest breed'.

6. Administered through a private corporation, Trinity House.

7. Groves and Ledyard (1977, 1980).

8. Bathurst (1999), pp. 59–61.

9. Buchanan and Tulloch (1962), Downs (1957), Buchanan and Tollison (1972, 1984).

10. The Prisoner's Dilemma was one of the problems devised in early exploration of game theory at the Rand Corporation after the Second World War; supposedly devised by Merrill Glood and Melvin Dresher, the problem was posed in story form by Albert Tucker to explain his research to Stanford psychologists.

11. Marwell and Ames (1981).

12. Youngson (1966), p. 160, considers that 'it looks well – better, perhaps, than if it had been finished'. I don't think so.

13. The 'folk theorem' of game theory (see e.g. Fudenberg and Tirole (1991), chapter 5), so called because its attribution is unclear, claims that all such strategies are potential Nash equilibria in an indefinitely repeated game. We behave as we are expected to.

14. Axelrod (1984, 1997).

15. See Basu (2000).

16. See Cronin (1991) for an explanation of these biological models; R. H. Frank (1988) for a development of their economic analogues. Gintis (2000) describes both.

17. The classic statement of group-selection arguments is Wynne-Edwards (1962), which helped provoke the decisive refutation by G. C. Williams (1966).

18. 'Lord, what can I do? I am spent! People will not obey me. I have been pulling down houses. But the fire overtakes us faster than we can do it': the Lord Mayor of London (on 2 September 1666), in Latham (1985), p. 660.

19. Titmuss (1970).

20. This kind of problem is not, of course, peculiarly French. It was equally 'unhelpful' for British civil servants to warn of the possible dangers of 'mad cow disease'. The cover-up does, however, seem to have been less egregious and, fortunately, the results less disastrous.

Chapter 21. Co-ordination

1. Kincaid (1986).
2. Levy (1989).
3. Prout (1922).
4. See Kelly (1998), Shapiro and Varian (1999).
5. Travers and Milgram (1969). The 'small world' phenomenon is well illustrated at ORACLE OF BACON[W] and in Watts (1999).
6. This vacuous phrase has been adopted as policy by the UK government.
7. This similarly vacuous concept is lauded by OECD (1975).
8. According to estimates by Dixon (1996), 36 per cent of expenditure under Superfund to that date related to transactions costs rather than to clearing up pollution.
9. Mnookin and Kornhauser (1979).

Chapter 22. The Knowledge Economy

1. See for example Shapiro and Varian (1999); also 'new economy' writers such as Kelly (1998), Leadbeater (2000) and Coyle (2001).
2. Bodanis (2000), R. W. Clark (1979).
3. The Bletchley Park project, once highly secret, has now generated an extensive literature – Hinsley and Stripp (1993), Enever (1994), Butters (2000) – and a film (*Enigma*).
4. In the last years of his life, Turing was a pathbreaker in the understanding of the mathematics of spontaneous order in non-linear dynamic systems of the kind described in Chapter 9. His paper on the chemical basis of morphogenesis was published in 1952. See Hodges (1992).
5. Watson (1968). Crick spent most of his career at the Salk Institute in California, but never undertook further work of comparable significance. Watson was a successful science administrator and fundraiser, and a leader of the Human Genome programme.
6. NOBEL[W].
7. Very little happened following Fleming's now famous discovery. The drug

could only be useful if it could be absorbed and produced in large quantities and Florey had difficulty securing even philanthropic funding for this research. Judson (1980).

8. Norman Borlang, an American whose principal work was undertaken at the International Maize and Wheat Center in Mexico, received the Nobel Peace Prize in 1970 for his contribution to the 'green revolution'.

9. Schwartz (2002), Fisher (1997), Godfrey and Sterling (2001).

10. Freiberger and Swaine (2000), Kaplan (1999).

11. Lucent was floated off from AT&T in 1996 at $27 per share. The share price reached a high of $84 in the bubble but in 2002 fell below $2.

12. Sheehan (1993).

13. Own calculations using data from NOBEL[W].

14. The vast majority of US higher education institutions are state controlled, but the major research centres – such as Harvard, Yale, Princeton, Chicago and Stanford – are private institutions which raise most of their own funding.

15. Read (1999).

16. The Broadcasting Act 1990 provided for compulsory licensing of this material and in March 1992 the Copyright Tribunal determined low royalties for this use.

17. S. Hartley (2001). Mrs Pearsall's own account is Pearsall (1990).

18. *Guardian*, 6 March 2001.

19. Stern Stewart. See Stern, Shiely and Ross (2001), Ehrbar (1998).

20. In 2001 the government settled its action in return for minor concessions by Microsoft after higher courts had criticized the conduct of presiding judge Jackson. A number of individual states continued to pursue the case.

21. B. Marshall (2002).

22. In 1929 merchandising rights to Pooh characters were sold to a New York entrepreneur, who subsequently licensed them to Disney. Copyright in the Pooh stories remained with the Pooh Property Trust, which sold these visual rights seventy years later.

23. See David Hume Institute (1997) for a sceptical review of current intellectual property law.

24. Baumol (2002).

Chapter 23. Poor States Stay Poor

1. Collins and Lapierre (1975).

2. On Mahalanobis, see Yergin and Stanislaw (1998), chapter 3, and Chakravarty (1988).

3. Rostow (1953).

4. Kotkin (2001).

5. Harrod (1939), Domar (1957). See Solow (1970) for an exposition (Growth Theory).

6. Lewis was also the only economist from a poor country – when he received his prize, he was vice-chancellor of the University of the West Indies, although his principal work was done in England. Amartya Sen is credited to India by the Nobel Prize Committee but his career has been spent in Britain and the United States.

7. Lewis and Schultz (1953).

8. Although India and China are among the largest recipients of aid, because of their size the figure per head is among the lowest. It is clearly an advantage to be a small country as an aid recipient.

9. Dalziel and Lattimore (1999).

10. Rosenstein-Rodan (1943, 1961).

11. 'It was in Cavite that I finally found a piece of unswooshed space, and I found it, oddly enough, in a Nike shoe factory': N. Klein (1999), p. 203.

12. The sad story of the Morogoro shoe factory is told in World Bank (1995).

13. World Bank (2002).

14. A moving obituary in *The Economist* (21 October 1999) concluded: 'he was a magnificent teacher: articulate, questioning, stimulating, caring. He should never have been given charge of an economy.'

15. See for example Desai (2001).

16. Life expectancy at birth in India has risen from 32 years at independence to 63 years today, partly driven by a fall in infant mortality from over 200 per 1,000 live births to below 70; Adlakha (1997), World Bank (2001).

17. Gidoomal (1997).

18. Kurtz is the central character of Joseph Conrad's masterpiece, *Heart of Darkness* (1902). Drawing on Conrad's own experience of the Congo, it is still an extraordinary evocation of the corrupting effect of resource-based wealth. Francis Ford Coppola's remarkable *Apocalypse Now* is based on *Heart of Darkness* and Michaela Wrong picked up the theme in her description of the Mobutu era, *In the Footsteps of Mr Kurtz* (2000).

19. Hochschild (1999) is a shocking account of the Congo under Leopold's rule.

20. The Danish architect Georg Hans Tesling constructed his estate.

21. This history is recounted in Wrong (2000).

22. *New York Times*, 14 September 1982.

23. And there is currently extensive discussion of a formal bankruptcy regime for countries: Rogoff and Zettelmayer (2002).

24. Wrong (2000), pp. 113-14.

25. Maier (2000).

26. Saudi Arabia derives 35 per cent of GDP and 85 per cent of government revenue from oil.

27. T. Friedman (1999), p. 350.

28. Ayittey (1998).

29. A. G. Frank (1967).

30. Prebisch (1950), Singer (1950). Dependency theory is still at the heart of ECLA thinking – see ECLA[W], C. Kay (1989).

31. Though diamond-rich Botswana has been the most successful economy in sub-Saharan Africa.

32. Cardoso and Faletto (1979).

33. Norberg-Hodge (1991).

34. Diamond (1997), pp. 352-3.

35. A long tradition in economics, though not a mainstream one, has seen demand as stimulated by supply. See Veblen (1899), chapter 16, or more recently Galbraith (1986): 'he or she surrenders to the will of the purveyor of the beer, cigarettes, detergent or political purpose.'

36. Turnbull (1961, 1973).

37. B. D. Smith (1995), Flannery (1973).

38. Thompson (1968), Mokyr (1999), Hartley and Crafts (2000), Hartwell (1971).

39. HAPPINESS[W].

40. Freeland (2000), pp. 67-8.

Chapter 24. Who Gets What?

1. Weber (1930, 1947).

2. See Welch (2001), chapter 26, for a description of this process, in which the golf club played a large role.

3. In the last days of the 1990s boom, several CEOs extracted hundreds of millions of dollars from their failing companies: *Financial Times*, 30 July–1 August 2002.

4. Frank and Cook (1995) provide an entertaining exposition of this phenomenon – and its relationship to the division of labour.

5. Afterwards, the successful will wish they had not agreed to this: this is why legal disputes between pop stars and their managers are almost routine.

6. This theory is due to Shubik (1959) and Scarf (1962).

7. The Thurn and Taxis family remains one of the richest in Europe as a result

of the communications monopoly it enjoyed in the Habsburg Empire for three centuries; THURN[W].

8. M. Friedman (1962), p. 142.

9. The ratio of the market value of companies to the value of their tangible assets rose to unprecedented levels during the bubble.

10. Bruck (1989).

11. W. Taylor (1990).

12. Chrystal (1991). In December 1997 Michael Eisner of Disney exercised options worth £348 million: Conyon and Murphy (2000).

13. Bevan (2001), chapter 9.

14. In 2001 the top ten in the Forbes list were Gates, Allen and Ballmer of Microsoft, Ellison of Oracle, Buffett and five members of the Walton family.

15. New England, New York and California account for almost a quarter of US population but only 371 of 3,244 Wal-Mart stores in 2001.

16. Lowenstein (1995).

17. BUFFETT[W].

18. Ortega (1999) provides a more sceptical account.

19. In 2000 action in the English courts and by his brother the Sultan finally brought Jefri's activities to a halt (*Newsweek*, 10 December 2000).

20. Lowenstein (1995), p. 4.

21. *Washington Post*, 4 December 1986.

Chapter 25. Places

1. In 2002 the European Commission proposed substantial reductions and redirection of agricultural support, but these seem likely to be defeated by opposition, particularly from France.

2. Graham (1998).

3. Freeland (2000), S. F. Cohen (2000).

Chapter 26. The American Business Model

1. M. Friedman (1962), p. 25. Friedman's book is probably the best description of the American business model within a framework of social and political philosophy. For a less restrained version, see Gilder (1984).

2. Attitudes to anti-trust litigation against Microsoft are a litmus test of this latter distinction. The editorial pages of the *Wall Street Journal* are passionate in their defence of the beleaguered Gates. Irwin Stelzer, who occupies the

role of ambassador to London for the ABM, takes the other side in his *Sunday Times* columns. Under Clinton's Democrats, the Justice Department pursued the issue vigorously until 2001 but Bush's Republican administration effectively abandoned the case.

3. Williamson (2000*b*), pp. 255–6.

4. An obvious feature of these policies is their consonance with the needs of US banks. This provoked a major row when Stiglitz (2002) drew attention to Stanley Fischer's move from the number two position at the IMF to a senior role in Citibank.

5. 'Changes of policy not in a free market direction are by definition not reforms': Robert Wade, in Chang, Palma and Whittaker (2001), p. 76.

6. Market fundamentalist opposition was led by Jeff Sachs (*Financial Times*, 11 December 1997) and the cheerleaders of the ABM; left opposition by virtually all the anti-capitalist opposition is discussed in the next chapter.

7. 'Even if I didn't much care for the dawn there isn't much I could do about it' (T. Friedman 1999, p. xviii).

8. See successive OECD country surveys, for example.

9. As in Evans *et al.* (1996), Douglas, Richardson and Robson (2002).

10. 'It is difficult to reach definite conclusions about why economic performance has not improved to a greater extent in the light of the substantial policy changes that have taken place, not least because it is hard to be precise about the counterfactual to be used for comparison': OECD (1999); quoted in Kay, *Financial Times*, 30 August 2000.

11. *Wall Street Journal*, 13 June 2002.

12. World Economic Forum (2002), IMD (2002).

13. There are some differences between the World Economic Forum and IMD, and Hong Kong and Singapore often rank ahead of the US in the former's assessment.

14. Economic organization is an influence on social cohesion and while this is hard to measure it is a metric on which both countries would score well.

15. In 1997 manufacturing was 16.6 per cent of US GDP and 19.3 per cent of GDP in the EU.

16. J. A. Kay (1996), chapter 10, provides an extended version of this argument.

17. Jorgensen (1987), Ullman (1988), Fischer (1988).

18. It is quite difficult to find people who acknowledge that their moral stance might require material sacrifice. After searching for quotations to exemplify these positions, I gave up.

19. Dunlap (1996), p. xii.

20. Cited in M. Lewis (1989), p. 54.

21. Rand (1990*a*, 1990*b*).

22. See e.g. OECD (2001) and, for a critique, Henderson (2001).

23. Wilson's observation was made in testimony to the Senate Armed Services Committee on his nomination as Secretary for Defense in the Eisenhower administration (quoted in the *New York Times*, 24 February 1953). It is often reproduced as 'what's good for General Motors is good for America', a significantly different statement.

24. Goethe (1971), p. 45.

25. *New York Times*, 13 September 1970; see also M. Friedman (1962), chapter VIII.

26. Attributed to Ian Gauld, taxonomist at the British Museum, in Vitullo-Martin and Moskin (1994).

27. Walzer (1981).

28. Crossen (2001), p. 213.

29. Wrong (2000), p. 20.

30. Kay, *Financial Times*, 23 July 2000.

31. Gates (1995, 1999).

32. Trump (1987), p. 1.

33. Lowenstein (1995), p. 20.

34. M. Lewis (1989), p. 88.

35. M. Friedman (1962), pp. 26–7.

36. Quoted in Freeland (2000), pp. 67–8.

37. 'I find it difficult to justify either accepting or rejecting [the capitalist ethic] or to justify any alternative principle. I am led to the view that it cannot in and of itself be regarded as an ethical principle; that it must be regarded as instrumental or a corollary of some other principle such as freedom' (M. Friedman 1962, pp. 165–6).

38. Turnbull (1973).

39. Tocqueville (2000 edn.).

Chapter 27. Beyond the American Business Model

1. Forrester, although over 80, has gone on in this vein, most recently in *Une étrange dictature* (2000). *L'Horreur economique* (1996) is available in English as *The Economic Horror*.

2. The situation is even worse than this suggests. After Jack Welch's autobiography, which is worth reading, the best selling pro-business book in Europe is *Who Moved My Cheese?* (Spencer Johnson 1999), whose large print,

vocabulary and sentence structure, plot and illustrations all appear aimed at people with the reading age of elementary school students.

3. Hertz (2001), pp. 6, 188.

4. See for example Coopey and Woodward (1996).

5. Magnusson (2000).

6. See e.g. Shanks (1961), Shonfield (1958, 1965), for an (astonishing today) description of the spirit of the times.

7. This remark is widely quoted but I have not found an original source.

8. The most extreme manifestation of this rationalist, technologically based optimism was the group around Robert Macnamara, which sought to apply techniques developed at the Ford Motor Company to the management of the Vietnam War. See e.g. Halberstam (1992).

9. Giddens (1998), pp. 66, 75–6.

10. 'Your representative owes you, not his industry only, but his judgement; and he betrays, instead of serving you, if he sacrifices it to your opinion': Burke, in Langford (1996), p. 69.

11. Attributed to Oscar Wilde.

12. The 'focus group' is a mechanism for achieving the worst of both worlds: it achieves the triviality and irrationality of participative democracy without the checks on the development of authoritarianism provided by periodic election.

13. Churchill commented: 'I'm told it's a blessing in disguise. If it is, it's very completely disguised': Cooper (1994).

14. T. Friedman (1999) entitles one chapter 'Buy Taiwan, Hold Italy, Sell France' – Bloomberg television criteria have it seems taken over international politics – and T. Frank (2001), pp. 73–8, has an entertaining compendium of anti-French jibes from American newspapers.

15. In 2000 average annual hours worked were 1,656 in France and 1,978 in the United States (source: ILO).

16. Such a book has not been written, but some good recent English-language books on the French exception include Jack (1999), Gordon and Meunier (2001), Zeldin (1997).

17. 'We [the servants] control all the wheels of the State from the Presidency of the Republic to the National Assembly where we are in the majority, passing through a cabinet composed for the most part of civil servants. We control also the judiciary, financial sector trades union and even economic powers; civil servants are at the head of public enterprises and the largest private enterprises as well. This all powerful position conferred on us can only be justified by an exceptional probity in our activities by pre-eminent human and moral qualities – those very qualities which resist selection through

competitive examination – and by constant concern to put the public service at the service of the public': Siedentop (2000), quoting Pierre Secret, *Le Figaro*, 18 June 1999.

18. The high-speed link from London to the coast will not be completed before 2007.

19. Westinghouse, the builder of these power stations, was bought in 1999 by a company owned by the British government.

20. The 'enarchs' are named after ENA, the École Nationale d'Administration, the most prestigious *grande école*.

21. The paradox – which game theory and bargaining theory reveal – is that if you must reach agreement, it becomes more difficult to reach agreement. It is the threat to walk away that forces reasonableness.

22. The experience of 1995 – when Chirac, newly elected, and his premier, Alain Juppé, attempted a Thatcherite confrontation with trade unions and lost – continues to be a major influence on French politics.

23. Crosland's book (1956) was the defining text for Labour's first attempt at modernization between the Attlee and Wilson governments.

24. Benn and Chitty (1996).

25. Giddens (1998), p. 66.

26. Greenspan in Rand (1967).

27. Statement to the French Foreign Minister, Pierre Laval, 13 May 1935, quoted Churchill (1948), chapter 8.

28. *Wall Street Journal*, 8 November 1999.

29. Wriston (1992), p. 45.

30. Friedman, *New York Times*, 13 September 1970.

31. Euchen (1981).

32. See Watrin (1999).

33. Thus Neaman (1990) describes the 'four fundamental pillars of the German *Sozialstaat* – old age pensions, health and accident insurance, employment creation and unemployment insurance, family support.'

34. Turner (2001), p. 372.

35. Classic accounts of redistributive market liberalism can be found in Meade (1964) and Brittan (1996); Turner (2001) is an excellent extended exposition.

36. Brittan (1996), pp. 55–6.

37. See Brittan (1968, 1973).

Chapter 28. The Embedded Market

1. This account owes much to Wolf (2002).

2. These followed many adverse comparisons made in the 1980s between the British and German systems, as in Prais (1983, 1984), Prais and Wagner (1984).

3. Wolf (2002), pp. 75–8.

4. This was also the effect of privatization: the former nationalized industries played a major role in training workers.

5. Even for the sober *Economist*, 'WorldCom's Internet expansion looks unstoppable': 11 September 1997; 'the Enron tale is every bit as remarkable as it seems': 1 June 2000.

6. Andersen was convicted in July 2002 for obstructing justice by destroying papers related to Enron accounts, and Scott Sullivan and David Myers, the senior financial officers of WorldCom, were arrested and charged shortly after the company collapsed.

7. The Dow-Jones index of US stocks reached an all-time high of 11723 on 12 January 2000. By 15 October 2001 (after 11 September and just before the collapse of Enron became evident) it had fallen to 9347 and in July 2002 closed below 7500.

8. Enron executives did go beyond common practice in appointing themselves as personal investors in the off-balance-sheet partnerships they established.

9. Kay, *Financial Times*, 28 April 1999.

10. Heneghan (2000).

11. If Muldoon was the worst Prime Minister of a rich state, Harding must have strong claims to have been the worst President.

12. Dershowitz (2001), Greene (2001), Gillman (2001).

13. Etzioni (1993, 1988).

14. C. Taylor (1989), p. 36.

15. Walzer (1981), p. 395.

16. Gray (1998).

17. 'One key reason why the presidents of large corporations do not, as some radical critics believe, control the United States is that they do not even succeed in controlling their own corporations; . . . that all too often, when imputed organizational skill and power are deployed and the desired effect follows, all that we have witnessed is the same kind of sequence as that to be observed when a clergyman is fortunate enough to pray for rain just before the unpredicted end of a drought': MacIntyre (1981), p. 75.

18. MacIntyre, 'A Partial Response to my Critics', in Horton and Mendus (1994), pp. 285–6.

19. Harvard Business School (1972).
20. Mill (1873).
21. Collins and Porras (1994).

Chapter 29. The Framework of Economic Policy

1. 'Chief executives were made the legal employers of the staff in their departments, with powers to hire and fire, set salaries, and negotiate conditions of employment. Performance distinguishes between the government's interest as owner seeking efficient use of its resources, and as purchaser of services from the department, seeking quality goods and services at the best prices': G. Scott, cited in Douglas, Richardson and Robson (2002), p. 118.
2. Administrative functions of British government – such as benefit payments or issuing passports – are undertaken by over 100 executive or 'next steps' agencies.
3. See the Learmont Report, in Home Office (1995).
4. 'We are committed to eradicating child poverty in 20 years and halving it in 10, to providing employment opportunities for all those who can work, and to breaking the cycle of disadvantage which can perpetuate the effects of poverty throughout people's lives, and from generation to generation': Department for Work and Pensions (2000), p. 1.
5. It is remarkable that Margaret Thatcher, a strongly authoritarian figure, was the most vigorous of modern political leaders in pursuing market-oriented policies. The most plausible explanation is that she simply did not understand the nature of the revolution she promoted. Certainly her lengthy autobiography never addresses the intellectual basis for her policies: the quality of ideas seems to be judged on a combination of her opinion of their proponent and their consonance with her previously expressed opinions.

On her election in 1979, Mrs Thatcher quoted St Francis's prayer: 'where there is discord may we bring harmony; where there is error may we bring truth; where there is doubt may we bring faith.' Little pluralism there – or afterwards.
6. Owen (1999), chapter 9.
7. Newbery and Pollitt (1997).
8. As Easterly (2001) notes (p. 241), it is true even today that development economics texts do not mention corruption, and are written as if government can be assumed to be disinterested. See e.g. Hayami (1997), Todaro (2002).
9. There has been growth in some very corrupt poor countries, most notably

Indonesia. Olson's (2000) distinction between roving and stationary bandits may be relevant here: the corrupt Suharto regime enjoyed power for over thirty years, and had some interest in enlarging the trough in which its snouts were invariably to be found. The equally long-lived regime of Mobutu, however, chose instead to destroy the economic infrastructure of the country.

10. See Yergin and Stanislaw (1998), pp. 11–12, for a discussion of this phrase, which was included in the British Labour Party's constitution until removed by New Labour in 1995.

11. This is true not just in Western Europe, but in poor countries and above all in the former Soviet bloc. When the Soviet Union collapsed its steel-making capacity exceeded that of the United States although its GDP was perhaps a tenth of the size (own data). Eastern European steel-making capacity depressed world prices and would have done so dramatically if it had ever worked properly.

12. Kay, Mayer and Thompson (1986).

13. Wallis and North (1986).

14. Hazledine (1996, 1998).

15. Direct costs of crime – police, courts, prisons – amount to 1.5 per cent of US GDP. Total costs – including private security costs and the opportunity cost of unproductive (imprisoned) labour – can hardly be less than 5 per cent of GDP.

16. Named after James Tobin of Yale University, Tobin taxes are simple sales taxes on cross-border currency trading; Tobin (1978, 1994), ul Haq, Kaul and Grunberg (1996), Eichengreen, Wyplosz and Tobin (1995).

17. While the impact of e-commerce on taxation has been exaggerated – like almost everything to do with e-commerce – the collapse of betting taxation in the UK is an illustration of these possible effects.

18. The passage in which Tom Wolfe's Master of the Universe attempts to explain investment banking to his 7-year-old daughter provides a devastating critique of modern financial services in five hundred words (Wolfe 1987, pp. 226–9).

Chapter 30. A Primer in Economic Policy

1. Caves and Porter (1977).

2. It is with these issues that current competition policy, which focuses on market shares and market power rather than on competition as a process, is typically concerned.

3. Hot coffee has been a problem ever since a US jury awarded $2.9 million

damages to a woman who had spilt a cup of McDonald's coffee over herself; *Wall Street Journal*, 1 September 1994, 2 December 1994.

4. The FSA imposed substantial fines on several leading retail providers, including the two largest, the Prudential and Legal and General.

5. A survey by *Health Which?* of complaints against GPs (12 October 1999) found 79 per cent were dissatisfied with the handling of their complaint. The legal service ombudsman, who oversees the Office of Supervision of Solicitors, states (11 July 2000) that the Office 'habitually takes far too long to do too little' and that there was a 'crisis in the organisation of governance of the legal profession'. She quoted a President of the Law Society who described complainants as 'whingers and grievance mongers'.

6. Kay and Vickers (1988).

7. Despite imaginative proposals to extend their scope, as in Shiller (1993).

8. Over 6 million US citizens are under some form of correctional supervision, of whom 2 million are actually in prison. The prison population of the EU is about 300,000.

9. Hensler *et al.* (2001).

10. 'The new equipment is so boring . . . that the children make up dangerous games, like crashing into the equipment with their bicycles': Howard (2001), p. 4.

11. Twenty years ago I wrote a book (Dilnot, Kay and Morris 1984) which took at face value the stated objectives of the British social security system and showed how benefits could be targeted to relieve poverty with minimum effect on work incentives. I regarded as self-evidently absurd a situation where most households simultaneously paid taxes and received benefits. However, what I derided was not a design flaw but a reflection of a sense of mutual obligations. The symbolism of a structure in which all pay and all receive was significant, as social, but not economic, commentators had understood.

12. In 1999 the major banks, led by Barclays, announced plans to introduce charges for the use of their machines by non-customers. Following extensive adverse publicity, two large but smaller banks (Halifax and Abbey National) scrapped all charges for machine use, and in July 2000 all banks followed suit.

13. See *Financial Times*, 3 December 1986, 26 January 1990.

14. T. Collins (1997), Currie (1994), Flowers (1996).

15. This was probably decisive in ending individual underwriting at Lloyd's.

16. I have written books on the tax and benefit system: Dilnot, Kay and Morris (1984), Kay and King (1990); while I don't now hold all the views I did then, I still urge readers to read (or, better still, buy) them.

17. See Chapter 6, n. 18.

18. See Easterly (2001) for a discussion of some of these issues.

Epilogue

1. Stiglitz (2002).
2. K. Rogoff, *An Open Letter to Joseph Stiglitz*, ROGOFF[W].
3. Bush's chief economic adviser, Laurence Lindsey, described the Enron collapse as a 'tribute to American capitalism': *Business Week*, 28 January 2002.

Glossary

absolute advantage *see* **competitive advantage**

arbitrage the activity of buying a product in one market to resell the identical product in another.

balance of payments the difference between a country's exports and imports (its current account surplus or deficit), which is necessarily matched by a growth or decline in its net asset position in the rest of the world.

bounded rationality choice from within a limited set of alternatives. Used in two different senses. The first (the original, due to Herbert Simon) assumes that the impossibility of assembling sufficient information constrains, largely arbitrarily, the possibilities considered and so people choose alternatives that are 'good enough'. The second (popularized by Oliver Williamson) supposes that rational choices are made from within a subset of all possibilities which is itself chosen rationally, i.e. balancing the costs of obtaining information against the benefits. The first interpretation effectively abandons conventional assumptions of rationality, the other transforms it into meta-rationality.

call option the right to buy a security at a fixed price (even if its market price has risen in the meantime). Thus the upside, but not the downside, of its movements is shared. In return for this, a premium is paid.

comparative advantage a country (or less commonly an individual) has a comparative advantage in the activities which it is relatively best at. See p. 70. Distinguish from competitive (absolute) advantage.

competitive advantage a firm has a competitive (absolute) advantage in activities which it performs better than other firms. Absolute (competitive) advantage governs the activities of firms, while comparative advantage governs the activities of countries and individuals. This is because firms with no competitive (absolute) advantages are pushed out of business, while countries and individuals with no competitive advantage are pushed into low-value activities in which they have comparative advantage.

competitive equilibrium a competitive market in which supply and demand are equal.

competitive market a market in which all buyers and sellers are sufficiently small that none has a significant effect on the price.

consumer surplus the difference between the maximum a purchaser would be willing to pay for a good and the price.

convexity a convex set has the property that any average of two points in the set is also in the set. A convex curve has the property that any line that joins two points on it lies above the curve. The practical implication of convexity is that averages are preferred to extremes.

derivative a security whose value is based on (derived from) the value of another security – see, for example, **put option** and **call option**.

division of labour the breaking down of tasks into a number of specialized activities.

economic rent the amount which a firm, individual or other resource is paid in an activity above what is needed to attract it to that activity. It is competition between buyers when the factor is scarce which creates economic rent.

economies of scale falling average costs of production which are the result of higher levels of output.

efficient market hypothesis the theory that information about the values of securities is fully incorporated in their prices. It takes a weak form (past data conveys no information), a semi-strong form (all publicly available information is incorporated) or a strong form (all information, whether public or not, is incorporated).

equity premium the difference between returns on stocks (shares) and returns on risk-free assets.

futures contract an agreement to buy or sell a commodity or security at a future date at a fixed price agreed now.

general (competitive) equilibrium a position in which all competitive markets in an economic system are simultaneously in equilibrium.

gross domestic product the total value of output (before depreciation) produced within the boundaries of a state.

gross national product the value of output (before depreciation) produced by factors of production owned by residents of a state. National and domestic products differ from each other by the amount of net property income from overseas.

incentive compatibility a property of allocation mechanisms under which no agent can gain an advantage by strategic behaviour.

information asymmetry a characteristic of a market in which one side (buyer or seller) is better informed about the properties of the good or service than the other (seller or buyer).

intellectual property rights created by copyright, patent or trademark legislation and associated regulations.

market anomalies observed deviations from the efficient market hypothesis.

mercantilism a theory of international trade (widely held before Adam Smith and still adhered to by some devotees of DIY economics) which draws an analogy between the exports and imports of states and the revenues and expenses of firms.

noise trader a buyer or seller (especially in securities markets) whose behaviour does not reflect views about the fundamental value (prospective earnings etc.) of what he or she is buying.

Pareto efficiency the property of an allocation of resources in which no one can be made better off without making someone else worse off.

Pareto improvement a change which makes some people better off and no one worse off.

path-dependency a dynamic process in which behaviour is affected indefinitely by initial conditions.

primary market the initial sale of a good or service (especially of a security).

productivity labour productivity is output per unit of labour (per head, per hour worked). Total factor productivity is output per unit of all inputs (including, in particular, capital inputs). Productivity without qualification usually (but not always) refers to labour productivity.

purchasing power parity the rate of exchange between different currencies at which a representative bundle of goods would cost the same in each country or currency zone.

put option the right to sell a security at a fixed price at a future date, even if its market price has subsequently fallen.

random walk theory the theory that future security price movements are independent of past movements.

secondary market (especially in securities markets) the resale of an item which has already been sold in a primary market.

winner's curse a property of allocation mechanisms in which the winner overpays for the good, service or security received. A failure of incentive compatibility.

References

Adams, J., 1995, *Risk*, London, UCL Press.

Adlakha, A., 1997, *International Brief: Population Trends in India*, US Department of Commerce.

Akerlof, G., 1970, 'The Market for Lemons: Quality Uncertainty and the Market Mechanism', *Quarterly Journal of Economics*, 84, August, 488–500.

—— 1984, *An Economic Theorist's Book of Tales*, Cambridge, Cambridge University Press.

Albert, M., 1990, *Capitalisme contre capitalisme*, Paris, Seuil; trans. P. Haviland as *Capitalism vs Capitalism*, London, Whurr, 1993.

Alchian, A. A., 1950, 'Uncertainty, Evolution and Economic Theory', *Journal of Political Economy*, 58, 211–21.

Allais, M., 1953, 'Le Comportement de l'homme rationnel devant le risque: critique des postulats et axioms de l'école américaine, *Econometrica*, 21 (4), October, 503–46.

Amsden, A. H., 1989, *Asia's Next Giant: South Korea and Late Industrialization*, New York and Oxford, Oxford University Press.

Aristotle, 1984, *Politics*, ed. J. Barnes, Princeton, Princeton University Press.

Arrow, K. J., 1950, 'A Difficulty in the Concept of Social Welfare', *Journal of Political Economy*, 58, 328–46.

—— 1951a, *Social Choice and Individual Values*, London, Chapman & Hall.

—— 1951b, *An Extension of the Basic Theorems of Classical Welfare Economics*, Berkeley, University of California Press.

—— 1971, *Essays in the Theory of Risk-bearing*, Amsterdam and London, North-Holland.

—— and Debreu, G., 1954, 'Existence of an Equilibrium for a Competitive Economy', *Econometrica*, 22 (3), July, 265–90.

—— and Hahn, F. H., 1971, *General Competitive Analysis*, Edinburgh, Oliver & Boyd.

Arthur, W. B., 1989, 'Competing Technologies, Increasing Returns, and Lock-in by Historical Events', *Economic Journal*, 99, March, 116–31.

Atkinson, A. B., 1970, 'On the Measurement of Inequality', *Journal of Economic Theory*, 2, 244–63.

—— 1983, *The Economics of Inequality*, Oxford, Oxford University Press.

Augar, P., 2000, *The Death of Gentlemanly Capitalism: The Rise and Fall of London's Investment Banks*, Harmondsworth, Penguin Books.

Aumann, R. J., 1964, 'Markets with a Continuum of Traders', *Econometrica*, 32, 39–50.

Axelrod, R., 1984, *The Evolution of Co-operation*, New York, Basic Books.

—— 1997, *The Complexity of Cooperation: Agent Based Models of Competition and Collaboration*, Princeton, Princeton University Press.

Ayittey, G. B. N., 1998, *Africa in Chaos*, Basingstoke, Macmillan.

Ball, D. B., 1991, *Financial Failure and Confederate Defeat*, Urbana, University of Illinois Press.

Bank of England, 1995, *Report of the Board of Banking Supervision: Inquiry into the Circumstances of the Collapse of Barings*, London, Bank of England.

Barth, J. R., 1991, *The Great Savings and Loan Debacle*, Washington, DC, American Enterprise Institute Press.

Barzel, Y., 1997, *Economic Analysis of Property Rights*, 2nd edn., Cambridge, Cambridge University Press.

Bass, T. A., 1999, *The Predictors*, London, Allen Lane.

Basu, K., 2000, *Prelude to Political Economy: A Study of the Social and Political Foundations of Economics*, Oxford, Oxford University Press.

Bathurst, B., 1999, *The Lighthouse Stevensons*, London, HarperCollins.

Bator, F. M., 1958, 'The Anatomy of Market Failure', *Quarterly Journal of Economics*, 72 (3), August, 351–79.

Baumol, W. J., 2002, *The Free-market Innovation Machine: Analysing the Growth Miracle of Capitalism*, Princeton and Oxford, Princeton University Press.

Becker, G. S., 1962, 'Irrational Behaviour and Economic Theory', *Journal of Political Economy*, 70, 1–13.

—— 1968, 'Crime and Punishment: An Economic Approach', *Journal of Political Economy*, 76 (2), March–April, 169–217.

—— 1973, 'A Theory of Marriage: Part I', *Journal of Political Economy*, 81 (4), July–August, 813–46.

—— 1974, 'A Theory of Marriage: Part II', *Journal of Political Economy*, 82 (2), March–April, S11–S26.

—— 1981, *A Treatise on the Family*, Cambridge, Mass., Harvard University Press.

—— 1993, 'The Economic Way of Looking at Behaviour (Nobel Lecture)', *Journal of Political Economy*, 101 (3), June, 385–409.

Belsky, G., and Gilovich, T., 2000, *Why Smart People Make Big Money Mistakes*, New York, Fireside.

Benartzi, S., and Thaler, R. H., 1995, 'Myopic Loss Aversion and the Equity Premium', *Quarterly Journal of Economics*, February, 73–92.

Benn, C., and Chitty, C., 1996, *Thirty Years On: Is Comprehensive Education Alive and Well or Struggling to Survive?*, Harmondsworth, Penguin.

Berlin, I., 2000, *The Power of Ideas*, ed. H. Hardy, London, Chatto & Windus.

Bernstein, P. L., 1996, *Against the Gods: The Remarkable Story of Risk*, New York and Chichester, John Wiley and Sons Inc.

Berry, C. J., 1997, *Social Theory of the Scottish Enlightenment*, Edinburgh, Edinburgh University Press.

Bertram, J. G., 1865, *Harvest of the Sea*, London, John Murray.

Bethell, L. (ed.), 1993, *Argentina since Independence*, Cambridge, Cambridge University Press.

Bevan, J., 2001, *The Rise and Fall of Marks and Spencer*, London, Profile.

Binmore, K. G., 1994, *Game Theory and the Social Contract*, Cambridge, Mass., MIT Press.

—— 1998, *Just Playing*, London and Cambridge, Mass., MIT Press.

Black, D., 1958, *The Theory of Committees and Elections*, Cambridge, Cambridge University Press.

Black, F., and Scholes, M., 1973, 'The Pricing of Options and Corporate Liabilities', *Journal of Political Economy*, 81, May–June, 637–59.

Blackmore, S., 1999, *The Meme Machine*, Oxford, Oxford University Press.

Blinder, A. S., 1974, 'The Economics of Brushing Teeth', *Journal of Political Economy*, 82, July–August, 887–91.

Bloomberg, M., and Walker, M., 2001, *Bloomberg on Bloomberg*, New York, Bloomberg.

Bobrow, M., and Thomas, S., 2001, 'Patents in a Genetic Age', *Nature*, 409, 15 February, 763–4.

Bodanis, D., 2000, $E=MC^2$: *A Biography of the World's Most Famous Equation*, London, Macmillan.

Borgers, T., and Dustmann, C., 2001, 'Strange Bids', *CEPR Discussion Paper*, 3072, November.

Borges, J. L., 1946, 'Of Exactitude in Science', in his *A Universal History of Infamy*, trans. N. T. di Giovanni, New York, Dutton, 1972.

Bower, T., 1995, *Maxwell: The Final Verdict*, London, HarperCollins.

—— 2001, *Fayed: The Unauthorized Biography*, London, Pan.

Bowlby, J., 1991, *Charles Darwin*, London, Pimlico.

Boyle, D., 2000, *The Tyranny of Numbers: Why Counting Can't Make Us Happy*, London, HarperCollins.

Brash, D. T., 1996, *New Zealand's Remarkable Reforms: 5th Annual Hayek Memorial Lecture*, London, Institute of Economic Affairs.

Brealey, R. A., and Myers, S. C., 1981–1999, *Principles of Corporate Finance*, 6 edns., New York and London, McGraw-Hill.

Breiter, H. C., *et al.*, 2001, 'Functional Imaging of Neural Responses to Expectancy and Experience of Monetary Gains and Losses', *Neuron*, 30, May, 619–39.

Brittan, S., 1968, *Left or Right: The Bogus Dilemma*, London, Secker & Warburg.

—— 1973, *Is There an Economic Consensus? An Attitude Survey*, London, Macmillan.

—— 1996, *Capitalism with a Human Face*, London, Fontana Press.

—— 1998, *Essays, Moral, Political, Economic*, Edinburgh, University of Edinburgh Press.

Broadie, A. (ed.), 1997, *The Scottish Enlightenment: An Anthology*, Edinburgh, Canongate.

Bruck, C., 1989, *The Predators' Ball: The Inside Story of Drexel Burnham and the Rise of the Junk Bond Raiders*, New York, Penguin.

Brunekreeft, G., 1997, *Coordination and Competition in the Electricity Pool of England and Wales*, Baden-Baden, Nomos-Verlag.

Buchan, J., 1997, *Frozen Desire: An Enquiry into the Meaning of Money*, London, Picador.

Buchanan, J., and Stubblebine, W. C., 1962, 'Externality', *Economica*, 29, 371–84.

—— and Tollison, R. D. (eds.), 1972, *Theory of Public Choice: Political Applications of Economics*, Ann Arbor, University of Michigan Press.

—— and Tollison, R. D. (eds.), 1984, *Theory of Public Choice: II*, Ann Arbor, University of Michigan Press.

—— and Tulloch, G., 1962, *The Calculus of Consent*, Ann Arbor, University of Michigan Press.

Buchet, M., 1993, *La Colombe d'Or: St Paul de Vence*, Paris, Éditions Assouline.

Buchholz, T., 1999, *New Ideas from Dead Economists*, New York, Plume.

Bulow, J., and Klemperer, P., 2002, 'Prices and the Winner's Curse', *Rand Journal of Economics*, 33 (1), Spring, 1–21.

Bunday, B. D., 1996, *An Introduction to Queuing Theory*, London, Arnold.

Burgess, S., and Rees, H., 1996, 'Job Tenure in Britain 1975–1992', *Economic Journal*, 106, 334–44.

Burn, D., 1978, *Nuclear Power and the Energy Crisis: Politics and the Atomic Industry*, London, Macmillan Press.

Butters, L., 2000, *Bletchley Park: Home of Station X*, Andover, Pitkin Unichrome.

Buzo, A., 1999, *The Guerrilla Dynasty: Politics and Leadership in North Korea*, Boulder, Colo., Westview Press.

Calavita, K., Pontell, H. N. and Tillman, R. H., 1997, *Big Money Game, Fraud and Politics in the Savings and Loan Crisis*, Berkeley and London, University of California Press.

Cannan, E., 1927, *An Economist's Protest*, London, P. S. King.

Capen, E., Clapp, R. and Campbell, N., 1971, 'Competitive Bidding in High-risk Situations', *Journal of Petroleum Technology*, 23 (1), 641–53.

Cardoso, F. H., and Faletto, E., 1979, *Dependency and Development in Latin America*, trans. M. M. Urquidi, Berkeley, University of California Press.

Carstens, P., 2001, *In the Company of Diamonds: De Beers, Kleinzee, and the Control of a Town*, Athens, Ohio, Ohio University Press.

Cassidy, J., 2002, *Dot.con: The Greatest Story Ever Sold*, London, Allen Lane.

Castles, Ian, 1998, 'The Mismeasurement of Nations: A Review Essay on the Human Development Report 1998', *Population and Development Review*, 24 (4), December, 831–45.

Caves, R., and Porter, M., 1977, 'From Entry Barriers to Mobility Barriers', *Quarterly Journal of Economics*, 91, 241–61.

Cellan-Jones, R., 2001, *Dot.bomb: The Rise and Fall of dot.com Britain*, London, Aurum Press.

Certeau, M. de, 1984, *The Practice of Everyday Life*, Berkeley, University of California Press.

Ceruzzi, P. E., 1998, *A History of Modern Computing*, Cambridge, Mass., and London, MIT Press.

Chakravarty, S., 1988, 'Mahalanobis, P. C.', in J. Eatwell, M. Milgate, and P. Newman (eds.), *The New Palgrave: A Dictionary of Economics*, Basingstoke, Palgrave Macmillan.

Chandler, Jr., A. D., 1963, *Strategy and Structure: Chapters in the History of the Industrial Enterprise*, Cambridge, Mass., MIT Press.

Chang, H. J., Palma, G. and Whittaker, D. H. (eds.), 2001, *Financial Liberalization and the Asian Crisis*, Basingstoke, Palgrave Macmillan.

Chang, J., 1992, *Wild Swans: Three Daughters of China*, London, Harper-Collins.

Chernow, R., 1998, *The Life of John D. Rockefeller*, London, Little, Brown.

Chrystal, G., 1991, *In Search of Excess*, New York, Norton.

Church, R., 1996, 'Deconstructing Nuffield: The Evolution of Managerial Culture in the British Motor Industry', *Economic History Review*, 3, 561–83.

Churchill, W. S., 1948, *The Second World War*, vol. 1: *The Gathering Storm*, London, Cassell.

Clark, A. E., and Oswald, A. J., 2002, 'A Simple Statistical Method for Measuring How Life Events Affect Happiness', *Working Paper, University of Warwick*.

Clark, R. W., 1979, *Einstein: The Life and Times*, London, Hodder & Stoughton.

Cohen, S. F., 2000, *Failed Crusade: America and the Tragedy of Post-Communist Russia*, New York and London, Norton.

Cohen, S. M., 1982, 'For General Electric, Planning Crowned with Success (sic)', *Planning Review*, March.

Collins, J. C., and Porras, J. I., 1994, *Built to Last: Successful Habits of Visionary Companies*, New York, HarperBusiness.

Collins, L., and Lapierre, D., 1975, *Freedom at Midnight*, London, Collins.

Collins, T., with Bickwell, D., 1997, *Crash: Ten Easy Ways to Avoid a Computer Disaster*, London, Simon & Schuster.

Condorcet, Marquis de, 1785, *Essai sur l'application de l'analyse à la probabilité des décisions rendues à la pluralité des vois*, Paris.

Conrad, J., 1973, *Heart of Darkness* (1902), Harmondsworth, Penguin Books.

Conyon, M. J., and Murphy, K. J., 2000, 'The Prince and the Pauper', *Economic Journal*, 110 (467), 640–71.

Cooper, D., 1994, 'Winston and Clementine', *Finest Hour* (journal of the Churchill Centre), 83, Second Quarter.

Coopey, R., and Woodward, N. (eds.), 1996, *Britain in the 1970s: The Troubled Economy*, London, UCL Press.

Coyle, D., 2001, *Paradoxes of Prosperity: Why the New Capitalism Benefits All*, New York and London, Texere.

Crabtree, J., Duffy, G. and Pearce, J. (eds.), 1987, *The Great Tin Crash*, London, Latin America Bureau.

Cronin, H., 1991, *The Ant and the Peacock*, Cambridge, Cambridge University Press.

Crosland, C. A. R., 1956, *The Future of Socialism*, London, Jonathan Cape.

Crossen, C., 2001, *The Rich and How They Got That Way*, London, Nicholas Brealey.

Csikszentmihalyi, M., 1992, *Flow: The Psychology of Happiness*, London, Rider.

—— 1997, *Living Well: The Psychology of Everyday Life*, London, Weidenfeld & Nicolson.

Currie, W., 1994, 'The Strategic Management of a Large Scale IT Project in the Financial Services Sector', *New Technology, Work and Employment*, 9, (1), 19–29.

Dalziel, P., and Lattimore, R., 1999, *The New Zealand Macroeconomy: A Briefing on the Reforms*, 3rd edn., Greenlane, New Zealand, and Oxford, Oxford University Press.

Darwin, C. R., 1859, *On the Origin of Species by Means of Natural Selection*, ed. G. Beer, Oxford, Oxford University Press, 1996.

Dasgupta, P., 1993, *An Inquiry into Wellbeing and Destitution*, Oxford, Clarendon Press.

David, F. N., 1993, *Games, Gods and Gambling*, Mineola, NY, Dover Publications.

David, P. A., 1985, 'Clio and the Economics of QWERTY', *American Economic Review*, 75 (2), May, 332–7.

David Hume Institute, 1997, *Innovation, Incentive and Reward*, Edinburgh, Edinburgh University Press.

Davidson, R. J., 2000, 'Affective Style, Psychopathology and Resilience', *American Psychologist*, November, 1196–214.

Davies, K., 2001, *The Sequence: Inside the Race for the Human Genome*, London, Weidenfeld & Nicolson.

Dawkins, R., 1989, *The Selfish Gene*, new edn., Oxford, Oxford University Press.
—— 1991, *The Blind Watchmaker*, new edn., London, Penguin Books.

Debreu, G., 1957, *Stochastic Choice and Cardinal Utility*, New Haven, Cowles Foundation, Yale University.
—— 1973, *Theory of Value: An Axiomatic Analysis of Economic Equilibrium*, New Haven, Yale University Press.

Del Mar, A., 1895, *History of Monetary Systems*, London, Effingham Wilson.

Demsetz, H., 1964, 'The Exchange and Enforcement of Property Rights', *Journal of Law and Economics*, October, 11–26.
—— 1967, 'Towards a Theory of Property Rights', *American Economic Review*, 57 (2), 347–59.

Denham, A., 2001, *Keith Joseph*, Chesham, Acumen.

Department for Work and Pensions, 2000, *The Changing Welfare State: Opportunity for All: One Year On: Making a Difference*, Second Annual Report, London, HMSO.

Department of Energy, 1976, *The Structure of the Electricity Supply Industry in England and Wales: Report of the Committee of Inquiry*, Cmnd. 6388, London, HMSO.

Dershowitz, A. M., 2001, *Supreme Injustice: How the High Court Hijacked Election 2000*, Oxford, Oxford University Press.

Desai, A. V., 2001, 'The Economics and Politics of Transition to an Open Market Economy', *Prime Minister's Advisory Council Report, Technical Paper*, 155.

Desmond, A., and Moore, J., 1991, *Darwin: The Life of a Tormented Evolutionist*, New York, W. W. Norton & Co. Inc.

Diamond, J. M., 1997, *Guns, Germs and Steel: The Fates of Human Societies*, London, Jonathan Cape.

Dickens, A. G., 1977, *The Age of Humanism and Reformation: Europe in the Fourteenth, Fifteenth and Sixteenth Centuries*, Englewood Cliffs, NJ, and London, Prentice-Hall.

DiClerico, R., 1990, *The American Presidents*, 3rd edn., Englewood Cliffs, NJ, and London, Prentice-Hall.

Dilnot, A. W., Kay, J. A. and Morris, C. N., 1984, *The Reform of Social Security*, Oxford, Clarendon Press.

Dimson, E., Marsh P. and Staunton, M., 2002, *Triumph of the Optimists: 101 Years of Global Investment Returns*, Princeton, Princeton University Press.

Dixit, A. K., and Nalebuff, B. J., 1991, *Thinking Strategically*, New York, W. W. Norton & Co. Inc.

Dixon, L. S., 1996, *Fixing Superfund*, Santa Monica, Calif., Rand Institute for Civil Justice.

Domar, E. D., 1957, *Essays in the Theory of Economic Growth*, New York, Oxford University Press.

Douglas, M., and Wildavsky, A., 1982, *Risk and Culture: An Essay on the Selection of Technical and Environmental Dangers*, Berkeley and London, University of California Press.

Douglas, R., Richardson, R. and Robson, S., 2002, *Spending Without Reform*, London, Reform.

Downs, A., 1957, *An Economic Analysis of Democracy*, New York, Harper and Row.

Dunham, M., 1963, *George Westinghouse: Young Inventor*, London, Athenaeum.

Dunlap, A. J., with Andelman, B., 1996, *Mean Business: How I Save Bad Companies and Make Good Companies Great*, New York, Fireside.

Durham, W. H., 1991, *Coevolution: Genes, Culture and Human Diversity*, Stanford, Calif., Stanford University Press.

Dworkin, R., 1977, *Taking Rights Seriously*, London, Duckworth.

—— 1984, 'Rights as Trumps', in J. Waldron (ed.), *Theories of Rights*, Oxford, Clarendon, 153–67.

Easterlin, R., 1974, 'Does Economic Growth Improve the Human Lot?', in P. A. David and W. B. Melvin (eds.), *Nations and Households and Economic Growth*, Palo Alto, Calif., Stanford University Press.

Easterly, W., 2001, *The Elusive Quest for Growth: Economists' Adventures and Misadventures in the Tropics*, Cambridge, Mass., and London, MIT Press.

Easton, B., 1994, 'Economic and Other Ideas behind the New Zealand Reforms', *Oxford Review of Economic Policy*, 10 (3), 78–94.

Eatwell, J., Milgate, M. and Newman, P. (eds.), 1988, *The New Palgrave: A Dictionary of Economics*, Basingstoke, Palgrave Macmillan.

Economist Intelligence Unit, 2002, *Country Profile: North Korea 2002/2003*, London, Economist Intelligence Unit.

'Éditions 1999', 1999, *Un ami de Cézanne et van Gogh: le docteur Gachet*, Paris, Éditions de la Réunion des Musées Nationaux.

Ehrbar, A., 1998, *EVA: The Real Key to Creating Wealth*, New York, John Wiley & Sons.

Eichengreen, B., Wyplosz, C. and Tobin, J., 1995, 'Two Cases for Sand in the Wheels of International Finance', *Economic Journal*, 105, January, 162–72.

Enever, T., 1994, *Britain's Best Kept Secret: Ultra's Base at Bletchley Park*, Stroud, Alan Sutton.

Engerman, S. L., and Zallman, R. Z., 1986, *Measuring the Transaction Sector* (NBER Studies in Income and Wealth), Chicago, University of Chicago Press.

Etcoff, N. L., 1994, 'Beauty and the Beholder', *Nature*, 368, 17 March.

Etzioni, A., 1988, *The Moral Dimension: Towards a New Economics*, New York, Free Press.

—— 1993, *Support of Community: The Reinvention of American Society*, New York, Touchstone.

Euchen, W., 1981, *The German Social Market Economies*, Oxford, Basil Blackwell.

Evans, L., Grimes, A., Wilkinson, B. and Teece, D., 1996, 'Economic Reform in New Zealand 1984–95: The Pursuit of Efficiency', *Journal of Economic Literature*, 34 (4), December, 1856–902.

Fama, E. F., and French, K. R., 2001, 'Disappearing Dividends', *Journal of Financial Economics*, 60, 3–43.

Fay, S., 1996, *The Collapse of Barings*, London, Arrow.

Fearon, P., and Moran, A., 1999, *Privatising Victoria's Electricity Distribution*, Melbourne, Institute of Public Affairs.

Ferguson, A., 1767, *An Essay on the History of Civil Society*, ed. Fania Oz-Salzberger, New York, Cambridge University Press, 1996.

Ferguson, N., 2001, *The Cash Nexus: Money and Power in the Modern World, 1700–2000*, London, Allen Lane The Penguin Press.

Firebaugh, G., 1999, 'Empirics of World Income Inequality', *American Journal of Sociology*, 104, May, 1597–630.

Fischer, S., 1988, 'Symposium on the Slowdown in Productivity Growth', *Journal of Economic Perspectives*, 2 (4) Fall, 3–7.

Fisher, D. E., 1997, *Tube: The Invention of Television*, Fort Washington, Pa., Harvest Books.

Flannery, K., 1973, 'The Origins of Agriculture', *Annual Reviews of Anthropology*, 2, 271–310.

Flatow, I., 1992, *They All Laughed – From Lightbulbs to Lasers: The Fascinating Stories Behind the Great Inventions that have Changed our Lives*, HarperCollins, New York, 1992.

Flowers, S., 1996, *Software Failure: Management Failure*, Chichester, Wiley.

Forrester, V., 1996, *L'Horreur économique*, Paris, Fayard, trans. as *The Economic Horror*, Cambridge, Polity Press, 1999.

—— 2000, *Une étrange dictature*, Paris, Fayard.

Forster, E. M., 1982, *Alexandria: A History and a Guide*, with an introduction by L. Durrell, new edn., London, Michael Haag.

Frank, A. G., 1967, *Capitalism and Underdevelopment in Latin America: Historical Studies of Chile and Brazil*, New York and London, Monthly Review Press.

—— 1969, *Latin America: Underdevelopment or Revolution: Essays on the Development of Underdevelopment and the Immediate Enemy*, New York and London, Monthly Review Press.

Frank, R. H., 1985, *Choosing the Right Pond*, New York, Oxford University Press.

—— 1988, *Passions within Reason: The Strategic Role of the Emotions*, New York and London, Alton.

—— and Cook, P. J., 1995, *The Winner-Take-All Society*, Harmondsworth, Penguin Books.

Frank, T., 2001, *One Market under God: Extreme Capitalism, Market Populism and the End of Economic Democracy*, London, Secker & Warburg.

Fraser, P. M., 1984, *Ptolemaic Alexandria*, Oxford, Clarendon Press.

Freedland, J., 1998, *Bring Home the Revolution: How Britain can Live the American Dream*, London, Fourth Estate.

Freedom House, 2001, *Freedom in the World: The Annual Survey of Political Rights and Civil Liberties*, New York, Freedom.

—— 2002, *Freedom in the World: The Annual Survey of Political Rights and Civil Liberties*, New York, Freedom.

Freeland, C., 2000, *Sale of the Century: The Inside Story of the Second Russian Revolution*, New York, Times Books.

Freiberger, P., and Swaine, M., 2000, *Fire in the Valley: The Making of the Personal Computer*, New York, McGraw-Hill.

Friedman, M., 1953, 'The Methodology of Positive Economics', in his *Essays in Positive Economics*, Chicago, Chicago University Press and Cambridge, Cambridge University Press, 3–43.

—— with Friedman, R. D., 1962, *Capitalism and Freedom*, Chicago and London, University of Chicago Press.

Friedman, T., 1999, *The Lexus and the Olive Tree*, London, HarperCollins.

Fry, M. (ed.), 1992, *Adam Smith's Legacy*, London, Routledge.

Fudenberg, D., and Tirole, J., 1991, *Game Theory*, Cambridge, Mass., MIT Press.

Fukuyama, F., 1989, 'The End of History', *National Interest*, Summer, 3–18.

—— 1992, *The End of History and the Last Man*, London, Hamilton.

Furbotn, E. G., and Pejovich, S., 1972, 'Property Rights and Economic Theory: A Survey of Recent Literature', *Journal of Economic Literature*, 10 (4), December, 1137–62.

Gachet, P., with comments by Mothe, A., 1994, *Les 70 jours de van Gogh à Auvers*, Saint-Ouen-L'Aumône, Éditions du Valhermeil.

Galbraith, J. K., 1986, *The Anatomy of Power*, London, Hamish Hamilton.

Gates, B., with Myhrvold, N. and Rinearson, P., 1995, *The Road Ahead*, London, Viking.

—— with Hemingway, C., 1999, *Business @ the Speed of Thought: Using a Digital Nervous System*, Harmondsworth, Penguin Books.

Geertz, C., 1973, *The Interpretation of Cultures*, New York, Basic Books.

Giddens, A., 1998, *The Third Way: The Renewal of Social Democracy*, Malden, Mass., and Cambridge, Polity Press.

Gidoomal, R., 1997, *The UK Maharajas: Inside the South Asian Success Story*, London, Nicholas Brealey.

Gigerenzer, G., and Selten, R. (eds.), 2001, *Bounded Rationality: The Adaptive Toolbox*, Cambridge, Mass., and London, MIT Press.

—— et al., 1999, *Simple Heuristics that Make us Smart*, New York, Oxford University Press.

Gilder, G. F., 1984, *The Spirit of Enterprise*, New York, Simon & Schuster.

Gillman, H., 2001, *The Votes that Counted: How the Court Decided the 2000 Presidential Election*, Chicago, University of Chicago Press.

Gintis, H., 2000, *Game Theory Evolving: A Problem Centered Introduction to Modeling Strategic Interaction*, Princeton, Princeton University Press.

Gladwell, M., 2000, *The Tipping Point: How Little Things can Make a Big Difference*, London, Little, Brown.

Gleick, J., 1988, *Chaos: Making a New Science*, London, Heinemann.

Godfrey, D. G., and Sterling, C. H., 2001, *Philo T. Farnsworth: The Father of Television*, Salt Lake City, University of Utah Press.

Goethe, J. W. von, 1971, *Elective Affinities* (1809), trans. with introduction by R. J. Hollingdale, London, Penguin.

Goodhart, C., 1984, *Monetary Theory and Practice: The UK Experience*, London, Macmillan.

Goold, M. and Campbell, A., 1987, *Strategies and Styles: The Role of the Centre in Managing Diversified Corporations*, Oxford, Basil Blackwell.

Gopnik, A., 2001, *Paris to the Moon*, London, Vintage.

Gordon, P. H., and Meunier, S., 2001, *The French Challenge: Adapting to Globalization*, Washington, DC, Brookings Institution Press.

Gottschalk, P., and Smeeding, T. M., 1997, 'Cross-national Comparisons of Earnings and Income Inequality', *Journal of Economic Literature*, 35, June, 633–87.

Graham, L. R., 1998, *What have we Learned about Science and Technology from the Russian Experience?*, Palo Alto, Calif., Stanford University Press.

Gray, J., 1993, *Beyond the New Right: Markets, Government and the Common Environment*, London and New York, Routledge.

—— 1998, *False Dawn: The Delusions of Global Capitalism*, London, Granta.

Green, R. J., 1995, 'The Cost of Nuclear Power Compared with Alternatives to the Magnox Programme', *Oxford Economic Papers*, 47, 513–24.

Greene, A., 2001, *Understanding the 2000 Election: A Guide to the Legal Battles that Decided the Presidency*, New York and London, New York University Press.

Greenfield, S. A., 2000, *The Private Life of the Brain*, London, Allen Lane Penguin.

Greenspan, A., 1963, 'The Assault on Integrity', in A. Rand, 1967, *Capitalism: The Unknown Ideal*, New York, Signet.

Gregory, T., 1962, *Ernest Oppenheimer and the Economic Development of Southern Africa*, Cape Town, Oxford University Press.

Grigg, D., 1992, *The Transformation of Agriculture in the West*, Oxford, Basil Blackwell.

Groves, T., and Ledyard, J. O., 1977, 'Optimal Allocation of Public Goods: A Solution to the Free Rider Problem', *Econometrica*, 45, 783–809.

—— and —— 1980, 'The Existence of Efficient and Incentive Compatible Equilibria with Public Goods', *Econometrica*, 48 (6), September, 1487–506.

Haigh, J., 1999, *Taking Chances: Winning with Probability*, Oxford, Oxford University Press.

Hair, P. E. H., 1971, 'Deaths from Violence in Britain: A Tentative Survey', *Population Studies*, 25 (1), 5–24.

Halberstam, D., 1987, *The Reckoning*, London, Bloomsbury Publishing.

—— 1992, *The Brightest and Best*, New York, Fawcett.

Hamermesh, D. S., and Soss, N. M., 1974, 'An Economic Theory of Suicide', *Journal of Political Economy*, 82 (1), January–February, 83–98.

Hamilton, W. O., 1964, 'The Genetical Evolution of Social Behaviour', *Journal of Theoretical Biology*, 7, 1–52.

Hannah, L., 1976, *The Rise of the Corporate Economy*, London, Methuen.

—— 1979, *Electricity before Nationalisation: A Study of the Development of the Electricity Supply Industry in Britain to 1948*, London, Macmillan.

—— 1982, *Engineers, Managers and Politicians: The First Fifteen Years of Nationalised Electricity Supply in Britain*, London, Macmillan.

Hardin, G., 1968, 'The Tragedy of the Commons', *Science*, 162, 1243–8.

Hardt, M., and Negri, A., 2000, *Empire*, Cambridge, Mass., and London, Harvard University Press.

Hardy, G. H., Littlewood, J. E. and Polya, G., 1934, *Inequalities*, Cambridge, Cambridge University Press.

Harkness, S., and Machin, S., 1999, *Graduate Earnings in Britain 1974–1995*, DfEE Research Report, 95, London, Department for Education and Employment.

Harrison, L. E., and Huntington, S. P. (eds.), 2000, *Culture Matters*, New York, Basic Books.

Harrod, R., 1939, 'An Essay in Dynamic Theory', *Economic Journal*, 49 (193), March, 14–33.

Hartley, K., and Crafts, N., 2000, 'Simulating the Two Views of the British Industrial Revolution', *Journal of Economic History*, 60 (3), September, 819–41.

Hartley, S., 2001, *Mrs P's Journey: The Remarkable Story of the Woman who Created the A–Z Map*, London, Simon & Schuster.

Hartwell, R. M., 1971, *The Industrial Revolution and Economic Growth*, London, Methuen.

Harvard Business School, 1972, *Prelude Corporation*, Harvard Business School Case Study, Cambridge, Mass., Harvard Business School.

Havel, V., 1985, *The Power of the Powerless: Citizens against the State in Central-eastern Europe*, London, Hutchinson.

Havermesh, R. B., 1986, *Making Strategy Work*, New York, Wiley.

Hay, K., and Moore, P., 1998, *The Caterpillar doesn't Know: How Personal Change is Creating Organizational Change*, New York, Free Press.

Hayami, Y., 1997, *Development Economics: From the Poverty to the Wealth of Nations*, Oxford, Clarendon Press.

Hazledine, T., 1996, 'The New Zealand Economic Revolution after Ten Years', *University of Auckland Department of Economics WP*, 161, November.

—— 1998, *Taking New Zealand Seriously: The Economics of Decency*, Auckland, New Zealand, HarperCollins New Zealand Ltd.

Heilbroner, R., 1955, *The Great Economists: Their Lives and their Conceptions of the World*, London, Eyre & Spottiswoode.

Henderson, D., 1977, 'Two British Errors: Their Probable Size and Some Possible Reasons', *Oxford Economic Papers*, 29 (2), 159–205.

—— 1986, *Innocence and Design: The Influence of Economic Ideas on Policy*, Oxford, Blackwell.

—— 2000, 'False Perspective: The UNDP View of the World', *World Economics*, 1 (1), January–March.

—— 2001, 'Misguided Virtue: False Notions of Corporate Social Responsibility', *Hobart Paper*, 142 (London, Institute of Economic Affairs).

Heneghan, T. (2000), *Unchained Eagle: Germany after the Wall*, London, Pearson Education.

Henney, A., 1988, *The Economic Failure of Nuclear Power in Britain*, London, Greenpeace.

Hensler, D., Carrol, S., White, M. and Cross, J., 2001, *Asbestos Litigation*, Santa Monica, Calif., US Rand Institute for Civil Justice.

Hertz, N., 2001, *The Silent Takeover: Global Capitalism and the Death of Democracy*, London, Heinemann.

Heston, A., and Summers, R., 1991, 'The Penn World Table (Mark 5): An Expanded Set of International Comparisons, 1950–1988', *Quarterly Journal of Economics*, 106 (2), May, 327–68.

Hicks, J. R., 1939, *Value and Capital: An Inquiry into Some Fundamental Principles of Economic Theory*, revised edn., Oxford, Clarendon Press, 1946.

Hiltzik, M. A., 2000, *Dealers of Lightning: Xerox PARC and the Dawn of the Computer Age*, London, Orion Business Books.

Hinsley, F. H., and Stripp, A. (eds.), 1993, *Codebreakers: The Inside Story of Bletchley Park*, Oxford, Oxford University Press.

Hird, J. A., 1994, *Superfund: The Political Economy of Environmental Risk*, London and Baltimore, Johns Hopkins University Press.

Hirsch, F., 1977, *Social Limits to Growth*, London, Routledge and Kegan Paul.

Hirschman, A. O., 1970, *Exit, Voice and Loyalty: Responses to Decline in Firms, Organizations, and States*, Cambridge, Mass., Harvard University Press.

Hochschild, A., 1999, *King Leopold's Ghost: A Story of Greed, Terror & Heroism in Colonial Africa*, London, Macmillan.

Hodges, A., 1992, *Alan Turing: The Enigma*, London, Vintage Books.

Hoffman, A., 2000, 'Standardised Capital Stock Estimates in Latin America: A 1950–94 Update', *Cambridge Journal of Economics*, 24, 45–86.

Home Office, 1995, *Review of Prison Service Security in England and Wales (the Learmont Report)*, London, HMSO.

Horton, J., and Mendus, S. (eds.), 1994, *After MacIntyre: Critical Perspectives on the Work of Alasdair MacIntyre*, Cambridge, Polity Press.

Hosking, G., 1992, *A History of the Soviet Union*, London, Fontana.

Howard, P. K., 2001, *The Lost Art of Drawing the Line*, New York, Random House.

Hume, D., 1779, *Dialogues Concerning Natural Religion*, London.

Hunt, L., and Heinrich, K., 1996, *Barings Lost: Nick Leeson and the Collapse of Barings PLC*, St Leonards NSW, Allen and Unwin.

Hutton, W., 1995, *The State We're In*, London, Jonathan Cape.

—— 2002, *The World We're In*, London, Little, Brown.

Ichbiah, D., and Knepper, S. L., 1991, *The Making of Microsoft: How Bill Gates and his Team Created the World's Most Successful Software Company*, Rocklin, Calif., Prima Publications.

IMD, 2002, *The World Competitiveness Report*, Lausanne, IMD.

Inglehart, R., and Baker, W. E., 2000, 'Economic Levels of 65 Societies, Superimposed on Two Dimensions of Cross-cultural Variation', *American Sociological Review*, 65, February, 19–51.

—— Basañez, M., Moreno, A. and Moreno, M., 1998, *Human Values and Beliefs: A Cross-cultural Sourcebook: Political, Religious, Sexual, and Economic Norms in 43 Societies*, Ann Arbor, University of Michigan Press.

Jack, A., 1999, *The French Exception*, London, Profile Books.

Jacobs, J., 1961, *The Death and Life of Great American Cities*, New York, Random.

James, K. R., 2000, 'The Price of Retail Investing in the UK', *FSA Occasional Paper*, 6, February.

James, O., 1998, *Britain on the Couch: Why We're Unhappier Compared with 1950 Despite being Richer: A Treatment for the Low-serotonin Society*, London, Arrow.

Jameson, F., 1992, *Postmodernism: Or the Cultural Logic of Late Capitalism*, London, Verso Books.

Jarvis, V., and Prais, S. J., 1997, 'The Quality of Manufactured Products in Britain and Germany', *International Review of Applied Economics*, 11 (3), 421–38.

Jasny, Naum, 1965, *Khrushchev's Crop Policy*, Glasgow, George Outram and Co.

Jay, P., 2000, *Road to Riches or the Wealth of Man*, London, Weidenfeld & Nicolson.

Jeffries, I., 2001, *Economies in Transition: A Guide to China, Cuba, Mongolia, North Korea and Vietnam at the Turn of the Twenty-first Century*, London, Routledge.

Jencks, C., 1986, *What is Post Modernism?*, New York, St Martin's Press.

Jensen, M., 1978, 'Some Anomalous Evidence Regarding Market Efficiency', *Journal of Financial Economics*, 6, 95–101.

Johnson, Spencer, 1999, *Who Moved my Cheese? An Amazing Way to Deal with Change in your Work and your Life*, London, Vermilion.

Johnson, Stephen, 2001, *Emergence: The Connected Lives of Ants, Brains, Cities and Software*, Harmondsworth, Penguin.

Jones-Lee, M. W., 1976, *The Value of Life: An Economic Analysis*, London, Martin Robertson.

Jorgensen, D. W., 1987, 'Productivity and US Economic Growth', Cambridge, Mass., Harvard University Press.

Josephson, P. R., 1995, '"Projects of the Century" in Soviet History: Large-scale Technologies from Lenin to Gorbachev', *Technology & Culture*, 36 (3), 519–59.

Judson, H. F., 1980, *The Search for Solutions*, London, Hutchinson.

Kagel, J. H., and Roth, A. E. (eds.), 1995, *The Handbook of Experimental Economics*, Princeton, Princeton University Press.

Kahneman, D., and Tversky, A. (eds.), 2000, *Choices, Values and Frames*, New York and Cambridge, Russell Sage Foundation and Cambridge University Press.

—— Kretsch, J. and Thaler, R., 1986, 'Fairness as a Constraint on Profit Seeking', *American Economic Review*, 76, 728–41.

Kakutani, S., 1941, 'A Generalization of Brouwer's Fixed Point Theorem', *Duke Mathematical Journal*, 8, 451–9.

Kakwani, N. C., 1980, *Income Inequality and Poverty: Methods of Estimation to Policy Applications*, New York, Oxford University Press.

Kanfer, S., 1993, *The Last Empire: De Beers, Diamonds and the World*, London, Hodder & Stoughton.

Kaplan, D. A., 1999, *The Silicon Boys and their Valley of Dreams*, New York, William Morrow & Co.

Karnow, S., 1973, *Mao and China: From Revolution to Revolution*, London, Macmillan.

Katzenstein, P. J., 1984, *Corporatism and Change: Austria, Switzerland and Politics of Industry*, London and Ithaca, NY, Cornell University Press.

Kauffman, S. A., 1995, *At Home in the Universe: The Search for Laws of Complexity*, New York and Oxford, Oxford University Press.

—— 2000, *Investigations*, Oxford, Oxford University Press.

Kay, C., 1989, *Latin American Theories of Development and Underdevelopment*, London, Routledge.

Kay, J. A., 1993, *Foundations of Corporate Success: How Business Strategies Add Value*, Oxford, Oxford University Press.

—— 1996, *The Business of Economics*, Oxford, Oxford University Press.

—— 1997, 'Regulation by Rules or Regulation by Values? Community Values and the Market Economy', *Social Market Foundation Occasional Paper* (London).

—— 1999, 'Regulation by Rules or by Values?', in A. Kilmarnock (ed.), *The Social Market and the State*, London, Social Market Foundation, 3–23.

—— 2000, 'Oxford: A Lost Cause?', *Prospect*.

—— and King, M. A., 1990, *The British Tax System*, 5th edn., Oxford, Oxford University Press.

—— Mayer, C. P. and Thompson, D. J., 1986, *Privatization and Regulation – the UK Experience*, Oxford, Oxford University Press.

—— and Vickers, J. S., 1988, 'Regulatory Reform in Britain', *Economic Policy*, 7, October, 285–351.

Kelly, K., 1998, *New Rules for the New Economy*, London, Fourth Estate.

Kendall, M., 1953, 'The Analysis of Economic Time Series, Part I: Prices', *Journal of the Royal Statistical Society*, 96, 11–25.

Kenrick, J., 1979, 'Expanding Imputed Values in the National Income and Product Accounts', *Review of Income and Wealth*, December, 349–63.

Keynes, J. M., 1936, *The General Theory of Employment, Interest and Money*, London, Macmillan.

Khrushchev, N., 1974, *Khrushchev Remembers*, vol. 2: *The Last Testament*, ed. and trans. S. Talbott, London, André Deutsch.

Kiel, L. D., and Elliott, E. W., 1996, *Chaos Theory in the Social Sciences: Foundations and Applications*, Ann Arbor, Michigan University Press.

Kilmarnock, A. (ed.), 1999, *The Social Market and the State*, London, Social Market Foundation.

Kincaid, P., 1986, *The Rule of the Road: An International Guide to History and Practice*, Westport, Conn., Greenwood Press.

Kirman, A., 1993, 'Ants, Rationality and Recruitment', *Quarterly Journal of Economics*, 108, February, 137–56.

Klein, G., 1998, *Sources of Power: How People Make Decisions*, Cambridge, Mass., and London, MIT Press.

Klein, N., 1999, *No Logo*, London, Flamingo.

Klopfenstein, B. C., 1989, *The Diffusion of the VCR into the United States*, London and Newbury Park, Calif., Sage Focus Editions.

Knight, F. H., 1921, *Risk, Uncertainty and Profit*, Boston and New York, Houghton Mifflin.

Koopmans, T. C., 1957, *Three Essays on the State of Economic Science*, New York, McGraw-Hill.

Kornai, J., 1992, *The Socialist System*, Oxford, Oxford University Press.

Kornicki, P. (ed.), 1998, *Meiji Japan: Political, Economic and Social History, 1868–1912*, London, Routledge.

Kotkin, S., 2001, *Armageddon Averted: The Soviet Collapse 1970–2000*, Oxford, Oxford University Press.

Krugman, P., 1994, 'The Myth of Asia's Miracle', *Foreign Affairs*, November/December.

—— 1995, *Development, Geography and Economic Theory*, Cambridge, Mass., MIT Press.

—— 1996, *The Self-organizing Economy*, Oxford and Cambridge, Mass., Blackwell.

Landais, B., 1999, *L'Affaire Gachet: L'audace des bandits*, Paris, Layeur.

Landes, D. S., 1998, *The Wealth and Poverty of Nations*, London, Little, Brown.

Lane, R. E., 1991, *The Market Experience*, Cambridge, Cambridge University Press.

Langford, P. (ed.), 1996, *The Writings and Speeches of Edmund Burke*, vol. 3: *Party, Parliament and the American War*, Oxford, Clarendon Press.

Langlois, J., Roggman, L. and Musselman, L., 1994, 'What is Average and what is not Average about Attractive Faces?', *Psychological Science*, 5, 214–20.

Lanjouw, P., and Stern, N. (eds.), 1998, *Economic Development in Palanpur over Five Decades*, Delhi, Oxford University Press.

Latham, R. (ed.), 1985, *The Shorter Pepys*, London, Bell & Hyman.

Lazear, E. P., 2000, 'Economic Imperialism', *Quarterly Journal of Economics*, February, 99–146.

Leacock, S. B., 1936, *Hellements of Hickonomicks in Hiccoughs of Verse Done in our Social Planning-mill*, New York, Dodd, Mead & Company.

Leadbeater, C., 2000, *Living on Thin Air: The New Economy*, London, Viking.

Ledyard, J. O., 1988, 'Market Failure', in J. Eatwell, M. Milgate and P. Newman (eds.), *The New Palgrave: A Dictionary of Economics*, Basingstoke, Palgrave Macmillan.

Leeson, N., with Whitley, E., 1996, *Rogue Trader*, London, Little, Brown.

Leijonhufvud, A., 1968, *On Keynesian Economics and the Economics of Keynes*, London and New York, Oxford University Press.

Lessig, L., Slaughter, A.-M. and Zittrain, J., 1999, 'Developments in the Law: The Law of Cyberspace', *Harvard Law Review*, 112, May, 1577–704.

Levine, I. E., 1962, *Inventive Wizard: George Westinghouse*, New York, Julian Messner.

Levy, M. R., 1989, *The VCR Age: Home Video and Mass Communication*, Newbury Park, Calif., Sage Publications.

Lewis, A., and Schultz, T. W., 1953, *The Economic Organization of Agriculture*, New York, McGraw-Hill.

Lewis, M., 1989, *Liar's Poker: Two Cities, True Greed*, London, Hodder & Stoughton.

—— 1999, *The New New Thing*, London, Hodder & Stoughton.

Lewis, W. A., 1954, 'Economic Development with Unlimited Supplies of Labour', *Manchester School*, 22, May, 139–91.

Liebowitz, S. J., and Margolis, S. E., 1990, 'The Fable of the Keys', *Journal of Law & Economics*, 33, April, 1–25.

Little, I., 1996, *Picking Winners: The East Asian Experience*, London, Social Market Foundation.

Loewenstein, G., 1999, 'Because it is There: The Challenge of Mountaineering for Utility Theory', *Kyklos*, 52, 315–44.

Lomborg, B., 2001, *The Skeptical Environmentalist: Measuring the Real State of the World*, Cambridge, Cambridge University Press.

Lowenstein, R., 1995, *Buffett: The Making of an American Capitalist*, London, Weidenfeld & Nicolson.

—— 2000, *When Genius Failed: The Rise and Fall of Long-term Capital Management*, London, Fourth Estate.

Lynch, L., and Kahn, M., 2000, *California's Electricity Options and Challenges*, San Francisco, California Public Utilities Commission.

Lynn, M., 1991, *The Billion-dollar Battle: Merck v Glaxo*, London, Heinemann.

Lyotard, J.-F., 1992, *The Postmodern Condition: A Report on Knowledge* (orig. pub. 1979), English translation, Manchester, Manchester University Press.

McCloskey, D. N., 1989, *The Open Fields of England: Rent, Risk, and the Rate of Interest 1300–1815*, Cambridge, Cambridge University Press.

—— 1991, 'The Prudent Peasant: New Findings on Open Fields', *Journal of Economic History*, 51 (2), June, 343–55.

MacFarquhar, R. (ed.), 1966, *China under Mao: Politics Takes Command*, Cambridge, Mass., MIT Press.

—— 1983, *The Origins of the Cultural Revolution*, vol. 2: *The Great Leap Forward, 1958–1960*, Oxford, Oxford University Press.

—— 1993, *The Politics of China, 1949–1989*, Cambridge, Cambridge University Press.

MacIntyre, A., 1981, *After Virtue: A Study in Moral Theory*, London, Duckworth.

Mackay, C., 1841, *Extraordinary Popular Delusions and the Madness of Crowds*, repr. Ware, Herts., Wordsworth Editions, 1995.

McMurrin, S. M. (ed.), 1981, *The Tanner Lectures on Human Values*, Salt Lake City, University of Utah Press.

McNeill, W. H., 1963, *The Rise of the West: A History of the Human Community*, Chicago and London, University of Chicago Press.

Macrae, N., 1992, *Johan von Neumann*, New York, Pantheon.

Maddison, A., 1993, *Monitoring the World Economy 1820–1992*, Paris, OECD.

—— 2001, *The World Economy: A Millennial Perspective*, Paris, OECD Development Centre Studies.

Magnusson, L., 2000, *An Economic History of Sweden*, London, Routledge.

Maier, K., 2000, *This House has Fallen: Midnight in Nigeria*, New York, Public Affairs.

Malkiel, B. G., 1996, *A Random Walk down Wall Street: Including a Life-cycle Guide to Personal Investing*, New York, W. W. Norton.

Malmsten, E., Portanger, E. and Drazin, C., 2002, *Boo Hoo: A Dot Com Story*, New York, Random House Business Books.

Maranell, G., and Dodder, R., 1970, 'Political Orientation and Evaluation of Presidential Prestige: A Study of American Historians', *Social Science Quarterly*, 51, Summer, 415–21.

Mardel, M., 1996, 'The Triumph of the New Economy', *Business Week*, 30 December, 70.

Marshall, A., 1925, *Correspondence with Professor A. L. Bowley*, London, Macmillan.

Marshall, B. (ed.), 2002, *Heliobacter Pioneers*, Carlton, Victoria, Blackwell Scientific.

Marshall, O., 2000, *English-speaking Communities in Latin America*, Basingstoke, Macmillan.

Marwell, G., and Ames, R., 1981, 'Economists Free Ride, Does Anyone Else?', *Journal of Public Economics*, 15, 295–310.

Marx, Karl, 1875, *Capital*, trans. D. McLellan, Oxford, Oxford University Press, 1999.

Maynard Smith, J., 1982, *Evolution and the Theory of Games*, Cambridge, Cambridge University Press.

Meade, J., 1964, *Efficiency, Equality and the Ownership of Property*, London, Allen & Unwin.

Meadows, D. H., Meadows, D. L., Randers, J. and Behrens, W. W., III, 1972, *The Limits to Growth*, New York, Signet Books.

Mehra, R., and Prescott, E. C., 1985, 'The Equity Premium: A Puzzle', *Journal of Monetary Economics*, 15, March, 145–61.

Melchior, A., Telle, K. and Wiig, H., 2000, *Globalisation and Inequality: World Income Distribution and Living Standards, 1960–1998*, Norwegian Institute of International Affairs, Royal Norwegian Ministry of Foreign Affairs Studies, Foreign Policy Issues, Report 6B.

Merriden, T., 2001, *Irresistible Forces: The Business Legacy of Napster and the Growth of the Underground Internet*, Oxford, Capstone.

Merton, R. K., 1936, 'Science, Technology and Society in Seventeenth-century England', in G. Sarton (ed.), *Osiris: Studies in the History and Philosophy of Science, and on the History of Learning and Culture*, vol. 4, Bruges, St Catherine Press.

—— 1996, *The Rise of Modern Science*, London, University of Chicago Press.

Milanovic, B., 1999, *True World Income Distribution, 1988 and 1993: First Calculation Based on Household Surveys Alone*, World Bank, Development Research Group.

Milgrom, P., and Roberts, J., 1992, *Economics Organization and Management*, London, Prentice-Hall International.

Mill, J. S., 1873, *Autobiography*, London, Social Reformer.

Miller, A., 2000, *The Crucible* (orig. pub. 1953), Harmondsworth, Penguin.

Ministry of Finance, 2002, *Economic Survey 2001–2002*, Government of India.

Mintzberg, H., 1994, *The Rise and Fall of Strategic Planning*, London, Prentice-Hall.

Mnookin, R., and Kornhauser, L., 1979, 'Bargaining in the Shadow of the Law', *Yale Law Journal*, 88, 950–97.

Mokyr, J. (ed.), 1999, *The British Industrial Revolution: An Economic Perspective*, 2nd edn., Boulder, Colo., and Oxford, Westview Press.

Monbiot, G., 2001, *Captive State: The Corporate Takeover of Britain*, London, Pan Books.

Monopolies Commission, 1972, *Beecham Group and Glaxo Group: Report on the Proposed Mergers*, London, HMSO.

Muthoo, A., 2000, 'A Non-technical Introduction to Bargaining Theory', *World Economics*, February.

Naim, M., 1999, 'Fads and Fashion in Economic Reforms: Washington Consensus or Washington Confusion', *Third World Quarterly*, 21 (3), 505–28.

Nasar, S., 1998, *A Beautiful Mind*, London, Faber.

National Audit Office, 2001, *Managing the Relationship to Secure a Successful Partnership in PFI Projects*, London, HMSO.

—— 2002, *The Financial Analysis for the London Underground Public Private Partnerships*, London, HMSO.

Neale, Alan D., and Goyder, D. G., 1980, *The Antitrust Laws of the United States of America*, Cambridge, Cambridge University Press.

Neaman, E. A., 1990, 'German Collectivism and the Welfare State', *Critical Review*, 4 (4), 608.

Nelson, P., 1974, 'Advertising as Information', *Journal of Political Economy*, 82 (4), July–August, 729–54.

Nelson, R., 1995, 'Recent Evolutionary Theorizing about Economic Change', *Journal of Economic Literature*, 39, 48–90.

—— and Winter, S. G., 1982, *An Evolutionary Theory of Economic Change*, Cambridge, Mass., and London, Belknap.

Newbery, D. M., and Pollitt, M. G., 1997, 'The Restructuring and Privatisation of the CEGB – Was it Worth It?', *Journal of Industrial Economics*, 45 (3), 269–303.

Norberg-Hodge, H., 1991, *Ancient Futures: Learning from Ladakh*, San Francisco, Calif., Sierra Club Books.

Nordhaus, William, 1997, 'Do Real-Output and Real-Wage Measures Capture Reality?: The History of Lighting Suggests Not', in Timothy Bresnehan and Robert Gordon (eds.), *The Economics of New Goods*, Chicago, University of Chicago Press.

Nordhaus, W. D., and Kokkelenberg, E. C. (eds.), 1999, *Natures' Numbers*, Washington, DC, National Academy Press.

North, D. C., 1990, *Institutions, Institutional Change and Economic Performance*, Cambridge, Cambridge University Press.

—— and Thomas, R. P., 1973, *The Rise of the Western World: A New Economic History*, Cambridge, Cambridge University Press.

Nozick, R., 1974, *Anarchy, State and Utopia*, Oxford, Blackwell.

Oakeshott, M. J., 1962, *Rationalism in Politics and Other Essays*, London, Methuen.

OECD, 1975, *The Polluter Pays Principle: Definition, Analysis, Implementation*, Paris, Organization for Economic Cooperation and Development.

OECD, 1993, *Improvement of Economic Forecasts*, Paris, Organization for Economic Cooperation and Development.

OECD, 1999, *OECD Economic Surveys: New Zealand 1999*, Paris, Organization for Economic Cooperation and Development.

OECD, 2001, *Corporate Social Responsibility: Partners for Progress*, Paris, Organization for Economic Cooperation and Development.

Office of Fair Trading, 2001, *The Role of Market Definition in Monopoly and Dominance Inquiries*, London, HMSO.

Olson, M., 1996, 'Big Bills Left on the Sidewalk: Why Some Nations are Rich, and Others Poor', *Journal of Economic Perspectives*, 10 (3), 3–24.

—— 2000, *Power and Prosperity: Outgrowing Communist and Capitalist Dictatorships*, New York, Basic Books.

—— and Satu, K., 2000, *A Not-so-dismal Science: A Broader View of Economies and Societies*, Oxford, Oxford University Press.

Ormerod, P., 1998, *Butterfly Economics: A New General Theory of Social and Economic Behaviour*, London, Faber & Faber.

O'Rourke, P. J., 1998, *Eat the Rich*, London, Picador.

Ortega, B., 1999, *In Sam We Trust: The Untold Story of Sam Walton, and how Wal-Mart is Devouring America*, London, Kogan Page.

Ostrom, E., 1990, *Governing the Commons: The Evolution of Institutions for Collective Action*, Cambridge, Cambridge University Press.

Oswald, A., 1997, 'Happiness and Economic Performance', *Economic Journal*, 107, 1815–31.

Owen, G., 1999, *From Empire to Europe: The Decline and Revival of British Industry since the Second World War*, London, HarperCollins.

Paley, W., 1802, *Natural Theology; or Evidences of the Existence and Attributes of the Deity, Collected from the Appearances of Nature*, London.

Patterson, D. E., and Shapiro, C., 2001, 'Trans-Atlantic Divergence in GE/Honeywell: Causes and Lessons', *Antitrust Magazine*, Fall, 18–25.

Pearce, D. W., 1992, 'Green Economics', *Environmental Values*, 1 (1), 3–13.

Pearsall, P., 1990, *A–Z Maps: The Personal Story, From Bedsitter to Household Name*, London, Geographers' A–Z Map Company.

Perrett, D. I., May, K. A. and Yoshikawa, S., 1994, 'Facial Shape and Judgements of Female Attractiveness', *Nature*, 368, 17 March, 239–42.

Pettigrew, A. M., 1985, *The Awakening Giant: Continuity and Change in Imperial Chemical Industries*, Oxford, Blackwell.

Pinker, S., 1994, *The Language Instinct: The New Science of Language and Mind*, Harmondsworth, Penguin Books.

Polanyi, K., 1945, *Origins of our Time: The Great Transformation*, London, Gollancz.

Pomeranz, K., 2000, *The Great Divergence: China, Europe and the Making of the Modern World Economy*, Princeton and Oxford, Princeton University Press.

Porter, M. E., 1990, *The Competitive Advantage of Nations*, London, Macmillan.

Posner, R. A., 1987, 'The Law and Economics Movement', *American Economic Review*, 77 (2), May, Papers and Proceedings of the Ninety-ninth Annual Meeting of the American Economic Association, 1–13.

—— 1998, *Economic Analysis of Law*, 5th edn., New York, Aspen Law & Business.

Prais, S. J., 1983, *Some Practical Aspects of Human Capital Investments: Training Standards in Five Occupations in Britain and Germany*, London, National Institute of Economic and Social Research.

—— 1984, *The Stock of Machinery in Britain, Germany and the United States*, London, National Institute of Economic and Social Research.

—— and Wagner, K., 1983, 'Schooling Standards in Britain and Germany: Some Summary Comparisons Bearing on Economic Efficiency', *National Institute Discussion Paper*, 60 (London).

Prebisch, R., 1950, *The Economic Development of Latin America and its Principal Problems*, New York, United Nations.

Pritchett, L., 1997, 'Divergence, Big Time', *Journal of Economic Perspectives*, 11 (3), Summer, 3–17.

Prout, H. G., 1922, *A Life of George Westinghouse*, London, Benn Brothers.

Putnam, R. D., 2000, *Bowling Alone: The Collapse and Revival of American Community*, New York and London, Simon & Schuster.

Quah, D., 1996, 'Twin Peaks: Growth and Convergence in Models of Distribution Dynamics', *Economic Journal*, 106 (437), July, 1045–55.

Rabin, M., 1998, 'Psychology and Economics', *Journal of Economic Literature*, 36, March, 11–46.

Radford, R. A., 1945, 'The Economic Organization of a POW Camp', *Economica*, November, 189–201.

Rand, A., 1967, *Capitalism: The Unknown Ideal*, New York, Signet.

—— 1990a, *Introduction to Objectivist Epistemology*, New York, Meridian Books.

—— 1990b, *The Voice of Reason: Essays in Objectivist Thought*, New York, Meridian Books.

Raphael, A., 1994, *Ultimate Risk*, London, Bantam Press.

Rapoport, A., 1985, 'Applications of Game Theoretic Concepts in Biology', *Bulletin of Mathematical Biology*, 47, 161–92.

Ravage, B., 1997, *George Westinghouse: A Genius for Invention*, Austin, Tex., Raintree-Steck-Vaughn.

Rawls, J., 1972, *A Theory of Justice*, Oxford, Clarendon.

Read, D., 1999, *The Power of News: The History of Reuters*, 2nd edn., Oxford, Oxford University Press.

Revesz, R. L., and Stewart, R. B. (eds.), 1995, *Analyzing Superfund: Economics, Science and Law*, Washington, DC, Resources for the Future.

Rhodes, M., 2000, 'Past Imperfect? The Performance of UK Equity Managed Funds', *FSA Occasional Paper Series*, 9, August.

Ricardo, D., 1817, *On the Principles of Political Economy and Taxation*, London.

Richardson, G. B., 1972, 'The Organization of Industry', *Economic Journal*, 82, 883–96.

Ridings, W., and McIver, S., 1997, *Rating the Presidents*, Secaucus, NJ, Citadel Press.

Ritter, J. R., 1991, 'The Long-run Performance of Initial Public Offerings', *Journal of Finance*, 46 (1), 3–27.

Robbins, L. C., 1935, *An Essay on the Nature and Significance of Economic Science*, London, Macmillan.

Rogoff, K., and Zettelmayer, J., 2002, 'Early Ideas on Sovereign Bankruptcy Reorganisation: A Survey', *IMF Working Paper*, 2/57.

Rohrbough, M. J., 1997, *Days of Gold: The California Gold Rush and the American Nation*, Berkeley and London, University of California Press.

Rosenberg, N., and Birdzell, L. E., Jr., 1986, *How the West Grew Rich: The Economic Transformation of the Industrial World*, New York, Basic Books.

Rosenstein-Rodan, P. N., 1943, 'Problems of Industrialisation of Eastern and Southeastern Europe', *Economic Journal*, 53, June–September, 202–11.

—— 1961, 'Notes on the Theory of the Big Push', in H. S. Ellis and H. C. Wallich (eds.), *Economic Development for Latin America*, New York, St Martin's Press, chapter VII B.1, pp. 342–5.

Rostow, W. W., 1953, *The Process of Economic Growth*, Oxford, Clarendon Press.

Rothschild, E., 2001, *Economic Sentiments, Adam Smith, Condorcet and the Enlightenment*, Cambridge, Mass., and London, Harvard University Press.

Roughley, T. C., 1951, *Fish and Fisheries of Australia*, London and Sydney, Angus & Robertson.

Rousseau, J.-J., 1913, *The Social Contract and Discourses* (1791), trans. G. D. H. Cole, London, J. M. Dent.

Rowley, E. E., 1994, *Hyperinflation in Germany: Perceptions of a Process*, Aldershot, Scolar Press.

Ruggles, Nancy D., and Ruggles, R., 1999, *National Accounting and Economic Policy: The United States and the UN Systems*, Cheltenham, Elgar.

Runciman, W. G., 1998, *The Social Animal*, London, HarperCollins.

Sachs, J., 2000, 'Notes on a New Sociology of Economic Development', in L. E. Harrison and S. P. Huntington (eds.), *Culture Matters*, New York, Basic Books, 29–43.

Sala-i-Martin, X., 2002, 'The "Disturbing Rise" of Global Income Inequality', *NBER Working Paper*, 8904, April.

Saltzman, C., 1999, *Portrait of Dr Gachet: The Story of a van Gogh Master-piece, Modernism, Money, Collectors, Dealers, Taste, Greed, and Loss*, New York, Viking.

Samuelson, P. A., 1947, *Foundations of Economic Analysis*, Cambridge, Mass., Harvard University Press.

—— 1993, 'Altruism as a Problem Involving Group versus Individual Selection in Economics and Biology', *American Economic Review*, 83 (2), May, 143–8.

Samuelsson, K., 1961, *Religion and Economic Action*, trans. E. G. French, ed. and introd. D. C. Coleman, Stockholm, Svenska Bokforlaget.

Scarf, H. E., 1962, *An Analysis of Markets with a Large Number of Partici-pants*, Philadelphia, Ivy Curtis Press.

Schlesinger, A., Jr., 1996, 'The Ultimate Approval Rating', *New York Times Magazine*, 15 December, 48–9.

Schultz, J. P., 1998, 'Inequality in the Distribution of Personal Income in the World: How it is Changing and Why', *Journal of Population Economics*, 11, 307–44.

Schumpeter, J. A., 1943, *Capitalism, Socialism and Democracy*, London, Allen & Unwin.

Schwartz, E. I., 2002, *The Last Lone Inventor: A Tale of Genius, Deceit, and the Birth of Television*, New York, HarperCollins.

Sen, A. K., 1970, *Collective Choice and Social Welfare*, San Francisco and London, Holden-Day.

—— 1987, *On Ethics and Economics*, Oxford, Basil Blackwell.

—— 1988, 'Rational Behaviour', in J. Eatwell, M. Milgate and P. Newman (eds.), *The New Palgrave: A Dictionary of Economics*, Basingstoke, Pal-grave Macmillan.

Servan-Schreiber, J.-J., 1967, *Le Défi américain*, Paris; English translation: *The American Challenge*, London, Hamish Hamilton, 1968.

Sewell, B., 1994, *The Reviews that Caused the Rumpus*, London, Bloomsbury.

Shanks, M., 1961, *The Stagnant Society: A Warning*, Harmondsworth, Penguin.

Shapiro, C., and Varian, H. R., 1999, *Information Rules: A Strategic Guide to the Network Economy*, Cambridge, Mass., Harvard Business Press.

Sheehan, H., 1993, *Marxism and the Philosophy of Science: A Critical His-tory*, Atlantic Highlands, NJ, Humanities Press International.

Shefrin, H., 2000, *Beyond Greed and Fear: Understanding Behavioral Finance and the Psychology of Investing*, Boston, Mass., and London, Harvard University Press.

Shiller, R. J., 1993, *Macro Markets: Creating Institutions for Managing Society's Largest Economic Risks*, Oxford, Clarendon Press.

—— 2000, *Irrational Exuberance*, Princeton and Chichester, Princeton University Press.

Shleifer, A., and Summers, L., 1988, 'Breach of Trust in Hostile Takeovers', in A. Auerbach (ed.), *Corporate Takeovers: Causes and Consequences*, London, University of Chicago Press.

Shleifer, A., 1999, *Inefficient Markets: An Introduction to Behavioral Finance*, Oxford, Oxford University Press.

Shonfield, A. A., 1958, *British Economic Policy since the War*, Harmondsworth, Penguin.

—— 1965, *Modern Capitalism*, London, Oxford University Press.

Shubik, M., 1959, 'Edgeworth Market Games', in A. W. Tucker and R. D. Luce (eds.), *Contributions to the Theory of Games*, volume 4, Princeton, Princeton University Press, pp. 207–78.

Shumway, N., 1991, *The Invention of Argentina*, Berkeley and Oxford, University of California Press.

Siedentop, L., 2000, *Democracy in Europe*, London, Allen Lane.

Siegel, J. J., 1998, *Stocks for the Long Run*, 2nd edn., New York and London, McGraw-Hill.

Simon, H. A., 1969, *The Sciences of the Artificial*, Cambridge, Mass., MIT Press.

Singer, H., 1950, 'The Distribution of Gains between Investing and Borrowing Countries', *American Economic Review*, 40, 473–85.

Smith, A., 1759, *The Theory of Moral Sentiments*, Indianapolis, Liberty Press, 1976.

—— 1976, *An Inquiry into the Nature and Causes of the Wealth of Nations*, ed. R. H. Campbell and A. S. Skinner, Oxford, Oxford University Press.

Smith, B. D., 1995, *The Emergence of Agriculture*, New York and Oxford, Scientific American Library.

Sokal, A. D., and Bricmont, J., 1998, *Intellectual Impostures: Postmodern Philosophers' Abuse of Science*, London, Profile Books Ltd.

Solow, R. M., 1970, *Growth Theory: An Exposition*, Oxford, Oxford University Press.

Soros, G., 1998, *The Crisis of Global Capitalism: Open Society Endangered*, New York, Public Affairs.

—— 2000, *Reforming Global Capitalism*, New York, Little, Brown.

Soto, H. de, 2000, *The Mystery of Capital: Why Capitalism Triumphs in the West and Fails Everywhere Else*, London, Bantam Press.

Spence, A. M., 1973, *Market Signalling: Information Transfer and Hiring and Related Process*, Cambridge, Mass., Harvard University Press.

Starmer, C., 2000, 'Developments in Non-expected Utility Theory', *Journal of Economic Literature*, 38, June, 332–82.

Steckel, R. H., 1995, 'Stature and the Standard of Living', *Journal of Economic Literature*, 33, December, 1903–40.

Stephens, P., 1996, *Politics and the Pound: The Conservatives' Struggle with Sterling*, London, Macmillan.

Stern, J. M., Shiely, J. S. and Ross, I., 2001, *The EVA Challenge: Implementing Value-Added Change in an Organization*, New York and Chichester, Wiley.

Stigler, G. J., 1981, 'Economics and Ethics', in S. M. McMurrin (ed.), *The Tanner Lectures on Human Values*, volume 2, Salt Lake City, University of Utah Press.

Stiglitz, J. E., 1994, *Whither Socialism?*, Cambridge, Mass., and London, MIT Press.

—— 2000, 'The Contributions of the Economics of Information to Twentieth Century Economics', *Quarterly Journal of Economics*, November, 1441–78.

—— 2002, *Globalization and its Discontents*, London, Penguin.

Stone, R., 1986, 'Nobel Memorial Lecture 1984: The Accounts of Society', *Journal of Applied Econometrics*, 1 (1), January, 5–28.

Strathern, P., 2001, *Dr Strangelove's Game: A Brief History of Economic Genius*, London, Hamish Hamilton.

Stringer, C., and Gamble, C., 1993, *In Search of the Neanderthals: Solving the Puzzle of Human Origins*, London, Thames & Hudson.

Sugden, R., 1989, 'Spontaneous Order', *Journal of Economic Perspectives*, 3 (4), Fall, 85–97.

Sulston, J., and Ferry, G., 2002, *The Common Thread: A Story of Science, Politics, Ethics and the Human Genome*, London, Bantam.

Suzuki, N., 1997, *Measuring the Degree of Competition in the US Milk Market*, London, National Research Institute of Agricultural Economics, MAFF.

Talbott, S., 1971, *Khrushchev Remembers*, London, André Deutsch.

Tattersall, I., 1995, *The Last Neanderthal*, New York, Macmillan.

Tawney, R. H., 1926, *Religion and the Rise of Capitalism*, London, John Murray.

Taylor, C., 1989, *Sources of the Self: The Making of the Modern Identity*, Cambridge, Cambridge University Press.

Taylor, P., and Joncker, L., 1978, 'Evolutionarily Stable Strategies and Game Dynamics', *Mathematical Biosciences*, 40, 145–56.

Taylor, W., 1990, 'Can Big Owners Make a Big Difference?', *Harvard Business Review*, September–October, 70–80.

Teiwes, F. C., with Sun, W., 1999, *China's Road to Disaster: Mao, Central Politicians, and Provincial Leaders in the Unfolding of the Great Leap Forward 1955–1959*, Armonk, NY, M. E. Sharpe.

Telser, L. G., 1980, 'A Theory of Self-enforcing Agreements', *Journal of Business*, 53 (1), 27–44.

Thaler, R. H., 1991, *The Winner's Curse: Paradoxes and Anomalies of Economic Life*, New York and Toronto, Free Press and Maxwell Macmillan.

Thatcher, M., 1993, *The Downing Street Years*, London, HarperCollins.

Thompson, E. P., 1968, *The Making of the English Working Class*, Harmondsworth, Penguin.

Thurow, L. C., 1999, *Building Wealth: The New Rules for Individuals, Companies, and Nations in a Knowledge-based Economy*, New York, Harper Business.

Titmuss, R. M., 1970, *The Gift Relationship: From Human Blood to Social Policy*, London, Allen & Unwin.

Tobin, J., 1978, 'A Proposal for International Monetary Reform', *Eastern Economic Journal*, 4, 153–9.

—— 1992, 'The Invisible Hand in Modern Microeconomics', in M. Fry (ed.), *Adam Smith's Legacy*, London, Routledge.

—— 1994, 'A Currency Transaction Tax, Why and How', CIDEI Conference on Globalization of Markets, Rome, *CIDEI WP*, 29.

—— and Nordhaus, W., 1972, *Is Growth Obsolete?*, New York, Economic Growth Colloquium.

Tocqueville, A. de, 2000 edn., *Democracy in America* (1835), ed. and trans. H. C. Mansfield and D. Winthrop, Chicago, University of Chicago Press.

Todaro, M. P., 1994, *Economic Development*, New York and London, Longman.

—— 2002, *Economic Development*, 7th edn., London, Pearson Education.

Transparency International, 2001, *Global Corruption Report*, Berlin, Transparency International.

Travers, J., and Milgram, S., 1969, 'An Experimental Study of the Small World Problem', *Sociometry*, 32 (4), December, 425–33.

Trump, D., with Schwartz, T., 1987, *Trump: The Art of the Deal*, London, Century.

Tsurumi, M. (ed.), 2001, *Financial Big Bang in Asia*, Aldershot, Ashgate.

Tudge, C., 1998, *Neanderthals, Bandits and Farmers: How Agriculture Really Began*, London, Weidenfeld & Nicolson.

Turnbull, C. D., 1961, *The Forest People*, new edn. 1993, London, Pimlico.

—— 1973, *The Mountain People*, new introd., 1994, London, Pimlico.

Turner, J. A., 2001, *Just Capital: The Liberal Economy*, London, Macmillan Publishing.

ul Haq, M., Kaul, I. and Grunberg, I. (eds.), 1996, *The Tobin Tax: Coping with Financial Volatility*, Oxford, Oxford University Press.

Ullman, J. E., 1988, *The Anatomy of Industrial Decline*, New York, Quorum.

United Nations Development Programme, 2002, *Human Development Report*, New York, Oxford University Press.

van de Stadt, H., Kapetyn, A. and van de Geer, S., 1985, 'The Relativity of Utility', *Review of Economics and Statistics*, 67, 179–87.

Veblen, T., 1899, *The Theory of the Leisure Class: An Economic Study of Institutions*, London, Routledge/Thoemmes Press, 1994.

Vickrey, W., 1961, 'Counterspeculation, Auctions and Competitive Sealed Tenders', *Journal of Finance*, 16, 8–37.

—— 1962, *Auction and Bidding Games*, Philadelphia, Ivy Curtis Press.

Vitullo-Martin, J., and Moskin, J. R. (eds.), 1994, *The Executive's Book of Quotations*, New York and Oxford, Oxford University Press.

Waldron, J. (ed.), 1984, *Theories of Rights*, Oxford, Oxford University Press.

Waldrop, M. M., 1994, *Complexity: The Emerging Science at the Edge of Order and Chaos*, Harmondsworth, Penguin.

Walker, D., and Coleridge, E. E., 1992, *Report on an Inquiry into Lloyd's Syndicate Participations and the LMX Spiral*, London, Lloyd's of London.

Wallis, J. J., and North, D. C., 1986, *Measuring the Transaction Sector in the American Economy, 1870–1970*, Chicago, Chicago University Press.

Walzer, M., 1981, 'Philosophy and Democracy', *Political Theory*, 9 (3), 379–99.

—— 1984, *Spheres of Justice: A Defence of Pluralism and Equality*, Oxford, Robertson.

Watrin, C., 1999, 'The Social Market Economy: The Main Ideas and their Influence on Economic Policy', in A. Kilmarnock (ed.), *The Social Market and the State*, London, Social Market Foundation.

Watson, J. D., 1968, *The Double Helix: A Personal Account of the Discovery of the Structure of DNA*, London, Weidenfeld & Nicolson.

Watts, D. J., 1999, *Small Worlds: The Dynamics of Networks between Order and Randomness*, Princeton and Chichester, Princeton University Press.

Weale, M., 1993, 'Fifty Years of National Income Accounting', *Economic Notes*, 22 (2), 178–99.

Weaver, W., 1948, 'Science and Complexity', *American Scientist*, 36, 536–44.

Weber, M., 1930, *The Protestant Work Ethic and the Spirit of Capitalism*, London, Allen & Unwin.

—— 1947, *The Theory of Social and Economic Organization*, trans. A. R. Henderson and T. Parsons, New York, Free Press of Glencoe.

Welch, J., with Byrne, J. A., 2001, *Jack: Straight from the Gut*, New York, Warner Books.

Weldon, F., 2001, *The Bulgari Connection*, London, Flamingo.

White, L. J., 1991, *The S & L Debacle: Public Policy Lessons for Bank and Thrift Regulation*, New York, Oxford University Press.

Widdig, B., 2001, *Culture and Inflation in Weimar Germany*, Berkeley and London, University of California Press.

Williams, G. C., 1966, *Adaptation and Natural Selection: A Critique of Some Current Evolutionary Thought*, Princeton, Princeton University Press.

Williams, R. E., 1997, *The Political Economy of the Common Market in Milk and Dairy Products in the European Union*, Rome, Food and Agriculture Organization of the United Nations.

Williamson, J., 2000a, 'What Should the World Bank Think about the Washington Consensus?', *World Bank Research Observer*, 15 (2), August, 251–64.

—— 2000b, *Exchange Rate Regimes for Emerging Markets: Revising the Intermediate Option*, Washington, DC, Institute for International Economics.

Williamson, O. E., 1975, *Markets and Hierarchies*, London, Collier Macmillan.

—— 1985, *The Economic Institutions of Capitalism: Firms, Markets, Relational Contracting*, London, Collier Macmillan.

—— and Winter, S. G. (eds.), 1991, *The Nature of the Firm: Origins, Evolution and Development*, Oxford and New York, Oxford University Press.

Wilson, E. O., 1971, *The Insect Societies*, Cambridge, Mass., Harvard University Press.

—— 1975, *Sociobiology, the New Synthesis*, Cambridge, Mass., Belknap Press of Harvard University Press.

—— 1998, *Consilience: The Unity of Knowledge*, London, Little, Brown.

WM Company, 2002, *A Comparison of Active and Passive Management of Unit Trusts*, Edinburgh, Virgin Money Personal Finance.

Wolf, A., 2002, *Does Education Matter? Myths about Education and Economic Growth*, London, Penguin.

Wolfe, T., 1987, *The Bonfire of the Vanities*, New York, Farrar, Straus, and Giroux.

Wolff, M., 1998, *Burn Rate: How I Survived the Gold Rush Years on the Internet*, London, Weidenfeld & Nicolson.

Woodward, B., 2000, *Maestro: Greenspan's Fed and the American Boom*, New York and London, Simon & Schuster.

World Bank, 1993, *The East Asian Miracle, Economic Growth and Public Policy*, Oxford, Oxford University Press.

—— 1995, *Bureaucrats in Business: The Economics and Politics of Government Ownership*, Oxford, Oxford University Press.

—— 1997, *Expanding the Measure of Wealth: Indicators of Environmentally Sustainable Development*, Washington DC, World Bank.

—— 2001, *2001 World Development Indicators*, Washington, DC, World Bank.

—— 2002, *Tanzania at the Turn of the Century: World Bank Country Study*, Washington, DC, World Bank.

World Bank Development Report, 1997, *The State in a Changing World*, Washington, DC, World Bank.

World Economic Forum, 2002, *The Global Competitiveness Report 2001–2002*, Geneva, World Economic Forum.

Wright, R., 1994, *The Moral Animal: Evolutionary Psychology and Everyday Life*, New York, Pantheon Books.

Wriston, W. B., 1992, *The Twilight of Sovereignty*, New York, Scribner.

Wrong, M., 2000, *In the Footsteps of Mr Kurtz: Living on the Brink of Disaster in the Congo*, London, Fourth Estate.

Wynne-Edwards, V. C., 1962, *Animal Dispersion in Relation to Social Behaviour*, London and Edinburgh, Oliver & Boyd.

Yergin, D. I., and Stanislaw, J., 1998, *The Commanding Heights: The Battle between Government and the Marketplace that is Remaking the Modern World*, New York, Simon & Schuster.

Young, A., 1995, 'The Tyranny of Numbers: Confronting the Statistical Realities of the East Asian Growth Experience', *Quarterly Journal of Economics*, 110, August, 641–80.

Youngson, A. J., 1959, *Possibilities of Economic Progress*, Cambridge, Cambridge University Press.

—— 1966, *The Making of Classical Edinburgh, 1750–1840*, Edinburgh, Edinburgh University Press.

Zahavi, A., 1975, 'Mate Selection – a Selection for a Handicap', *Journal of Theoretical Biology*, 53, 205–14.

Zeldin, T., 1997, *The French*, Illinois, Harlan Davidson.

Index